MW01142945

PUZZLE PIECE PHONICS

DEDICATION

We dedicate this book to all of our teacher friends in North Carolina. Your dedication, creativity, and passion shine through every day in the students you've impacted.

ACKNOWLEDGMENTS

We are grateful for the support of the following educational leaders:

Barb Falkenbury
Reading Specialist
Cannon School
Concord, North Carolina

James Garvin
Principal and Educational Leader
Reid Park Academy
Charlotte, North Carolina

Kindergarten

PUZZLE PIECE PHONICS

Teacher's Guide

Word Study for the Balanced Literacy Classroom

Carolyn Banuelos

Danielle James

Elise Lund

resources.corwin.com/puzzlepiecephonics-gradeK

A SAGE Publishing Company

FOR INFORMATION:

Corwin

A SAGE Company

2455 Teller Road

Thousand Oaks, California 91320

(800) 233-9936

www.corwin.com

SAGE Publications Ltd.

1 Oliver's Yard

55 City Road

London EC1Y 1SP

United Kingdom

SAGE Publications India Pvt. Ltd.

B 1/I 1 Mohan Cooperative Industrial Area

Mathura Road, New Delhi 110 044

India

SAGE Publications Asia-Pacific Pte. Ltd.

3 Church Street

#10-04 Samsung Hub

Singapore 049483

Director and Publisher,
Corwin Classroom: Lisa Luedeke

Senior Acquisitions Editor: Wendy Murray

Editorial Development Manager: Julie Nemer

Editorial Assistant: Sharon Wu

Production Editor: Melanie Birdsall

Copy Editor: Melinda Masson

Typesetter: Integra

Proofreader: Theresa Kay

Cover and Interior Designer: Gail Buschman

Marketing Manager: Brian Grimm

Copyright © 2019 by Corwin

All rights reserved. When forms and sample documents are included, their use is authorized only by educators, local school sites, and/or noncommercial or nonprofit entities that have purchased the book. Except for that usage, no part of this book may be reproduced or utilized in any form or by any means, electronic or mechanical, including photocopying, recording, or by any information storage and retrieval system, without permission in writing from the publisher.

All trademarks depicted within this book, including trademarks appearing as part of a screenshot, figure, or other image, are included solely for the purpose of illustration and are the property of their respective holders. The use of the trademarks in no way indicates any relationship with, or endorsement by, the holders of said trademarks.

Art Explosion is a registered trademark of Nova Development.

Printed in the United States of America

Library of Congress Cataloging-in-Publication Data

Names: Banuelos, Carolyn, author. | James, Danielle, author. | Lund, Elise, author.

Title: Puzzle piece phonics teacher's guide, kindergarten : word study for the balanced literacy classroom / Carolyn Banuelos, Danielle James, Elise Lund.

Description: Thousand Oaks, California : Corwin, [2018]

Identifiers: LCCN 2017058388 | ISBN 9781506364513 (spiral : alk. paper)

Subjects: LCSH: Reading (Kindergarten) | Reading—Phonetic method. |

Reading—Color aids.

Classification: LCC LB1181.2 .B36 2018 | DDC 372.4—dc23 LC record available at https://lccn.loc.gov/2017058388

This book is printed on acid-free paper.

18 19 20 21 22 10 9 8 7 6 5 4 3 2 1

SUSTAINABLE FORESTRY INITIATIVE

Certified Sourcing
www.sfiprogram.org
SFI-01268

SFI label applies to text stock

DISCLAIMER: This book may direct you to access third-party content via web links, QR codes, or other scannable technologies, which are provided for your reference by the author(s). Corwin makes no guarantee that such third-party content will be available for your use and encourages you to review the terms and conditions of such third-party content. Corwin takes no responsibility and assumes no liability for your use of any third-party content, nor does Corwin approve, sponsor, endorse, verify, or certify such third-party content.

CONTENTS

Consonants

Short Vowels

Visit the companion website at
resources.corwin.com/puzzlepiecephonics-gradeK
for downloadable Weekly Celebration certificates,
Word Explorer poster teaching tips, and more resources.

INTRODUCTION

A Letter From Carolyn, Danielle, and Elise

Dear Teachers,

Welcome to *Puzzle Piece Phonics*. We are very excited to share our love of word study with you. We are three teachers who developed this comprehensive resource when we worked together through the transition from the North Carolina Standard Course of Study to the Common Core State Standards (CCSS). It came about from a moment of near panic when we were sitting at a table in the library after school, and it seemed to hit us at the same time how much more the CCSS expected of students. We looked at each other and wondered, how are we ever going to get our students from "here" to "there"? But then we called on our various strengths—our creativity, our curricular understanding, our practicality, and our can-do personalities—and generated *Puzzle Piece Phonics*.

Carolyn Banuelos

In the years since, each of us adapted *Puzzle Piece Phonics* to fit our classrooms and made sure it can work anywhere, to meet the needs of all our diverse students, and embodies the vision of Balanced Literacy. We enjoy making it our own, and we have seen success with all of our students. Now it's your turn!

DOABLE DIFFERENTIATION

What sets this resource apart is that it meets the needs of students working on very different levels. Some students need to overcome gaps to meet grade-level expectations, whereas other students need to exceed grade-level expectations to achieve one year's growth. With *Puzzle Piece Phonics*, differentiating learning for students is not an add-on but a central part of its design so that all students make great strides in the course of the year. Students learn new skills during whole-group lessons, then immediately apply them at their individual working level through the differentiated components, including weekly sorts, fluency poems, and Practice Pieces. As Wiley Blevins says in *A Fresh Look at Phonics* (2017), "The goal is to challenge those students who already know the phonics skills you might be introducing to the whole group and to provide successful and purposeful learning for those students whose skill level is lacking" (p. 34). *Puzzle Piece Phonics* will help you meet this goal.

Danielle James

In addition, we provide suggestions throughout for how you might adapt the plan. For example, you might want to switch the tasks for the day. You can also change the level on which students are working by telling them to turn to the next page. We are constantly reminded of the need for flexible groups, yet the reality of daily life in a classroom can make flexible grouping difficult. With *Puzzle Piece Phonics*, all students are focusing on the same weekly spelling patterns, and therefore movement between groups can be fluid. All students experience success either on or above grade level. As they grow their knowledge, students can easily begin working in a new group the next week without having to learn new routines and content.

Elise Lund

COLORFUL PUZZLE PIECES

Our program is designed for *all* students to develop a complete, well-rounded understanding of the major concepts of phonics. To make these concepts more concrete for children, we have created big puzzle pieces that create a classroom display. There is a puzzle piece for each sound and spelling pattern. Students can look up at the display at any time for reference.

The pieces hook together into the Puzzle Piece Families. Each piece shows an image of an object, the spelling, and the sound pattern to help demonstrate the key rules of phonics. There is also a motion that corresponds with each puzzle piece, helps students retain the sounds and spellings, and helps teachers give quick student signals. Each week, students study a few of the puzzle pieces, and the interactive use of the pieces engages their auditory, visual, tactile, and kinesthetic modes of learning. See pages I-5 to I-8 for more how-tos!

DEVELOPMENTALLY APPROPRIATE INSTRUCTIONAL DESIGN

As teachers, we noticed the flaws in the phonics resources we used, and so in this program we designed a scope and sequence that reflects how students best acquire phonics knowledge. The gist? Slow and steady wins the race. Connections to previous learning and immediate, daily application of concepts to authentic reading and writing are essential. When young learners themselves come to see that the phonics and word study work they do is all of a piece with the reading and writing they do throughout the literacy block, it helps them progress. Specifically:

- Similar patterns are studied in succession so students can connect their learning to previously taught concepts. Focus patterns are studied for one week at a time so students have ample opportunities to practice and apply spelling patterns.
- Repeated practice with a variety of tasks builds the confidence necessary for students to apply phonics knowledge outside of the word study block.
- Students constantly read and write words that contain the weekly focus patterns in a variety of authentic contexts, including fluency poems, Comprehension Checks, and Practice Pieces.

EASY ONGOING ASSESSMENT

Puzzle Piece Phonics holds students accountable for applying instructional content. Our program includes formal and informal assessment points. There are Spelling Checks, Comprehension Checks, and informal observations throughout the week. Students have the opportunity to self-check their work while completing Practice Pieces so they know where they are in developing their understanding of the focus patterns. They reflect on their progress toward mastery with the focus patterns for the week and become self-directed learners. Assessments and Practice Pieces can be shared with families so they are able to see student progress and hold students accountable for the skills taught in school.

RESEARCH-BASED APPROACHES TO WORD STUDY

You will notice that *Puzzle Piece Phonics* does not include a take-home list of spelling words for students. Why? Because research in the last two decades has proven that systematic instruction on phonics patterns is more effective at promoting growth in reading and spelling than non-phonics-based approaches (National Reading Panel, 2000). Instead, students learn spelling and phonics patterns as a natural part of reading and writing. They study specific patterns through the puzzle pieces and then apply the patterns to read and write both studied and new words. Balanced Literacy requires that word study is not taught in isolation. The skills students learn during word study become a tool for successful reading and writing all day long.

STUDENT NOTEBOOKS

Through our program, students will understand phonics patterns, read for meaning, build their vocabularies, and apply knowledge of word structure to decode and encode words. Word study is only a portion of the day, but the skills learned during this time lead to success in all content areas. Using their Learner's Notebooks and Fluency Notebooks, students learn to have fun with language, and you will watch their excitement grow as they understand more and more of what they encounter in print. Phonics is one piece of understanding print. However, students also need to develop their vocabularies and their understanding of word structure. Vocabulary is embedded in the weekly sorts and introduced in the blending lines. Students not only read and spell the words, but they also apply them correctly in context. Students learn how to break words into syllables and add endings to change their meanings. To make word study a part of all of the components of Balanced Literacy, we found it necessary to extend the word study block. By doing this, students' success in all content areas was evident.

A USER-FRIENDLY GUIDE

There will be a lot of wonderful learning happening in your classroom! However, it will be fun and easy for you to manage. As teachers, we know what it's like to open up an implementation guide that is so long and complex that you don't even bother reading it. So, we have written this streamlined Teacher's Guide with simple directions for implementing the daily lessons. Follow the routines, and they will become second nature to you and your students.

Planning word study is a matter of changing the words from week to week. *Puzzle Piece Phonics* is designed to inspire, challenge, and support students without creating more work for teachers.

Phonics can easily become the forgotten piece of Balanced Literacy. However, by making word work the center of literacy instruction, all of the other skills fall into place. This has happened in our classrooms over the past few years, and we are excited for it to begin in yours!

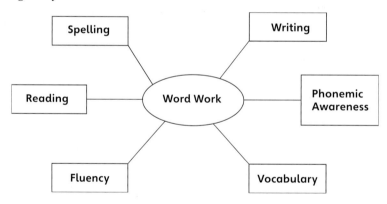

Happy word working!

Carolyn, Danielle, and Elise

REFERENCES

Blevins, W. (2017). *A fresh look at phonics: Common causes of failure and 7 ingredients for success.* Thousand Oaks, CA: Corwin.

National Reading Panel. (2000). *Report of the National Reading Panel: Teaching children to read: An evidence-based assessment of the scientific research literature on reading and its implications for reading instruction: Reports of the subgroups.* Washington, DC: National Institute of Child Health and Human Development, National Institutes of Health.

Features of the Puzzle Pieces

Kindergarteners love, love, love using the puzzle pieces as they learn. Here is how the pieces work.

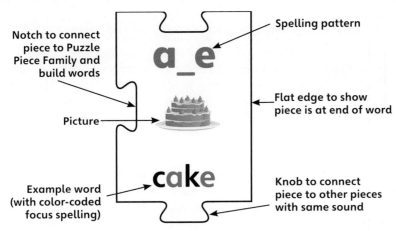

Notch to connect piece to Puzzle Piece Family and build words

Spelling pattern

Flat edge to show piece is at end of word

Picture

Example word (with color-coded focus spelling)

Knob to connect piece to other pieces with same sound

Color Codes of the Puzzle Pieces

The color codes help students organize their understandings about what makes up a word.

Red	consonants	**Muted Blue**	short *o* vowel families
Blue	short vowels	**Muted Blue**	short *u* vowel families
Muted Blue	short *a* vowel families	Orange	digraphs
Muted Blue	short *e* vowel families	**Purple**	blends
Muted Blue	short *i* vowel families	Green	long vowels

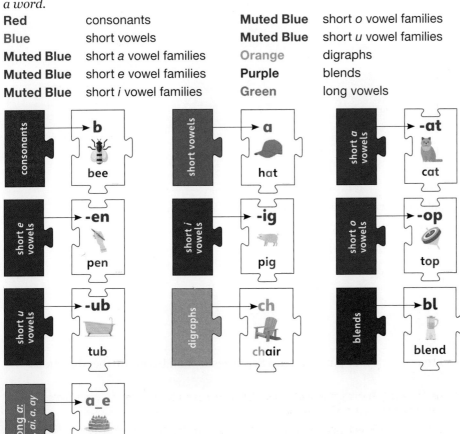

How to Prepare the Puzzle Pieces

Prior to implementing the Puzzle Piece Phonics lessons in your classroom, follow the steps below to prepare your puzzle pieces.

1. After removing the pieces from packaging, cut around the thick black lines of each piece.

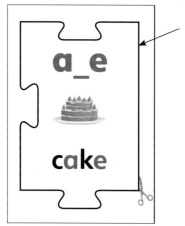

2. Once pieces are cut out, laminate the pieces.

(Lamination is optional. If you do not have access to laminate your pieces, they will still hold up throughout the year.)

3. Cut excess lamination off each puzzle piece.

4. Decide on an adhesive to display your cut pieces.

   Suggestions:
   - Masking tape
   - Hot glue
   - Sticky putty
   - Hooks
   - Poster strips
   - Double-sided tape

Now you're ready to **display** and **teach** with your puzzle pieces! See pages I-7 and I-8 for further directions.

How to Display the Puzzle Pieces

The puzzle pieces become part of a classroom reference wall once they have been formally studied and prominently displayed for a week.

The puzzle pieces connect horizontally in Puzzle Piece Families.

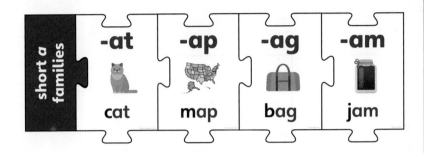

You can connect the puzzle pieces that represent the short *a* families after teaching all of them in Concept 4.

The puzzle pieces connect vertically to other puzzle pieces that represent the same sound.

You can connect the puzzle pieces that represent long *a* to present in the classroom. In kindergarten, students are formally taught only the *a_e* puzzle piece, but you can show students the various spellings of long *a* by connecting the pieces vertically.

How to Teach With the Puzzle Pieces

The puzzle pieces are prominently displayed and support the work of you and your students during the week they are formally studied.

Introduce the focus puzzle pieces each week during the **Big Reveal**. Continue to display them prominently at the front of the classroom.

Display the *hat* and *bed* puzzle pieces at the front of the classroom during Concept 3, Week 1.

Build words with the focus puzzle pieces during the week.

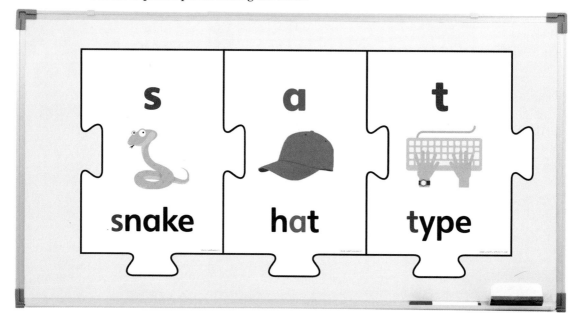

Display the *snake*, *hat*, and *type* pieces to build the word *sat*.

Getting Ready to Teach

The Instructional Routines and Student Activities

Instructional routines are a cornerstone of *Puzzle Piece Phonics*. They require minimal teacher talk so that word study can move at a brisk pace. Students will know what is expected of them, and they can be active participants. They will learn quickly that the one doing the talking is the one doing the learning!

This section is meant to get you up to speed with the steps in the routines and day-to-day flow. Follow the routines outlined in this section, and your instruction will be research-based and you will use your word study time efficiently. This section is also a good go-to place for professional development conversations. Return to it when you need to brush up on particular routines, as routines change, or as new routines are introduced.

You will find the following description of each routine:

- **What Is It?**—a brief overview of each component, how often it is completed, and how long it takes
- **Learning Outcomes**—goals for students
- **Purpose**—the rationale behind each component
- **Basic Routine**—explicit, step-by-step directions for implementing each routine

Other resources in this section to help you pace your teaching include the following:

- **Kindergarten: Word Study Sound Pacing**—the scope and sequence of the program
- **Kindergarten: Sight Word Pacing**—a week-by-week list of the sight words introduced
- **The Sound Pieces With Motions Chart**—a map of the puzzle pieces that outlines the components of each piece and shows how they should be displayed in your classroom

Once you are familiar with the routines described here, you're ready to begin the scope and sequence. There are ten concepts in all, spanning approximately thirty-six weeks of instruction. You'll notice each concept opens with a Preparing for Your Week section to plan weekly instruction. These sections supplement the routines outlined here. They include tips for management and differentiation to help you personalize the routines for your students. Use this section to put your own spin on things.

Do not underestimate the importance of making *Puzzle Piece Phonics* your own. As the National Reading Panel (NRP) found, scripted phonics programs that underestimate the value of teacher judgment are largely ineffective. The NRP (2000) recommends phonics programs that "maintain consistency of instruction and at the same time encourage unique contributions from teachers" (pp. 2–135). *Puzzle Piece Phonics* will allow you to meet the recommendations of the NRP. Simply balance following the routines with fidelity with making it fit for you!

The Puzzle Pieces

WHAT IS IT?

The puzzle pieces are used as a classroom reference wall; they match the weekly word sorts and appear in the Learner's Notebook. Each puzzle piece represents one sound/ spelling pattern. The puzzle pieces show the spelling, a picture of one word that has that spelling, and the written word with that spelling. The focus pattern appears in bold and is color-coded within the example word. There is a motion for each puzzle piece that helps students remember the example word on the puzzle piece. The motions help engage learners and aid retention. The reference Puzzle Pieces only have the lowercase letter(s) representing the focus sound(s). This is so students can build words using the Puzzle Pieces. In the back of the Puzzle Piece pack, there are upper-case letter cards. Teachers may use these cards during instruction to show the uppercase letter that matches each Puzzle Piece.

The focus spellings at the top of the puzzle pieces are color-coded:

Red	consonants	**Muted Blue**	short *o* vowel families
Blue	short vowels	**Muted Blue**	short *u* vowel families
Muted Blue	short *a* vowel families	**Orange**	digraphs
Muted Blue	short *e* vowel families	**Purple**	blends
Muted Blue	short *i* vowel families	**Green**	long vowels

LEARNING OUTCOMES

Students will

- Reference the puzzle pieces to understand how and when certain spellings can be applied
- Reference the puzzle pieces to make connections between spellings that follow similar patterns

PURPOSE

The puzzle pieces help students learn the major patterns of phonics. The pieces fit in specific ways to demonstrate those patterns:

- **Vertically:** The spellings of a particular sound connect vertically. Students will see these vertical connections in first and second grade. For example, the *a_e, a, ay,* and *ai* patterns can all be used to represent the long *a* sound. They snap together vertically. This helps students understand that the long *a* sound can be represented in any of those ways.
- **Horizontally:** Similar patterns connect horizontally. For example, all of the pieces in the vowel_e family connect horizontally. This helps students understand that the vowel_e rule applies to long *a, e, i, o,* and *u*.

The puzzle pieces also help students understand how and when various patterns can be applied. For example:

- Spellings that are only used at the beginning of a word have a straight edge on the left side. No pieces can be physically placed before that spelling. This helps students recognize that those spellings (such as *tr* and *dr*) always come at the beginning of a word.
- Spellings that are only used at the end of a word have a straight edge on the right side. No pieces can be physically placed after that spelling. This shows that these spellings (such as *at, ap,* and *ag*) can only come at the end of a word.
- The vowel_e spellings have an opening on the top. The bottom side of a consonant piece sticks out and can be inserted into the opening to create a vowel_e pattern (e.g., the bottom of the *no* piece snaps into the top of the *bone* piece to form the o_e spelling in the word *bone*).

BASIC ROUTINE

Teachers hang the puzzle pieces on the classroom wall from the beginning of the school year. They are introduced in families. See the Puzzle Piece Family routine section on page I-11 for more information.

The Puzzle Piece Family Routine

WHAT IS IT?

The Puzzle Piece Family routine should take no longer than five minutes and is completed on the first day of each new concept. It is the scope and sequence of the program. The families reflect the major concepts of word study and phonics: building the sorting routine, letters (consonants and short vowels), short vowels, short *a* families, short *e* families, short *i* families, short *o* families, short *u* families, mixed short vowel families, and vowel_*e*. The puzzle pieces are designed to physically link together in families to facilitate learning. The concepts are organized to teach these families.

LEARNING OUTCOMES

Students will

- Identify the connection between focus patterns that follow the same phonics pattern
- Identify the Puzzle Piece Families, including
  - Winter things and food things—explain that objects can be sorted into categories
  - Letters—the building blocks of words
  - Short vowels—vowels that are closed in by consonants
  - Short vowel families—groups of rhyming words that are spelled with the consonant, vowel, consonant (CVC) or consonant, vowel, consonant, consonant (CVCC) patterns
  - Vowel_*e* patterns—a vowel that is followed by a consonant plus *e* and produces the long vowel sound

PURPOSE

The Puzzle Piece Families are taught in successive weeks to allow students to grasp the beginning concepts of phonics and apply prior learning. With each new concept/family taught, the teacher explicitly states to students that they are learning a *new* type of pattern. This explicitness helps students organize words into categories and use what they already know to tackle untaught patterns in new words.

BASIC ROUTINE

The introduction of the Puzzle Piece Family occurs as you begin the instruction outlined in Week 1, Day 1 of each concept. The teacher introduces the family before the Big Reveal. The routine changes depending on the phonics concept being taught in that concept.

In general, the routine is as follows:

1. The teacher writes the Puzzle Piece Family words on the board.
2. The teacher points to the words and reads them aloud.
3. The teacher points to one word and says the word.
4. The teacher motions for students to repeat the word.
5. The teacher repeats Steps 3–4 with the remaining words.
6. The students discuss patterns they notice within the words.
7. The teacher facilitates a discussion about the words, and leads students to discovering the new Puzzle Piece Family.

Follow the specific instructions outlined in Week 1, Day 1 of each concept.

The Big Reveal

WHAT IS IT?

The Big Reveal is a two- to three-minute dynamic introduction to the components of each puzzle piece for the week. Students get excited about the weekly focus patterns and make connections to the major concepts of the current concept.

LEARNING OUTCOMES

Students will

- Learn the names of the weekly puzzle pieces
- Learn the sounds of the weekly puzzle pieces
- Learn the motions of the weekly puzzle pieces
- Learn the spellings of the weekly puzzle pieces
- Connect the weekly puzzle pieces to previously learned puzzle pieces
- Quickly recognize the sounds, motions, and spellings of the puzzle pieces by the end of the week

PURPOSE

The purpose of the Big Reveal is to familiarize students with the puzzle pieces they will study all week. During the Big Reveal, students will begin to develop their schema for the weekly puzzle pieces.

BASIC ROUTINE

In Concept 2, the Big Reveal occurs on the first two or three days of each week. In the remaining concepts, the Big Reveal occurs on the first day of each week. The teacher holds up a piece and introduces its name, sound, motion, and spelling. The routine changes depending on the focus skills.

Each routine contains four components:

1. The name of each puzzle piece
2. The sound of each puzzle piece
3. The motion of each puzzle piece
4. The spelling of each puzzle piece

Puzzle Piece Review

WHAT IS IT?

The Puzzle Piece Review is a one- to three-minute recap done on Days 3–5 or 4–5 in Concept 2 and on Days 2–5 in Concepts 1 and 3–10. The teacher and students repeat the names, sounds, motions, and spellings of the weekly puzzle pieces.

LEARNING OUTCOMES

Students will

- Review the names, sounds, motions, and spellings of the weekly puzzle pieces
- Develop fluency in recalling the features of the weekly focus patterns

PURPOSE

The purpose of the Puzzle Piece Review is to focus students on word study and to develop students' automaticity with the weekly focus patterns.

BASIC ROUTINE

The Puzzle Piece Review has many options. Follow the specific instructions outlined in the Daily Lessons.

Preassessments

WHAT IS IT?

Preassessments are quick checks that vary in time. They are given prior to the start of a new concept and challenge students to write words with patterns that have not yet been formally taught.

LEARNING OUTCOMES

Students will

- Show their existing knowledge of the sound spelling patterns

PURPOSE

These formative assessments help the teacher form student groups for word sorting or change the makeup of groups. The information also helps teachers determine the focus of lessons for each group.

There are five preassessments:

The first preassessment is given during Concept 1. This is an initial check to see students' knowledge of letter identification, sound, and formation.

The second preassessment is given during Concept 2. It assesses students' knowledge of short vowels because flexible, differentiated groups may need to be adjusted. Short vowels will be formally studied in Concepts 3–9.

The third preassessment is given during Concept 3. It assesses students' knowledge of word families because differentiated groups may need to be adjusted. Word families will be formally introduced in Concepts 4–8.

The fourth preassessment is given during Concept 7. It assesses students' knowledge of mixed short vowels and consonants because flexible, differentiated groups may need to be adjusted prior to Concept 8, when students will work with all of the short vowels at one time.

The fifth preassessment is given during Concept 9. It assesses students' knowledge of short vowels and vowel_e because flexible, differentiated groups may need to be adjusted. Vowel_e will be formally introduced in Concept 10.

A rubric for grading each preassessment can be found in the Preparing for Your Week section of the week in which it is given.

BASIC ROUTINE

Before giving the preassessment, explain to students that the purpose of the preassessment is to see what students already know.

Follow this routine:

1. The teacher tells students which number the class is on.
2. The teacher says the word represented by the picture.
3. The students write the sounds they hear in that word.
4. The teacher repeats Steps 1–3 until all words have been dictated.

The time for this routine varies depending on your students. If needed, preassessments can be completed in multiple sessions.

Postassessments

WHAT IS IT?

Postassessments are quick checks that vary in time. They are designed to determine if students have mastered the spelling patterns that have been formally introduced in previous concepts. There is only one version of each postassessment. It tests the kindergarten standards, and it does not include any skills students working with the enriched words may have been exposed to.

LEARNING OUTCOMES

Students will

- Show which of the formally introduced sound spelling patterns they have mastered
- Meet with their teacher in a conference to discuss how they performed, and use the information to reflect on their work
- Set a Word Work goal for upcoming concepts
- Continue to goal-set so they feel confident going into the five postassessments given throughout the year

PURPOSE

The purpose is for teachers and students to know which spelling patterns students have mastered. Teachers can use the data as the basis of a one-on-one conference with each student. Conferences can be used to set goals for word study, guide student writing, or recommend books that might be a good fit for individual students. They are also a time for teachers to provide praise for students when seeing students apply word study skills in other content areas. Conferences can be an opportunity for teachers to nudge students to go beyond their current working level.

Teachers use the data for follow-up instruction. They can reteach students who need remediation and enrich students who need an extension.

There are five postassessments:

The first postassessment is given at the end of Concept 2. It assesses consonant and short vowel sounds.

The second postassessment is given at the end of Concept 3. It assesses short vowels.

The third postassessment is given at the end of Concept 8. It assesses word families.

The fourth postassessment is given during Concept 9. It assesses mixed short vowels and consonants.

The fifth postassessment is given during Concept 10. It is a summative assessment of all the kindergarten spelling patterns including consonants, short vowels, and vowel_*e*.

BASIC ROUTINE

Before giving the postassessment, explain to students that this assessment covers the spelling patterns they have learned and allows them to apply their knowledge. They should take this assessment seriously so both the teacher and students can see the students' progress.

Follow this routine:

1. The teacher tells students which number the class is on.
2. The teacher says the word represented by the picture.
3. The students write the sounds they hear in that word.
4. The teacher repeats Steps 1–3 until all words have been dictated.

The time for this routine varies depending on your students. If needed, postassessments can be completed in multiple sessions.

Phonemic Awareness

WHAT IS IT?

The Phonemic Awareness routine takes two minutes and is done each day as a warm-up. Students practice hearing and manipulating sounds in spoken words. They are not writing down sounds they hear; phonemic awareness is all auditory and spoken.

LEARNING OUTCOMES

Students will

- Listen for rhyming words
- Isolate initial sounds in words
- Segment words into sounds
- Orally break words into syllables
- Change initial, medial, and final sounds in words
- Compare and contrast spoken words
- Identify short vowels and long vowels

PURPOSE

The purpose is for students to practice isolating and pronouncing phonemes in spoken words. Later, when writing, students will *segment* the sounds they hear within words before they represent the sounds using spelling patterns. Then, when reading, students *blend* segmented phonemes to decode unknown words. Teachers can assess students' mastery of isolating and blending sounds during phonemic awareness.

BASIC ROUTINE

Each day your class warms up by orally manipulating words. The routine changes depending on the focus skills and student need.

Follow this routine:

1. The teacher gives directions and models the Phonemic Awareness activity.
2. The students practice the skill using the listed words.

Follow the specific instructions outlined in the Teacher's Guide.

Word or Letter? Routine

For Concept I, Week 2

WHAT IS IT?

Word or Letter? is a three- to five-minute activity done on Days 1–4. Students will look at words and letters displayed on the board. Students will interact with the words and letters by circling letters and underlining words.

LEARNING OUTCOMES

Students will

- Identify words
- Identify letters
- Circle letters and underline words

PURPOSE

The purpose of the Word or Letter? activity is for students to identify that words are made up of letters. By completing this guided practice as a class, students will apply this understanding during their sorting and Spelling Check for the week.

(Continued)

BASIC ROUTINE   See the weekly lessons in the Teacher's Guide for direction on which word(s) and letter(s) to display.

Students and teacher will follow this routine:

1. The teacher will display the daily words and letters on the board.
2. The students will read the words and letters to themselves.
3. The teacher will call on one student to come up to the board and choose to circle a letter or underline a word.
4. The student will circle a letter or underline a word.
5. The teacher and students will review the action taken and give a thumbs-up if they agree or a thumbs-down if they disagree.
6. The teacher will correct the action if needed.
7. The teacher and students will identify the letter or read the word.
8. The teacher and students will follow Steps 3–7 until all of the words and letters are underlined or circled.

Supported Blending

WHAT IS IT?   The Supported Blending routine takes ten minutes or less and is done on Days 1–4 of Concepts 1 and 2. Students produce one or some of the sounds within a word. The teacher then provides the remaining sounds within the word. Students blend together the sounds they produced with those produced by the teacher to form a full word.

LEARNING OUTCOMES   Students will

- Look at a spelling pattern and orally produce the corresponding sound
- Listen to the teacher-produced sounds
- Put together the student-produced and teacher-produced sounds
- Learn how to put sounds together to make new words

PURPOSE   Before students are fully able to blend words, they need frequent modeling and practice with isolating sounds in words and putting them back together. When we tell students to "sound out" a word, we are asking them to blend the sounds of each spelling pattern within the word. This allows them to decode (or read) the word. Supported Blending provides modeling and practice with this skill. Kindergarten students initially use the Supported Blending routine before vowel sounds have been formally introduced.

Supported Blending also allows students to practice word attack strategies. Students must be able to decode some words with patterns that have not been formally introduced.

BASIC ROUTINE

There are two or three supported blending lines each day. Regardless of the number of syllables, follow this routine:

1. The teacher writes the blending line.
2. The teacher places one finger under the first spelling in the first word (e.g., place one finger under *m* for the spelling of /m/).
3. The teacher cues the students by saying, "Sound."
4. The students orally produce the sound of the first spelling.
5. The teacher drags his or her finger under the remainder of the word (e.g., under *op* in *mop*).
6. The teacher says the remainder of the word (e.g., say "/ŏp/").
7. The teacher places his or her finger back under the first spelling in the word.
8. The teacher drags his or her finger underneath all of the spellings in the word and cues the students by saying, "Blend."
9. The students link the first sound that they produce with the remainder of the word that the teacher produces.
10. The teacher places his or her hand below the middle of the word
11. The teacher cues the students to read the word again by saying, "Word."
12. The students repeat the word.
13. The teacher and students repeat Steps 2–12 until all words in a line have been decoded.
14. The teacher places his or her finger underneath the first word on the line and cues the students to reread all of the words by saying, "Read the line."
15. The students read all of the words in the line as the teacher places his or her hand below each one. The teacher may provide additional assistance by continuing to produce the remaining part of each word.
16. The teacher and students discuss the focus of that line (see the "discuss" box in the Daily Lessons).

After decoding the blending lines, write the sight word of the week.

1. The teacher places his or her hand below the word.
2. The teacher says the word.
3. The students repeat the word.
4. The students orally spell the word.

Blending

WHAT IS IT?

The Blending routine takes ten minutes or less, and is done on Days 1–4 beginning in Concept 3. Students look at a word, say the sounds of each spelling pattern within the word, and put them back together to decode the word. Words on each blending line have a specific focus: a particular puzzle piece, initial sound, final sound, or previously learned concept. Sight words and a sentence containing words related to the focus patterns follow the blending lines.

(Continued)

LEARNING OUTCOMES	Students will

Students will

- Look at a spelling pattern and orally produce the corresponding sound
- Put together the sounds in syllables and words
- Discuss patterns they notice within the blending lines
- Read sight words
- Apply their knowledge of phonics to decode a sentence

PURPOSE

Blending is the teacher's opportunity to model the process of decoding words. It takes students time and practice to internalize the process as it includes multiple steps:

- Chunking a word into syllables
- Saying the sound of each spelling pattern within a syllable
- Putting the sounds in a syllable together
- Putting the syllables in a word together

Students should be held accountable for systematically decoding words using this routine when reading independently and when reading with support. Blending also gives students the opportunity to discuss related words.

BASIC ROUTINE

There are three blending lines each day.

Follow this routine:

1. The teacher writes the blending line.
2. The teacher places the corresponding number of fingers under the first spelling in the word (e.g., place one finger under the *m* for the spelling of /m/ in *mat*).
3. The teacher cues the students by saying, "Sound."
4. The students orally produce the sound of the first spelling.
5. The teacher places the corresponding number of fingers under the second spelling in the word (e.g., place one finger under the *a* for the spelling of /ă/ in *mat*).
6. The teacher cues the students by saying, "Sound."
7. The students orally produce the sound of the second spelling.
8. Continue with this process until students produce the vowel sound.
9. The teacher will place his or her finger back under the first spelling in the word.
10. The teacher will drag his or her finger underneath the spellings decoded so far (not the entire word—stop at the vowel; e.g., drag under the letters *m* and *a*).
11. The teacher will cue the students by saying, "Blend."
12. The students will orally produce the sounds of the spellings through the vowel (e.g., say "/mă/").
13. The teacher and students will continue with the process until the sounds of any consonant sounds after the vowel have been produced.
14. The teacher will place his or her finger back under the first spelling in the word.
15. The teacher will drag his or her finger underneath all of the spellings in the word and cue the students by saying, "Blend."
16. The teacher will place his or her hand below the middle of the word.
17. The teacher will cue the students to read the word again by saying, "Word."
18. The students will say the word one more time.
19. The teacher and students will follow this routine until all words in a line have been decoded.

BASIC ROUTINE (Continued)	20. The teacher will place his or her finger underneath the first word on the line and cue the students to reread all of the words by saying, "Read the line."
	21. The students will read all of the words in the line as the teacher places his or her hand below each one.
	22. The teacher and students will discuss the focus of that line (see the "discuss" box in the Daily Lessons).

After decoding the blending lines, write the one or two sight words of the week.

1. The teacher will place his or her hand below the first word.
2. The teacher will say the word.
3. The students will repeat the word.
4. The students will orally spell the word.
5. The teacher and students will follow this routine until all words have been read and spelled.

After reviewing the sight words, write the sentence of the day:

1. The teacher writes the sentence.
2. The teacher reviews any challenging words with students, modeling word attack strategies.
3. The teacher tells the students to silently read the sentence and give a "thumbs-up" when they are finished.
4. The teacher cues the students to chorally read the sentence.
5. The teacher places his or her hand below each word.
6. The students chorally read each word in the sentence.

Sight Words Routine

WHAT IS IT?	The Sight Words routine takes one minute and is part of the Blending routine. There are one or two focus sight words each week. They are introduced and reviewed during Blending and Dictation.
LEARNING OUTCOMES	Students will • Recognize sight words • Read sight words • Spell sight words • Retain knowledge of sight words previously introduced
PURPOSE	Books are made up of sight words and regularly spelled words. Students will become successful readers if they recognize and read sight words within three to five seconds. Students should not decode sight words, especially since they are sometimes spelled irregularly (e.g., *said*).
	Students also need to be able to spell sight words so writing is not as labor intensive. Knowing how to spell sight words without thinking allows students to concentrate on words that require encoding. Continuously review the spelling of sight words and hold students accountable for this expectation.

(Continued)

BASIC ROUTINE   The weekly sight words are introduced and reviewed after the blending lines.

Follow this routine:

1. The teacher places his or her hand below the first word.
2. The teacher says the word.
3. The students repeat the word.
4. The students orally spell the word.
5. Repeat Steps 1–4 until all words have been read and spelled.

Letter Formation

WHAT IS IT?   Letter Formation is direct instruction on the formation of consonants and vowels in Concept 2. The teacher models the formation of one uppercase and one lowercase letter each day. Students then practice forming two lines of uppercase and two lines of lowercase letters.

LEARNING OUTCOMES   Students will

- Identify uppercase and lowercase letters
- Correctly form uppercase and lowercase letters

PURPOSE   The purpose of Letter Formation is to teach students to identify and correctly form uppercase and lowercase letters. Students will likely need instruction on how to correctly use the lines on a page in order to develop age-appropriate handwriting. Letter Formation also helps students identify the features of letters (lines, curves, and circles) that will allow them to quickly identify letters when reading.

BASIC ROUTINE   Students will learn the formation of one uppercase and one lowercase letter each day.

Follow this routine:

1. The students will take out their Learner's Notebooks and turn to today's Letter Formation.
2. The teacher will identify the letter he or she will model (e.g., say, "This letter is uppercase *d*").
3. The teacher will form the letter, saying aloud the specific prompts in the Teacher's Guide (see the Daily Lessons for specific prompts).
4. The teacher prompts students to practice forming the uppercase letter on the provided lines in the Learner's Notebook. He or she will circulate, monitor, and assist students as needed.
5. The teacher will call the group back together.
6. The teacher will identify the next letter he or she will model (e.g., say, "This letter is lowercase *d*").
7. The teacher will form the letter, saying aloud the specific prompts in the Teacher's Guide (see the Daily Lessons for specific prompts).
8. The teacher prompts students to practice forming the lowercase letter on the provided lines in the Learner's Notebook. He or she will circulate, monitor, and assist students as needed.

Dictation

WHAT IS IT?

The Dictation routine takes no longer than ten minutes and is completed on Days 1 and 3 (after Concept 2). Students encode words with the weekly focus patterns as they are said aloud by the teacher. In Concept 2, students record only the initial or medial (short vowel) sound in the words. Beginning in Concept 3, students are held accountable for identifying and recording all of the sounds in the words.

LEARNING OUTCOMES

Students will

- Hear the sounds in words
- Reference the puzzle pieces and connect the sounds they hear to the spellings they see
- Write the letters that represent the sounds they hear
- Correctly spell sight words
- Apply the conventions of the English language to write sentences
- Self-check their work for common errors

PURPOSE

The purpose of Dictation is to teach students to encode words. Dictation is the teacher's opportunity to model counting the sounds in a word and recording the letter that represents that sound. In Concept 2, students record only the initial, final (in the case of /x/), or medial (short vowel) sound in the words. Beginning in Concept 3, students are held accountable for identifying and recording all of the sounds in the words. This format allows students to gain confidence as responsibility is gradually released to them.

Dictation includes a simple sentence beginning in Concept 9. Writing a sentence holds students accountable for applying their knowledge of phonics beyond writing one word at a time. Many students will be conscientious of the focus patterns within word study, but they will not naturally transfer this knowledge to their other writing. This is true of sight words as well. Transcribing a sentence gives students an opportunity to listen for words with the focus patterns among other words.

BASIC ROUTINE

Dictation is composed of words that students tap out with support, words that students tap out independently, one sight word, and later one sentence. Students also self-check their work.

Follow these routines for each part of Dictation.

Recording Initial or Medial Sounds (Concept 2), Words 1–2

1. The students will take out their Learner's Notebooks and turn to today's Dictation.
2. The teacher will say the word (e.g., say "tiger" or "hat").
3. The teacher will use the word in a sentence (e.g., say, "I saw a tiger at the zoo" or "I have a baseball hat").
4. The teacher will repeat the word (e.g., say "tiger" or "hat").
5. The teacher will say, "Tell me the first/vowel sound you hear in _____."
6. The teacher and students will isolate the first sound or the vowel sound in the word (e.g., say, "/t/ *iger*" or "/h/ /ă/ /ă/ /ă/ /t/").
7. The teacher will say, "Point to the first/vowel sound you hear in _____" (e.g., say, "Point to the first sound you hear in *tiger*" or "Point to the vowel sound you hear in *hat*").
8. The teacher and students will point to the puzzle piece that represents the first sound or vowel sound in the word while simultaneously saying the sound (e.g., point to the type piece and say "/t/" or point to the hat piece and say "/ă/").

(Continued)

9. The teacher will say, "Write the letter _____" (e.g., say, "Write the letter *t*" or "Write the letter *a*").
10. The students will write the letter (e.g., students will write *t* or *a*).
11. The students will move to the next line in their Learner's Notebook.
12. The teacher and students will follow Steps 2–11 for the second word.

Recording Initial or Medial Sounds (Concept 2), Words 3–5

1. The teacher will say the word (e.g., say "tiger" or "hat").
2. The teacher will use the word in a sentence (e.g., say, "I saw a tiger at the zoo" or "I have a baseball hat").
3. The teacher will repeat the word (e.g., say "tiger" or "hat").
4. The teacher will say, "Write the first/vowel sound you hear in _____" (e.g., say, "Write the first sound you hear in *tiger*" or "Write the vowel sound you hear in *hat*").
5. The students will write the letter (e.g., students will write *t* or *a*)

Sight Word

1. The teacher will say the word (e.g., say "a").
2. The teacher will use the word in a sentence (e.g., say, "May I please have a cookie?").
3. The teacher will repeat the word (e.g., say "a").
4. The teacher will say, "Write _____" (e.g., say, "Write *a*").
5. The students will write the word referencing the word wall as needed (e.g., look at and write *a*).

Recording Full Words (Concepts 3–10), Words 1–2

1. The students take out their Learner's Notebooks and turn to today's Dictation.
2. The teacher says the word (e.g., say "rip").
3. The teacher uses the word in a sentence (e.g., say, "There is a rip in my paper").
4. The teacher repeats the word (e.g., say "rip").
5. The teacher says, "Tap out the sounds you hear in _____."
6. The teacher and students tap out the sounds in the word (e.g., say, "/r/ /ĭ/ /p/").
7. The teacher says, "Point to the sounds you hear in _____" (e.g., say, "Point to the sounds you hear in *rip*").
8. The teacher and students point to the puzzle pieces that represent the sounds in the word while simultaneously saying each sound (e.g., point to the *run* piece and say "/r/," point to the *zip* piece and say "/ĭ/," and point to the *pop* piece and say "/p/").
9. The teacher says, "Write _____" (e.g., say, "Write *rip*").
10. The students write the word (e.g., students will write *rip*).
11. The students move to the next line in their Learner's Notebook.
12. The teacher and students repeat Steps 2–11 for the second word.

BASIC ROUTINE
(Continued)

Recording Full Words (Concepts 3–10), Word 3 or Words 3–4

1. The teacher says the word (e.g., say "rip").
2. The teacher uses the word in a sentence (e.g., say, "There is a rip in my paper").
3. The teacher repeats the word (e.g., say "rip").
4. The teacher says, "Write _____" (e.g., say, "Write *rip*").
5. The students write the word independently using the routine practiced with the first two words (e.g., students will write *rip*).
6. The students move to the next line in their Learner's Notebook.

Sentence

1. The teacher will say the entire sentence (e.g., say, "The cup is big").
2. The teacher will slowly say each word in the sentence, pausing for several seconds in between each word (e.g., say, "The ... cup ... is ... big").
3. The students will record the words in the sentence in order, being mindful of sight words, focus patterns, and writing conventions introduced so far.

Checking the Words

1. The teacher will say the word (e.g., say "rip").
2. The teacher will write the word (e.g., write *rip*).
3. The students will check every letter in the word. If a student makes an error, he or she will cross off the word and write it correctly next to it (e.g., the student will write ~~rep~~ then *rip*).
4. The teacher will review the focus pattern in the word (e.g., say, "*Rip* is in the *–ip* family").
5. The teacher will say the sight word (e.g., say "a").
6. The teacher will write the sight word (e.g., write *a*).
7. The teacher will point to the sight word on the word wall.
8. The students will check every letter in the word. If a student makes an error, he or she will cross off the word and write it correctly next to it (e.g., the student will write ~~an~~ then *a*).

Checking the Sentence

1. The teacher will write the sentence (e.g., say, "The cup is big").
2. The students will place a check over every word and convention in the sentence (e.g., students will write, "The$^{\checkmark\checkmark}$ cup$^{\checkmark}$ is$^{\checkmark}$ big$^{\checkmark.\checkmark}$").
3. The teacher will review the focus patterns, sight words, and conventions in the sentence (e.g., say, "Check the capital *T*. Check your spelling of *cup* and *big*. Check that you have a period.").

Quick Switch

WHAT IS IT?

The Quick Switch routine takes seven to ten minutes and is completed on Days 2 and 4 starting in Concept 3. Teachers say words containing the weekly focus patterns, and students manipulate the sounds within those words. The result is a list of words tied together by similar sounds.

(Continued)

LEARNING OUTCOMES	Students will
	• Hear the sounds in words
	• Write the letters that represent the sounds they hear
	• Listen for similarities and differences between two words
	• Use one word to assist them in writing another word

PURPOSE	The purpose of Quick Switch is for students to see the relationships among similar words. They apply spelling patterns from familiar words to spell unknown words. Students also learn that changing one letter or sound completely alters the meaning of the word.

BASIC ROUTINE	Quick Switch consists of a list of five words that are dictated.
	Follow this routine:

1. The students will take out their Learner's Notebooks and turn to today's Quick Switch.
2. The teacher will say the first word (e.g., say "tag").
3. The teacher will prompt students to segment the word (e.g., say, "What sounds do you hear in *tag*?").
4. The students will tap out the sounds in the word (e.g., say, "/t/ /ă/ /g/").
5. The students will write the sounds they hear on line 1 (e.g., students will write "*t, a, g*").
6. The teacher will record the correct spelling of the first word (e.g., write *tag*).
7. The teacher asks, "How would we change _____ to _____?" (e.g., say, "How would we change *tag* to *bag*?").
8. The teacher will call on a student or prompt students to share with a partner to identify the changing target sound.
9. The teacher will say, "To change _____ to _____, we change _____ to _____" (e.g., say, "To change *tag* to *bag*, we change *t* to *b*").
10. The teacher will prompt students to record the new word on line 2.
11. The teacher and students will follow Steps 7–8 to Quick Switch words 3–5.

Sometimes, students will have to change more than one letter to go from one word to the next. Assist students with these changes. See the Daily Lessons for specific notes.

Grouping With Combined Picture and Word Cards Sorting Routine

For Concept I

WHAT IS IT?	Grouping With Combined Picture and Word Cards is a five- to ten-minute activity done on Days 1–4. Students look at the combined picture and word card and place the card under the correct category header. Students create two groups (categories) of words during this activity.

LEARNING OUTCOMES	Students will
	• Look at the picture
	• Read the matching word on the combined word and picture card
	• Identify that pictures/words can be grouped into categories

PURPOSE	The purpose of the Grouping With Combined Picture and Word Cards sorting routine is for students to group pictures/words under category headers. Students will complete this sorting routine at the start of the year during Concept 1. Students will begin to understand the concept of sorting and feel confident in their ability to find similarities and categorize.
BASIC ROUTINE	There is one sort per week that students will use.

Students will sort using the following routine:

1. Remove their headers from their bags (example: school things, pool things).
2. Lay their headers at the top of their work space.
3. Retrieve one combined picture and word card at a time from their bags.
4. Look at the combined picture and word card that was retrieved from their bags and decide which category the card belongs under (e.g., look at *desk* and think where to place it).
5. Place the combined picture and word card under the header category it belongs to (e.g., student places *desk* under "school things" header).
6. Choose another combined picture and word card from their bags and repeat Steps 4–5.
7. Follow this routine until all of their weekly combined picture and word cards are placed in the categories.

Sorting With Combined Picture and Word Cards Routine

For Concept 2

WHAT IS IT?	Sorting With Combined Picture and Word Cards occurs on Days 1–4 and often takes five to ten minutes—five minutes once students get the hang of it. Students say words represented by pictures and words. They match the cards to headers that represent the weekly focus patterns.
LEARNING OUTCOMES	Students will

- Tap out sounds in words represented by pictures and words
- Hear the focus pattern in each word represented by the card
- Connect the focus pattern in each word to the appropriate sort header
- Identify consonant and short vowel sounds

PURPOSE	The purpose of Sorting With Combined Picture and Word Cards is for students to build the habit of tapping out the sounds in words. Students practice matching the focus pattern found within their word to the weekly focus header. Students repeatedly say and hear the focus patterns.

(Continued)

BASIC ROUTINE   There is only one combined picture and word sort per week. All students will use the same sort.

Students will sort using the following routine:

1.   The students will remove their headers from their bags.
2.   The students will lay their headers across the top of their work space, side by side.
3.   The students will retrieve one picture and word card at a time from their bags.
4.   The students will look at the card that was retrieved from their bags and isolate the focus sound in the word (e.g., students will say, "/ă/ *sk*").
5.   The students will say the word aloud to themselves (e.g., students will say "ask").
6.   The students will find the header that matches their card, point to it, say the word represented by their picture, and tap out the header (e.g., students will point to the header *hat*, say "hat," and say "/h/ /ă/ /t/").
7.   The students will say their chosen word (e.g., students will say "ask").
8.   The students will say their matching header (e.g., students will say "hat").
9.   The students will repeat the focus sound in the word represented by the chosen picture and matching header three times (e.g., students will say "/ă/ /ă/ /ă/").
10.   The students will say the spelling of the focus pattern found in the word represented by their chosen card and the matching header (e.g., students will say "short *a*").
11.   The students will lay their chosen card underneath the matching header.
12.   The students will choose another picture from their bags and repeat Steps 4–11.
13.   The students will follow this routine until all of their weekly cards are placed underneath the appropriate headers.

Engraining this routine in your students will lead to their success as the program progresses.

Sorting With Separate Picture and Word Cards Routine

For Concepts 3 and 10

WHAT IS IT?   Sorting With Separate Picture and Word Cards is a five- to ten-minute activity done on Days 1–4. Students match pictures to printed words that represent each picture. They then sort the pictures and words under headers that represent the weekly focus patterns.

LEARNING OUTCOMES   Students will
- Tap out sounds in words
- Hear the focus pattern in each word and picture
- Connect the focus sound and spelling in each word to the appropriate sort header
- Identify consonants, short vowels, and long vowels

PURPOSE	The purpose of Sorting With Separate Picture and Word Cards is to transition students from isolating single sounds in words to segmenting and reading full words. Matching pictures to words supports students as they build independence reading CVC and vowel_e words.
BASIC ROUTINE	Each week there are two sets of sorts. Each set is composed of one group of pictures and one group of words. The pictures and words match. One set meets grade-level expectations (Group 1), and one set provides enrichment (Group 2). Beginning in Concept 3, Week 1, be sure to flexibly group students and let them know which sort they will use for the week.

Students will sort using the following routine:

1. The students remove their headers from their bags.
2. The students lay their headers across the top of their work space, side by side.
3. The students make a stack of pictures (so that one picture can be seen at a time) and a column of words (so that all words can be seen at a time).
4. The students retrieve one picture from their stack of pictures.
5. The students look at the picture and tap out the sounds in the word represented by the picture (e.g., the students say "/p/ /ŏ/ /t/").
6. The students say the word represented by the picture aloud (e.g., the students say "pot").
7. The students find the header that matches their picture, point to it, and read the header (e.g., the students point to the header *log* and say "log").
8. The students say the word represented by the picture (e.g., the students say "pot").
9. The students say the matching header (e.g., the students say "log").
10. The students repeat the focus sound in the picture and matching header three times (e.g., the students say "/ŏ/ /ŏ/ /ŏ/").
11. The students say the spelling of the focus pattern found in the word represented by the picture and in the matching header (e.g., the students say "short *o*").
12. The students sort the picture underneath the matching header.
13. The students find the printed word that matches the picture from their column of printed words.
14. The students sort their printed word next to the matching picture underneath the header.
15. The students choose another picture from their stack of pictures and repeat Steps 4–14 until all of their weekly pictures and words are sorted underneath the appropriate headers.

Sorting With Words Routine

For Concepts 4–9

WHAT IS IT?	Sorting With Words is a five- to ten-minute activity done on Days 1–4. Students tap out the sounds in their words. They then sort the words under headers that represent the weekly focus patterns.

(Continued)

LEARNING OUTCOMES	Students will • Tap out sounds in words • Hear the focus pattern in each word • Connect the sound they hear to the spelling pattern used in the word • Connect the focus patterns in each word to the appropriate sort header • Identify consonants and short vowels
PURPOSE	The purpose of Sorting With Words is for students to repeatedly say, hear, and read the focus patterns of the week. Students build mastery of the focus patterns through repeated practice. They quickly recognize and are able to sound out the weekly focus patterns, wherever the patterns appear. Students also begin to recognize the puzzle pieces as a reference point. The headers, which are the same as the puzzle pieces, reinforce the weekly focus patterns. When the headers are put away, the puzzle pieces remain as a connection that students can apply to encode and decode new words. They carry over this knowledge to read and write words both within word study and authentically at other times of day.
BASIC ROUTINE	In Concepts 4–8, there is one new sort each week that contains words with the focus patterns. If students do not master the first sort for each concept during week 1, then they will continue to work with the same sort the following week until mastery. In Concept 9, there are differentiated word sorts each week. Students follow this routine:

1. The students remove their headers from their bags.
2. The students lay their headers across the top of their work space, side by side.
3. The students retrieve one word from their bags.
4. The students look at the word and tap out the sounds in the word (e.g., the students say "/c/ /ŏ/ /b/").
5. The students read the word aloud (e.g., the students say "cob").
6. The students find the header that matches the word, point to it, and read the header (e.g., the students point to the header *knob* and say "knob").
7. The students say the word (e.g., the students say "cob").
8. The students say the matching header (e.g., the students say "knob").
9. The students repeat the focus sound in the chosen word and matching header three times (e.g., the students say "/ŏb/ /ŏb/ /ŏb/").
10. The students say the spelling of the focus pattern found in the word and matching header (e.g., the students say "_ob").
11. The students sort the word underneath the matching header.
12. The students choose another word from their bags and repeat Steps 4–11 until all of their weekly words are sorted underneath the appropriate headers.

Practice Pieces

WHAT IS IT?	Practice Pieces are various routines that take fifteen minutes and are completed on Days 1–4. They help students apply the weekly focus patterns in authentic activities.

LEARNING OUTCOMES	Students will

Students will

- Read and write their weekly words
- Apply the weekly focus patterns within new contexts
- Build accountability for reading and writing the focus patterns as they mindfully practice

PURPOSE

The purpose of the Practice Pieces is for students to build fluency in reading and writing the focus patterns of the week. Phonics instruction is most effective when students immediately apply what they have been learning to read and write. Practice Pieces are students' independent practice for the day and give them that opportunity for application.

As students complete weekly Spelling Checks, they will also learn the importance of study skills, and they will take ownership of their performance. Encourage students to reflect on their work for the week and how it affected their weekly Spelling Check. Reflection will help students take their Practice Pieces seriously.

BASIC ROUTINE

Practice Pieces are typically the same week to week so students can attend to their weekly focus patterns, rather than learn a new routine. Find which Practice Pieces work best for your class, but don't be afraid to switch things up as needed. See the Teacher's Guide and the Tips for Management and Differentiation sections for notes about any changes or additional Practice Pieces.

The options include the following:

- Quick Color
- Careful Cut
- Add Two
- Make a New Category
- Glue Words
- Create a Scene
- Highlighter Hunt
- Grab and Write
- Letter Matrix
- Fluency Drill
- Read and Trade
- Act It Out
- Spell It Out
- Glue, Draw a Picture
- Create a Puzzle Piece
- Color-Code Writing
- Super Sentences
- Labeling the Room
- Word Hunt
- Partner Spell
- Rainbow Write
- Sort Your Own Way

See explanations of each Practice Piece at the end of this section (pages I-37–I-60).

Fluency: Choral Reading Routine

For Concept I

WHAT IS IT?

Fluency is a fifteen-minute activity that is completed on Days 1–4. In Concept 1, students will chorally read repetitive poems as a class.

LEARNING OUTCOMES

Students will

- Listen to a poem and fill in the blanks to connect language to their experiences
- Read words accurately
- Read at a natural pace
- Read with expression

PURPOSE

The purpose of this choral reading is for students to enjoy language with their classmates, become familiar with print, and practice the three major components of reading fluency:

- Reading the words accurately
- Reading at a natural pace
- Reading with expression

Choral reading supports students as they are beginning to see themselves as readers. All students experience success so that they can begin the year with excitement.

BASIC ROUTINE

There are two poems per week in the Fluency Notebook. You will introduce the poems and give students the opportunity to repeatedly read them.

Follow this routine to introduce poems:

1. Select the poem you will read for the day.
2. Instruct students to open their Fluency Notebooks to the poem or display an enlarged version of the poem in front of the class.
3. Tell students the title of the poem and read it all the way through.
4. Invite students to help you read the poem.
5. Teach the signals "My Turn" (point to yourself) and "Your Turn" (hold your hand out to the students, palm up).
6. Signal "My Turn" and read the first part of the poem (as much or as little as you think students can remember).
7. Signal "Your Turn" and reread the first part of the poem with students.
8. Continue signaling "My Turn" and "Your Turn" until the poem is complete. If necessary, stop and reread parts or combine smaller sections before rereading the full poem.
9. Point out any blanks to students. Call on students to fill in the blanks and write the suggestions on the lines.
10. Reread the full poem and celebrate students as readers.

BASIC ROUTINE **(Continued)**	Follow this routine to reread poems:

1. Select the poem you will read for the day.
2. Instruct students to open their Fluency Notebooks to the poem or display an enlarged version of the poem in front of the class.
3. If necessary, read the poem aloud to students first, either in its entirety or in smaller sections.
4. Cue students to chorally read the poem as a class.
5. Reread the poem several times in a variety of fun, interesting formats. You can call on girls or boys, have a helper point to the words while the class reads, or read it in different voices.
6. Celebrate students as readers.

Fluency: Chants and Alliteration Couplets Routine

For Concept 2

WHAT IS IT?	Fluency is a fifteen-minute activity that is completed on Days 1–4. In Concept 2, students will complete and repeatedly read chants that highlight the focus sounds. They will also repeatedly read couplets with alliteration.
LEARNING OUTCOMES	Students will • Listen to a poem and fill in the blanks to connect language to their experiences and weekly sort words • Read words accurately • Read at a natural pace • Read with expression • Identify examples of words with the focus patterns
PURPOSE	The chants and alliteration couplets help students continue growing in their confidence as readers. They are simple, allowing students to memorize them throughout the week. Students can then independently read the chants and couplets, matching spoken words to print and identifying the focus patterns within words.
BASIC ROUTINE	There is one chant and one couplet for each weekly focus sound, for a total of three chants and three couplets. You will introduce the chants and couplets and give students the opportunity to repeatedly read them. Follow this routine to introduce chants and couplets:

1. Select the chant or couplet you will read for the day.
2. Instruct students to open their Fluency Notebooks to the chant or couplet or display an enlarged version of it in front of the class.
3. Tell students the title or the focus pattern and read the chant or couplet all the way through.
4. Invite students to help you read the chant or couplet.
5. Review the signals "My Turn" (point to yourself) and "Your Turn" (hold your hand out to the students, palm up).

(Continued)

6. Signal "My Turn" and read the first part of the chant or couplet (as much or as little as you think students can remember).
7. Signal "Your Turn" and reread the first part of the chant or couplet with students.
8. Continue signaling "My Turn" and "Your Turn" until the chant or couplet is complete. If necessary, stop and reread parts or combine smaller sections before rereading the full poem.
9. Point out any blanks to students. Call on students to fill in the blanks and write the suggestions on the lines. Suggestions should begin with the focus sound.
10. Reread the full chant or couplet and celebrate students as readers.

Follow this routine to reread chants and couplets:

1. Select the chant or couplet you will read for the day.
2. Instruct students to open their Fluency Notebooks to the chant or couplet or display an enlarged version of it in front of the class.
3. If necessary, read the chant or couplet aloud to students first, either in its entirety or in smaller sections.
4. Cue students to chorally read the chant or couplet as a class.
5. Reread the poem several times in a variety of fun, interesting formats. You can call on girls or boys, have a helper point to the words while the class reads, or read it in different voices.
6. Celebrate students as readers.

As the week progresses, students may be ready to independently select and read from their fluency materials with a partner. Assign students partners and circulate, listen, or gather a small group of students for extra support as needed.

Fluency: Passages Routine

For Concept 3

WHAT IS IT?
Fluency is a fifteen-minute activity that is completed on Days 1–4. In Concept 3, students will repeatedly read one of two weekly passages.

LEARNING OUTCOMES
Students will

- Apply their knowledge of sounds and spellings to decode unfamiliar words
- Read words accurately
- Read at a natural pace
- Read with expression

PURPOSE
Fluency passages are short, highly decodable texts that allow students to take on more responsibility for independently reading. As students master the passage throughout the week, they will be practicing the three major components of reading fluency:

- Reading the words accurately
- Reading at a natural pace
- Reading with expression

Students will also build confidence in themselves as readers and see that they can read on their own.

BASIC ROUTINE　　There are two passages per week in the Fluency Notebook. One of the passages is written for students in Group 1. One of the passages is written for students in Group 2. Introduce the passages to your class or to small groups of students. Then circulate and listen to partners read, or gather a small group of students who need additional support.

Students will follow this routine:

1. Students turn to the assigned page within the Fluency Notebook.
2. Students read the passage aloud with a partner at least three times.
3. Students continue to practice the passage until they have achieved fluency.
4. Students may return to previously assigned passages to maintain fluency.

Fluency: Short Vowel Poems Routine

For Concepts 4–10

WHAT IS IT?　　Fluency is a fifteen-minute activity that is completed on Days 1–4. In Concepts 4–10, students repeatedly read one of two differentiated poems with the weekly focus patterns in context.

LEARNING OUTCOMES　　Students will

- Apply their knowledge of sounds and spellings to decode unfamiliar words
- Read words accurately
- Read at a natural pace
- Read with expression

PURPOSE　　The short vowel poems will help students continue to practice the three components of reading fluency. As they repeatedly read the poems throughout the week, students become more familiar with each one. They add expression and personalize how they read the poems. Students begin to see themselves as readers, and reading as enjoyable.

BASIC ROUTINE　　There are two poems per week in the Fluency Notebook. One of the poems is written for students in Group 1. One of the poems is written for students in Group 2.

Introduce the poems to your class or to small groups of students. Then circulate and listen to partners read, or gather a small group of students who need additional support.

Students will follow this routine:

1. Students will turn to the assigned page within the Fluency Notebook.
2. Students will read the poem aloud at least three times.
3. Students will continue to practice the daily poem until they have achieved fluency.
4. Students may return to previously assigned poems to maintain fluency.

Spelling Checks

WHAT IS IT?

Spelling Checks are formal assessments that take ten minutes and are completed on Day 5. They assess students' mastery of the weekly focus patterns. Spelling Checks are not traditional spelling tests, as students are not encouraged to memorize specific words. Instead, students are expected to represent initial consonant sounds (Concept 2) or to tap out words, reference the puzzle pieces, and record some of their weekly words (Concepts 3–10).

LEARNING OUTCOMES

Students will

- Isolate and record initial consonants
- Spell weekly words phonetically
- Apply the conventions of the English language to write a sentence (beginning in Concept 3)

PURPOSE

Spelling Checks serve a purpose for students and teachers as well as families:

- **Students** mindfully complete their Practice Pieces when they understand that repeated practice leads to success on their Spelling Checks.
- **Teachers** have a record of student mastery, which they can use to form differentiated word study groups and to communicate with families.
- **Families** are able to see grade-level expectations as well as student progress.

The goal of the Spelling Check is to ensure that students are able to transfer each concept independently to their own writing. Students must apply what they have learned each week in order to retain their knowledge. However, avoid this check becoming stressful for them. Students are developing spelling, and representing sounds within words is the first step toward full understanding. You can adjust grading expectations to meet the needs of your students and reflect their progress. For example, in Concept 3, you can hold students accountable for recording the vowel sound and wait until Concept 4 to require students to tap out and represent full words.

BASIC ROUTINE

In Concepts 2 and 4–8 during Week 1, all students will record the same sounds or words for the Spelling Check. Follow this routine:

1. Students get out their Learner's Notebooks and pull out the page for this week's Spelling Check.
2. The teacher says sound 1 or word 1 isolated and in a sentence.
3. The students record the sound or word.
4. The teacher and students continue until the five sounds or words have been recorded.
5. The teacher says the sentence (beginning in Concept 3) and slowly repeats it.
6. The students record the sentence.
7. The teacher instructs students to check over their work.

There are two differentiated Spelling Checks in Concept 3, Concepts 4–8 during Week 2, Concept 9, and Concept 10.

Follow this routine:

1. Students get out their Learner's Notebooks and pull out the page for this week's Spelling Check.
2. The teacher assigns students seats based on their word study groups (place students with the same words in the same area of the room).

BASIC ROUTINE (Continued)	3. Students move into their assigned groups, taking their Spelling Checks and a pencil.

3. Students move into their assigned groups, taking their Spelling Checks and a pencil.
4. The teacher moves to the group of students in Group 1 and says word 1 isolated and in a sentence.
5. The students in Group 1 record the word.
6. The teacher moves to Group 2 and says word 1 isolated and in a sentence.
7. The students in Group 2 record the word.
8. The teacher and students follow Steps 4–7 with the remaining words for Groups 1 and 2.
9. The teacher moves to Group 1, says the sentence, and slowly repeats it.
10. The students in Group 1 record the sentence.
11. The teacher moves to Group 2, says the sentence, and slowly repeats it.
12. The students in Group 2 record the sentence.
13. The teacher instructs students to check over their work.

Use teacher discretion when implementing and grading Spelling Checks.

Handwriting Check

WHAT IS IT?

The Handwriting Check is a five-minute formal assessment of students' letter formation. The teacher models the upper- and lowercase formation of the weekly letters. Then students independently record three of each letter.

LEARNING OUTCOMES

Students will

- Form uppercase letters
- Form lowercase letters
- Correctly use handwriting paper

PURPOSE

Handwriting Checks allow teachers to assess students' developing letter formation. Teachers can use the checks to hold one-on-one conferences with students, report progress to families, and plan small-group remediation.

BASIC ROUTINE

Students will complete the Handwriting Check one time per week.

Follow this routine:

1. The students will locate their Handwriting Checks for the week.
2. The teacher will write the first letter on the board and say, "This is uppercase/lowercase _____" (e.g., say, "This is uppercase *D*").
3. The teacher will prompt students to record three copies of the first letter (e.g., say, "Write three uppercase *D*s").
4. The students will record three copies of the first letter.
5. The teacher and students will repeat Steps 2–4 with the remaining letters.
6. The teacher will prompt students to check over their work and turn it in.

Comprehension Check

WHAT IS IT?

The Comprehension Check should take no longer than fifteen minutes and is completed on Day 5. Students complete a cold read of a text that contains words with the weekly focus patterns, sight words, and previously taught patterns. Students will look at a picture and select the sentence that matches the picture. Later in the year, students will answer questions about the text.

LEARNING OUTCOMES

Students will
- Apply phonics patterns and word attack strategies to decode words
- Apply knowledge of sight words
- Answer within- and beyond-the-text questions to show understanding of the text

PURPOSE

The purpose of the Comprehension Check builds throughout the year.

- In Concept 3, students focus on word attack strategies. They use their knowledge of the sight words and focus patterns taught, in order to circle a sentence that matches a picture.
- In Concepts 4–8, students reference the text in order to answer within-the-text questions.
- In Concepts 9–10, students are introduced to beyond-the-text questions, which require them to use their own knowledge that connects to the text in order to answer the questions.

Although they differ in strategy, all Comprehension Checks focus on sight word mastery and word attack strategies. They can be used as a formal assessment or as an opportunity for students to practice applying their new skills.

BASIC ROUTINE

Follow this routine:

1. The students locate their Comprehension Checks for the week.
2. The students look at the picture for the first section of the passage.
3. The students will identify the sentence that matches the picture. If needed, you can tell students, "Find the sentence that says …" and read the correct sentence.
4. The students will complete Steps 2–3 for the next two sections of text.
5. The students read the first comprehension question.
6. The students will use their background knowledge or the text to answer the question.
7. The students answer the comprehension question by either drawing a picture, circling the answer, or filling in the blank.
8. The students repeat Steps 5–8 until all of the comprehension questions have been answered.

Quick Color

PURPOSE

The purpose of Quick Color is for students to prepare their materials for the week. Students sort and manipulate their words all week long. One student's words can become lost or mixed up with another student's words. Quick Color helps students identify that the words with a certain color on the back belong to them.

Beginning in Concept 3, Week 1, there are two sorts for the week. Be sure students know which sort they will use before completing Quick Color.

Students will

1. Locate the correct sort for the week in their Learner's Notebooks
2. Remove the sorts from their Learner's Notebooks
3. Quickly "scribble-scrabble" over the back of their page with one color of crayon
4. Make sure that each word has some bit of color on it

**WHAT TO
WATCH FOR**

• This activity should not take more than two minutes. Students should not color the entire sheet. They should be putting messy marks as an organizational tool for the week.

MODIFICATIONS

• There are no modifications for this Practice Piece.

EXTENSIONS

• There are no extensions for this Practice Piece.

Careful Cut

PURPOSE

The purpose of Careful Cut is for students to prepare their materials for the week.

Students will

1. Cut around the sort
2. Cut the sort into vertical columns
3. Cut the vertical columns horizontally to create a single word
4. Place the cut words in their word bags

**WHAT TO
WATCH FOR**

- Encourage students to systematically cut the words rather than cutting them individually. This saves instructional time.

MODIFICATIONS

- Highlight vertical lines that need to be cut in one color and horizontal lines that need to be cut in another color. Tell students which color to cut first and second. This will guide students to create single words.

EXTENSIONS

- There are no extensions for this Practice Piece.

Add Two

PURPOSE

The purpose of Add Two is for students to identify additional items that fit into specific categories. Students practice grouping together like objects.

Students will

1. Lay their weekly headers at the top of their work space
2. Identify the two weekly categories
3. Select one category to focus on
4. Identify two items that fit into that category
5. Draw or label a card for each item
6. Add the cards to the category
7. Repeat Steps 4–6 for the second category

WHAT TO WATCH FOR

- Students may want to draw items that do not fit into specific categories. Monitor and support students' work as necessary.

MODIFICATIONS

- Students may initially struggle to identify additional objects that fit into specific categories. You can complete this activity as a class or generate a list together and allow students to select which objects to add to their categories.

EXTENSIONS

- Students can create additional cards for each category.
- Students can label their picture cards.

Make a New Category

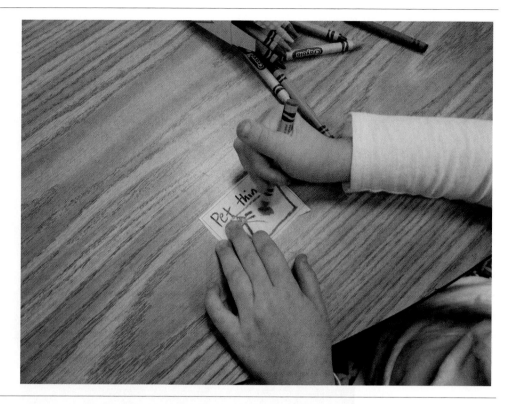

PURPOSE

The purpose of Make a New Category is for students to further practice sorting and categorizing objects.

Students will

1. Lay their weekly headers at the top of their work space
2. Identify the two weekly categories
3. Choose a new category of items to add to their sort
4. Draw or label a header for the new category
5. Draw or label cards for items that belong in that category

WHAT TO WATCH FOR

- Students may struggle with the concept of a category. Discuss this word with students and practice coming up with categories and objects within those categories as a class before releasing responsibility to students.

MODIFICATIONS

- You can complete this activity as a whole group or with small groups of students.
- If students struggle to draw or label their cards or headers, you can take dictation.

EXTENSIONS

- Students can create two additional categories to add.

Glue Words

PURPOSE

The purpose of this activity is for students to keep their words and/or pictures for future reference. Students can take their words home for continued practice.

Students will

1. Get a piece of paper
2. Pick up their sort header from their desk and glue it to their paper
3. Create a long line of glue underneath the sort header
4. Quickly pick up one word and/or picture from their desks and apply it to the glue line
5. Follow Steps 2–4 until all words have been glued

WHAT TO WATCH FOR

• Help students organize their work space so their words do not become unsorted while gluing.

MODIFICATIONS

• The teacher can create the glue line.

EXTENSIONS

• Students can create a plan for practicing their words at home.

Create a Scene

PURPOSE

The purpose of Create a Scene is for students to think about the meaning of their words and connect them to create a picture. Students will glue their words to a blank sheet of paper, making them easier to take home.

Students will

1. Get a blank sheet of paper, a glue stick, and their bag of words and pictures
2. Decide on a scene to create using their words
3. Lay the words on their papers to create the scene
4. Glue the words down
5. Draw details/add to the picture to enhance the scene

WHAT TO WATCH FOR

- Students may need instruction and modeling to know how to use a glue stick properly.

MODIFICATIONS

- You can complete this activity as a class or with a small group of students.
- You can limit students to only working with a few words within one category, rather than looking at their full bank of words.

EXTENSIONS

- Students can label parts of their completed scene.
- Students can create two separate scenes using words from the two categories.

Highlighter Hunt

PURPOSE

The purpose of Highlighter Hunt is for students to identify the focus pattern within each weekly word.

Students will

1. Lay each sort header out in front of them
2. Take one word at a time out of their bags
3. Say the word out loud
4. Identify the focus pattern within the word
5. Highlight the letters that make up the focus pattern

WHAT TO WATCH FOR

- Students may make a mistake when working with materials other than pencils. Decide how you want students to fix errors and teach your expectation before students begin working.

MODIFICATIONS

- Help the students underline the focus spellings in pencil. Then have students independently trace over the spellings with a highlighter.

EXTENSIONS

- Extensions are embedded within the differentiation of the sorts. Students in Group 2 will examine longer words in order to find the focus patterns.

Grab and Write

PURPOSE

The purpose of Grab and Write is for students to practice letter identification and formation.

Students will

1. Get a sheet of handwriting paper, a pencil, and their bag of words
2. Take one word at a time out of their bags
3. Identify the first letter (or last letter in the case of /x/) in the word
4. Record the letter on their sheet of paper using correct letter formation
5. Set the word aside
6. Select a new word and repeat Steps 3–5

**WHAT TO
WATCH FOR**

- Students may need additional modeling of letter formation before beginning this activity.

MODIFICATIONS

- You can provide students with a prepared paper that has the weekly letters formed with dotted lines or in highlighter. As students select words, they can match the first letter on a word card to the letters on their paper and trace them.

EXTENSIONS

- Students can write the uppercase and lowercase versions of each letter.
- Students can record additional letters within words that have been studied in previous weeks.

Letter Matrix

Letter Matrix: d, t, and a

| D d dig | T t type | A a hat |

t	H	a	A	i
P	d	S	g	T
j	M	T	D	p
a	l	d	a	L
r	T	C	w	d
D	F	t	m	z
t	J	A	k	A

PURPOSE

The purpose of Letter Matrix is for students to practice letter identification.

Students will

1. Open their Learner's Notebooks to today's Letter Matrix and take out a crayon
2. Search for the uppercase and lowercase versions of the focus letters of the week
3. Color in the letters with a crayon as they find them

WHAT TO WATCH FOR

- Students may need modeling to understand how to search the matrix and appropriately color the letters. You can complete a Letter Matrix together as a class, calling on volunteers to search for and color in the letters.

MODIFICATIONS

- It may help students to look at a smaller version of the letter matrix. You can cover part of the page with sticky notes or a sheet of paper and help students search within a smaller space.

EXTENSIONS

- Students can search for letters that have been previously studied in the matrix and color them in a different color.
- Students can color-code uppercase and lowercase letters.

Fluency Drill

Bb

Bob bought a big box of books at the shop.

Bob browsed the books until Ben said stop.

PURPOSE

The purpose of the Fluency Drill is for students to practice letter sounds and identification.

Students will

1. Open their Fluency Notebooks to the chants and alliteration couplets for the week and take out a pencil.
2. Search for the chants and alliteration couplets for uppercase and lowercase versions of the focus letters for the week.
3. Circle and produce the sounds of the letters as they find them.

**WHAT TO
WATCH FOR**

- This task requires students to multitask. They must search for the focus letters, circle them, and produce their sound. At first, students may need modeling and practice to master this procedure. Over time, you should look for your students' fluency to build.

MODIFICATIONS

- Students may need to attend to one task at a time. They can first search the chant or alliteration couplet and circle any of the weekly letters. Then they can return to the chant or couplet a second time to produce the sound of the circled letters. If students need further support, you can write the letters on a whiteboard as students find them. After searching the chant or couplet, have students look at the whiteboard and produce the sounds of the recorded letters.

EXTENSIONS

- Students can test their growing fluency. You can see how many letters and sounds they can identify in one minute.

Read and Trade

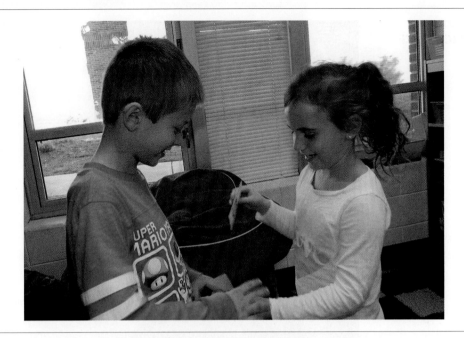

PURPOSE

The purpose of Read and Trade is for students to interact with one another while practicing reading their weekly words.

Materials

1. Flashcards with the weekly words
2. A sheet of paper and pencil for each student

Follow this routine:

1. The teacher will gather the class and give each student a flashcard with one of the weekly words.
2. The teacher will give students the signal to stand up and find a partner.
3. Students will partner up, showing each other the word on their flashcards.
4. Partner A will read the word on partner B's card.
5. Partner B will read the word on partner A's card.
6. The two students will trade cards and move to find another partner.
7. The teacher will call time, and students will return to their seats with the flashcard that is currently in their hands.
8. The students will draw the word that is on their flashcard.

**WHAT TO
WATCH FOR**

- Students may forget to trade cards or to read their partner's flashcard instead of their own. Practice these procedures several times before playing Read and Trade.

MODIFICATIONS

- You can teach students that if their partner is unable to read the word, they can give a helpful hint or read the word to the student. Then the student should repeat the word.
- You can pull a small group of students to play with a limited set of words. If your whole class would benefit from repeated exposure to the same words, then you can write the same few words on a class set of flashcards. The class can play with a limited set of words.

EXTENSIONS

- You can add additional words that include the focus patterns but are not included in the weekly sorts. Challenge students to decode the new words.

Act It Out

PURPOSE

The purpose of Act It Out is for students to interact with one another while practicing reading their weekly words.

Follow this routine:

1. The teacher will place students in partners. One partner from each group will bring his or her bag of words.
2. Partners will choose one word from the bag.
3. Partners will read the word and act out its meaning together.
4. Partners will place the word off to the side.
5. Partners will select a new word and repeat Steps 3–4 until all words have been read or time is called.

WHAT TO WATCH FOR

- Students will likely need modeling to understand how to act out words. Complete this activity several times as a class before transitioning students into partner work.

MODIFICATIONS

- You can complete this activity with a small group of students.
- You can give students a limited set of words to work with. Create actions for the words together first, and then allow students to select words and repeat the actions with a partner.

EXTENSIONS

- If students finish acting out their weekly words quickly, challenge them to act out a poem in their Fluency Notebook.

Spell It Out

STUDENT PRACTICE PIECE

PURPOSE

The purpose of Spell It Out is for students to apply their understanding of the weekly focus patterns to spell new words.

Students will

1. Open their Learner's Notebooks to today's Spell It Out and take out a pencil
2. Look at the picture that represents the first word
3. Break the word into sounds and reference the puzzle pieces to identify the sounds
4. Record the sounds, writing the word
5. Repeat Steps 2–4 for the remaining words

WHAT TO WATCH FOR

- Students may not know the meaning of the pictures. Show students the page in the Learner's Notebook and identify each picture before beginning. Then circulate, repeat the pictures, and help students tap out words.

MODIFICATIONS

- You can complete this activity with a small group of students. Tap out the sounds and reference the puzzle pieces together. If necessary, write the words in highlighter and have students trace them.
- Students can focus on recording only the initial sound or the vowel sound of words.

EXTENSIONS

- Students can write simple sentences using the words.

Glue, Draw a Picture

PURPOSE

The purpose of Glue, Draw a Picture is for students to practice reading their weekly words and make connections to their meanings.

Students will

1. Get out their bag of words, a blank sheet of paper, and a pencil
2. Remove one word at a time from their bags
3. Glue the word to their paper
4. Read the word and draw a picture of it
5. Repeat Steps 2–4 with the remaining words

WHAT TO WATCH FOR

- You may need to model for students how to set up their papers. Students will likely run out of space if they haphazardly glue the words to the page. Model for students how to neatly glue the words in columns while saving enough space to draw a picture.

MODIFICATIONS

- You can complete this activity with a small group of students. Read each word together, then have students create their pictures.

EXTENSIONS

- Students can create and label a scene using their words.

Create a Puzzle Piece

PURPOSE

The purpose of Create a Puzzle Piece is to allow students to connect the focus patterns to a word that is significant to them. Students are also able to be creative and make another resource for future reference.

Students will

1. Draw a puzzle piece outline
2. Select one of their sort headers
3. Decide a new name for the piece
4. Create a new piece that shows its spelling, picture, and name and follows the format of the existing puzzle pieces

WHAT TO WATCH FOR

- For this to be a proper reference point, the name of the puzzle piece the student creates must be spelled correctly. Students might want to use a word that is not found in their weekly sort as their new name for the puzzle piece. Help students check their spelling of words, if this is the case.

MODIFICATIONS

- Limit students to the words contained in their weekly sort.

EXTENSIONS

- Students can create a motion for their puzzle piece.
- Students can write words that contain the focus spelling pattern of that piece on the back.

Color-Code Writing

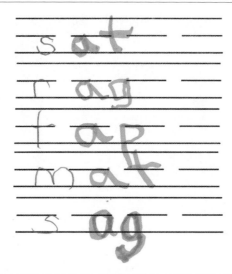

PURPOSE

The purpose of Color-Code Writing is for students to recognize the focus spelling patterns and to make them stand out. Once words within the weekly sort have been color-coded, students will be able to clearly see where the spelling patterns are located within their words.

Students will

1. Take out a pencil and one marker, crayon, or colored pencil
2. Get a piece of paper
3. Create one column on their paper for each focus spelling pattern that week (The columns will match the sort headers for the week; for example, if the sort headers are short *a* and short *e*, then students will create a short *a* column and a short *e* column.)
4. Read their first word
5. Write their first word entirely in pencil in the correct column
6. Identify which letters make up the focus pattern
7. Trace over the letters that make up the focus pattern with their marker, crayon, or colored pencil
8. Repeat Steps 3–7 with their remaining words until all words have been written

WHAT TO WATCH FOR

- Students may make a mistake when working with materials other than pencils. Decide how you want students to fix errors, and teach your expectation before students begin working.

MODIFICATIONS

- Prerecord all letters except for those that make up the focus pattern (e.g., in the word *cat*, record the *c* and *t* in the short *a* column). When students complete this activity, they will follow the same routine but only record the focus spelling (e.g., the student will write *a* in the short *a* column to complete the word *cat*).

EXTENSIONS

- To make the activity more challenging, require students to look at the word, read it and say the focus spelling pattern, then flip the word over. They will write the word in Color-Code Writing without looking. Then students will flip the word back over and check their work. If you choose to use this extension, make sure you have taught students how to carefully check their work and address any mistakes.

Super Sentences

PURPOSE

The purpose of Super Sentences is to give students the opportunity to use their weekly words in context. Students must know the meaning of the words to complete this activity. As the year progresses, vocabulary words are embedded into the curriculum with increasing frequency. Students can use their weekly words in a creative way while also demonstrating understanding of their meaning.

Students will

1. Get a piece of paper
2. Look at their words for the week
3. Select a word to use in a sentence
4. Orally construct a sentence that contains the word
5. Record the sentence on a sheet of paper
6. Circle their weekly word within the sentence
7. Repeat Steps 1–5 until the practice time ends

**WHAT TO
WATCH FOR**

- This activity provides students an opportunity to apply all of the expectations for conventions in kindergarten. Standards require that students spell untaught words phonetically and sight words correctly. Students should also correctly use punctuation and capital letters at this time. Hold students accountable for the phonics patterns, sight words, and conventions that have been taught up to this point.
- Explain to students that Super Sentences show the meaning of the word. For example, "I see a leaf" does not explain the meaning of the word *leaf*. Model how to write a sentence with meaning. For example, "The red leaf fell off the tree" shows that the student knows that leaves are on trees.
- As the year progresses, teach students that Super Sentences contain two or more details. A sentence sounds like "I saw a black cat." A Super Sentence sounds like "I saw a black cat running up the tree!" Students will become more creative as the teacher models Super Sentences and other students share what they have created.

| MODIFICATIONS | • Give students a cloze (a list of sentences that are each missing one of their weekly words). They will read the sentences, look at their weekly words, and fill in the blank with the word that makes sense. |
| | • Students may select a word that they have difficulty applying to a new sentence. Teach students that they can move on to another word and return to that one if there is time. Encourage students to recognize when they have spent too long thinking of a sentence with one word. |

EXTENSIONS	• Students can write a story using the words for the week. Ask students to circle words that could go together in a story, and brainstorm a story line with those words. Encourage students to write a story that makes sense and has a beginning, middle, and end. Students can work with members of their sort group to co-write a story as well.
	• Students can work with a partner to build on each other's sentences. One partner will write a sentence starter containing the weekly word (e.g., "I have a pet cat …"), and the other partner will add a detail to the sentence (e.g., "I have a pet cat that likes to chase yarn").
	• Students can swap papers with a partner and peer edit.

Labeling the Room

| PURPOSE | The purpose of Labeling the Room is to give students an opportunity to match their pictures and word sort cards to specific items in the classroom. Students will make connections that their words represent meaning. They will show this meaning by pointing out items to label in their everyday school lives. |

Follow this routine:

1. The teacher will ask students to think about their sort cards for the week.
2. The teacher will read off the weekly pictures/words.
3. Students will walk around or point to items in the room that can be labeled from this week's sort.
4. The teacher will label the item by writing on a notecard and taping the notecard to the specific item.
5. The teacher and students will read and make the connection from their sort to their classroom item.

| WHAT TO WATCH FOR | • Students may mix up homophones. If this occurs, take the opportunity as a teaching moment to explain the different meanings of a specific word. |
| | • Students may suggest words that do not contain any focus patterns. If this occurs, the teacher can give hints or a suggestion on another classroom item to label. |

| MODIFICATIONS | • The teacher can create premade labeling cards. These will assist students in labeling the room. They will not need to brainstorm words; they can use the card and match it to the item in the room. |

- Student may not have many words from their weekly sort that can be labeled in the room. If this occurs, ask students to think beyond their sorts and think about the week's focus. Students can make suggestions to label items in the room that contain the sort's focus of the week.
- The teacher can guide students to tap out the sounds in all the labeled objects.

Word Hunt

STUDENT PRACTICE PIECE

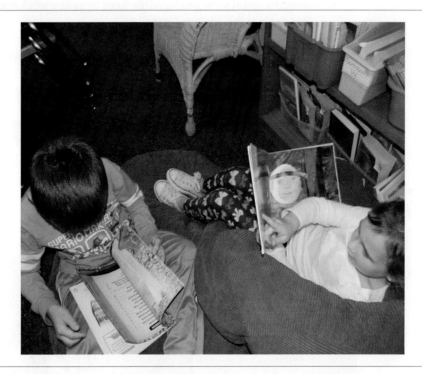

PURPOSE

The purpose of the Word Hunt is to give students an opportunity to locate specific words within books and the classroom environment. Students will decode the focus patterns within new words. They must also determine which words have the focus pattern in them and which words do not.

Students will

1. Get a piece of paper
2. Divide their paper into as many columns as there are sort headers for that week
3. Label each column with one sort header
4. Walk around the room, explore books, or reference their fluency poems in search of words that contain their focus patterns
5. Identify words that have the focus patterns within them
6. Write the words that they find under the appropriate header
7. Continue the activity until the time is up

WHAT TO WATCH FOR	• Students may hear the focus sound within a word, but the word does not contain the focus spelling. For example, students may attempt to record the word *science* under *i_e* because they hear the long *i* sound and they see *i* and *e* together. However, this is not a spelling of *i_e*.
	• Some spelling patterns will be difficult to find in books and around the room (e.g., *e_e*). Encourage students to look in their Fluency Notebooks or prepare word lists ahead of time when you know a pattern is difficult to find.
MODIFICATIONS	• Students can look at premade word cards with new words that contain the focus patterns.
	• Students can review the blending lines from the week and pull out the words that contain the focus patterns.
EXTENSIONS	• Students can look for "rule breakers." For example, *have* contains the *a_e* pattern that usually produces a long *a* sound.
	• Students can look for items that have the focus pattern in their name but are not labeled. For example, *trash can* contains the short *a* pattern, but it may not be labeled. Students can look up the correct spelling of the item before deciding whether or not to record its name on their papers.

Partner Spell

STUDENT PRACTICE PIECE

PURPOSE

The purpose of this activity is to give students a chance to hear and spell their weekly words with a partner. Students are able to teach one another, which facilitates their own learning of the patterns.

Follow this routine:

1. The students will get their word study bags and paper and a pencil or a whiteboard and marker.
2. The students will find their partners and sit face-to-face.
3. Partners will remove their weekly headers.
4. Each partner will place the headers in front of him- or herself.
5. Each partner will remove all of his or her words from his or her bag and stack them together.
6. Partner 1 will read the first word that is on the top of his or her stack to partner 2.
7. Partner 2 will tap out the word that was read by partner 1 orally.
8. Partner 2 will identify the focus sound that is within the word that partner 1 read aloud.
9. Partner 2 will point to the appropriate header in front of him- or herself.
10. Partner 1 will say "correct" or "try again" until partner 2 correctly identifies the weekly header.
11. Partner 2 will write the word on his or her paper or whiteboard.
12. Partner 2 will show his or her paper or whiteboard to partner 1.
13. Partner 1 will say "correct" or "try again" until partner 2 correctly spells the word.
14. Partner 1 will place the word back in his or her bag.
15. Partner 2 will read the first word that is on the top of his or her stack to partner 1.
16. Partner 1 will tap out the word that was read by partner 2 orally.
17. Partner 1 will identify the focus sound that is within the word that partner 2 read aloud.
18. Partner 1 will point to the appropriate header in front of him- or herself.
19. Partner 2 will say "correct" or "try again" until partner 1 correctly identifies the weekly header.
20. Partner 1 will write the word on his or her paper or whiteboard.
21. Partner 1 will show his or her paper or whiteboard to partner 2.
22. Partner 2 will say "correct" or "try again" until partner 1 correctly spells the word.
23. Partner 2 will place the word back in his or her bag.
24. The partners will repeat Steps 6–23 until their stacks of weekly words have been spelled.

WHAT TO WATCH FOR

- Assign a consistent phonics partner for this practice. This allows the students to build a relationship and a routine together over each week. They learn how to support and teach one another.
- Model how to be a supportive partner during this activity. You can have a "fish bowl" where the class sits in a circle around two students as they successfully move through the activity. Give students possible prompts to help their partner.
- Remind students to keep their weekly words separate from their partners'. If words become mixed up, students can check the color on the back of the word.

| MODIFICATIONS | • Students can use one set of words. They will work together to read the word and tap it out. Then they will flip over the word and work together to write the word. |
| | • Students can identify and write only the focus sound in their weekly words. |

| EXTENSIONS | • Partner 1 can write a sentence with a missing word. The missing word will be from the weekly sort. Partner 2 must complete the sentence by identifying and correctly spelling the missing word. |

Rainbow Write

STUDENT PRACTICE PIECE

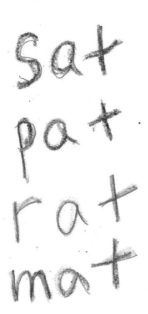

| PURPOSE | The purpose of Rainbow Write is to give students a fun way to practice repeatedly writing their weekly words.

Students will |
	1. Choose three to five colors of crayons or colored pencils
	2. Write their first word in their first color
	3. Trace over their first word in the remaining two to four colors
	4. Follow Steps 2 and 3 until all of their words have been written

| WHAT TO WATCH FOR | • This activity should be completed with crayons or colored pencils. If students use markers, then the dark colors will saturate into the felt of the lighter colors and ruin the markers. Students may also create holes in their paper. |
| | • Teach students how to organize their papers for this activity. They can use a ruler to create lines or boxes. Students will need enough space to repeatedly trace over each word. |

MODIFICATIONS	•	Write students' weekly words in pencil on their Rainbow Write paper. Students will repeatedly trace over your writing to complete the activity.
EXTENSIONS	•	Students can organize their work by choosing three to five colors for one focus pattern or sort header and another three to five colors for other focus patterns or sort headers. Once the Rainbow Write is complete, students will be able to clearly see the different focus patterns.

Sort Your Own Way

STUDENT PRACTICE PIECE

PURPOSE

The purpose of Sort Your Own Way is to give students an opportunity to creatively work with their words. Students will become accustomed to using the sort headers to group their words. Sort Your Own Way extends the sort by asking students to find a different "fit" for their words. All of the sorts are closed sorts (the headers tell students how they must sort the words). This Practice Piece turns the closed sort into an open sort in which students get to pick how to sort their words.

Students will

1. Take out their weekly words but leave their sort headers in their bags
2. Spread the words out on their work space so all of them can be seen
3. Look for words that have something in common and form groups
4. Record their groups
5. Write the new rule that explains each group

WHAT TO WATCH FOR	•	Students will need you to model how you think through the process of creating new groups. Students have been looking specifically at the focus patterns within their words. They will naturally look for the patterns within them. You need to model how to take the same set of words and group them by meaning, word type, or additional phonics patterns.
	•	Students may have difficulty finding a new way to sort. You may need to suggest possible ways students can sort their words. Ideas include the following:

- Sort by word meaning (animals, things found outside, things that scare me, etc.)
- Sort by word type (noun, adjective, verb, etc.)
- Sort by initial sound
- Sort by endings (*–ed, –ing*)
- Sort by number of syllables
- Sort by blends or digraphs
- Sort by medial sounds
- Sort by final sound
- Sort by vowel type
- Sort by previously learned focus patterns
- Sort alphabetically

MODIFICATIONS	•	Students can complete this activity with a limited set of words.
	•	Create groups that follow a new rule ahead of time. Students can match their weekly words to the new groups.

EXTENSIONS	•	Students can brainstorm other words that belong in their groups but are not included in their weekly sort.
	•	Students can walk around the room and try to guess how other students sorted.
	•	Group the words in a new way ahead of time. Challenge students to figure out your new rule for sorting.
	•	Challenge students to sort their words in as few groups as possible. It is more difficult to generate a rule that encompasses a larger number of words than many groups that include a small number of words.

Scope and Sequence Resources

Kindergarten: Word Study Pacing

WEEK	WEEKLY FOCUS	TYPE OF SORT
CONCEPT I: BUILDING THE SORTING ROUTINE		
Week 1	School Things, Pool Things	Combined Picture and Word Cards Sort
Week 2	Word or Letter	
CONCEPT 2: LETTER IDENTIFICATION, FORMATION, AND SOUND		
Week 3	/d/, /t/, /ă/	Combined Picture and Word Cards Sort
Week 4	/m/, /s/, /ă/	
Week 5	/b/, /c/, /ĕ/	
Week 6	/g/, /p/, /ĕ/	
Week 7	/w/, /n/, /ĭ/	
Week 8	/q/, /f/, /r/, /ĭ/	
Week 9	/x/, /k/, /ŏ/	
Week 10	/l/, /j/, /ŏ/	
Week 11	/v/, /h/, /ŭ/	
Week 12	/y/, /z/, /ŭ/	
CONCEPT 3: SHORT VOWELS		
Week 13	Short *a*, Short *e*	Differentiated Separate Picture and Word Cards Sort
Week 14	Short *e*, Short *o*	
Week 15	Short *o*, Short *i*	
Week 16	Short *i*, Short *u*	
Week 17	Short *u*, Short *a*	
CONCEPT 4: SHORT A FAMILIES		
Week 18	–*at*, –*ap*, –*ag*	One Word Sort—on the second week of families, students who did not master the week before will continue with the first week's sort
Week 19	–*am*, –*an*, –*and*	

WEEK	WEEKLY FOCUS	TYPE OF SORT
CONCEPT 5: SHORT *E* FAMILIES		
Week 20	*–et, –ed, –en*	One Word Sort—on the second week of families, students who did not master the week before will continue with the first week's sort
Week 21	*–ell, –eck, –est*	
CONCEPT 6: SHORT *I* FAMILIES		
Week 22	*–it, –in, –ip*	One Word Sort—on the second week of families, students who did not master the week before will continue with the first week's sort
Week 23	*–ick, –ill, –ig*	
CONCEPT 7: SHORT *O* FAMILIES		
Week 24	*–op, –ot, –ob*	One Word Sort—on the second week of families, students who did not master the week before will continue with the first week's sort
Week 25	*–ong, –ock, –og*	
CONCEPT 8: SHORT *U* FAMILIES		
Week 26	*–ub, –un, –ut*	One Word Sort—on the second week of families, students who did not master the week before will continue with the first week's sort
Week 27	*–uff, –uck, –unk*	
CONCEPT 9: MIXED SHORT VOWEL REVIEW		
Week 28	*–ap, –ep, –ip, –op, –up*	Differentiated Word Sorts
Week 29	*–am, –em, –im, –om, –um*	
Week 30	*–an, –en, –in, –on, –un*	
Week 31	*–ast, –est, –ist, –ost, –ust*	
CONCEPT 10: SHORT VOWELS AND VOWEL_*E*		
Week 32	Short *a, a_e*	Differentiated Separate Picture and Word Cards Sort
Week 33	Short *e, e_e*	
Week 34	Short *i, i_e*	
Week 35	Short *o, o_e*	
Week 36	Short *u, u_e*	

Kindergarten: Sight Word Pacing

CONCEPT	WEEK	SIGHT WORDS
Concept 1: Building the Sorting Routine	Week 1	none
	Week 2	none
Concept 2: Letter Identification, Formation, and Sound	Week 1	*a*
	Week 2	*at*
	Week 3	*be*
	Week 4	*he*
	Week 5	*I*
	Week 6	*it*
	Week 7	*on*
	Week 8	*no*
	Week 9	*up*
	Week 10	*us*
Concept 3: Short Vowels	Week 1	*can, is*
	Week 2	*see, in*
	Week 3	*to, you*
	Week 4	*for, go*
	Week 5	*or, if*
Concept 4: Short *a* Families	Week 1	*we, and*
	Week 2	*big, the*

CONCEPT	WEEK	SIGHT WORDS
Concept 5: Short *e* Families	Week 1	*ten, red*
	Week 2	*said, she*
Concept 6: Short *i* Families	Week 1	*sit, very*
	Week 2	*six, as*
Concept 7: Short *o* Families	Week 1	*not, off*
	Week 2	*got, hot*
Concept 8: Short *u* Families	Week 1	*run, ran*
	Week 2	*its, ask*
Concept 9: Mixed Short Vowel Review	Week 1	*how, why*
	Week 2	*what, who*
	Week 3	*when, where*
	Week 4	*under, over*
Concept 10: Short Vowels and Vowel_e	Week 1	*have, ate*
	Week 2	*eat, done*
	Week 3	review
	Week 4	review
	Week 5	review

Sound Pieces With Motions Chart

CONSONANTS				
b **bee** (Pretend your pointer finger is a bee, fly it through the air, and say "/b/.")	**c** **cow** (Create two fists with your hands, move them up and down to pretend to milk a cow, and say "/k/.")	**d** **dig** (Pretend you are digging a hole and say "/d/.")	**f** **fan** (Use your hand to fan your face and say "/f/.")	**g** **gum** (Create a mouth with one hand, chomp it open and closed, and say "/g/.")
	c **cent** (Pretend you are holding a handful of coins. Shake your hand from left to right and say "/s/.")			**g** **gem** (Cup your hands together like you are holding a pile of gems, lightly bounce them up and down, and say "/j/.")
h **hot** (Stick your tongue out, fan your face, and say "/h/.")	**j** **jingle** (Pretend you are holding a bell, ring the bell, and say "/j/.")	**k** **kick** (Pretend you are kicking a ball by moving your foot from front to back and say "/k/.")	**l** **lollipop** (Pretend you are licking a lollipop. As you are licking the lollipop, say "/l/.")	**m** **mop** (Pretend you are holding a mop and mopping up something on the floor. As you mop up the mess, say "/m/.")

Bee: istock.com/adekvat; Cow: istock.com/vectorikart; Dig: istock.com/mutsMaks; Fan: istock.com/zzve; Gum: istock.com/elinedesignservices; Cent: istock.com/graphicgeoff; Gem: istock.com/ AnnaRassadnikova; Hot: istock.com/terdpong2; Jingle: istock.com/LeshkaSmok; Kick: istock.com/pijama6l; Lollipop: istock.com/PandaVector; Mop: istock.com/mhatzapa

	–dge	**–ck**		
	badge	clock		
	(Pretend there is a badge in your hand, place it on your shirt, and say "/j/.")	(Pretend your arm is the hand of a clock. Move it left to right in front of you and say "tick-tock, tick-tock, tick-tock." Then say "/k/.")		

n	**p**	**q**	**r**	**s**
no	pop	quiet	run	snake
(Give a thumbs-down with both hands and say "/n/.")	(Create an oval shape with your hands by placing your fingertips together. Pull your fingertips apart quickly and say "/p/.")	(Hold your index finger over your lips and whisper the sound "/q/.")	(Bend your arms at the elbow and make a fist with your hands. Move your bent arms forward and backward to create a running motion. As you are moving your arms, say "/r/.")	(Put your arms together and move them to create a slithering motion. As you are moving your arms, say "/s/.")

t	**v**	**w**	**x**	**y**
type	violin	wiggle	mix	yes
(Place both hands in front of you and curl your fingers. Pretend there is a keyboard in front of you and move your fingers up and down to create a typing motion. As you are pretend typing, say "/t/.")	(Place your right arm straight out in front of you. Move your left hand back and forth over your right elbow and pretend to play a violin. While strumming, say "/v/.")	(In a sitting position or a standing position, quickly move your body back and forth to create a wiggle motion. As you are wiggling, say "/w/.")	(Bend your left arm at the elbow and pretend to hold a bowl. With your right hand, pretend to be mixing in the bowl. As you are mixing, say "/x/.")	(Give a thumbs-up with both hands and say "/y/.")

Badge: istock.com/bsd555; Clock:istock.com/Alaskastockpictures; No: istock.com/FARBAI; Pop: istock.com/wissanu99; Quiet: istock.com/Sara Showalter; Run: istock.com/graphic-bee; Snake: istock.com/kwansrn; Type: istock.com/ShowVectorStudio; Violin: istock.com/TopVectors; Wiggle: istock.com/graphic-bee; Mix: istock.com/vasilyevalara; Yes: istock.com/S-S-S

CONSONANTS (Continued)				
z 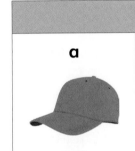 **zoom** (Stretch out the fingers on your right hand and push them together so there are no gaps. Move your hand quickly from one side of your body to the other and say "/z/.")				

SHORT VOWELS

a **hat** (Tap your head and say "/ă/.")	**e** **bed** (Fold your hands, rest your head on your hands, and say "/ĕ/.")	**i**  **zip** (Pretend to zip up your coat. Move your hand up and say "/ĭ/.")	**o** **log** (Pretend to be a frog jumping on a log. Bounce up and down and say "/ŏ/.")	**u** **sun** (Branch out your fingers, make a circular motion in front of your body, and say "/ŭ/.")

SHORT A FAMILIES

–at **cat** (With your right hand, stroke the air like you are petting a cat and say "/ăt/.")	**–ap** **map** (Hold your left hand out so that you are looking at your palm and point your right index finger. Drag your finger across your left palm like you are following a road on a map. As you are dragging your finger, say "/ăp/.")	**–ag** **bag** (Place two fisted hands together so that your index fingers are touching. Move your hands apart right to left and say "/ăg/.")	**–am** **jam** (Pretend to hold a knife in your right hand and a piece of toast in your left hand. Use your right hand to pretend to spread jam on your left hand and say "/ăm/.")	**–an** **man** (Point your index finger straight out, place it underneath your nose to make a mustache, and say "/ăn/.")	**–and** **band** (Pretend you are holding an instrument in front of your face with both hands, wiggle your fingers, and say "/ănd/.")

Zoom: istock.com/funnybank; Hat: istock.com/stevezmina1; Bed: istock.com/vasilyevalara; Zip: istock.com/pe-art; Log: istock.com/bennyb; Sun: istock.com/StudioBarcelona; Cat: istock.com/Nadzeya_Dzivakova; Map: istock.com/Irma Burns; Bag: istock.com/missbobit; Jam: istock.com/muzzza; Man: istock.com/rafyfane; Band: istock.com/lenm

SHORT *E* FAMILIES

–et	**–ed**	**–en**	**–ell**	**–eck**	**–est**
net	red	pen	bell	neck	nest
(Create a fist with your right hand, move it in a figure eight motion, and say "/ĕt/.")	(Pinch your rosy cheeks and say "/ĕd/.")	(Pretend to hold a pen in the air, write the letters e and n, and say "/ĕn/.")	(Pretend to hold a bell, move your wrist right to left, and say "/ĕl/.")	(Touch your neck with both your right and left hands and say "/ĕk/.")	(Pretend to flap your arms like a bird and say "/ĕst/.")

SHORT *I* FAMILIES

–it	**–in**	**–ip**	**–ick**	**–ill**	**–ig**
sit	pin	hip	sick	grill	pig
(Pretend to sit in a chair and say "/ĭt/.")	(Poke your arm gently and say "/ĭn/.")	(Put your hands on your hips and say "/ĭp/.")	(Put the palm of your hand to your forehead and say "/ĭk/.")	(Pretend to hold a spatula in one hand, move it up and down, and say "/ĭl/.")	(Scrunch your nose up and say "/ĭg/.")

SHORT *O* FAMILIES

–op	**–ot**	**–ob**	**–ong**	**–ock**	**–og**
top	pot	knob	tong	lock	dog
(Place your thumb and index finger together and point them toward the ground. Then make a flicking motion and say "/ŏp/.")	(Clasp your hands together in front of your body, move them away from your body to create a circle with your arms, and say "/ŏt/.")	(Pretend to be holding a doorknob, twist your wrist right and left, and say "/ŏb/.")	(Place your fingers straight out and together. Move your thumb away from your fingers to create a snapping motion and say "/ŏng/.")	(Pretend to be holding a lock in your left hand. With your right hand touching your left, twist your right hand to the right and say "/ŏk/.")	(Stick your tongue out, breathe heavily, and say "/ŏg/.")

Net: istock.com/mocoo; Red: istock.com/MaksimYremenko; Pen: istock.com/pe-art; Bell: istock.com/Quarta_; Neck: istock.com/passengerz; Nest: istock.com/StudioBarcelona; Sit: istock.com/pijama61; Pin: istock.com/jane_Kelly; Hip: istock.com/MichikoDesign; Sick: istock.com/pijama61; Grill: istock.com/nicolecioe; Pig: istock.com/Nadzeya_Dzivakova; Top: istock.com/chdwh; Pot: istock.com/johnnylemonseed; Knob: istock.com/wektorygrafika; Tong: istock.com/adekvat; Lock: istock.com/luplupme; Dog: istock.com/TopVectors

SHORT *U* FAMILIES

–ub

tub

(Pretend to be washing your hair and say "/ŭb/.")

–un

bun

(Lay your hands flat in front of you with the palms facing each other. Clap your hands together and say "/ŭn/.")

–ut

cut

(Create the peace sign with your index and middle finger. Move them away from each other and back together again. Then say "/ŭt/.")

–uff

fluff

(Pretend you are holding a fluffy bunny in your arms, pet the bunny, and say "/ŭf/.")

–uck

duck

(Create a *V* with your hands touching at your wrist. Place the *V* at your mouth, move your hands together in a snapping motion, and say "/ŭk/.")

–unk

bunk

(Pretend you are climbing a ladder with your hands only and say "/ŭnk/.")

DIGRAPHS

ch

chair

(Squat down and pretend you are sitting in a chair. While you are pretending to sit, say "/ch/.")

sh

shoe

(Bend over, pretend to tie your shoe, and say "/sh/.")

ph

dolphin

(Make your right hand flat and put your fingers together. Move your hand up and down in a rolling motion to create a dolphin jumping. As you move your hand, say "/f/.")

th

thumb

(Give a thumbs-up with your right hand. Point to the thumb of your right hand with your left index finger. As you point, say "/th/.")

wh

whale

(Create fists with both of your hands and place them on top of your head. Burst your fists open and move them up and away from your head to make a blowhole motion. As you burst your fists, say "/wh/.")

Tub: istock.com/Photoplotnikov; Bun: istock.com/Photoplotnikov; Cut: istock.com/Janista; Fluff: istock.com/djvstock; Duck: istock.com/graphic-bee; Bunk: istock .com/keko-ka; Chair: istock.com/Rusanovska; Shoe: istock.com/macrovector; Dolphin: istock.com/jodol9; Thumb: istock.com/Aerial3; Whale: istock.com/llyaf

BLENDS

st	bl	fr	ft	fl	nk
stop	**blend**	**frog**	**gift**	**flag**	**sink**
(Stretch your arm out in front of you, bend your wrist so that your finger-tips are pointing up, and say "/st/.")	(Fan both hands out in front of you. Shake your fingers and have them touch each other. While your fingers meet, say "/bl/.")	(Place your left hand with your palm down in front of you. Bounce two fingers from your right hand up and down on top of your left hand to pretend to make a frog. While bouncing your hand, say "/fr/.")	(Pretend you are opening a gift and say "/ft/.")	(Pretend your arm is a flag, wave it back and forth, and say "/fl/.")	(Pretend you are washing your hands in a sink and say "/nk/.")

ng	mp	tr	dr	cr	
ring	**jump**	**truck**	**drum**	**crack**	
(Pretend you are wearing a ring, rub your ring finger, and say "/ng/.")	(Jump into the air and say "/mp/.")	(Create fists with both of your hands and place them in front of you with your fingers facing each other. Move your fists up and down to pretend to drive a truck. As you are driving, say "/tr/.")	(Create a fist with both of your hands and place them in front of you. Flick your right wrist up and down. Then flick your left wrist up and down. As you are flicking your wrist, say "/dr/.")	(Flatten your hands with your palms facing down and put them side by side. Keep your hands flat, but move the pinkie side down to pretend to crack the surface made by your hands. While making the crack, say "/cr/.")	

Stop: istock.com/treemouse; Blend: istock.com/Iryna Alekseienko; Frog: istock.com/Glenne82; Gift: istock.com/UrchenkoJulia; Flag: istock.com/boris64; Sink: istock.com/kathykonkle; Ring: istock.com/runeer; Jump: istock.com/pijama61; Truck: istock.com/TopVectors; Drum: istock.com/Lanaclipart; Crack: istock.com/kgtoh

LONG VOWELS				
long *a*: *a_e, ai,* *a, ay*	**long *e*:** *e_e, ee, ea,* *ie, e, ey, y*	**long *i*:** *i_e, ie, i, igh*	**long *o*:** *o_e, oa,* *o, ow*	**long *u*:** *u_e, ue,* *u, ew*
a_e cake	**e_e** Pete	**i_e** bike	**o_e** bone	**u_e** cube
(Point your index finger forward, swipe it into a pretend bowl in a scooping motion, and say "/ā/.")	(Create a waving motion with your right hand and say "/ē/.")	(Put your arms in front of you, create a fist on each hand, and say "/ī/.")	(Create a fist with both of your hands, put your fists near your mouth, and say "/ō/.")	(Make an *L* with the thumb and pointer finger on your right and left hands. Put them together to create a rectangle. Move the rectangle forward and backward and say "/ū/.")

Cake: istock.com/Tomacco; Pete: istock.com/pijama61; Bike: istock.com/heather_mcgrath; Bone: istock.com/adekvat; Cube: istock.com/Physicx

Concept 1 Overview:

Building the Sorting Routine (Sorting Into Identified Categories)

istock.com/UberImages

WELCOME BACK TO SCHOOL!

This is the launching week for *Puzzle Piece Phonics*! Students are getting introduced to many school routines. One of these routines is for word study. These two weeks of Concept 1 are meant for you and your students to get back into the school "groove." Word study lessons are light and have parts that can be omitted if you need additional time for back-to-school routines.

GOALS FOR THE CONCEPT

Students will
- Sort items into categories
- Recognize letters
- Recognize words
- Identify that all words are made up of letters
- Build word study routines
- Read with fluency

WEEKS FOR THIS CONCEPT

Week 1: School Things, Pool Things
Week 2: Word or Letter

Preparing for Your Week

Resources

HEADERS

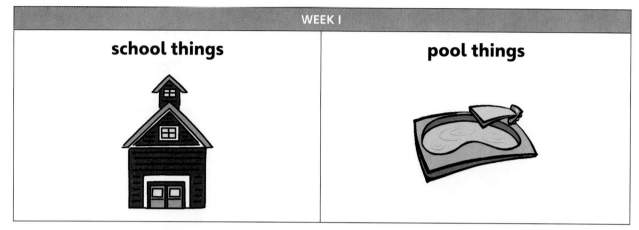

WEEK 1	
school things	pool things

Preparing for Your Week

PREASSESSMENT DIRECTIONS

Complete this assessment any day during Concept 1, Weeks 1 and 2. Instruct students to turn to **page 1 in the Learner's Notebook**. Explain to students that they are not expected to spell the words correctly—you want to see what they already know about spelling patterns. Tell students the check is used to see what they know about letters, sounds, and letter formation. There is a whole-group section and an individual section. For the whole-group section, split up the rows and complete on different days. For the individual section, work with students one-on-one to complete. A blackline master of this initial check is available at resources.corwin.com/puzzlepiecephonics-gradeK.

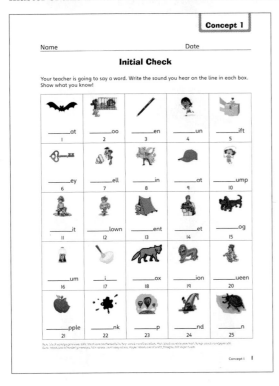

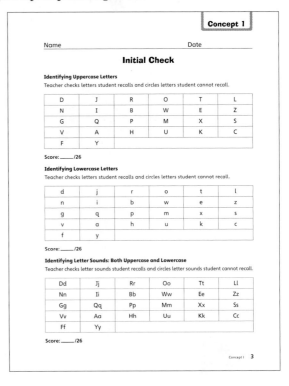

Preparing for Your Week

PREASSESSMENT: INITIAL CHECK

ANSWER KEY				
1. bat	2. zoo	3. pen	4. run	5. gift
6. key	7. yell	8. win	9. hat	10. jump
11. sit	12. clown	13. tent	14. vet	15. dog
16. gum	17. mix	18. fox	19. lion	20. queen
21. apple	22. ink	23. up	24. end	25. on

Run: istock.com/graphic-bee; Gift: istock.com/UrchenkoJulia; Key: istock.com/DavidGoh; Hat: istock.com/stevezmina1; Jump: istock.com/pijama61; Gum: istock.com/elinedesignservices; Mix: istock.com/vasilyevalara; Apple: istock.com/CandO_Designs; Ink: clipart.com

EVALUATING THE ASSESSMENT:
WHAT TO LOOK FOR

Skills to look for in the whole-group section include

- Initial sounds and final sound of /x/
- Knowledge of consonants
- Knowledge of short vowels

Skills to look for in the individual section include

- Identifying uppercase letters
- Identifying lowercase letters
- Identifying consonant and short vowel sounds
- Forming uppercase letters
- Forming lowercase letters

TIPS FOR SCORING

Whole-group part: Give students one point for each letter they write correctly to spell the word represented by the picture.

Individual part: Give students one point for each letter they identify and form. See student scoring pages in the Learner's Notebook.

Preparing for Your Week

CORRESPONDING *LEARNER'S NOTEBOOK PAGES*

| | Week 1 | Concept 1 |

Name _____ Date _____

Weekly Sort

school things	pool things	sunglasses
pencil	swimsuit	backpack
crayons	floats	sunscreen
books	ball	calculator

Concept I   **7**

Preparing for Your Week

CORRESPONDING *FLUENCY NOTEBOOK* PAGES

I'm at School

I'm at school!

I'm at school!

This is what I see.

This is what I see.

I see _____.

I see _____.

I see _____.

I see _____.

I am at school.

I am at school.

And I see _____.

I'm at the Pool

I'm at the pool!

I'm at the pool!

This is what I see.

This is what I see.

I see _____.

I see _____.

I see _____.

I see _____.

I am at the pool.

I am at the pool.

And I see _____.

Preparing for Your Week

Tips for Management and Differentiation

Refer to this section and to resources.corwin.com/puzzlepiecephonics-gradeK for resources and ideas to deepen your students' learning throughout the week. Feel free to put your own spin on the routines, too. For daily lesson plans, see pages 8–12 of this Teacher's Guide.

TIPS FOR PHONEMIC AWARENESS	• The focus for this week is words that rhyme. Before starting the Phonemic Awareness activity, explain to students that this warm-up is just for their ears! They have to listen and think about the sounds in the words said. • Explain to students that words that rhyme have the same ending sounds. • If you notice your students need additional practice with identifying rhyming words, you can extend the activity with similar words. • To extend the activity, ask students to think of an additional word that rhymes. Or if words do not rhyme, ask them to think of a rhyming word.
TIPS FOR THE PUZZLE PIECE REVIEW	• There are no sounds pieces this week. Students are learning the sorting routine and working on sorting pictures into categories. • Each day students will play a game of Categories. The teacher will say the category and a group of four words. Students will think of the four words and share out which word does not fit into the category. • Model and set expectations for students when working with a word study partner. • Take this time to list more words that could be put into a category together—for example, *couch, chair, TV, coffee table, lamp*. Ask students which category all of these words could fit into (living room things).
TIPS FOR INITIAL ASSESSMENT	• This is the first week of school. It is your time to assess students and see what they have come to school knowing. Some of your students will come in as readers, and some students won't even know what a letter is. This first week gives you time to get to know the needs of your class. • Break up the initial check according to how it works for your class. We recommend completing one row of the whole-group part each day. Some students may need one-on-one attention for the whole-group part.
TIPS FOR SORTING	• Model and positively reinforce the sorting routine repeatedly throughout the week. Students should see that you will consistently enforce the sorting routine this year! • Take the time to visit with each student to make sure all are understanding the meaning of the picture. • Explain to students that the word is listed under the picture. This will help students understand the written meaning of the picture.
TIPS FOR THE PRACTICE PIECES	• Keep in mind that the routines may take more time at this point in the year than they will once your students are familiar with word study. If you are short on time, feel free to skip the Practice Pieces for the day. • Be sure to give your students multiple opportunities to see how the Practice Pieces should be completed. If necessary, you can introduce only one or two of the Practice Piece routines. Complete them as a class first, then give students time to practice independently. • During each activity, students will be focusing on knowing which category their picture belongs to. Adapt the activities to work for your class.
TIPS FOR FLUENCY	• This week students will read open-ended poems in which they can fill in the blank with their sort pictures. The poems are very repetitive and are meant to be interactive. Students will need support with the sight words in the poems.

Day 1

THE PUZZLE PIECE FAMILY

Launch Concept 1: Building the Sorting Routine by following the Puzzle Piece Family routine found on page I-11 of the Introduction.

1. Show students pictures of the following:

A scarf
A snowman
A snowflake
A tree with no leaves on its branches
Mittens

2. Have students discuss what all the pictures have in common (winter things).

3. Show students pictures of the following:

Pizza
Spaghetti
A hot dog
Grilled cheese
An apple

4. Have students discuss what all the pictures have in common (food things).

5. Facilitate a discussion that leads them to discover the Puzzle Piece Family: Sorting items into categories. Explain to students that sorting items into categories will help them to build the sorting routine for word study this year.

PHONEMIC AWARENESS: LISTEN

1. Give the directions. Say, "I am going to say two words. Your job is to tell me if the two words rhyme. For example, if I say '*me, key*,' you say 'yes!' If I say '*dad, mop*,' you say 'no.'"

2. Say the following pairs of words:

go, row (yes)   hi, to (no)   bike, like (yes)   lap, sap (yes)   pop, rug (no)

THE BIG REVEAL

1. Say, "Let's make a list of things you could find at school."

2. Say, "Now, let's make a list of things you could find at the pool."

3. Say, "Great job! This week we are going to build our sorting routine for word study. You will sort the pictures for your sort into two categories: school things and pool things."

INITIAL ASSESSMENT

1. Use this time to complete the initial assessment for your students.

PRACTICE: COMPLETE YOUR WORK ON YOUR OWN

1. Have students turn to page 7 of the Learner's Notebook.

2. Instruct students to tear out the sort and complete the following Practice Pieces: Quick Color, Careful Cut, and Grouping With Combined Picture and Word Cards (see further directions on pages I-37, I-38, and I-24 of the Introduction).

3. Circulate as students work, which usually takes fifteen minutes, and coach as needed.

FLUENCY: READING LIKE YOU'RE SPEAKING

1. Have students turn to page 1 in the Fluency Notebook.

2. Have students read one or more of the following poems: "I'm at School" and "I'm at the Pool."

3. Circulate and listen to students read or gather a small group of students who need additional support.

Day 2

PHONEMIC AWARENESS: LISTEN

1. Give the directions. Say, "I am going to say two words. Your job is to tell me if the two words rhyme. For example, if I say 'me, key,' you say 'yes!' If I say 'dad, mop,' you say 'no.'"

2. Say the following pairs of words:

run, sun (yes)   no, look (no)   sky, fly (yes)
duck, yuck (yes) free, tree (yes)

PUZZLE PIECE REVIEW

1. Say, "Tell a partner one thing you can find at **school**."

2. Say, "Tell a partner one thing you can find at the **pool**."

3. Say, "This week we are sorting words into categories. To practice, I am going to say a group of four words. You tell me the word that does not fit into the category."

    1.   Category: **Animals**
        zebra, giraffe, flip-flop, panda (word that does not fit: *flip-flop*)

    2.   Category: **Food**
        tacos, hat, pizza, salad (word that does not fit: *hat*)

    3.   Category: **Clothes**
        shirt, dress, pants, dog (word that does not fit: *dog*)

INITIAL ASSESSMENT

1. Use this time to complete the initial assessment for your students.

SORT: WHAT IS YOUR FOCUS PATTERN?

1. Have students take out their bag of pictures and words (created on Day 1) and follow the Grouping With Combined Picture and Word Cards routine on page I-24 of the Introduction.

PRACTICE: COMPLETE YOUR WORK ON YOUR OWN

1. Students will follow the Add Two routine on page I-39 of the Introduction.

2. Circulate as students work, which usually takes fifteen minutes, and coach as needed.

FLUENCY: READING LIKE YOU'RE SPEAKING

1. Have students turn to page 1 in the Fluency Notebook.

2. Have students read one or more of the following poems: "I'm at School" and "I'm at the Pool."

3. Circulate and listen to students read or gather a small group of students who need additional support.

Day 3

PHONEMIC AWARENESS: LISTEN

1. Give the directions. Say, "I am going to say two words. Your job is to tell me if the two words rhyme. For example, if I say '*me, key,*' you say 'yes!' If I say '*dad, mop,*' you say 'no.'"

2. Say the following pairs of words:

cook, fun (no)   go, snow (yes)   dog, low (no)
yes, mess (yes)   dot, bought (yes)

PUZZLE PIECE REVIEW

1. Say, "Tell a partner one thing you can find at **school**."

2. Say, "Tell a partner one thing you can find at the **pool**."

3. Say, "This week we are sorting words into categories. To practice, I am going to say a group of four words. You tell me the word that does not fit into the category."

    1.   Category: **Drinks**
       soda, water, tea, hamburger (word that does not fit: *hamburger*)

    2.   Category: **Pets**
       fish, notebook, cat, hamster (word that does not fit: *notebook*)

    3.   Category: **Instruments**
       piano, flute, drums, monkey bars (word that does not fit: *monkey bars*)

INITIAL ASSESSMENT

1. Use this time to complete the initial assessment for your students.

SORT: WHAT IS YOUR FOCUS PATTERN?

1. Have students take out their bag of pictures and words (created on Day 1) and follow the Grouping With Combined Picture and Word Cards routine on page I-24 of the Introduction.

PRACTICE: COMPLETE YOUR WORK ON YOUR OWN

1. Students will follow the Make a New Category routine on page I-40 of the Introduction.

2. Circulate as students work, which usually takes fifteen minutes, and coach as needed.

FLUENCY: READING LIKE YOU'RE SPEAKING

1. Have students turn to page 1 in the Fluency Notebook.

2. Have students read one or more of the following poems: "I'm at School" and "I'm at the Pool."

3. Circulate and listen to students read or gather a small group of students who need additional support.

PHONEMIC AWARENESS: LISTEN

1. Give the directions. Say, "I am going to say two words. Your job is to tell me if the two words rhyme. For example, if I say '*me, key*,' you say 'yes!' If I say '*dad, mop*,' you say 'no.'"

2. Say the following pairs of words:

wood, could (yes)   my, lie (yes)   for, core (yes)
do, go (no)   say, day (yes)

PUZZLE PIECE REVIEW

1. Say, "Tell a partner one thing you can find at **school**."

2. Say, "Tell a partner one thing you can find at the **pool**."

3. Say, "This week we are sorting words into categories. To practice, I am going to say a group of four words. You tell me the word that does not fit into the category."

   1. Category: **Birds**
      penguin, bear, pelican, seagull (word that does not fit: *bear*)

   2. Category: **Numbers**
      two, five, popcorn, twelve (word that does not fit: *popcorn*)

   3. Category: **Names**
      Fred, Kelly, Victor, French fries (word that does not fit: *French fries*)

INITIAL ASSESSMENT

1. Use this time to complete the initial assessment for your students.

SORT: WHAT IS YOUR FOCUS PATTERN?

1. Have students take out their bag of pictures and words (created on Day 1) and follow the Grouping With Combined Picture and Word Cards routine on page I-24 of the Introduction.

PRACTICE: COMPLETE YOUR WORK ON YOUR OWN

1. Have students complete the following Practice Pieces: Glue Words (on page I-41 of the Introduction) and Create a Scene (on page I-42 of the Introduction).

2. Circulate as students work, which usually takes fifteen minutes, and coach as needed.

FLUENCY: READING LIKE YOU'RE SPEAKING

1. Have students turn to page 1 in the Fluency Notebook.

2. Have students read one or more of the following poems: "I'm at School" and "I'm at the Pool."

3. Circulate and listen to students read or gather a small group of students who need additional support.

Day 5

PHONEMIC AWARENESS: LISTEN	**1.** Give the directions. Say, "I am going to say two words. Your job is to tell me if the two words rhyme. For example, if I say '*me, key*,' you say 'yes!' If I say '*dad, mop*,' you say 'no.'"
	2. Say the following pairs of words:

much, mud (no)   toe, sew (yes)   did, talk (no)
punch, lunch (yes)   hi, by (yes)

REVIEW PATTERNS OF THE WEEK	**1.** Say, "Tell a partner one thing you can find at **school**."
	2. Say, "Tell a partner one thing you can find at the **pool**."
	3. Say, "This week we are sorting words into categories. To practice, I am going to say a group of four words. You tell me the word that does not fit into the category."

    1.   Category: **Transportation**
        table, bus, car, bike (word that does not fit: *table*)

    2.   Category: **Letters**
        A, G, T, watermelon (word that does not fit: *watermelon*)

    3.   Category: **Vegetables**
        peas, pasta, lettuce, squash (word that does not fit: *pasta*)

INITIAL ASSESSMENT	**1.** Use this time to complete the initial assessment for your students.
LABELING THE ROOM	**1.** Label the classroom with things found from this week's sort.
FLUENCY: READING LIKE YOU'RE SPEAKING	**1.** Have students turn to page 1 in the Fluency Notebook.
	2. Have students read one or more of the following poems: "I'm at School" and "I'm at the Pool."
	3. Circulate and listen to students read or gather a small group of students who need additional support.
WEEKLY CELEBRATION	**1.** Display the celebratory message: "Welcome back to school! You are a superstar sorter!"
	2. Encourage students to work together to read the message.
	3. Have students copy the message onto their weekly certificate (see resources .corwin.com/puzzlepiecephonics-gradeK) and place it somewhere to take home.

Preparing for Your Week

Resources

HEADERS

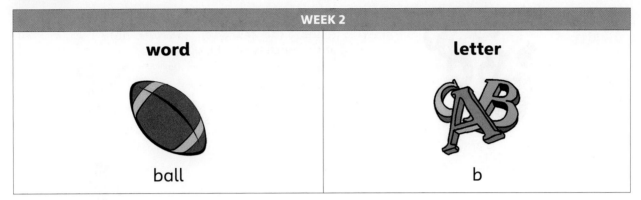

WEEK 2	
word ball	**letter** b

CORRESPONDING *LEARNER'S NOTEBOOK* PAGES

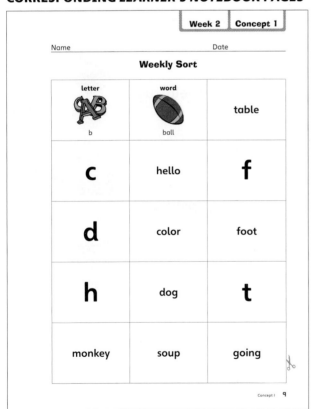

Preparing for Your Week

CORRESPONDING *FLUENCY NOTEBOOK PAGES*

Alphabet Song

a, b, c, d, e, f, g,

h, i, j, k,

l, m, n, o, p,

q, r, s,

t, u, v,

w, x,

y, and z

Now I said my ABCs, and now I will say them backward!

z, y, x, w, v, u, t,

s, r, q,

p, o, n, m,

l, k, j,

i, h, g,

f, e, d,

c, b, and a

Now I said my backward ABCs, and now I am done!

Letters Make Words

c   a   t   spells cat

d   o   g   spells dog

r   u   g   spells rug

b   e   d   spells bed

k   i   d   spells kid

_____   _____   _____

spells _____

Bed: istock.com/vasilyevalara

Preparing for Your Week

Tips for Management and Differentiation

Refer to this section and to resources.corwin.com/puzzlepiecephonics-gradeK for resources and ideas to deepen your students' learning throughout the week. Feel free to put your own spin on the routines, too. For daily lesson plans, see pages 16–20 of this Teacher's Guide.

TIPS FOR PHONEMIC AWARENESS	• The focus for this week is words that rhyme. Before starting the Phonemic Awareness activity, explain to students that this warm-up is just for their ears! They have to listen and think about the sounds in the words said. • Explain to students that words that rhyme have the same ending sounds. • If you notice your students need additional practice with identifying rhyming words, you can extend the activity with similar words. • To extend the activity, ask students to think of an additional word that rhymes. Or if words do not rhyme, ask them to think of a rhyming word.
TIPS FOR THE PUZZLE PIECE REVIEW	• There are no sound pieces this week. Students are learning the sorting routine and working on sorting letters and words. • Model and set expectations for students when working with a word study partner. • Take this time to review the alphabet. During the Puzzle Piece Review each day, have students sing different alphabet songs. Be sure to point to the consonant and short vowel pieces when saying the name of the letter.
TIPS FOR INITIAL ASSESSMENT	• This is the second week of school. It is your time to assess students and see what they have come to school knowing. Some of your students will come in as readers, and some students won't even know what a letter is. These early weeks gives you time to get to know the needs of your class. • Break up the initial check according to how it works for your class. We recommend completing one row of the whole-group part each day. Some students may need one-on-one attention for the whole-group part.
TIPS FOR SORTING	• Model and positively reinforce the sorting routine repeatedly throughout the week. Students should see that you will consistently enforce the sorting routine this year! • Take the time to visit with each student to make sure all are understanding the meaning of *letter* and *word*. Explain to students that words are made up of letters.
TIPS FOR THE PRACTICE PIECES	• Keep in mind that the routines may take more time at this point in the year than they will once your students are familiar with word study. If you are short on time, feel free to skip the Practice Pieces for the day. • Be sure to give your students multiple opportunities to see how the Practice Pieces should be completed. If necessary, you can introduce only one or two of the Practice Piece routines. Complete them as a class first, then give students time to practice independently.
TIPS FOR FLUENCY	• This week students will read basic poems. The poems are very repetitive and are meant to be interactive. Students will need support with the sight words in the poems.
TIPS FOR SPELLING CHECK	• Review the directions with students. Make sure they understand how to circle letters and underline words. • Use teacher discretion when grading the Spelling Check.

PHONEMIC AWARENESS: LISTEN

1. Give the directions. Say, "I am going to say two words. Your job is to tell me if the two words rhyme. For example, if I say '*me, key,*' you say 'yes!' If I say '*dad, mop,*' you say 'no.'"

2. Say the following pairs of words:

loop, pool (no) fight, bite (yes) up, pup (yes)
glow, fall (no) her, him (no)

THE BIG REVEAL

1. Say, "Let's say all of our letters." Lead the class in saying the ABCs by pointing to the consonant and short vowel puzzle pieces.

2. Say, "Let's make a list of **letters**."

3. Say, "Now, let's make a list of **words**."

4. Ask students, "What do you notice about all of the **words** that we listed?" (All of the words are made up of the **letters** of the alphabet.)

5. Say, "Great job! This week we are going to build our sorting routine for word study. You will sort **letters** or **words**."

WORD OR LETTER?

1. Write the following letters and words on the board. Have students come up and circle the letters and underline the words.

popcorn

y

quiet

fort

d

INITIAL ASSESSMENT

1. Use this time to complete the initial assessment for your students.

PRACTICE: COMPLETE YOUR WORK ON YOUR OWN

1. Have students turn to page 9 of the Learner's Notebook.

2. Instruct students to tear out the sort and complete the following Practice Pieces: Quick Color, Careful Cut, and Grouping With Combined Picture and Word Cards (see further directions on pages I-37, I-38, and I-24 of the Introduction).

3. Circulate as students work, which usually takes fifteen minutes, and coach as needed.

FLUENCY: READING LIKE YOU'RE SPEAKING

1. Have students turn to page 2 in the Fluency Notebook.

2. Have students read one or more of the following poems: "Alphabet Song" and "Letters Make Words."

3. Circulate and listen to students read or gather a small group of students who need additional support.

Day 2

PHONEMIC AWARENESS: LISTEN	**1.** Give the directions. Say, "I am going to say two words. Your job is to tell me if the two words rhyme. For example, if I say '*me, key*,' you say 'yes!' If I say '*dad, mop*,' you say 'no.'"
	2. Say the following pairs of words:
	cut, hut (yes) pie, pay (no) plane, rain (yes) dip, hip (yes) throw, fox (no)

PUZZLE PIECE REVIEW	**1.** Say, "Let's say our alphabet!" Lead the class in saying the ABCs by pointing to the consonant and short vowel puzzle pieces.
	2. Say, "Tell a partner one letter."
	3. Say, "Tell a partner one word."

WORD OR LETTER?	**1.** Write the following letters and words on the board. Have students come up and circle the letters and underline the words.
	x
	costume
	lollipop
	n
	v

INITIAL ASSESSMENT	**1.** Use this time to complete the initial assessment for your students.

SORT: WHAT IS YOUR FOCUS PATTERN?	**1.** Have students take out their bag of pictures and words (created on Day 1) and follow the Grouping With Combined Picture and Word Cards routine on page I-24 of the Introduction.

PRACTICE: COMPLETE YOUR WORK ON YOUR OWN	**1.** Students will follow the Add Two routine on page I-39 of the Introduction.
	2. Circulate as students work, which usually takes fifteen minutes, and coach as needed.

FLUENCY: READING LIKE YOU'RE SPEAKING	**1.** Have students turn to page 2 in the Fluency Notebook.
	2. Have students read one or more of the following poems: "Alphabet Song" and "Letters Make Words."
	3. Circulate and listen to students read or gather a small group of students who need additional support.

Day 3

PHONEMIC AWARENESS: LISTEN

1. Give the directions. Say, "I am going to say two words. Your job is to tell me if the two words rhyme. For example, if I say '*me, key*,' you say 'yes!' If I say '*dad, mop*,' you say 'no.'"

2. Say the following pairs of words:

buy, nose (no)   pop, stop (yes)   mouse, house (yes)
do, to (yes)   mix, hit (no)

PUZZLE PIECE REVIEW

1. Say, "Let's say our alphabet!" Lead the class in saying the ABCs by pointing to the consonant and short vowel puzzle pieces.

2. Say, "Tell a partner one letter."

3. Say, "Tell a partner one word."

WORD OR LETTER?

1. Write the following letters and words on the board. Have students come up and circle the letters and underline the words.

> bowl
>
> r
>
> h
>
> rope
>
> tent

INITIAL ASSESSMENT

1. Use this time to complete the initial assessment for your students.

SORT: WHAT IS YOUR FOCUS PATTERN?

1. Have students take out their bag of pictures and words (created on Day 1) and follow the Grouping With Combined Picture and Word Cards routine on page I-24 of the Introduction.

PRACTICE: COMPLETE YOUR WORK ON YOUR OWN

1. Students will follow the Make a New Category routine on page I-40 of the Introduction.

2. Circulate as students work, which usually takes fifteen minutes, and coach as needed.

FLUENCY: READING LIKE YOU'RE SPEAKING

1. Have students turn to page 2 in the Fluency Notebook.

2. Have students read one or more of the following poems: "Alphabet Song" and "Letters Make Words."

3. Circulate and listen to students read or gather a small group of students who need additional support.

PHONEMIC AWARENESS: LISTEN

1. Give the directions. Say, "I am going to say two words. Your job is to tell me if the two words rhyme. For example, if I say '*me, key*,' you say 'yes!' If I say '*dad, mop*,' you say 'no.'"

2. Say the following pairs of words:

coy, soy (yes)   pit, kit (yes)   did, close (no)
sweep, sleep (yes)   kick, lock (no)

PUZZLE PIECE REVIEW

1. Say, "Let's say our alphabet!" Lead the class in saying the ABCs by pointing to the consonant and short vowel puzzle pieces.

2. Say, "Tell a partner one letter."

3. Say, "Tell a partner one word."

WORD OR LETTER?

1. Write the following letters and words on the board. Have students come up and circle the letters and underline the words.

truck

food

o

c

watermelon

INITIAL ASSESSMENT

1. Use this time to complete the initial assessment for your students.

SORT: WHAT IS YOUR FOCUS PATTERN?

1. Have students take out their bag of pictures and words (created on Day 1) and follow the Grouping With Combined Picture and Word Cards routine on page I-24 of the Introduction.

PRACTICE: COMPLETE YOUR WORK ON YOUR OWN

1. Have students complete the following Practice Pieces: Glue Words (on page I-41 of the Introduction) and Create a Scene (on page I-42 of the Introduction).

2. Circulate as students work, which usually takes fifteen minutes, and coach as needed.

FLUENCY: READING LIKE YOU'RE SPEAKING

1. Have students turn to page 2 in the Fluency Notebook.

2. Have students read one or more of the following poems: "Alphabet Song" and "Letters Make Words."

3. Circulate and listen to students read or gather a small group of students who need additional support.

Day 5

PHONEMIC AWARENESS: LISTEN

1. Give the directions. Say, "I am going to say two words. Your job is to tell me if the two words rhyme. For example, if I say '*me, key,*' you say 'yes!' If I say '*dad, mop,*' you say 'no.'"

2. Say the following pairs of words:

splash, rash (yes)   row, day (no)   math, path (yes)
cat, mat (yes)   get, not (no)

REVIEW PATTERNS OF THE WEEK

1. Say, "Let's say our alphabet!" Lead the class in saying the ABCs by pointing to the consonant and short vowel puzzle pieces.

2. Say, "Tell a partner one letter."

3. Say, "Tell a partner one word."

SPELLING CHECK

1. Follow the Spelling Check routine on page I-34 of the Introduction.

2. Have students turn to page 11 of the Learner's Notebook.

3. Say, "Circle the letters on the page and underline the words."

Words for the Spelling Check

I. m	6. g
2. monkey	7. t
3. h	8. going
4. s	9. color
5. soup	10. c

4. See page 15 of the Teacher's Guide for tips on grading the Spelling Check.

LABELING THE ROOM

1. Label objects around the classroom. Identify the labels as words, and point out the letters that make up each word.

FLUENCY: READING LIKE YOU'RE SPEAKING

1. Have students turn to page 2 in the Fluency Notebook.

2. Have students read one or more of the following poems: "Alphabet Song" and "Letters Make Words."

3. Circulate and listen to students read or gather a small group of students who need additional support.

WEEKLY CELEBRATION

1. Display the celebratory message: "Good job! You know that words are made of letters!"

2. Encourage students to work together to read the message.

3. Have students copy the message onto their weekly certificate (see resources .corwin.com/puzzlepiecephonics-gradeK) and place it somewhere to take home.

Concept 2 Overview:

Letter Identification, Formation, and Sound

istock.com/skynesher

WHAT ARE LETTERS?

This concept is all about uppercase and lowercase letters. Students will identify letters, form letters, and recognize the sounds of letters. Concept 1 allowed you to get to know your students and identify which word study needs they have. Concept 2 introduces all of the major content that students are expected to master in kindergarten: consonants and short vowels.

Use this concept as an introduction and to solidify the understanding that words are made up of sounds that are represented by letters. After Concept 2, kindergarteners will continue to be immersed in consonants and short vowels. Be rest assured that students will have ample opportunities to master consonants and short vowels throughout all of kindergarten, even if they do not by the end of Concept 2. Concept 2 is meant to build the foundation for successful readers.

GOALS FOR THE CONCEPT

Students will
- Identify uppercase and lowercase letters
- Form uppercase and lowercase letters
- Recognize sounds of letters
- Understand that all words are made up of letters
- Build word study routines
- Read with fluency

WEEKS FOR THIS CONCEPT

Week 1: *Dd, Tt, Aa*
Week 2: *Mm, Ss, Aa*
Week 3: *Bb, Cc, Ee*
Week 4: *Gg, Pp, Ee*
Week 5: *Ww, Nn, Ii*
Week 6: *Qq, Ff, Rr, Ii*
Week 7: *Xx, Kk, Oo*
Week 8: *Ll, Jj, Oo*
Week 9: *Vv, Hh, Uu*
Week 10: *Yy, Zz, Uu*

Resources

PUZZLE PIECES

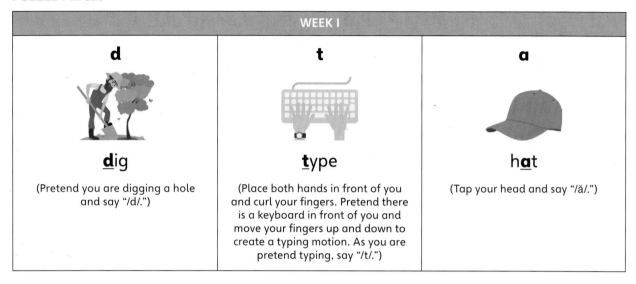

WEEK 1
d / **dig** (Pretend you are digging a hole and say "/d/.")	**t** / **type** (Place both hands in front of you and curl your fingers. Pretend there is a keyboard in front of you and move your fingers up and down to create a typing motion. As you are pretend typing, say "/t/.")	**a** / **hat** (Tap your head and say "/ă/.")

CORRESPONDING *LEARNER'S NOTEBOOK PAGES*

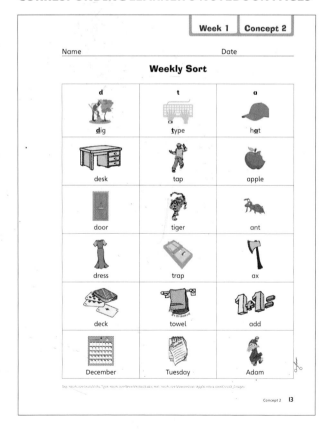

Dig: istock.com/mutsMaks; Type: istock.com/ShowVectorStudio; Hat: istock.com/stevezmina1

Preparing for Your Week

CORRESPONDING *FLUENCY NOTEBOOK* PAGES

Dig

d d d Dig!

d d d Dig!

I found a

_____.

I found a

_____.

d d d Dig!

d d d Dig!

I found a

_____.

I found a

_____.

d d d Dig!

d d d Dig!

Dig: istock.com/mutsMaks

Type

t t t Type!

t t t Type!

I type about a

_____.

I type about a

_____.

t t t Type!

t t t Type!

I type about a

_____.

I type about a

_____.

t t t Type!

t t t Type!

Type: istock.com/ShowVectorStudio

Hat

a a a Hat!

a a a Hat!

A(n) _____

is in my hat!

A(n) _____

is in my hat!

a a a Hat!

a a a Hat!

A(n) _____

is in my hat!

A(n) _____

is in my hat!

a a a Hat!

a a a Hat!

Hat: istock.com/stevezmina1

Dd

Don't, dog, don't! Don't do that, dog.

Don't, dog, don't! Don't eat that frog!

Tt

Tiptoe, tiptoe, tap tap tap.

Tom tiptoes and taps to get that rat!

Aa

Animals, animals are everywhere.

Animals, animals hang in the air.

Preparing for Your Week

Tips for Management and Differentiation

Refer to this section and to resources.corwin.com/puzzlepiecephonics-gradeK for resources and ideas to deepen your students' learning throughout the week. Feel free to put your own spin on the routines, too. For daily lesson plans, see pages 26–33 of this Teacher's Guide.

TIPS FOR PHONEMIC AWARENESS	• The focus for this week is segmenting words into their onset and rime. The student's job is to hear the onset and rime and put the word back together. • If you notice your students need additional practice, extend the activity with additional words. • Students may incorporate the rhyming Phonemic Awareness activity from last week and say a word that rhymes with the put-together word.
TIPS FOR THE PUZZLE PIECE REVIEW	• This week on Days 1–3 you are introducing students to a new puzzle piece. Be sure to spend enough time introducing the piece so students understand their focus for that day. • The reference Puzzle Pieces only have the lowercase letter representing the focus sound. This is so students can build words using the Puzzle Pieces. In the back of the Puzzle Piece pack, you will find uppercase letter cards. Cut these out and use them with the Puzzle Pieces to show the uppercase letter formation for each piece.
TIPS FOR SUPPORTED BLENDING	• This is the first time your kindergarteners will be exposed to blending. Follow the Supported Blending routine and hold students accountable for producing the initial sounds for each word. • Reblend lines if necessary.
TIPS FOR FORMATION	• Encourage students to circle the letter on the row that they feel they formed the best. Have them try to duplicate the letter. • Go around with a highlighter to help students who are struggling with their letters. • Have a station in your room with sand for students to practice forming their letters in. • Students may reverse the lowercase *d*. To help them in knowing which way the letter *d* is to be written, show students a visual representation. They can create a drum with their left hand by making a circle with their fingers. Then, they can create a drumstick with the pointer finger of their right hand. Have students join the drum with the drumstick to see the lowercase letter *d*.
TIPS FOR DICTATION	• If students are struggling to identify the initial sound of a word, tell students to write the letter that says "/d/," "/t/," or "/ă/."

Preparing for Your Week

TIPS FOR SORTING

- Model and positively reinforce the sorting routine repeatedly throughout the week. Students should see that you will consistently enforce the sorting routine this year!
- This week students are sorting their pictures and words with the three headers. On Days 1–3, students will only be sorting with one header. Instruct students to place any unused picture and word cards and headers back into their word sort bags.
- On Day 2, if students can handle sorting both *Dd* and *Tt*, allow them to build off what they learned on Day 1. The same applies for Day 3.
- The sort contains words with authentic capitalization. Review the picture and word cards with students and go over this week's capitalized words.

TIPS FOR THE PRACTICE PIECES

- Keep in mind that the routines may take more time at this point in the year than they will once your students are familiar with word study.
- Be sure to give your students multiple opportunities to see how the Practice Pieces should be completed. If necessary, you can introduce only one or two of the Practice Piece routines. Complete them as a class first, then give students time to practice independently.
- This Practice Piece time can be your opportunity to create fun, authentic experiences with letters.
  - **Dd**: Have students fill in an uppercase *D* and lowercase *d* with dots.
  - **Tt**: Have students fill in an uppercase *T* and lowercase *t* with toothpicks.
  - **Aa**: Have students fill in an uppercase *A* and lowercase *a* with apple stamps.
  - Make it fun for your students using the supplies you have!

TIPS FOR FLUENCY

- This week students will read open-ended chants in which they can fill in the blank with their sort pictures. The chants are very repetitive and are meant to be interactive. Students will need support with the sight words in the chants.
- Students can read their chants and couplets to a partner.
- Students can pull out pictures from their sort bags to fill in the blanks during the chants.

TIPS FOR SPELLING CHECK

- Review the directions with students. They are writing the letter that represents the sound you dictate.
- Use teacher discretion when grading the Spelling Check.

Day 1

THE PUZZLE PIECE FAMILY

Launch Concept 2: Letter Identification, Formation, and Sound by following the Puzzle Piece Family routine found on page I-11 of the Introduction.

1. Show students the following letters:

b	t
w	e
a	m
s	f
d	l

2. Have students identify the names of the letters.

3. Facilitate a discussion that leads them to discover the Puzzle Piece Family: Letters.

PHONEMIC AWARENESS: LISTEN

1. Say, "I am going to break a word into two parts. Your job is to put the word back together. For example, if I say '/b/ [pause] –at,' you say '_bat._'"

2. Say the following words:

/t/ –ap (tap)   /h/ –it (hit)   /b/ –ack (back)   /l/ –it (lit)   /p/ –op (pop)

THE BIG REVEAL

1. Hold up the _dig_ puzzle piece and say, "This is the _dig_ piece. It represents the letter _d._ The dig piece says '/d/ /d/ /d/' like at the beginning of the word _dig._ Pretend you are digging a hole and say '/d/.' We will study this letter and sound all week. Let's make a list of words that have the _dig_ sound in them" (record the words).

SUPPORTED BLENDING: PUTTING SOUNDS TOGETHER TO MAKE NEW WORDS

1. Follow the Supported Blending routine on page 1-16 of the Introduction.

2. Display the following words on the board one line at a time. Facilitate a discussion about the blending line focus after each line.

3. Then display the weekly sight word.

| dig | dot | dad | Discuss: initial sound of /d/. |
| desk | door | dress | Discuss: initial sound of /d/. |

Sight Word: a

FORMATION: WRITING LETTERS

1. Have students turn to page 15 of the Learner's Notebook.

2. Model forming uppercase letter _D_ and lowercase letter _d._

Uppercase Formation	**Lowercase Formation**
Your pencil starts at the top line.	Your pencil starts at the top line.
Form a straight line down to the bottom line.	Form a straight line down to the bottom line.
Pick your pencil up.	Pick your pencil up.
Your pencil starts at the top line.	Your pencil starts at the middle line.
Form a curved line down to the bottom line.	Form a curved line down to the bottom line.
Pick your pencil up.	Pick your pencil up.

3. Assist students in forming two lines of uppercase _D_s.

4. Assist students in forming two lines of lowercase _d_s.

Day 1 (Continued)

**PRACTICE:
COMPLETE
YOUR WORK ON
YOUR OWN**

1. Have students turn to page 13 of the Learner's Notebook.

2. Instruct students to tear out the sort and complete the following Practice Pieces: Quick Color, Careful Cut, and Sorting With Combined Picture and Word Cards (see further directions on pages I-37, I-38, and I-25 of the Introduction).

3. Instruct students that they are only using the *dig* header and words with the letter *d*.

4. Circulate as students work, which usually takes fifteen minutes, and coach as needed.

**FLUENCY:
READING LIKE
YOU'RE SPEAKING**

1. Have students turn to page 3 in the Fluency Notebook.

2. Have students read one or more of the following chants: "Dig," "Type," and "Hat."

3. Circulate and listen to students read or gather a small group of students who need additional support.

Day 2

PHONEMIC AWARENESS: LISTEN

1. Give the directions. Say, "I am going to break a word into two parts. Your job is to put the word back together. For example, if I say '/b/ [pause] –at,' you say 'bat.'"

2. Say the following words:

/m/ –ap (map)   /ch/ –ick (chick)   /s/ –it (sit)
/h/ –ot (hot)   /j/ –ug (jug)

THE BIG REVEAL

1. Say, "Yesterday we learned the *dig* puzzle piece. It represents the letter *d*. The dig piece says '/d/ /d/ /d/' like at the beginning of the word *dig*. Let's all do the motion for the *dig* piece together."

2. Hold up the *type* puzzle piece and say, "This is the *type* piece. It represents the letter *t*. The type piece says '/t/ /t/ /t/' like at the beginning of the word *type*. Place both hands in front of you and curl your fingers. Pretend there is a keyboard in front of you and move your fingers up and down to create a typing motion. As you are pretend typing, say '/t/.' We will study this sound all week. Let's make a list of words that have the *type* sound in them" (record the words).

SUPPORTED BLENDING: PUTTING SOUNDS TOGETHER TO MAKE NEW WORDS

1. Follow the Supported Blending routine on page 1-16 of the Introduction.

2. Display the following words on the board one line at a time. Facilitate a discussion about the blending line focus after each line.

3. Then display the weekly sight word.

| type | tap | tub | Discuss: initial sound of /t/. |
| trap | towel | tiger | Discuss: initial sound of /t/. |

Sight Word: a

FORMATION: WRITING LETTERS

1. Have students turn to page 16 of the Learner's Notebook.

2. Model forming uppercase letter *T* and lowercase letter *t*.

Uppercase Formation	**Lowercase Formation**
Your pencil starts at the top line.	Your pencil starts at the top line.
Form a straight line down to the bottom line.	Form a straight line down to the bottom line.
Pick your pencil up.	Pick your pencil up.
Your pencil starts at the top line to the left.	Your pencil starts at the middle line to the left.
Form a straight line on the top line.	Form a straight line on the middle line.
Pick your pencil up.	Pick your pencil up.

3. Assist students in forming two lines of uppercase *T*s.

4. Assist students in forming two lines of lowercase *t*s.

SORT: WHAT IS YOUR FOCUS PATTERN?

1. Have students take out their bag of pictures (created on Day 1) and follow the Sorting With Combined Picture and Word Cards routine on page 1-25 of the Introduction.

2. Instruct students that they are only using the *type* header and words with the letter *t*.

Day 2 (Continued)

PRACTICE: COMPLETE YOUR WORK ON YOUR OWN	**1.** Students will follow the Grab and Write routine on page I-44 of the Introduction. **2.** Circulate as students work, which usually takes fifteen minutes, and coach as needed.
FLUENCY: READING LIKE YOU'RE SPEAKING	**1.** Have students turn to page 3 in the Fluency Notebook. **2.** Have students read one or more of the following chants: "Dig," "Type," and "Hat." **3.** Circulate and listen to students read or gather a small group of students who need additional support.

Day 3

PHONEMIC AWARENESS: **LISTEN**

1. Give the directions. Say, "I am going to break a word into two parts. Your job is to put the word back together. For example, if I say '/b/ [pause] –at,' you say 'bat.'"

2. Say the following words:

/l/ –og (log)   /f/ –it (fit)   /v/ –et (vet)
/w/ –ill (will)   /n/ –ot (not)

THE BIG REVEAL

1. Say, "On Day 1 we learned the *dig* puzzle piece. It represents the letter *d*. The dig piece says '/d/ /d/ /d/' like at the beginning of the word *dig*. Let's all do the motion for the *dig* piece together."

2. Say, "Yesterday we learned the *type* puzzle piece. It represents the letter *t*. The type piece says '/t/ /t/ /t/' like at the beginning of the word *type*. Let's all do the motion for the *type* piece together."

3. Hold up the *hat* puzzle piece and say, "This is the *hat* piece. It represents the letter *a*. The hat piece says '/ă/ /ă/ /ă/' like in the middle of the word *hat*. Tap your head and say '/ă/.' We will study this sound all week. Let's make a list of words that have the *hat* sound in them" (record the words).

SUPPORTED BLENDING: **PUTTING SOUNDS TOGETHER TO MAKE NEW WORDS**

1. Follow the Supported Blending routine on page I-16 of the Introduction.

2. Display the following words on the board one line at a time. Facilitate a discussion about the blending line focus after each line.

3. Then display the weekly sight word.

ant	add	ask	Discuss: initial sound of /ă/
apple	at	Alex	Discuss: initial sound of /ă/; capital A in the name *Alex*

Sight Word: a

FORMATION: **WRITING LETTERS**

1. Have students turn to page 17 of the Learner's Notebook.

2. Model forming uppercase letter *A* and lowercase letter *a*.

Uppercase Formation

Your pencil starts at the top line.

Form a straight, diagonal line down to the bottom line, left.

Pick your pencil up.

Your pencil starts at the top line.

Form a straight, diagonal line down to the bottom line, right.

Pick your pencil up.

Your pencil starts at the middle line.

Form a straight line connecting the two diagonal lines.

Pick your pencil up.

Lowercase Formation

Your pencil starts at the middle line.

Form a circle.

Pick your pencil up.

Your pencil starts at the middle line.

Form a straight line down to the bottom line.

Pick your pencil up.

3. Assist students in forming two lines of uppercase *A*s.

4. Assist students in forming two lines of lowercase *a*s.

Day 3 (Continued)

SORT: WHAT IS YOUR FOCUS PATTERN?	**1.** Have students take out their bag of pictures (created on Day 1) and follow the Sorting With Combined Picture and Word Cards routine on page I-25 of the Introduction.
	2. Instruct students that they are only using the *hat* header and words with the letter *a*.
PRACTICE: COMPLETE YOUR WORK ON YOUR OWN	**1.** Have students turn to page 18 in the Learner's Notebook.
	2. Students will complete the Letter Matrix routine found on page I-45 of the Introduction.
	3. Circulate as students work, which usually takes fifteen minutes, and coach as needed.
FLUENCY: READING LIKE YOU'RE SPEAKING	**1.** Have students turn to page 3 in the Fluency Notebook.
	2. Have students read one or more of the following chants: "Dig," "Type," and "Hat."
	3. Circulate and listen to students read or gather a small group of students who need additional support.

Day 4

PHONEMIC AWARENESS: LISTEN	**1.** Give the directions. Say, "I am going to break a word into two parts. Your job is to put the word back together. For example, if I say '/b/ [pause] –at,' you say 'bat.'" **2.** Say the following words: /y/ –es (yes) /j/ –ig (jig) /f/ –uss (fuss) /h/ –ut (hut) /b/ –id (bid)
PUZZLE PIECE REVIEW 	**1.** Say, "When I point to the piece, you tell me its name" (*dig, type, hat*). **2.** Say, "When I point to the piece, you tell me its sound" (/d/, /t/, /ă/). **3.** Say, "When I point to the piece, you tell me its spelling" (*d, t, a*). **4.** Say, "Write the spellings in the air with your finger" (students will form the letters *d, t,* and *a*).
SUPPORTED BLENDING: PUTTING SOUNDS TOGETHER TO MAKE NEW WORDS	**1.** Follow the Supported Blending routine on page I-16 of the Introduction. **2.** Display the following words on the board one line at a time. Facilitate a discussion about the blending line focus after each line. **3.** Then display the weekly sight word.

dig	desk	December	Discuss: initial sound of /d/; capital *D* in the name of the month
type	Tuesday	tiger	Discuss: initial sound of /t/; capital *T* in the name of the day
add	Adam	ask	Discuss: initial sound of /ă/; capital *A* in the name *Adam*

Sight Word: a

DICTATION: STRETCH OUT YOUR WORDS	**1.** Have students turn to page 19 of the Learner's Notebook. **2.** Follow the Dictation routine on page I-21 of the Introduction to dictate the following words: I. tiger 2. desk 3. towel 4. ask 5. Tuesday **Sight Word: a** **3.** Hold students accountable for recording the initial sound in each word in their Learner's Notebook.
SORT: WHAT IS YOUR FOCUS PATTERN?	**1.** Have students take out their bag of pictures and words (created on Day 1) and follow the Sorting With Combined Picture and Word Cards routine on page I-25 of the Introduction.
PRACTICE: COMPLETE YOUR WORK ON YOUR OWN	**1.** Have students complete the following Practice Pieces: Glue Words (on page I-41 of the Introduction) and Fluency Drill (on page I-46 of the Introduction). **2.** Circulate as students work, which usually takes fifteen minutes, and coach as needed.
FLUENCY: READING LIKE YOU'RE SPEAKING	**1.** Have students turn to page 3 in the Fluency Notebook. **2.** Have students read one or more of the following chants: "Dig," "Type," and "Hat." **3.** Circulate and listen to students read or gather a small group of students who need additional support.

Day 5

PHONEMIC AWARENESS: LISTEN

1. Give the directions. Say, "I am going to break a word into two parts. Your job is to put the word back together. For example, if I say '/b/ [pause] –at,' you say 'bat.'"

2. Say the following words:

| /g/ –ap (gap) | /r/ –ut (rut) | /t/ –uck (tuck) | /j/ –og (jog) | /z/ –ip (zip) |

REVIEW PATTERNS OF THE WEEK

1. Say, "Find a partner."

2. Say, "Tell your partner the names of this week's pieces" (*dig, type, hat*).

3. Say, "Tell your partner the sounds of this week's pieces" (/d/, /t/, /ă/).

4. Say, "Tell your partner the spellings of this week's pieces" (*d, t, a*).

5. Say, "Write the spellings on your partner's back with your finger" (students will form the letters *d, t,* and *a*).

SPELLING CHECK

1. Follow the Spelling Check routine on page I-34 of the Introduction.

2. Have students turn to page 21 of the Learner's Notebook.

3. Say, "Write the letter that represents the sound you hear."

4. Dictate the following sounds (repeat the sound if needed):

1. /d/
2. /ă/
3. /d/
4. /t/
5. /ă/

Sight Word: a

LABELING THE ROOM

1. Label the classroom with things found from this week's sort.

HANDWRITING CHECK

1. Have students turn to page 22 in the Learner's Notebook.

2. Model and have students form the following letters:

1. Three uppercase *D*s
2. Three lowercase *d*s
3. Three uppercase *T*s
4. Three lowercase *t*s
5. Three uppercase *A*s
6. Three lowercase *a*s

WEEKLY CELEBRATION

1. Display the celebratory message: "Dynamite! You learned the *dig, type,* and *hat* puzzle pieces!"

2. Encourage students to work together to read the message.

3. Have students copy the message onto their weekly certificate (see resources .corwin.com/puzzlepiecephonics-gradeK) and place it somewhere to take home.

Preparing for Your Week

Resources

PUZZLE PIECES

WEEK 2		
m	**s**	**a**
mop	**s**nake	h**a**t
(Pretend you are holding a mop and mopping up something on the floor. As you mop up the mess, say "/m/.")	(Put your arms together and move them to create a slithering motion. As you are moving your arms, say "/s/.")	(Tap your head and say "/ă/.")

CORRESPONDING *LEARNER'S NOTEBOOK PAGES*

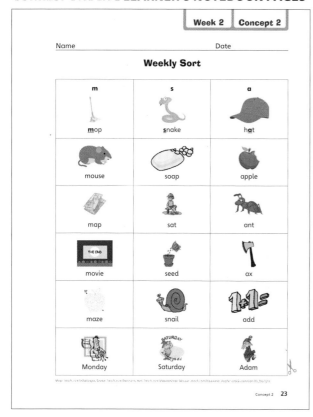

Mop: istock.com/mhatzapa; Snake: istock.com/kwansrn; Hat: istock.com/stevezmina1

Preparing for Your Week

CORRESPONDING *FLUENCY NOTEBOOK PAGES*

Mop

m m m Mop!
m m m Mop!

I mop up the

_____.

I mop up the

_____.

m m m Mop!
m m m Mop!

I mop up the

_____.

I mop up the

_____.

m m m Mop!
m m m Mop!

Mop: istock.com/mhatzapa

Snake

s s s Snake!
s s s Snake!

The snake ate

_____.

The snake ate

_____.

s s s Snake!
s s s Snake!

The snake ate

_____.

The snake ate

_____.

s s s Snake!
s s s Snake!

Snake: istock.com/kwansrn

Hat

a a a Hat!
a a a Hat!

A(n) _____

is in my hat!

A(n) _____

is in my hat!

a a a Hat!
a a a Hat!

A(n) _____

is in my hat!

A(n) _____

is in my hat!

a a a Hat!
a a a Hat!

Hat: istock.com/stevezmina1

Mm

Mix, mix, mix. Molly makes muffins.

Munch, munch, munch. Mike eats dozens.

Mix: istock.com/vasilyevalara

Ss

Sally sips strawberry soda while having fun.

Sally sips slowly under the sizzling sun.

Aa

Animals, animals are everywhere.

Animals, animals hang in the air.

Preparing for Your Week

Tips for Management and Differentiation

Refer to this section and to resources.corwin.com/puzzlepiecephonics-gradeK for resources and ideas to deepen your students' learning throughout the week. Feel free to put your own spin on the routines, too. For daily lesson plans, see pages 38–44 of this Teacher's Guide.

TIPS FOR PHONEMIC AWARENESS
- The focus for this week is segmenting words into their onset and rime. The student's job is to hear the onset and rime and put the word back together.
- If you notice your students need additional practice, extend the activity with additional words.
- Students may incorporate the rhyming Phonemic Awareness activity from last week and say a word that rhymes with the put-together word.

TIPS FOR THE PUZZLE PIECE REVIEW
- This week on Days 1 and 2 you are introducing students to a new puzzle piece. Be sure to spend enough time introducing the piece so students understand their focus for that day.
- The reference Puzzle Pieces only have the lowercase letter representing the focus sound. This is so students can build words using the Puzzle Pieces. In the back of the Puzzle Piece pack, you will find uppercase letter cards. Cut these out and use them with the Puzzle Pieces to show the uppercase letter formation for each piece.

TIPS FOR SUPPORTED BLENDING
- Follow the Supported Blending routine and hold students accountable for producing the initial sounds for each word.
- Reblend lines if necessary.
- If students do not have the attention span to blend the review line, you may omit the third line from the blending routine.

TIPS FOR FORMATION
- Encourage students to circle the letter on the row that they feel they formed the best. Have them try to duplicate the letter.
- Go around with a highlighter to help students who are struggling with their letters.
- Have a station in your room with sand for students to practice forming their letters in.
- Students may need extra direction in forming the letter *s*.

TIPS FOR DICTATION
- If students are struggling to identify the initial sound of a word, isolate the sound for students and tell them to record that specific sound.

TIPS FOR SORTING
- This week students are sorting their pictures and words with the three headers. On Days 1 and 2, students will only be sorting with two headers. Instruct students to place any unused picture and word cards and headers back into their word sort bags.
- On Day 2, if students can handle sorting *Mm, Ss,* and *Aa*, allow them to build off what they learned last week and on Day 1.
- The sort contains words with authentic capitalization. Review the picture and word cards with students and go over this week's capitalized words.

Preparing for Your Week

TIPS FOR THE PRACTICE PIECES

- Keep in mind that the routines may take more time at this point in the year than they will once your students are familiar with word study.
- Be sure to give your students multiple opportunities to see how the Practice Pieces should be completed. If necessary, you can introduce only one or two of the Practice Piece routines. Complete them as a class first, then give students time to practice independently.
- This Practice Piece time can be your opportunity to create fun, authentic experiences with letters.
  - **Mm:** Have students fill in an uppercase *M* and lowercase *m* with marshmallows.
  - **Ss:** Have students fill in an uppercase *S* and lowercase *s* with sand.
  - **Aa:** Have students fill in an uppercase *A* and lowercase *a* with apple stamps.
  - Make it fun for your students using the supplies you have!

TIPS FOR FLUENCY

- This week students will read open-ended chants in which they can fill in the blank with their sort pictures. The chants are very repetitive and are meant to be interactive. Students will need support with the sight words in the chants.
- Students can illustrate other parts of the poems.
- Students can read their chants and couplets to a partner.
- Students can pull out pictures from their sort bags to fill in the blanks during the chants.
- Students may circle the letters of the week in each couplet.

TIPS FOR SPELLING CHECK

- Review the directions with students. They are writing the letter that represents the sound you dictate.
- Use teacher discretion when grading the Spelling Check.

PHONEMIC AWARENESS: LISTEN

1. Give the directions. Say, "I am going to break a word into two parts. Your job is to put the word back together. For example, if I say '/b/ [pause] –at,' you say 'bat.'"

2. Say the following words:

/p/ –up (pup)   /sh/ –op (shop)   /t/ –im (Tim)
/m/ –ight (might)   /s/ –it (sit)

THE BIG REVEAL

1. Hold up the *mop* puzzle piece and say, "This is the *mop* piece. It represents the letter *m*. The *mop* piece says '/m/ /m/ /m/' like at the beginning of the word *mop*. Pretend you are holding a mop and mopping up something on the floor. As you mop up the mess, say '/m/.' We will study this letter and sound all week. Let's make a list of words that have the *mop* sound in them" (record the words).

SUPPORTED BLENDING: PUTTING SOUNDS TOGETHER TO MAKE NEW WORDS

1. Follow the Supported Blending routine on page I-16 of the Introduction.

2. Display the following words on the board one line at a time. Facilitate a discussion about the blending line focus after each line.

3. Then display the weekly sight word.

mop	maze	map	Discuss: initial sound of /m/
mouse	milk	mug	Discuss: initial sound of /m/
tap	deck	ant	Discuss: review of sounds from previous weeks

Sight Word: at

FORMATION: WRITING LETTERS

1. Have students turn to page 25 of the Learner's Notebook.

2. Model forming uppercase letter *M* and lowercase letter *m*.

Uppercase Formation

Your pencil starts at the top line.

Form a straight line down to the bottom line.

Pick your pencil up.

Your pencil starts at the top line.

Form a diagonal line to the middle line, right.

Pick your pencil up.

Your pencil starts at the top line, to the right.

Form a diagonal line to the middle, left.

Pick your pencil up.

Your pencil starts at the top line.

Form a straight line down to the bottom line.

Pick your pencil up.

Lowercase Formation

Your pencil starts at the middle line.

Form a straight line down to the bottom line.

Pick your pencil up.

Your pencil starts just below the middle line.

Form a hump, then another hump all the way down to the bottom line, right.

Pick your pencil up.

3. Assist students in forming two lines of uppercase *M*s.

4. Assist students in forming two lines of lowercase *m*s.

Day 1 (Continued)

PRACTICE:
COMPLETE
YOUR WORK ON
YOUR OWN

1. Have students turn to page 23 of the Learner's Notebook.

2. Instruct students to tear out the sort and complete the following Practice Pieces: Quick Color, Careful Cut, and Sorting With Combined Picture and Word Cards (see further directions on pages I-37, I-38, and I-25 of the Introduction).

3. Instruct students that they are only using the *mop* and *hat* headers and words with the letters *m* and *a*.

4. Circulate as students work, which usually takes fifteen minutes, and coach as needed.

FLUENCY:
READING LIKE
YOU'RE SPEAKING

1. Have students turn to page 5 in the Fluency Notebook.

2. Have students read one or more of the following chants: "Mop," "Snake," and "Hat."

3. Circulate and listen to students read or gather a small group of students who need additional support.

Day 2

PHONEMIC AWARENESS: LISTEN

1. Say, "I am going to break a word into two parts. Your job is to put the word back together. For example, if I say '/b/ [pause] –at,' you say 'bat.'"

2. Say the following words:

/h/ –am (ham)   /f/ –it (fit)   /b/ –ook (book)
/p/ –ot (pot)   /m/ –ade (made)

THE BIG REVEAL

1. Say, "Yesterday we learned the *mop* piece. It represents the letter *m*. The mop piece says '/m/ /m/ /m/' like at the beginning of the word *mop*. Let's all do the motion for the *mop* piece together."

2. Hold up the *snake* puzzle piece and say, "This is the *snake* piece. It represents the letter *s*. The *snake* piece says '/s/ /s/ /s/' like at the beginning of the word *snake*. Put your arms together and move them to create a slithering motion. As you are moving your arms, say '/s/.' We will study this sound all week. Let's make a list of words that have the *snake* sound in them" (record the words).

SUPPORTED BLENDING: PUTTING SOUNDS TOGETHER TO MAKE NEW WORDS

1. Follow the Supported Blending routine on page I-16 of the Introduction.

2. Display the following words on the board one line at a time. Facilitate a discussion about the blending line focus after each line.

3. Then display the weekly sight word.

sat	snake	seed	Discuss: initial sound of /s/
soap	sit	side	Discuss: initial sound of /s/
tiger	donut	atlas	Discuss: review of sounds from previous weeks

Sight Word: at

FORMATION: WRITING LETTERS

1. Have students turn to page 26 of the Learner's Notebook.

2. Model forming uppercase letter *S* and lowercase letter *s*.

Uppercase Formation	**Lowercase Formation**
Your pencil starts just below the top line.	Your pencil starts just below the middle line.
Form a curved line to the middle line.	Form a curved line to in between the middle and bottom lines.
Form a curved line to just above the bottom line.	Form a curved line to just above the bottom line.
Pick your pencil up.	Pick your pencil up.

3. Assist students in forming two lines of uppercase *S*s.

4. Assist students in forming two lines of lowercase *s*s.

SORT: WHAT IS YOUR FOCUS PATTERN?

1. Have students take out their bag of pictures (created on Day 1) and follow the Sorting With Combined Picture and Word Cards routine on page I-25 of the Introduction.

2. Instruct students that they are only using the *snake* and *hat* headers and words with the letters *s* and *a*.

| **PRACTICE: COMPLETE YOUR WORK ON YOUR OWN** | **1.** Students will follow the Grab and Write routine on page I-44 of the Introduction. |
| | **2.** Circulate as students work, which usually takes fifteen minutes, and coach as needed. |

FLUENCY: READING LIKE YOU'RE SPEAKING	**1.** Have students turn to page 5 in the Fluency Notebook.
	2. Have students read one or more of the following chants: "Mop," "Snake," and "Hat."
	3. Circulate and listen to students read or gather a small group of students who need additional support.

Day 3

PHONEMIC AWARENESS: LISTEN

1. Give the directions. Say, "I am going to break a word into two parts. Your job is to put the word back together. For example, if I say '/b/ [pause] –at,' you say 'bat.'"

2. Say the following words:

/b/ –ag (bag)   /th/ –ud (thud)   /z/ –oo (zoo)
/l/ –ink (link)   /y/ –um (yum)

PUZZLE PIECE REVIEW

1. Say, "When I point to the piece, you tell me its name" (*mop, snake, hat*).

2. Say, "When I point to the piece, you tell me its sound" (/m/, /s/, /ă/).

3. Say, "When I point to the piece, you tell me its spelling" (*m, s, a*).

4. Say, "Write the spellings in the air with your finger" (students will form the letters *m, s,* and *a*).

SUPPORTED BLENDING: PUTTING SOUNDS TOGETHER TO MAKE NEW WORDS

1. Follow the Supported Blending routine on page I-16 of the Introduction.

2. Display the following words on the board one line at a time. Facilitate a discussion about the blending line focus after each line.

3. Then display the weekly sight word.

apple	snail	movie	Discuss: initial sounds of /ă/, /s/, and /m/
maze	seed	Seth	Discuss: initial sounds of /m/ and /s/; capital *S* in the name *Seth*
add	timer	dock	Discuss: review of sounds from previous weeks

Sight Word: at

DICTATION: STRETCH OUT YOUR WORDS

1. Have students turn to page 27 of the Learner's Notebook.

2. Follow the Dictation routine on page I-21 of the Introduction to dictate the following words:

I. snake   2. mop   3. ten   4. dunk   5. Monday

Sight Word: at

3. Hold students accountable for recording the initial sound in each word in their Learner's Notebook.

SORT: WHAT IS YOUR FOCUS PATTERN?

1. Have students take out their bag of pictures (created on Day 1) and follow the Sorting With Combined Picture and Word Cards routine on page I-25 of the Introduction.

PRACTICE: COMPLETE YOUR WORK ON YOUR OWN

1. Have students turn to page 28 in the Learner's Notebook.

2. Students will complete the Letter Matrix routine found on page I-45 of the Introduction.

3. Circulate as students work, which usually takes fifteen minutes, and coach as needed.

FLUENCY: READING LIKE YOU'RE SPEAKING

1. Have students turn to page 5 in the Fluency Notebook.

2. Have students read one or more of the following chants: "Mop," "Snake," and "Hat."

3. Circulate and listen to students read or gather a small group of students who need additional support.

PHONEMIC AWARENESS: LISTEN

1. Give the directions. Say, "I am going to break a word into two parts. Your job is to put the word back together. For example, if I say '/b/ [pause] –at,' you say 'bat.'"

2. Say the following words:

/t/ –all (tall)   /h/ –igh (high)   /m/ –ob (mob)   /d/ –esk (desk)   /f/ –it (fit)

PUZZLE PIECE REVIEW

1. Say, "When I point to the piece, you tell me its name" (mop, snake, hat).

2. Say, "When I point to the piece, you tell me its sound" (/m/, /s/, /ă/).

3. Say, "When I point to the piece, you tell me its spelling" (m, s, a).

4. Say, "Write the spellings in the air with your finger" (students will form the letters m, s, and a).

SUPPORTED BLENDING: PUTTING SOUNDS TOGETHER TO MAKE NEW WORDS

1. Follow the Supported Blending routine on page I-16 of the Introduction.

2. Display the following words on the board one line at a time. Facilitate a discussion about the blending line focus after each line.

3. Then display the weekly sight word.

ask	sled	moment	Discuss: initial sounds of /ă/, /s/, and /m/
snake	monkey	ant	Discuss: initial sounds of /s/, /m/, and /ă/
Saturday	Monday	Sunday	Discuss: initial sounds of /s/ and /m/; capital S and M in the names of the days

Sight Word: at

DICTATION: STRETCH OUT YOUR WORDS

1. Have students turn to page 29 of the Learner's Notebook.

2. Follow the Dictation routine on page I-21 of the Introduction to dictate the following words:

l. soup   2. dent   3. milk   4. apple   5. Saturday

Sight Word: at

3. Hold students accountable for recording the initial sound in each word in their Learner's Notebook.

SORT: WHAT IS YOUR FOCUS PATTERN?

1. Have students take out their bag of pictures and words (created on Day 1) and follow the Sorting With Combined Picture and Word Cards routine on page I-25 of the Introduction.

PRACTICE: COMPLETE YOUR WORK ON YOUR OWN

1. Have students complete the following Practice Pieces: Glue Words (on page I-41 of the Introduction) and Fluency Drill (on page I-46 of the Introduction).

2. Circulate as students work, which usually takes fifteen minutes, and coach as needed.

FLUENCY: READING LIKE YOU'RE SPEAKING

1. Have students turn to page 5 in the Fluency Notebook.

2. Have students read one or more of the following chants: "Mop," "Snake," and "Hat."

3. Circulate and listen to students read or gather a small group of students who need additional support.

Day 5

PHONEMIC AWARENESS: LISTEN

1. Say, "I am going to break a word into two parts. Your job is to put the word back together. For example, if I say '/b/ [pause] –at,' you say 'bat.'"

2. Say the following words:

/s/ –od (sod)   /k/ –it (kit)   /d/ –uck (duck)   /n/ –est (nest)   /r/ –oll (roll)

REVIEW PATTERNS OF THE WEEK

1. Say, "Find a partner."

2. Say, "Tell your partner the names of this week's pieces" (*mop, snake, hat*).

3. Say, "Tell your partner the sounds of this week's pieces" (/m/, /s/, /ă/).

4. Say, "Tell your partner the spellings of this week's pieces" (*m, s, a*).

5. Say, "Write the spellings on your partner's back with your finger" (students will form the letters *m, s,* and *a*).

SPELLING CHECK

1. Follow the Spelling Check routine on page I-34 of the Introduction.

2. Have students turn to page 31 of the Learner's Notebook.

3. Say, "Write the letter that represents the sound you hear."

4. Dictate the following sounds (repeat the sound if needed):

I. /ă/

2. /s/

3. /d/

4. /m/

5. /t/

Sight Word: at

LABELING THE ROOM

1. Label the classroom with things found from this week's sort.

HANDWRITING CHECK

1. Have students turn to page 32 in the Learner's Notebook.

2. Model and have students form the following letters:

1. Three uppercase *M*s

2. Three lowercase *m*s

3. Three uppercase *S*s

4. Three lowercase *s*s

5. Three uppercase *A*s

6. Three lowercase *a*s

WEEKLY CELEBRATION

1. Display the celebratory message: "Magnificent! You learned the *mop, snake,* and *hat* puzzle pieces!"

2. Encourage students to work together to read the message.

3. Have students copy the message onto their weekly certificate (see resources .corwin.com/puzzlepiecephonics-gradeK) and place it somewhere to take home.

Resources

PUZZLE PIECES

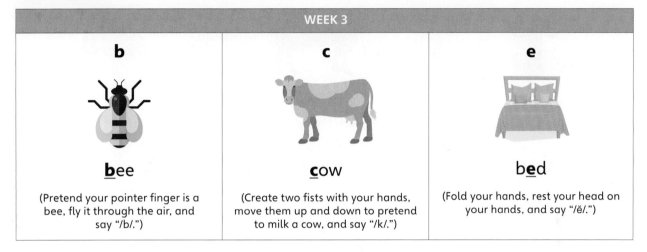

WEEK 3		
b	**c**	**e**
bee	**c**ow	b**e**d
(Pretend your pointer finger is a bee, fly it through the air, and say "/b/.")	(Create two fists with your hands, move them up and down to pretend to milk a cow, and say "/k/.")	(Fold your hands, rest your head on your hands, and say "/ĕ/.")

CORRESPONDING *LEARNER'S NOTEBOOK* PAGES

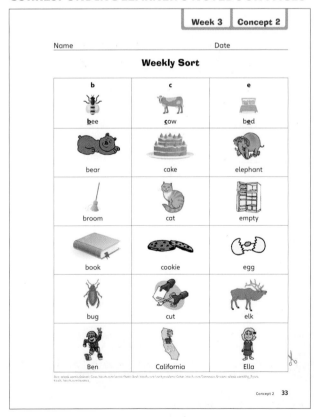

Bee: istock.com/adekvat; Cow: istock.com/vectorikart; Bed: istock.com/vasilyevalara

Preparing for Your Week

CORRESPONDING *FLUENCY NOTEBOOK PAGES*

Bee

b b b Bee!
b b b Bee!

The bee sees a

_____.

The bee sees a

_____.

b b b Bee!
b b b Bee!

The bee sees a

_____.

The bee sees a

_____.

b b b Bee!
b b b Bee!

Bee: istock.com/adekvat

Cow

k k k Cow!
k k k Cow!

Cow eats

_____.

Cow eats

_____.

k k k Cow!
k k k Cow!

Cow eats

_____.

Cow eats

_____.

k k k Cow!
k k k Cow!

Cow: istock.com/vectorikart

Bed

e e e Bed!
e e e Bed!

An _____

is in bed!

An _____

is in bed!

e e e Bed!
e e e Bed!

An _____

is in bed!

An _____

is in bed!

e e e Bed!
e e e Bed!

Bed: istock.com/vasilyevalara

Bb

Bob bought a big box of books at the shop.

Bob browsed the books until Ben said stop.

Cc

Cooks are in the kitchen—what will they bake?

Cutting carrots, stirring batter for a carrot cake!

Ee

Effie asked Erin, "Do rainbows ever end?"

Erin told Effie, "Yes, but you'll always be my friend."

Preparing for Your Week

Tips for Management and Differentiation

Refer to this section and to resources.corwin.com/puzzlepiecephonics-gradeK for resources and ideas to deepen your students' learning throughout the week. Feel free to put your own spin on the routines, too. For daily lesson plans, see pages 49–55 of this Teacher's Guide.

TIPS FOR PHONEMIC AWARENESS	• In previous weeks, students have heard the onset and rime and put the word back together. This week, students will be doing the opposite. They will hear a complete word and segment the word into its onset and rime. • If you notice your students need additional practice, extend the activity with additional words.
TIPS FOR THE PUZZLE PIECE REVIEW	• This week on Days 1–3 you are introducing students to a new puzzle piece. Be sure to spend enough time introducing the piece so students understand their focus for that day. • Have students work with the same partner each day to build a word study relationship.
TIPS FOR SUPPORTED BLENDING	• Follow the Supported Blending routine on page I-16 of the Introduction and hold students accountable for producing the initial sounds for each word. • Reblend lines if necessary.
TIPS FOR FORMATION	• Encourage students to circle the letter on the row that they feel they formed the best. Have them try to duplicate the letter. • Go around with a highlighter to help students who are struggling with their letters. • Have a station in your room with sand for students to practice forming their letters in.
TIPS FOR DICTATION	• If students are struggling to identify the initial sound of a word, tell students to write the letter that says "/b/," "/k/," or "/ĕ/."
TIPS FOR SORTING	• This week students are sorting their pictures and words with the three headers. On Days 1–3, students will only be sorting with one header. Instruct students to place any unused picture and word cards and headers back into their word sort bags. • On Day 2, if students can handle sorting both *Bb* and *Cc*, allow them to build off what they learned on Day 1. The same applies for Day 3. • The sort contains words with authentic capitalization. Review the picture and word cards with students and go over this week's capitalized words.

TIPS FOR THE PRACTICE PIECES	• This Practice Piece time can be your opportunity to create fun, authentic experiences with letters.
	   • **Bb:** Have students fill in an uppercase *B* and lowercase *b* with beans.
	   • **Cc:** Have students fill in an uppercase *C* and lowercase *c* with cow spots.
	   • **Ee:** Have students fill in an uppercase *E* and lowercase *e* with elephant print stamps.
	   • Make it fun for your students using the supplies you have!

(Continued)

Preparing for Your Week

TIPS FOR FLUENCY	• This week students will read open-ended chants in which they can fill in the blank with their sort pictures. The chants are very repetitive and are meant to be interactive. Students will need support with the sight words in the chants.
	• Students can illustrate other parts of the chants.
	• Students can read their chants and couplets to a partner.
	• Students can pull out pictures from their sort bags to fill in the blanks during the chants.
	• Students may circle the letters of the week in each couplet.
TIPS FOR SPELLING CHECK	• Review the directions with students. They are writing the letter that represents the sound you dictate.
	• Use teacher discretion when grading the Spelling Check.

PHONEMIC AWARENESS: LISTEN	**1.** Give the directions. Say, "I am going to say a word. Your job is to break the word into two parts. For example, if I say 'bat,' you say '/b/ [pause] –at.'"
	2. Say the following words:
	cup (/k/ –up)　lost (/l/ –ost)　for (/f/ –or)　did (/d/ –id)　big (/b/ –ig)

THE BIG REVEAL

1. Hold up the *bee* puzzle piece and say, "This is the *bee* piece. It represents the letter *b*. The *bee* piece says '/b/ /b/ /b/' like at the beginning of the word *bee*. Pretend your pointer finger is a bee, fly it through the air, and say '/b/.' We will study this letter and sound all week. Let's make a list of words that have the *bee* sound in them" (record the words).

SUPPORTED BLENDING: PUTTING SOUNDS TOGETHER TO MAKE NEW WORDS

1. Follow the Supported Blending routine on page I-16 of the Introduction.

2. Display the following words on the board one line at a time. Facilitate a discussion about the blending line focus after each line.

3. Then display the weekly sight word.

bee　　　bug　　book　　Discuss: initial sound of /b/

bad　　　boy　　boat　　Discuss: initial sound of /b/

Sight Word: be

FORMATION: WRITING LETTERS

1. Have students turn to page 35 of the Learner's Notebook.

2. Model forming uppercase letter *B* and lowercase letter *b*.

Uppercase Formation	**Lowercase Formation**
Your pencil starts at the top line.	Your pencil starts at the top line.
Form a straight line down to the bottom line.	Form a straight line down to the bottom line.
Pick your pencil up.	Pick your pencil up.
Your pencil starts at the top line.	Your pencil starts at the middle line.
Form a curved line to the middle line.	Form a curved line to the bottom line.
Form a curved line to the bottom line.	Pick your pencil up.
Pick your pencil up.	

3. Assist students in forming two lines of uppercase *B*s.

4. Assist students in forming two lines of lowercase *b*s.

PRACTICE: COMPLETE YOUR WORK ON YOUR OWN

1. Have students turn to page 33 of the Learner's Notebook.

2. Instruct students to tear out the sort and complete the following Practice Pieces: Quick Color, Careful Cut, and Sorting With Combined Picture and Word Cards (see further directions on pages I-37, I-38, and I-25 of the Introduction).

3. Instruct students that they are only using the *bee* header and words with the letter *b*.

4. Circulate as students work, which usually takes fifteen minutes, and coach as needed.

FLUENCY: READING LIKE YOU'RE SPEAKING

1. Have students turn to page 7 in the Fluency Notebook.

2. Have students read one or more of the following chants: "Bee," "Cow," and "Bed."

3. Circulate and listen to students read or gather a small group of students who need additional support.

PHONEMIC AWARENESS: LISTEN	**1.** Give the directions. Say, "I am going to say a word. Your job is to break the word into two parts. For example, if I say '*bat*,' you say '/b/ [pause] –*at*.'"
	2. Say the following words:

dock (/d/ –ock)   pop (/p/ –op)   light (/l/ –ight)
dog (/d/ –og)   hit (/h/ –it)

THE BIG REVEAL	**1.** Say, "Yesterday we learned the *bee* piece. It represents the letter *b*. The bee piece says '/b/ /b/ /b/' like at the beginning of the word *bee*. Let's all do the motion for the *bee* piece together."
	2. Hold up the *cow* puzzle piece and say, "This is the *cow* piece. It represents the letter *c*. The *cow* piece says '/k/ /k/ /k/' like at the beginning of the word *cow*. Create two fists with your hands, move them up and down to pretend to milk a cow, and say '/k/.' We will study this sound all week. Let's make a list of words that have the *cow* sound in them" (record the words).

SUPPORTED BLENDING: PUTTING SOUNDS TOGETHER TO MAKE NEW WORDS	**1.** Follow the Supported Blending routine on page I-16 of the Introduction.
	2. Display the following words on the board one line at a time. Facilitate a discussion about the blending line focus after each line.
	3. Then display the weekly sight word.

cow	**cat**	**cut**	Discuss: initial sound of /k/
cake	**cup**	**clip**	Discuss: initial sound of /k/

Sight Word: be

FORMATION: WRITING LETTERS	**1.** Have students turn to page 36 of the Learner's Notebook.
	2. Model forming uppercase letter *C* and lowercase letter *c*.

Uppercase Formation	**Lowercase Formation**
Your pencil starts just below the top line.	Your pencil starts just below the middle line.
Form a curved line down to the bottom line.	Form a curved line down to the bottom line.
Continue the curve back up to just above the bottom line.	Continue the curve back up to just above the bottom line.
Pick your pencil up.	Pick your pencil up.

3. Assist students in forming two lines of uppercase *C*s.

4. Assist students in forming two lines of lowercase *c*s.

SORT: WHAT IS YOUR FOCUS PATTERN?	**1.** Have students take out their bag of pictures (created on Day 1) and follow the Sorting With Combined Picture and Word Cards routine on page I-25 of the Introduction.
	2. Instruct students that they are only using the *cow* header and words with the letter *c*.

PRACTICE:
COMPLETE
YOUR WORK ON
YOUR OWN

1. Students will follow the Grab and Write routine on page I-44 of the Introduction.

2. Circulate as students work, which usually takes fifteen minutes, and coach as needed.

FLUENCY:
READING LIKE
YOU'RE SPEAKING

1. Have students turn to page 7 in the Fluency Notebook.

2. Have students read one or more of the following chants: "Bee," "Cow," and "Bed."

3. Circulate and listen to students read or gather a small group of students who need additional support.

Day 3

PHONEMIC AWARENESS: LISTEN

1. Say, "I am going to say a word. Your job is to break the word into two parts. For example, if I say '*bat*,' you say '/b/ [pause] *–at*.'"

2. Say the following words:

lunch (/l/ –unch)   camp (/k/ –amp)   vet (/v/ –et)
loop (/l/ –oop)   rat (/r/ –at)

THE BIG REVEAL

1. Say, "On Day 1, we learned the *bee* piece. It represents the letter *b*. The bee piece says '/b/ /b/ /b/' like at the beginning of the word *bee*. Let's all do the motion for the *bee* piece together."

2. Say, "Yesterday, we learned the *cow* piece. It represents the letter *c*. The cow piece says '/k/ /k/ /k/' like at the beginning of the word *cow*. Let's all do the motion for the *cow* piece together."

3. Hold up the *bed* puzzle piece and say, "This is the *bed* piece. It represents the letter *e*. The *bed* piece says '/ĕ/ /ĕ/ /ĕ/' like in the middle of the word *bed*. Fold your hands, rest your head on your hands, and say '/ĕ/.' We will study this sound all week. Let's make a list of words that have the *bed* sound in them" (record the words).

SUPPORTED BLENDING: PUTTING SOUNDS TOGETHER TO MAKE NEW WORDS

1. Follow the Supported Blending routine on page I-16 of the Introduction.

2. Display the following words on the board one line at a time. Facilitate a discussion about the blending line focus after each line.

3. Then display the weekly sight word.

elk	egg	elephant	Discuss: initial sound of /ĕ/
empty	end	Ella	Discuss: initial sound of /ĕ/; capital *E* in the name *Ella*

Sight Word: be

FORMATION: WRITING LETTERS

1. Have students turn to page 37 of the Learner's Notebook.

2. Model forming uppercase letter *E* and lowercase *e*.

Uppercase Formation

Your pencil starts at the top line.

Form a straight line down to the bottom line.

Pick your pencil up.

Your pencil starts at the top line.

Form a straight line on the top line, right.

Pick your pencil up.

Your pencil starts on the middle line.

Form a straight line on the middle line, right.

Pick your pencil up.

Your pencil starts on the bottom line, right.

Form a straight line on the bottom line.

Pick your pencil up.

Lowercase Formation

Your pencil starts just below the middle line.

Form a straight, horizontal line.

Move your pencil up and create a curved line that touches the middle line.

Continue the curve back up to just above the bottom line.

Pick your pencil up.

3. Assist students in forming two lines of uppercase *E*s.

4. Assist students in forming two lines of lowercase *e*s.

SORT: WHAT IS YOUR FOCUS PATTERN?

1. Have students take out their bag of pictures (created on Day 1) and follow the Sorting With Combined Picture and Word Cards routine on page I-25 of the Introduction.

2. Instruct students that they are only using the *bed* header and words with the letter *e*.

PRACTICE: COMPLETE YOUR WORK ON YOUR OWN

1. Have students turn to page 38 in the Learner's Notebook.

2. Students will complete the Letter Matrix routine found on page I-45 of the Introduction.

3. Circulate as students work, which usually takes fifteen minutes, and coach as needed.

FLUENCY: READING LIKE YOU'RE SPEAKING

1. Have students turn to page 7 in the Fluency Notebook.

2. Have students read one or more of the following chants: "Bee," "Cow," and "Bed."

3. Circulate and listen to students read or gather a small group of students who need additional support.

Day 4

PHONEMIC AWARENESS: LISTEN

1. Give the directions. Say, "I am going to say a word. Your job is to break the word into two parts. For example, if I say '*bat,*' you say '/b/ [pause] –*at.*'"

2. Say the following words:

bit (/b/ –it)   food (/f/ –ood)   boy (/b/ –oy)   dig (/d/ –ig)   yet (/y/ –et)

PUZZLE PIECE REVIEW

1. Say, "When I point to the piece, you tell me its name" (*bee, cow, bed*).

2. Say, "When I point to the piece, you tell me its sound" (/b/, /k/, /ĕ/).

3. Say, "When I point to the piece, you tell me its spelling" (*b, c, e*).

4. Say, "Write the spellings in the air with your finger" (students will form the letters *b, c,* and *e*).

SUPPORTED BLENDING: PUTTING SOUNDS TOGETHER TO MAKE NEW WORDS

1. Follow the Supported Blending routine on page I-16 of the Introduction.

2. Display the following words on the board one line at a time. Facilitate a discussion about the blending line focus after each line.

3. Then display the weekly sight word.

bear	broom	book	Discuss: initial sound of /b/
cookie	cut	California	Discuss: initial sound of /k/; capital C in the name of the state, *California*
empty	elk	egg	Discuss: initial sound of /ĕ/

Sight Word: be

DICTATION: STRETCH OUT YOUR WORDS

1. Have students turn to page 39 of the Learner's Notebook.

2. Follow the Dictation routine on page I-21 of the Introduction to dictate the following words:

l. cow   2. bee   3. cookie   4. empty   5. Ben

Sight Word: be

3. Hold students accountable for recording the initial sound in each word in their Learner's Notebook.

SORT: WHAT IS YOUR FOCUS PATTERN?

1. Have students take out their bag of pictures and words (created on Day 1) and follow the Sorting With Combined Picture and Word Cards routine on page I-25 of the Introduction.

PRACTICE: COMPLETE YOUR WORK ON YOUR OWN

1. Have students complete the following Practice Pieces: Glue Words (on page I-41 of the Introduction) and Fluency Drill (on page I-46 of the Introduction).

2. Circulate as students work, which usually takes fifteen minutes, and coach as needed.

FLUENCY: READING LIKE YOU'RE SPEAKING

1. Have students turn to page 7 in the Fluency Notebook.

2. Have students read one or more of the following chants: "Bee," "Cow," and "Bed."

3. Circulate and listen to students read or gather a small group of students who need additional support.

PHONEMIC AWARENESS: LISTEN	**1.** Give the directions. Say, "I am going to say a word. Your job is to break the word into two parts. For example, if I say '*bat,*' you say '/b/ [pause] –*at.*'"
	2. Say the following words:

call (/k/ –all)   big (/b/ –ig)   core (/k/ –ore)   dim (/d/ –im)   go (/g/ –o)

REVIEW PATTERNS OF THE WEEK	**1.** Say, "Find a partner."
	2. Say, "Tell your partner the names of this week's pieces" (*bee, cow, bed*).
	3. Say, "Tell your partner the sounds of this week's pieces" (/b/, /k/, /ĕ/).
	4. Say, "Tell your partner the spellings of this week's pieces" (*b, c, e*).
	5. Say, "Write the spellings on your partner's back with your finger" (students will form the letters *b, c,* and *e*).

SPELLING CHECK	**1.** Follow the Spelling Check routine on page I-34 of the Introduction.
	2. Have students turn to page 41 of the Learner's Notebook.
	3. Say, "Write the letter that represents the sound you hear."
	4. Dictate the following sounds (repeat the sound if needed):

1. /b/
2. /ĕ/
3. /k/
4. /ĕ/
5. /k/

Sight Word: be

LABELING THE ROOM	**1.** Label the classroom with things found from this week's sort.

HANDWRITING CHECK	**1.** Have students turn to page 42 in the Learner's Notebook.
	2. Model and have students form the following letters:

1. Three uppercase *B*s
2. Three lowercase *b*s
3. Three uppercase *C*s
4. Three lowercase *c*s
5. Three uppercase *E*s
6. Three lowercase *e*s

WEEKLY CELEBRATION	**1.** Display the celebratory message: "Cowabunga! You learned the *bee, cow,* and *bed* puzzle pieces!"
	2. Encourage students to work together to read the message.
	3. Have students copy the message onto their weekly certificate (see resources .corwin.com/puzzlepiecephonics-gradeK) and place it somewhere to take home.

Preparing for Your Week

Resources

PUZZLE PIECES

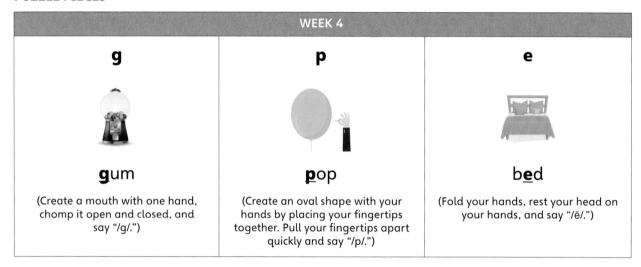

WEEK 4		
g	**p**	**e**
gum	**p**op	b**e**d
(Create a mouth with one hand, chomp it open and closed, and say "/g/.")	(Create an oval shape with your hands by placing your fingertips together. Pull your fingertips apart quickly and say "/p/.")	(Fold your hands, rest your head on your hands, and say "/ĕ/.")

CORRESPONDING *LEARNER'S NOTEBOOK* PAGES

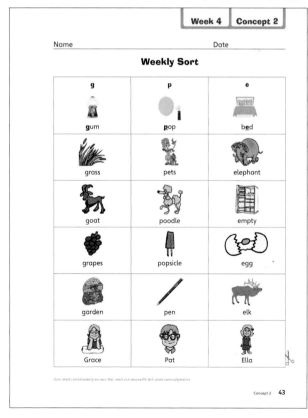

Gum: istock.com/elinedesignservices; Pop: istock.com/wissanu99; Bed: istock.com/vasilyevalara

Preparing for Your Week

CORRESPONDING *FLUENCY NOTEBOOK PAGES*

Gum

g g g Gum!
g g g Gum!

The _____

gave me gum!

The _____

gave me gum!

g g g Gum!
g g g Gum!

The _____

gave me gum!

The _____

gave me gum!

g g g Gum!
g g g Gum!

Gum: istock.com/elinedesignservices

Pop

p p p Pop!
p p p Pop!

Pop goes the

_____.

Pop goes the

_____.

p p p Pop!
p p p Pop!

Pop goes the

_____.

Pop goes the

_____.

p p p Pop!
p p p Pop!

Pop: istock.com/wissanu99

Bed

e e e Bed!
e e e Bed!

A(n) _____

is in bed!

A(n) _____

is in bed!

e e e Bed!
e e e Bed!

A(n) _____

is in bed!

A(n) _____

is in bed!

e e e Bed!
e e e Bed!

Bed: istock.com/vasilyevalara

Gg

Glug, glug, glug. Greg gobbles grapes.

Glug, glug, glug. Grapes taste great!

Pp

Pitter patter, pitter patter. Penguins parade on ice.

Pitter patter, pitter patter. Penguins play so nice.

Ee

Effie asked Erin, "Do rainbows ever end?"

Erin told Effie, "Yes, but you'll always be my friend."

Preparing for Your Week

Tips for Management and Differentiation

Refer to this section and to resources.corwin.com/puzzlepiecephonics-gradeK for resources and ideas to deepen your students' learning throughout the week. Feel free to put your own spin on the routines, too. For daily lesson plans, see pages 60–66 of this Teacher's Guide.

TIPS FOR PHONEMIC AWARENESS	• This week, students will continue to hear a complete word and segment the word into its onset and rime. • If you notice your students need additional practice, extend the activity with more words.
TIPS FOR THE PUZZLE PIECE REVIEW	• This week on Days 1 and 2 you are introducing students to a new puzzle piece. Be sure to spend enough time introducing the piece so students understand their focus for that day. • Have students work with the same partner each day to build a word study relationship.
TIPS FOR SUPPORTED BLENDING	• Follow the Supported Blending routine on page I-16 of the Introduction and hold students accountable for producing the initial sounds for each word. • Reblend lines if necessary. • If students do not have the attention span to blend the review line, you may omit the third line from the blending routine.
TIPS FOR FORMATION	• Encourage students to circle the letter on the row that they feel they formed the best. Have them try to duplicate the letter. • Go around with a highlighter to help students who are struggling with their letters. • Have a station in your room with sand for students to practice forming their letters in.
TIPS FOR DICTATION	• If students are struggling to identify the initial sound of a word, isolate the sound for students and tell them to record that specific sound.
TIPS FOR SORTING	• This week students are sorting their pictures and words with the three headers. On Days 1 and 2, students will only be sorting with two headers. Instruct students to place any unused picture and word cards and headers back into their word sort bags. • On Day 2, if students can handle sorting *Gg, Pp,* and *Ee*, allow them to build off what they learned last week and on Day 1. • The sort contains words with authentic capitalization. Review the picture and word cards with students and go over this week's capitalized words.

TIPS FOR THE PRACTICE PIECES	• This Practice Piece time can be your opportunity to create fun, authentic experiences with letters.
	   • **Gg:** Have students fill in an uppercase *G* and lowercase *g* with gumballs.
	   • **Pp:** Have students fill in an uppercase *P* and lowercase *p* with popcorn.
	   • **Ee:** Have students fill in an uppercase *E* and lowercase *e* with elephant print stamps.
	• Make it fun for your students using the supplies you have!

Preparing for Your Week

TIPS FOR FLUENCY

- This week students will read open-ended chants in which they can fill in the blank with their sort pictures. The chants are very repetitive and are meant to be interactive. Students will need support with the sight words in the chants.
- Students can illustrate other parts of the chants.
- Students can read their chants and couplets to a partner.
- Students can pull out pictures from their sort bags to fill in the blanks during the chants.
- Students may circle the letters of the week in each couplet.

TIPS FOR SPELLING CHECK

- Review the directions with students. They are writing the letter that represents the sound you dictate.
- Use teacher discretion when grading the Spelling Check.

Day 1

PHONEMIC AWARENESS: LISTEN

1. Give the directions. Say, "I am going to say a word. Your job is to break the word into two parts. For example, if I say '*bat*,' you say '/b/ [pause] –*at*.'"

2. Say the following words:

cat (/k/ –at)   pest (/p/ –est)   tide (/t/ –ide)
fix (/f/ –ix)   sound (/s/ –ound)

THE BIG REVEAL

1. Hold up the *gum* puzzle piece and say, "This is the *gum* piece. It represents the letter *g*. The *gum* piece says '/g/ /g/ /g/' like at the beginning of the word *gum*. Create a mouth with one hand, chomp it open and closed, and say '/g/.' We will study this letter and sound all week. Let's make a list of words that have the *gum* sound in them" (record the words).

SUPPORTED BLENDING: PUTTING SOUNDS TOGETHER TO MAKE NEW WORDS

1. Follow the Supported Blending routine on page I-16 of the Introduction.

2. Display the following words on the board one line at a time. Facilitate a discussion about the blending line focus after each line.

3. Then display the weekly sight word.

gum	grass	goat	Discuss: initial sound of /g/
get	grip	got	Discuss: initial sound of /g/
cookie	empty	bug	Discuss: review of sounds from previous weeks

Sight Word: he

FORMATION: WRITING LETTERS

1. Have students turn to page 45 of the Learner's Notebook.

2. Model forming uppercase letter *G* and lowercase letter *g*.

Uppercase Formation

Your pencil starts just below the top line.

Form a curved line down to the bottom line.

Continue to make the curved line come up just below the middle line.

Form a straight horizontal line to the left.

Pick your pencil up.

Lowercase Formation

Your pencil starts at the middle line.

Form a circle.

Pick your pencil up.

Your pencil starts at the middle line.

Form a straight line down that goes underneath the bottom line.

Continue the line by making a curve to the left.

Pick your pencil up.

3. Assist students in forming two lines of uppercase *G*s.

4. Assist students in forming two lines of lowercase *g*s.

Day 1 (Continued)

PRACTICE: COMPLETE YOUR WORK ON YOUR OWN

1. Have students turn to page 43 of the Learner's Notebook.

2. Instruct students to tear out the sort and complete the following Practice Pieces: Quick Color, Careful Cut, and Sorting With Combined Picture and Word Cards (see further directions on pages I-37, I-38, and I-25 of the Introduction).

3. Instruct students that they are only using the *gum* and *bed* headers and words with the letters *g* and *e*.

4. Circulate as students work, which usually takes fifteen minutes, and coach as needed.

FLUENCY: READING LIKE YOU'RE SPEAKING

1. Have students turn to page 9 in the Fluency Notebook.

2. Have students read one or more of the following chants: "Gum," "Pop," and "Bed."

3. Circulate and listen to students read or gather a small group of students who need additional support.

Day 2

PHONEMIC AWARENESS: LISTEN

1. Give the directions. Say, "I am going to say a word. Your job is to break the word into two parts. For example, if I say '*bat*,' you say '/b/ [pause] –*at*.'"

2. Say the following words:

neck (/n/ –eck)   kid (/k/ –id)   short (/sh/ –ort)
mix (/m/ –ix)   pipe (/p/ –ipe)

THE BIG REVEAL

1. Say, "Yesterday we learned the *gum* piece. It represents the letter *g*. The *gum* piece says '/g/ /g/ /g/' like at the beginning of the word *gum*. Let's all do the motion for the *gum* piece together."

2. Hold up the *pop* puzzle piece and say, "This is the *pop* piece. It represents the letter *p*. The pop piece says '/p/ /p/ /p/' like at the beginning and at the end of the word *pop*. Create an oval shape with your hands by placing your fingertips together. Pull your fingertips apart quickly and say '/p/.' We will study this sound all week. Let's make a list of words that have the *pop* sound in them" (record the words).

SUPPORTED BLENDING: PUTTING SOUNDS TOGETHER TO MAKE NEW WORDS

1. Follow the Supported Blending routine on page I-16 of the Introduction.

2. Display the following words on the board one line at a time. Facilitate a discussion about the blending line focus after each line.

3. Then display the weekly sight word.

pop	**play**	**pen**	Discuss: initial sound of /p/
poodle	**put**	**pink**	Discuss: initial sound of /p/
Ella	**coat**	**bear**	Discuss: review of sounds for previous weeks; capital *E* in the name *Ella*

Sight Word: he

FORMATION: WRITING LETTERS

1. Have students turn to page 46 of the Learner's Notebook.

2. Model forming uppercase letter *P* and lowercase letter *p*.

Uppercase Formation	**Lowercase Formation**
Your pencil starts at the top line.	Your pencil starts at the middle line.
Form a straight line down to the bottom line.	Form a straight line down to underneath the bottom line.
Pick your pencil up.	Pick your pencil up.
Your pencil starts at the top line.	Your pencil starts at the middle line.
Form a curved line to the middle line.	Form a curved line to the bottom line.
Pick your pencil up.	Pick your pencil up.

3. Assist students in forming two lines of uppercase *P*s.

4. Assist students in forming two lines of lowercase *p*s.

SORT: WHAT IS YOUR FOCUS PATTERN?

1. Have students take out their bag of pictures (created on Day 1) and follow the Sorting With Combined Picture and Word Cards routine on page I-25 of the Introduction.

2. Instruct students that they are only using the *pop* and *bed* headers and words with the letters *p* and *e*.

Day 2 (Continued)

PRACTICE: COMPLETE YOUR WORK ON YOUR OWN	**1.** Students will follow the Grab and Write routine on page I-44 of the Introduction. **2.** Circulate as students work, which usually takes fifteen minutes, and coach as needed.
FLUENCY: READING LIKE YOU'RE SPEAKING	**1.** Have students turn to page 9 in the Fluency Notebook. **2.** Have students read one or more of the following chants: "Gum," "Pop," and "Bed." **3.** Circulate and listen to students read or gather a small group of students who need additional support.

Day 3

PHONEMIC AWARENESS: LISTEN

1. Give the directions. Say, "I am going to say a word. Your job is to break the word into two parts. For example, if I say '*bat*,' you say '/b/ [pause] –*at*.'"

2. Say the following words:

top (/t/ –op)   bunch (/b/ –unch)   sick (/s/ –ick)
fell (/f/ –ell)   new (/n/ –ew)

PUZZLE PIECE REVIEW

1. Say, "When I point to the piece, you tell me its name" (*gum, pop, bed*).

2. Say, "When I point to the piece, you tell me its sound" (/g/, /p/, /ĕ/).

3. Say, "When I point to the piece, you tell me its spelling" (*g, p, e*).

4. Say, "Write the spellings in the air with your finger" (students will form the letters *g, p,* and *e*).

SUPPORTED BLENDING: PUTTING SOUNDS TOGETHER TO MAKE NEW WORDS

1. Follow the Supported Blending routine on page I-16 of the Introduction.

2. Display the following words on the board one line at a time. Facilitate a discussion about the blending line focus after each line.

3. Then display the weekly sight word.

bet	pet	set	Discuss: word family –*et* and the sound of /ĕt/
pat	bat	cat	Discuss: word family –*at* and the sound of /ăt/
got	pot	cot	Discuss: word family –*ot* and the sound of /ŏt/

Sight Word: he

DICTATION: STRETCH OUT YOUR WORDS

1. Have students turn to page 47 of the Learner's Notebook.

2. Follow the Dictation routine on page I-21 of the Introduction to dictate the following words:

I. pop 2. gum 3. elk 4. cake 5. Ella

Sight Word: he

3. Hold students accountable for recording the initial sound in each word in their Learner's Notebook.

SORT: WHAT IS YOUR FOCUS PATTERN?

1. Have students take out their bag of pictures (created on Day 1) and follow the Sorting With Combined Picture and Word Cards routine on page I-25 of the Introduction.

PRACTICE: COMPLETE YOUR WORK ON YOUR OWN

1. Have students turn to page 48 in the Learner's Notebook.

2. Students will complete the Letter Matrix routine found on page I-45 of the Introduction.

3. Circulate as students work, which usually takes fifteen minutes, and coach as needed.

FLUENCY: READING LIKE YOU'RE SPEAKING

1. Have students turn to page 9 in the Fluency Notebook.

2. Have students read one or more of the following chants: "Gum," "Pop," and "Bed."

3. Circulate and listen to students read or gather a small group of students who need additional support.

PHONEMIC AWARENESS: LISTEN	**1.** Give the directions. Say, "I am going to say a word. Your job is to break the word into two parts. For example, if I say '*bat*,' you say '/b/ [pause] –*at*.'"
	2. Say the following words:
	<center>**taught (/t/ –aught) mom (/m/ –om) give (/g/ –iv)** **hope (/h/ –ope) zip (/z/ –ip)**</center>

PUZZLE PIECE REVIEW	**1.** Say, "When I point to the piece, you tell me its name" (*gum, pop, bed*).
	2. Say, "When I point to the piece, you tell me its sound" (/g/, /p/, /ĕ/).
	3. Say, "When I point to the piece, you tell me its spelling" (*g, p, e*).
	4. Say, "Write the spellings in the air with your finger" (students will form the letters *g, p,* and *e*).

SUPPORTED BLENDING: PUTTING SOUNDS TOGETHER TO MAKE NEW WORDS	**1.** Follow the Supported Blending routine on page I-16 of the Introduction.
	2. Display the following words on the board one line at a time. Facilitate a discussion about the blending line focus after each line.
	3. Then display the weekly sight word.

popsicle	**garden**	**grapes**	Discuss: initial sounds of /p/ and /g/
Grace	**Pat**	**Ella**	Discuss: initial sounds of /g/, /p/, and /ĕ/; capital *G, P,* and *E* at the beginning of each name
poodle	**gather**	**egg**	Discuss: initial sounds of /p/, /g/, and /ĕ/

Sight Word: he

DICTATION: STRETCH OUT YOUR WORDS	**1.** Have students turn to page 49 of the Learner's Notebook.
	2. Follow the Dictation routine on page I-21 of the Introduction to dictate the following words:
	<blockquote>I. pets 2. goat 3. California 4. bug 5. elephant **Sight Word: he**</blockquote>
	3. Hold students accountable for recording the initial sound in each word in their Learner's Notebook.

SORT: WHAT IS YOUR FOCUS PATTERN?	**1.** Have students take out their bag of pictures and words (created on Day 1) and follow the Sorting With Combined Picture and Word Cards routine on page I-25 of the Introduction.

PRACTICE: COMPLETE YOUR WORK ON YOUR OWN	**1.** Have students complete the following Practice Pieces: Glue Words (on page I-41 of the Introduction) and Fluency Drill (on page I-46 of the Introduction).
	2. Circulate as students work, which usually takes fifteen minutes, and coach as needed.

FLUENCY: READING LIKE YOU'RE SPEAKING	**1.** Have students turn to page 9 in the Fluency Notebook.
	2. Have students read one or more of the following chants: "Gum," "Pop," and "Bed."
	3. Circulate and listen to students read or gather a small group of students who need additional support.

Day 5

PHONEMIC AWARENESS: LISTEN

1. Give the directions. Say, "I am going to say a word. Your job is to break the word into two parts. For example, if I say '*bat*,' you say '/b/ [pause] –*at*.'"

2. Say the following words:

go (/g/ –o)   pull (/p/ –ull)   right (/r/ –ight)
leak (/l/ –eak)   jump (/j/ –ump)

REVIEW PATTERNS OF THE WEEK

1. Say, "Find a partner."

2. Say, "Tell your partner the names of this week's pieces" (*gum, pop, bed*).

3. Say, "Tell your partner the sounds of this week's pieces" (/g/, /p/, /ĕ/).

4. Say, "Tell your partner the spellings of this week's pieces" (*g, p, e*).

5. Say, "Write the spellings on your partner's back with your finger" (students will form the letters *g, p,* and *e*).

SPELLING CHECK

1. Follow the Spelling Check routine on page I-34 of the Introduction.

2. Have students turn to page 51 of the Learner's Notebook.

3. Say, "Write the letter that represents the sound you hear."

4. Dictate the following sounds (repeat the sound if needed):

1. /b/

2. /ĕ/

3. /g/

4. /p/

5. /k/

Sight Word: he

LABELING THE ROOM

1. Label the classroom with things found from this week's sort.

HANDWRITING CHECK

1. Have students turn to page 52 in the Learner's Notebook.

2. Model and have students form the following letters:

1. Three uppercase *G*s

2. Three lowercase *g*s

3. Three uppercase *P*s

4. Three lowercase *p*s

5. Three uppercase *E*s

6. Three lowercase *e*s

WEEKLY CELEBRATION

1. Display the celebratory message: "Great job! You learned the *gum, pop,* and *bed* puzzle pieces!"

2. Encourage students to work together to read the message.

3. Have students copy the message onto their weekly certificate (see resources .corwin.com/puzzlepiecephonics-gradeK) and place it somewhere to take home.

Preparing for Your Week

Resources

PUZZLE PIECES

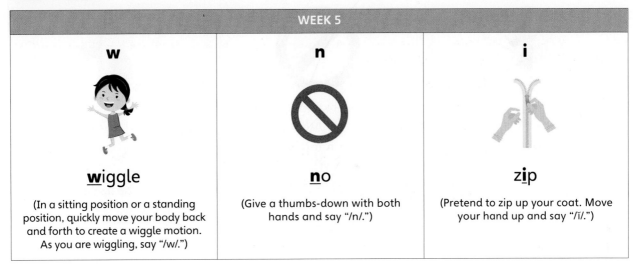

WEEK 5		
w	**n**	**i**
wiggle	**n**o	z**i**p
(In a sitting position or a standing position, quickly move your body back and forth to create a wiggle motion. As you are wiggling, say "/w/.")	(Give a thumbs-down with both hands and say "/n/.")	(Pretend to zip up your coat. Move your hand up and say "/ĭ/.")

CORRESPONDING *LEARNER'S NOTEBOOK* PAGES

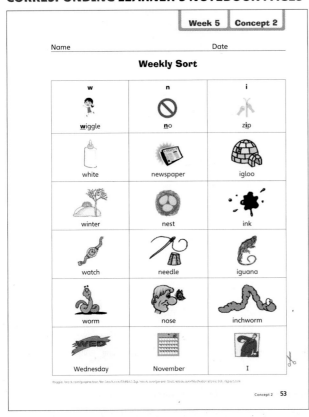

Week 5	Concept 2

Name _____ Date _____

Letter Matrix: *w, n,* and *i*

w	n	i
wiggle	**n**o	z**i**p

W	F	r	n	N
n	w	I	A	i
I	e	n	W	p
K	w	H	i	N
n	W	I	J	L
i	z	N	w	I
N	w	W	l	i

58   PUZZLE PIECE PHONICS LEARNER'S NOTEBOOK, KINDERGARTEN

Wiggle: istock.com/graphic-bee; No: istock.com/FARBAI; Zip: istock.com/pe-art

Preparing for Your Week

CORRESPONDING *FLUENCY NOTEBOOK PAGES*

Wiggle

w w w Wiggle!

w w w Wiggle!

Watch _____

wiggle!

Watch _____

wiggle!

w w w Wiggle!

w w w Wiggle!

Watch _____

wiggle!

Watch _____

wiggle!

w w w Wiggle!

w w w Wiggle!

Wiggle: istock.com/graphic-bee

No

n n n No!

n n n No!

Can I have a(n)

_____? No!

Can I have a(n)

_____? No!

n n n No!

n n n No!

Can I have a(n)

_____? No!

Can I have a(n)

_____? No!

n n n No!

n n n No!

No: istock.com/FARBAI

Zip

i i i Zip!

i i i Zip!

Zip up the

_____.

Zip up the

_____.

i i i Zip!

i i i Zip!

Zip up the

_____.

Zip up the

_____.

i i i Zip!

i i i Zip!

Zip: istock.com/pe-art

Ww

Wanda works weaving winter whites,

While watching the windy weather at night.

Nn

"My favorite number is nine," said Nan.

"Nineteen is my favorite number," said Jan.

Ii

I invented ice cream that never melts.

The ice is the coldest I've ever felt!

Preparing for Your Week

Tips for Management and Differentiation

Refer to this section and to resources.corwin.com/puzzlepiecephonics-gradeK for resources and ideas to deepen your students' learning throughout the week. Feel free to put your own spin on the routines, too. For daily lesson plans, see pages 71–79 of this Teacher's Guide.

TIPS FOR PHONEMIC AWARENESS	• In previous weeks, students have been working on segmenting the onset and rime of words. This week they will hear each segmented sound of a word and put the word back together. • If you notice your students need additional practice, extend the activity with additional words.
TIPS FOR THE PUZZLE PIECE REVIEW	• This week on Days 1–3 you are introducing students to a new puzzle piece. Be sure to spend enough time introducing the piece so students understand their focus for that day. • Have students work with the same partner each day to build a word study relationship.
TIPS FOR SUPPORTED BLENDING	• Follow the Supported Blending routine on page I-16 of the Introduction and hold students accountable for producing the initial sounds for each word. • Reblend lines if necessary. • Review the sight word *I*. This sight word is always capitalized because it is a "stand-alone *I*."
TIPS FOR FORMATION	• Encourage students to circle the letter on the row that they feel they formed the best. Have them try to duplicate the letter. • Go around with a highlighter to help students who are struggling with their letters. • Have a station in your room with sand for students to practice forming their letters in.
TIPS FOR DICTATION	• If students are struggling to identify the initial sound of a word, tell students to write the letter that says "/w/," "/n/," or "/ĭ/."
TIPS FOR SORTING	• This week students are sorting their pictures and words with the three headers. On Days 1–3, students will only be sorting with one header. Instruct students to place any unused picture and word cards and headers back into their word sort bags. • On Day 2, if students can handle sorting both *Ww* and *Nn*, allow them to build off what they learned on Day 1. The same applies for Day 3. • Take the time to visit with each student to make sure all are understanding the meaning of the picture. • The sort contains words with authentic capitalization. Review the picture and word cards with students and go over this week's capitalized words.

(Continued)

Preparing for Your Week

TIPS FOR THE PRACTICE PIECES

- This Practice Piece time can be your opportunity to create fun, authentic experiences with letters.
  - **Ww:** Have students fill in an uppercase *W* and lowercase *w* with gummy worms.
  - **Nn:** Have students fill in an uppercase *N* and lowercase *n* with noodles.
  - **Ii:** Have students fill in an uppercase *I* and lowercase *i* with stamps and ink.
  - Make it fun for your students using the supplies you have!

TIPS FOR FLUENCY

- This week students will read open-ended chants in which they can fill in the blank with their sort pictures.
  The chants are very repetitive and are meant to be interactive. Students will need support with the sight words in the chants.
- Students can illustrate other parts of the chants.
- Students can read their chants and couplets to a partner.
- Students can pull out pictures from their sort bags to fill in the blanks during the chants.
- Students may circle the letters of the week in each couplet.

TIPS FOR SPELLING CHECK

- Review the directions with students. They are writing the letter that represents the sound you dictate.
- Use teacher discretion when grading the Spelling Check.

PHONEMIC AWARENESS: LISTEN	**1.** Give the directions. Say, "I am going to say all of the sounds in a word. Your job is to put all the sounds back together and say the word. For example, if I say '/b/ /ă/ /t/,' you say 'bat.'"

2. Say the following groups of sounds:

/f/ /ŭ/ /n/ (fun)   /t/ /ŏ/ /p/ (top)   /s/ /ĭ/ /t/ (sit)
/h/ /ŭ/ /t/ (hut)   /t/ /ă/ /d/ (tad)

THE BIG REVEAL	**1.** Hold up the *wiggle* puzzle piece and say, "This is the *wiggle* piece. It represents the letter *w*. The *wiggle* piece says '/w/ /w/ /w/' like at the beginning of the word *wiggle*. In a sitting position or a standing position, quickly move your body back and forth to create a wiggle motion. As you are wiggling, say '/w/.' We will study this letter and sound all week. Let's make a list of words that have the *wiggle* sound in them" (record the words).

SUPPORTED BLENDING: PUTTING SOUNDS TOGETHER TO MAKE NEW WORDS	**1.** Follow the Supported Blending routine on page I-16 of the Introduction.
	2. Display the following words on the board one line at a time. Facilitate a discussion about the blending line focus after each line.
	3. Then display the weekly sight word.

wig	win	way	Discuss: initial sound of /w/
winter	watch	worm	Discuss: initial sound of /w/

Sight Word: I

FORMATION: WRITING LETTERS	**1.** Have students turn to page 55 of the Learner's Notebook.
	2. Model forming uppercase letter *W* and lowercase letter *w*.

Uppercase Formation	**Lowercase Formation**
Your pencil starts at the top line.	Your pencil starts at the middle line.
Form a slanted line down to the bottom line, right.	Form a slanted line down to the bottom line, right.
Pick your pencil up.	Pick your pencil up.
Your pencil starts at the middle line, to the right.	Your pencil starts at the middle line, to the right.
Form a slanted line down to the bottom line, left.	Form a slanted line down to the bottom line, left.
Pick your pencil up.	Pick your pencil up.
Your pencil starts at the middle line.	Your pencil starts at the middle line.
Form a slanted line down to the bottom line, right.	Form a slanted line down to the bottom line, right.
Pick your pencil up.	Pick your pencil up.
Your pencil starts at the top line, to the left.	Your pencil starts at the middle line, to the right.
Form a slanted line down to the bottom line, left.	Form a slanted line down to the bottom line, left.
Pick your pencil up.	Pick your pencil up.

(Continued)

Day 1 (Continued)

FORMATION: WRITING LETTERS (Continued)	**3.** Assist students in forming two lines of uppercase *W*s. **4.** Assist students in forming two lines of lowercase *w*s.
PRACTICE: COMPLETE YOUR WORK ON YOUR OWN	**1.** Have students turn to page 53 of the Learner's Notebook. **2.** Instruct students to tear out the sort and complete the following Practice Pieces: Quick Color, Careful Cut, and Sorting With Combined Picture and Word Cards (see further directions on pages I-37, I-38, and I-25 of the Introduction). **3.** Instruct students that they are only using the *wiggle* header and words with the letter *w*. **4.** Circulate as students work, which usually takes fifteen minutes, and coach as needed.
FLUENCY: READING LIKE YOU'RE SPEAKING	**1.** Have students turn to page 11 in the Fluency Notebook. **2.** Have students read one or more of the following chants: "Wiggle," "No," and "Zip." **3.** Circulate and listen to students read or gather a small group of students who need additional support.

PHONEMIC AWARENESS: LISTEN	**1.** Give the directions. Say, "I am going to say all of the sounds in a word. Your job is to put all the sounds back together and say the word. For example, if I say '/b/ /ă/ /t/,' you say '*bat*.'"

2. Say the following groups of sounds:

/d/ /ŏ/ /g/ (dog)   /f/ /ĭ/ /n/ (fin)   /p/ /ŏ/ /p/ (pop)
/h/ /ĕ/ /n/ (hen)   /l/ /ă/ /b/ (lab)

THE BIG REVEAL	**1.** Say, "Yesterday we learned the *wiggle* piece. It represents the letter *w*. The wiggle piece says '/w/ /w/ /w/' like at the beginning of the word *wiggle*. Let's all do the motion for the *wiggle* piece together."

2. Hold up the *no* puzzle piece and say, "This is the *no* piece. It represents the letter *n*. The *no* piece says '/n/ /n/ /n/' like at the beginning of the word *no*. Give a thumbs-down with both hands and say '/n/.' We will study this sound all week. Let's make a list of words that have the *no* sound in them" (record the words).

SUPPORTED BLENDING: PUTTING SOUNDS TOGETHER TO MAKE NEW WORDS	**1.** Follow the Supported Blending routine on page I-16 of the Introduction.

2. Display the following words on the board one line at a time. Facilitate a discussion about the blending line focus after each line.

3. Then display the weekly sight word.

no	**net**	**nap**	Discuss: initial sound of /n/
nest	**nose**	**needle**	Discuss: initial sound of /n/

Sight Word: I

FORMATION: WRITING LETTERS	**1.** Have students turn to page 56 of the Learner's Notebook.

2. Model forming uppercase letter *N* and lowercase letter *n*.

Uppercase Formation

Your pencil starts at the top line.

Form a straight line down to the bottom line.

Pick your pencil up.

Your pencil starts at the top line.

Form a slanted line down to the bottom line, right.

Pick your pencil up.

Your pencil starts at the top line, to the right.

Form a straight line down to the bottom line.

Lowercase Formation

Your pencil starts at the middle line.

Form a straight line down to the bottom line.

Pick your pencil up.

Your pencil starts just below the middle line.

Form a hump, then a straight line all the way down to the bottom line.

Pick your pencil up.

3. Assist students in forming two lines of uppercase *N*s.

4. Assist students in forming two lines of lowercase *n*s.

(Continued)

Day 2 (Continued)

SORT: WHAT IS YOUR FOCUS PATTERN?	**1.** Have students take out their bag of pictures (created on Day 1) and follow the Sorting With Combined Picture and Word Cards routine on page I-25 of the Introduction. **2.** Instruct students that they are only using the *no* header and words with the letter *n*.
PRACTICE: COMPLETE YOUR WORK ON YOUR OWN	**1.** Students will follow the Grab and Write routine on page I-44 of the Introduction. **2.** Circulate as students work, which usually takes fifteen minutes, and coach as needed.
FLUENCY: READING LIKE YOU'RE SPEAKING	**1.** Have students turn to page 11 in the Fluency Notebook. **2.** Have students read one or more of the following chants: "Wiggle," "No," and "Zip." **3.** Circulate and listen to students read or gather a small group of students who need additional support.

PHONEMIC AWARENESS: LISTEN

1. Give the directions. Say, "I am going to say all of the sounds in a word. Your job is to put all the sounds back together and say the word. For example, if I say '/b/ /ă/ /t/,' you say 'bat.'"

2. Say the following groups of sounds:

/y/ /ĕ/ /l/ (yell)   /g/ /ă/ /p/ (gap)   /t/ /ĭ/ /n/ (tin)
/s/ /ă/ /d/ (sad)   /m/ /ŏ/ /s/ (moss)

THE BIG REVEAL

1. Say, "On Day 1, we learned the *wiggle* piece. It represents the letter *w*. The *wiggle* piece says '/w/ /w/ /w/' like at the beginning of the word *wiggle*. Let's all do the motion for the *wiggle* piece together."

2. Say, "Yesterday, we learned the *no* piece. It represents the letter *n*. The *no* piece says '/n/ /n/ /n/' like at the beginning of the word *no*. Let's all do the motion for the *no* piece together."

3. Hold up the *zip* puzzle piece and say, "This is the *zip* piece. It represents the letter *i*. The *zip* piece says '/ĭ/ /ĭ/ /ĭ/' like in the middle of the word *zip*. Pretend to zip up your coat. Move your hand up and say '/ĭ/.' We will study this sound all week. Let's make a list of words that have the *zip* sound in them" (record the words).

SUPPORTED BLENDING: PUTTING SOUNDS TOGETHER TO MAKE NEW WORDS

1. Follow the Supported Blending routine on page I-16 of the Introduction.

2. Display the following words on the board one line at a time. Facilitate a discussion about the blending line focus after each line.

3. Then display the weekly sight word.

| ink | ill | inch | Discuss: initial sound of /ĭ/ |
| igloo | it | in | Discuss: initial sound of /ĭ/ |

Sight Word: **I**

FORMATION: WRITING LETTERS

1. Have students turn to page 57 of the Learner's Notebook.

2. Model forming uppercase letter *I* and lowercase letter *i*.

Uppercase Formation

Your pencil starts at the top line.

Form a straight line down to the bottom line.

Pick your pencil up.

Your pencil starts at the top line, to the left.

Form a straight line on the top line.

Pick your pencil up.

Your pencil starts on the bottom line.

Form a straight line on the bottom line, to the left.

Pick your pencil up.

Lowercase Formation

Your pencil starts at the middle line.

Form a straight line down to the bottom line.

Pick your pencil up.

Your pencil starts halfway between the top line and the middle line.

Make a dot.

Pick your pencil up.

3. Assist students in forming two lines of uppercase *I*s.

4. Assist students in forming two lines of lowercase *i*s.

(Continued)

Day 3 (Continued)

SORT: WHAT IS YOUR FOCUS PATTERN?	**1.** Have students take out their bag of pictures (created on Day 1) and follow the Sorting With Combined Picture and Word Cards routine on page I-25 of the Introduction.
	2. Instruct students that they are only using the *zip* header and words with the letter *i*.
PRACTICE: COMPLETE YOUR WORK ON YOUR OWN	**1.** Have students turn to page 58 in the Learner's Notebook.
	2. Students will complete the Letter Matrix routine found on page I-45 of the Introduction.
	3. Circulate as students work, which usually takes fifteen minutes, and coach as needed.
FLUENCY: READING LIKE YOU'RE SPEAKING	**1.** Have students turn to page 11 in the Fluency Notebook.
	2. Have students read one or more of the following chants: "Wiggle," "No," and "Zip."
	3. Circulate and listen to students read or gather a small group of students who need additional support.

PHONEMIC AWARENESS: LISTEN

1. Give the directions. Say, "I am going to say all of the sounds in a word. Your job is to put all the sounds back together and say the word. For example, if I say '/b/ /ă/ /t/,' you say '*bat*.'"

2. Say the following groups of sounds:

/d/ /ĕ/ /n/ (den)   /b/ /ĭ/ /d/ (bid)   /r/ /ŏ/ /b/ (rob)
/k/ /ĭ/ /d/ (kid)   /m/ /ĭ/ /t/ (mitt)

PUZZLE PIECE REVIEW

1. Say, "When I point to the piece, you tell me its name" (*wiggle, no, zip*).

2. Say, "When I point to the piece, you tell me its sound" (/w/, /n/, /ĭ/).

3. Say, "When I point to the piece, you tell me its spelling" (*w, n, i*).

4. Say, "Write the spellings in the air with your finger" (students will form the letters *w, n,* and *i*).

SUPPORTED BLENDING: PUTTING SOUNDS TOGETHER TO MAKE NEW WORDS

1. Follow the Supported Blending routine on page I-16 of the Introduction.

2. Display the following words on the board one line at a time. Facilitate a discussion about the blending line focus after each line.

3. Then display the weekly sight word.

winter	nest	iguana	Discuss: initial sounds of /w/, /n/, and /ĭ/
I	Wednesday	November	Discuss: initial sounds of /w/ and /n/; capital *I* in *I*; capital *W* in the day *Wednesday*; capital *N* in the month *November*
nose	watch	igloo	Discuss: initial sounds of /n/, /w/, and /ĭ/

Sight Word: I

DICTATION: STRETCH OUT YOUR WORDS

1. Have students turn to page 59 of the Learner's Notebook.

2. Follow the Dictation routine on page I-21 of the Introduction to dictate the following words:

I. will   2. iguana   3. November   4. no   5. worm

Sight Word: I

3. Hold students accountable for recording the initial sound in each word in their Learner's Notebook.

SORT: WHAT IS YOUR FOCUS PATTERN?

1. Have students take out their bag of pictures and words (created on Day 1) and follow the Sorting With Combined Picture and Word Cards routine on page I-25 of the Introduction.

(Continued)

Day 4 (Continued)

PRACTICE:
COMPLETE
YOUR WORK ON
YOUR OWN

1. Have students complete the following Practice Pieces: Glue Words (on page I-41 of the Introduction) and Fluency Drill (on page I-46 of the Introduction).

2. Circulate as students work, which usually takes fifteen minutes, and coach as needed.

FLUENCY:
READING LIKE
YOU'RE SPEAKING

1. Have students turn to page 11 in the Fluency Notebook.

2. Have students read one or more of the following chants: "Wiggle," "No," and "Zip."

3. Circulate and listen to students read or gather a small group of students who need additional support.

PHONEMIC AWARENESS: LISTEN

1. Give the directions. Say, "I am going to say all of the sounds in a word. Your job is to put all the sounds back together and say the word. For example, if I say '/b/ /ă/ /t/,' you say '*bat*.'"

2. Say the following groups of words:

/w/ /ĕ/ /l/ (well)   /h/ /ĭ/ /m/ (him)   /p/ /ŏ/ /d/ (pod)
/j/ /ĭ/ /l/ (Jill)   /v/ /ĕ/ /t/ (vet)

REVIEW PATTERNS OF THE WEEK

1. Say, "Find a partner."

2. Say, "Tell your partner the names of this week's pieces" (*wiggle, no, zip*).

3. Say, "Tell your partner the sounds of this week's pieces" (/w/, /n/, /ĭ/).

4. Say, "Tell your partner the spellings of this week's pieces" (*w, n, i*).

5. Say, "Write the spellings on your partner's back with your finger" (students will form the letters *w, n,* and *i*).

SPELLING CHECK

1. Follow the Spelling Check routine on page I-34 of the Introduction.

2. Have students turn to page 61 of the Learner's Notebook.

3. Say, "Write the letter that represents the sound you hear."

4. Dictate the following sounds (repeat the sound if needed):

1. /n/
2. /ĭ/
3. /w/
4. /ĭ/
5. /n/

Sight Word: I

LABELING THE ROOM

1. Label the classroom with things found from this week's sort.

HANDWRITING CHECK

1. Have students turn to page 62 in the Learner's Notebook.

2. Model and have students form the following letters:

1. Three uppercase *W*s
2. Three lowercase *w*s
3. Three uppercase *N*s
4. Three lowercase *n*s
5. Three uppercase *I*s
6. Three lowercase *i*s

WEEKLY CELEBRATION

1. Display the celebratory message: "Wahoo! You learned the *wiggle, no,* and *zip* puzzle pieces!"

2. Encourage students to work together to read the message.

3. Have students copy the message onto their weekly certificate (see resources .corwin.com/puzzlepiecephonics-gradeK) and place it somewhere to take home.

Preparing for Your Week

Resources

PUZZLE PIECES

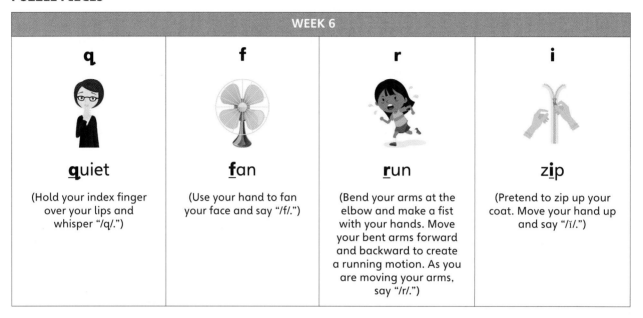

WEEK 6

q	f	r	i
quiet	**f**an	**r**un	z**i**p
(Hold your index finger over your lips and whisper "/q/.")	(Use your hand to fan your face and say "/f/.")	(Bend your arms at the elbow and make a fist with your hands. Move your bent arms forward and backward to create a running motion. As you are moving your arms, say "/r/.")	(Pretend to zip up your coat. Move your hand up and say "/ĭ/.")

CORRESPONDING *LEARNER'S NOTEBOOK* PAGES

Week 6	Concept 2

Name _____ Date _____

Letter Matrix: *q, f, r,* and *i*

q	f	r	i
quiet	fan	run	zip

i	R	G	q	F
r	Z	Q	f	I
v	y	I	r	q
Q	F	o	i	f
M	t	i	P	R
F	r	b	Q	h
f	I	R	L	q

68 PUZZLE PIECE PHONICS LEARNER'S NOTEBOOK, KINDERGARTEN

Quiet: istock.com/Sara Showalter; Fan: istock.com/zzve; Run: istock.com/graphic-bee; Zip: istock.com/pe-art

Preparing for Your Week

CORRESPONDING *FLUENCY NOTEBOOK PAGES*

Quiet	**Fan**	**Run**	**Zip**

Quiet	Fan	Run	Zip
q q q Quiet! q q q Quiet!	f f f Fan! f f f Fan!	r r r Run! r r r Run!	i i i Zip! i i i Zip!
Can the _____ please be quiet?	The fan cools _____.	Run, run, _____!	Zip up the _____.
Can the _____ please be quiet?	The fan cools _____.	Run, run, _____!	Zip up the _____.
q q q Quiet! q q q Quiet!	f f f Fan! f f f Fan!	r r r Run! r r r Run!	i i i Zip! i i i Zip!
Can the _____ please be quiet?	The fan cools _____.	Run, run, _____!	Zip up the _____.
Can the _____ please be quiet?	The fan cools _____.	Run, run, _____!	Zip up the _____.
q q q Quiet! q q q Quiet!	f f f Fan! f f f Fan!	r r r Run! r r r Run!	i i i Zip! i i i Zip!

Quiet: istock.com/Sara Showalter   Fan: istock.com/zzve   Run: istock.com/graphic-bee   Zip: istock.com/pe-art

Qq	**Ff**	**Rr**	**Ii**

Qq	Ff	Rr	Ii
Quick, quick! The queen is on her way! Quick, quick! The queen quietly waves!	"Fe Fi Fo Fum!" The friendly giant chants to me. "Fe Fi Fo Fum!" I chant back full of glee.	"Do raccoons eat raisins?" I ask Fran. "I've seen them eat rice and raisins from my trash can!"	I invented ice cream that never melts. The ice is the coldest I've ever felt!

Preparing for Your Week

Tips for Management and Differentiation

Refer to this section and to resources.corwin.com/puzzlepiecephonics-gradeK for resources and ideas to deepen your students' learning throughout the week. Feel free to put your own spin on the routines, too. For daily lesson plans, see pages 84–91 of this Teacher's Guide.

TIPS FOR PHONEMIC AWARENESS	• This week, students will continue to hear each segmented sound of a word and put the word back together. • If you notice your students need additional practice, extend the activity with more words.
TIPS FOR THE PUZZLE PIECE REVIEW	• This week on Days 1–3 you are introducing students to a new puzzle piece. Be sure to spend enough time introducing the piece so students understand their focus for that day. • Have students work with the same partner each day to build a word study relationship.
TIPS FOR SUPPORTED BLENDING	• Follow the Supported Blending routine on page I-16 of the Introduction and hold students accountable for producing the initial sounds for each word. The third line of blending is a review of previous sounds and spellings taught. • Reblend lines if necessary. • If students do not have the attention span to blend the review line, you may omit the third line from the Blending routine.
TIPS FOR FORMATION	• Encourage students to circle the letter on the row that they feel they formed the best. Have them try to duplicate the letter. • Go around with a highlighter to help students who are struggling with their letters. • Have a station in your room with sand for students to practice forming their letters in. • If students are struggling with forming letters, relate the current letter to a previous formation. For example, if students are having a hard time forming the uppercase *R*, compare this to the formation of the uppercase *P*.
TIPS FOR DICTATION	• If students are struggling to identify the initial sound of a word, isolate the sound for students and tell them to record that specific sound.
TIPS FOR SORTING	• This week students are sorting their pictures and words with the four headers. On Days 1–3, students will only be sorting with two headers. Instruct students to place any unused picture and word cards and headers back into their word sort bags. • On Day 2, if students can handle sorting *Qq, Ff,* and *Ii,* allow them to build off what they learned last week and on Day 1. The same applies for Day 3. • Take the time to visit with each student to make sure all are understanding the meaning of the picture. • The sort contains words with authentic capitalization. Review the picture and word cards with students and go over this week's capitalized words.

Preparing for Your Week

TIPS FOR THE PRACTICE PIECES	• This Practice Piece time can be your opportunity to create fun, authentic experiences with letters.

- **Qq:** Have students fill in an uppercase *Q* and lowercase *q* with quilt squares.
- **Ff:** Have students fill in an uppercase *F* and lowercase *f* with fish.
- **Rr:** Have students fill in an uppercase *R* and lowercase *r* with ribbon.
- **Ii:** Have students fill in an uppercase *I* and lowercase *i* with stamps and ink.
- Make it fun for your students using the supplies you have!

TIPS FOR FLUENCY

- This week students will read open-ended chants in which they can fill in the blank with their sort pictures. The chants are very repetitive and are meant to be interactive. Students will need support with the sight words in the chants.
- Students can illustrate other parts of the chants.
- Students can read their chants and couplets to a partner.
- Students can pull out pictures from their sort bags to fill in the blanks during the chants.
- Students may circle the letters of the week in each couplet.

TIPS FOR SPELLING CHECK

- Review the directions with students. They are writing the letter that represents the sound you dictate.
- Use teacher discretion when grading the Spelling Check.

Day 1

PHONEMIC AWARENESS: LISTEN

1. Give the directions. Say, "I am going to say all of the sounds in a word. Your job is to put all the sounds back together and say the word. For example, if I say '/b/ /ă/ /t/,' you say '*bat*.'"

2. Say the following groups of sounds:

/f/ /ĭ/ /t/ (fit)   /s/ /ŭ/ /n/ (sun)   /r/ /ă/ /p/ (rap)
/p/ /ĕ/ /n/ (pen)   /l/ /ĭ/ /k/ (lick)

THE BIG REVEAL

1. Hold up the *quiet* puzzle piece and say, "This is the *quiet* piece. It represents the letter *q*. The *quiet* piece says '/q/ /q/ /q/' like at the beginning of the word *quiet*. Hold your index finger over your lips and whisper '/q/.' We will study this letter and sound all week. Let's make a list of words that have the *quiet* sound in them" (record the words).

SUPPORTED BLENDING: PUTTING SOUNDS TOGETHER TO MAKE NEW WORDS

1. Follow the Supported Blending routine on page I-16 of the Introduction.

2. Display the following words on the board one line at a time. Facilitate a discussion about the blending line focus after each line.

3. Then display the weekly sight word.

quiet	queen	quilt	Discuss: initial sound of /q/
quiz	quack	Quinn	Discuss: initial sound of /q/; capital *Q* in the name *Quinn*
winner	igloo	note	Discuss: review of sounds from previous weeks

Sight Word: it

FORMATION: WRITING LETTERS

1. Have students turn to page 65 of the Learner's Notebook.

2. Model forming uppercase letter *Q* and lowercase letter *q*.

Uppercase Formation	**Lowercase Formation**
Your pencil starts at the top line.	Your pencil starts at the middle line.
Form an oval that touches the bottom line and comes back up to the top line.	Form a circle that touches the bottom line and comes back up to the middle line.
Pick your pencil up.	Pick your pencil up.
Your pencil starts in between the middle and bottom lines.	Your pencil starts at the middle line, to the right of the circle.
Form a slanted line to the bottom line, right.	Form a straight line down to underneath the bottom line. Form a slanted line up to the right.
Pick your pencil up.	Pick your pencil up.

3. Assist students in forming two lines of uppercase *Q*s.

4. Assist students in forming two lines of lowercase *q*s.

**PRACTICE:
COMPLETE
YOUR WORK ON
YOUR OWN**

1. Have students turn to page 63 of the Learner's Notebook.

2. Instruct students to tear out the sort and complete the following Practice Pieces: Quick Color, Careful Cut, and Sorting With Combined Picture and Word Cards (see further directions on pages I-37, I-38, and I-25 of the Introduction).

3. Instruct students that they are only using the *quiet* and *zip* headers and words with the letters *q* and *i*.

4. Circulate as students work, which usually takes fifteen minutes, and coach as needed.

**FLUENCY:
READING LIKE
YOU'RE SPEAKING**

1. Have students turn to page 13 in the Fluency Notebook.

2. Have students read one or more of the following chants: "Quiet," "Fan," "Run," and "Zip."

3. Circulate and listen to students read or gather a small group of students who need additional support.

PHONEMIC AWARENESS: LISTEN

1. Give the directions. Say, "I am going to say all of the sounds in a word. Your job is to put all the sounds back together and say the word. For example, if I say '/b/ /ă/ /t/,' you say '*bat*.'"

2. Say the following groups of sounds:

/b/ /ĭ/ /l/ (bill)   /g/ /ŭ/ /m/ (gum)   /h/ /ŏ/ /p/ (hop)
/z/ /ĕ/ /n/ (zen)   /h/ /ĭ/ /d/ (hid)

THE BIG REVEAL

1. Say, "Yesterday we learned the *quiet* piece. It represents the letter *q*. The *quiet* piece says '/q/ /q/ /q/' like at the beginning of the word *quiet*. Let's all do the motion for the *quiet* piece together."

2. Hold up the *fan* puzzle piece and say, "This is the *fan* piece. It represents the letter *f*. The *fan* piece says '/f/ /f/ /f/' like at the beginning of the word *fan*. Use your hand to fan your face and say '/f/.' We will study this letter and sound all week. Let's make a list of words that have the *fan* sound in them" (record the words).

SUPPORTED BLENDING: PUTTING SOUNDS TOGETHER TO MAKE NEW WORDS

1. Follow the Supported Blending routine on page I-16 of the Introduction.

2. Display the following words on the board one line at a time. Facilitate a discussion about the blending line focus after each line.

3. Then display the weekly sight word.

fan	fun	fin	Discuss: initial sound of /f/
fish	full	foot	Discuss: initial sound of /f/
India	walk	never	Discuss: review of sounds from previous weeks

Sight Word: it

FORMATION: WRITING LETTERS

1. Have students turn to page 66 of the Learner's Notebook.

2. Model forming uppercase letter *F* and lowercase letter *f*.

Uppercase Formation

Your pencil starts at the top line.

Form a straight line down to the bottom line.

Pick your pencil up.

Your pencil starts at the top line.

Form a straight, horizontal line to the right.

Pick your pencil up.

Your pencil starts at the middle line.

Form a straight, horizontal line to the right.

Pick your pencil up.

Lowercase Formation

Your pencil starts in between the top and middle lines.

Form a curved line up that touches the top line. Continue the line straight down to the bottom line.

Pick your pencil up.

Your pencil starts at the middle line, to the left.

Form a straight, horizontal line to the right.

Pick your pencil up.

3. Assist students in forming two lines of uppercase *F*s.

4. Assist students in forming two lines of lowercase *f*s.

Day 2 (Continued)

SORT: WHAT IS YOUR FOCUS PATTERN?	**1.** Have students take out their bag of pictures (created on Day 1) and follow the Sorting With Combined Picture and Word Cards routine on page I-25 of the Introduction. **2.** Instruct students that they are only using the *fan* and *zip* headers and words with the letters *f* and *i*.
PRACTICE: COMPLETE YOUR WORK ON YOUR OWN	**1.** Students will follow the Grab and Write routine on page I-44 of the Introduction. **2.** Circulate as students work, which usually takes fifteen minutes, and coach as needed.
FLUENCY: READING LIKE YOU'RE SPEAKING	**1.** Have students turn to page 13 in the Fluency Notebook. **2.** Have students read one or more of the following chants: "Quiet," "Fan," "Run," and "Zip." **3.** Circulate and listen to students read or gather a small group of students who need additional support.

Day 3

PHONEMIC AWARENESS: LISTEN

1. Give the directions. Say, "I am going to say all of the sounds in a word. Your job is to put all the sounds back together and say the word. For example, if I say '/b/ /ă/ /t/,' you say 'bat.'"

2. Say the following groups of sounds:

/f/ /ŏ/ /t/ (fought)   /v/ /ă/ /n/ (van)   /h/ /ĕ/ /n/ (hen)
/d/ /ă/ /d/ (dad)   /g/ /ŭ/ /s/ (Gus)

THE BIG REVEAL

1. Say, "On Day 1, we learned the *quiet* piece. It represents the letter *q*. The *quiet* piece says '/q/ /q/ /q/' like at the beginning of the word *quiet*. Let's all do the motion for the *quiet* piece together."

2. Say, "Yesterday, we learned the *fan* piece. It represents the letter *f*. The *fan* piece says '/f/ /f/ /f/' like at the beginning of the word *fan*. Let's all do the motion for the *fan* piece together."

3. Hold up the *run* puzzle piece and say, "This is the *run* piece. It represents the letter *r*. The *run* piece says '/r/ /r/ /r/' like at the beginning of the word *run*. Bend your arms at the elbow and make a fist with your hands. Move your bent arms forward and backward to create a running motion. As you are moving your arms, say '/r/.' We will study this letter and sound all week. Let's make a list of words that have the *run* sound in them" (record the words).

SUPPORTED BLENDING: PUTTING SOUNDS TOGETHER TO MAKE NEW WORDS

1. Follow the Supported Blending routine on page I-16 of the Introduction.

2. Display the following words on the board one line at a time. Facilitate a discussion about the blending line focus after each line.

3. Then display the weekly sight word.

run	row	rat	Discuss: initial sound of /r/
rabbit	rooster	ram	Discuss: initial sound of /r/
water	neck	win	Discuss: review of sounds from previous weeks

Sight Word: **it**

FORMATION: WRITING LETTERS

1. Have students turn to page 67 of the Learner's Notebook.

2. Model forming uppercase letter *R* and lowercase letter *r*.

Uppercase Formation

Your pencil starts at the top line.

Form a straight line down to the bottom line.

Pick your pencil up.

Your pencil starts at the top line.

Form a curved line to the middle line.

Pick your pencil up.

Your pencil starts at the middle line.

Form a slanted line down to the bottom line, right.

Pick your pencil up.

Lowercase Formation

Your pencil starts at the middle line.

Form a straight line down to the bottom line.

Pick your pencil up.

Your pencil starts just below the middle line.

Form a curved line to the right.

Pick your pencil up.

3. Assist students in forming two lines of uppercase *R*s.

4. Assist students in forming two lines of lowercase *r*s.

Day 3 (Continued)

SORT: WHAT IS YOUR FOCUS PATTERN?	**1.** Have students take out their bag of pictures (created on Day 1) and follow the Sorting With Combined Picture and Word Cards routine on page I-25 of the Introduction.
	2. Instruct students that they are only using the *run* and *zip* headers and words with the letters *r* and *i*.
PRACTICE: COMPLETE YOUR WORK ON YOUR OWN	**1.** Have students turn to page 68 in the Learner's Notebook.
	2. Students will complete the Letter Matrix routine found on page I-45 of the Introduction.
	3. Circulate as students work, which usually takes fifteen minutes, and coach as needed.
FLUENCY: READING LIKE YOU'RE SPEAKING	**1.** Have students turn to page 13 in the Fluency Notebook.
	2. Have students read one or more of the following chants: "Quiet," "Fan," "Run," and "Zip."
	3. Circulate and listen to students read or gather a small group of students who need additional support.

Day 4

PHONEMIC AWARENESS: LISTEN

1. Give the directions. Say, "I am going to say all of the sounds in a word. Your job is to put all the sounds back together and say the word. For example, if I say '/b/ /ă/ /t/,' you say 'bat.'"

2. Say the following groups of sounds:

/m/ /ĕ/ /n/ (men)   /p/ /ŏ/ /d/ (pod)   /l/ /ă/ /p/ (lap)
/j/ /ĭ/ /g/ (jig)   /s/ /ĕ/ /l/ (sell)

PUZZLE PIECE REVIEW

1. Say, "When I point to the piece, you tell me its name" (*quiet, fan, run, zip*).

2. Say, "When I point to the piece, you tell me its sound" (/q/, /f/, /r/, /ĭ/).

3. Say, "When I point to the piece, you tell me its spelling" (*q, f, r, i*).

4. Say, "Write the spellings in the air with your finger" (students will form the letters *q, f, r,* and *i*).

SUPPORTED BLENDING: PUTTING SOUNDS TOGETHER TO MAKE NEW WORDS

1. Follow the Supported Blending routine on page I-16 of the Introduction.

2. Display the following words on the board one line at a time. Facilitate a discussion about the blending line focus after each line.

3. Then display the weekly sight word.

quit	fit	pit	Discuss: word family *–it* and the sound of /ĭt/
rat	fat	pat	Discuss: word family *–at* and the sound of /ăt/
quick	Rick	sick	Discuss: word family *–ick* and the sound of /ĭck/; capital *R* in the name *Rick*

Sight Word: it

DICTATION: STRETCH OUT YOUR WORDS

1. Have students turn to page 69 of the Learner's Notebook.

2. Follow the Dictation routine on page I-21 of the Introduction to dictate the following words:

l. quilt   2. rabbit   3. inchworm   4. Friday   5. radio

Sight Word: it

3. Hold students accountable for recording the initial sound in each word in their Learner's Notebook.

SORT: WHAT IS YOUR FOCUS PATTERN?

1. Have students take out their bag of pictures and words (created on Day 1) and follow the Sorting With Combined Picture and Word Cards routine on page I-25 of the Introduction.

PRACTICE: COMPLETE YOUR WORK ON YOUR OWN

1. Have students complete the following Practice Pieces: Glue Words (on page I-41 of the Introduction) and Fluency Drill (on page I-46 of the Introduction).

2. Circulate as students work, which usually takes fifteen minutes, and coach as needed.

FLUENCY: READING LIKE YOU'RE SPEAKING

1. Have students turn to page 13 in the Fluency Notebook.

2. Have students read one or more of the following chants: "Quiet," "Fan," "Run," and "Zip."

3. Circulate and listen to students read or gather a small group of students who need additional support.

PHONEMIC AWARENESS: LISTEN

1. Give the directions. Say, "I am going to say all of the sounds in a word. Your job is to put all the sounds back together and say the word. For example, if I say '/b/ /ă/ /t/,' you say '*bat.*'"

2. Say the following groups of sounds:

/h/ /ŏ/ /t/ (hot)   /m/ /ĭ/ /x/ (mix)   /k/ /ŭ/ /p/ (cup)
/h/ /ă/ /t/ (hat)   /y/ /ĕ/ /s/ (yes)

REVIEW PATTERNS OF THE WEEK

1. Say, "Find a partner."

2. Say, "Tell your partner the names of this week's pieces" (*quiet, fan, run, zip*).

3. Say, "Tell your partner the sounds of this week's pieces" (/q/, /f/, /r/, /ĭ/).

4. Say, "Tell your partner the spellings of this week's pieces" (*q, f, r, i*).

5. Say, "Write the spellings on your partner's back with your finger" (students will form the letters *q, f, r,* and *i*).

SPELLING CHECK

1. Follow the Spelling Check routine on page I-34 of the Introduction.

2. Have students turn to page 71 of the Learner's Notebook.

3. Say, "Write the letter that represents the sound you hear."

4. Dictate the following sounds (repeat the sound if needed):

1. /r/
2. /f/
3. /ĭ/
4. /q/
5. /n/

Sight Word: it

LABELING THE ROOM

1. Label the classroom with things found from this week's sort.

HANDWRITING CHECK

1. Have students turn to page 72 in the Learner's Notebook.

2. Model and have students form the following letters:

1. Three uppercase *Q*s
2. Three lowercase *q*s
3. Three uppercase *F*s
4. Three lowercase *f*s
5. Three uppercase *R*s
6. Three lowercase *r*s

WEEKLY CELEBRATION

1. Display the celebratory message: "Fantastic! You learned the *quiet, fan,* and *run* puzzle pieces!"

2. Encourage students to work together to read the message.

3. Have students copy the message onto their weekly certificate (see resources .corwin.com/puzzlepiecephonics-gradeK) and place it somewhere to take home.

Preparing for Your Week

Resources

PUZZLE PIECES

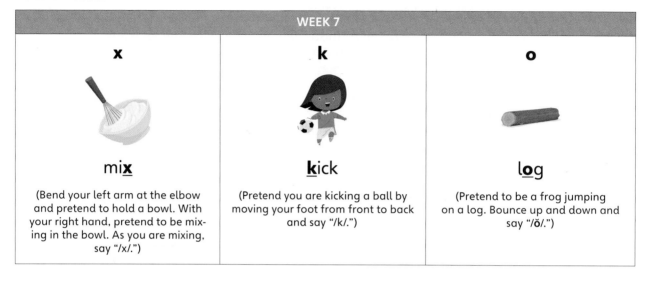

WEEK 7		
x	**k**	**o**
mi**x**	**k**ick	l**o**g
(Bend your left arm at the elbow and pretend to hold a bowl. With your right hand, pretend to be mixing in the bowl. As you are mixing, say "/x/.")	(Pretend you are kicking a ball by moving your foot from front to back and say "/k/.")	(Pretend to be a frog jumping on a log. Bounce up and down and say "/ŏ/.")

CORRESPONDING *LEARNER'S NOTEBOOK PAGES*

Mix: istock.com/vasilyevalara; Kick: istock.com/pijama61; Log: istock.com/bennyb

Preparing for Your Week

CORRESPONDING *FLUENCY NOTEBOOK PAGES*

Mix

x x x Mix!
x x x Mix!

I mix up the

_____.

I mix up the

_____.

x x x Mix!
x x x Mix!

I mix up the

_____.

I mix up the

_____.

x x x Mix!
x x x Mix!

Mix: istock.com/vasilyevalara

Kick

k k k Kick!
k k k Kick!

Don't kick the

_____.

Don't kick the

_____.

k k k Kick!
k k k Kick!

Don't kick the

_____.

Don't kick the

_____.

k k k Kick!
k k k Kick!

Kick: istock.com/pijama61

Log

o o o Log!
o o o Log!

A(n) _____

is hiding in the log!

A(n) _____

is hiding in the log!

o o o Log!
o o o Log!

A(n) _____

is hiding in the log!

A(n) _____

is hiding in the log!

o o o Log!
o o o Log!

Log: istock.com/bennyb

Xx

Max has exciting news to share with us.

He can play his sax while wearing a tux!

Kk

The kitty kissed the king on the nose.

The king tickled the kitten's soft toes.

Oo

Oh no! My dog is lost in the fog.

Hurray! I found him next to the bog.

Tips for Management and Differentiation

Refer to this section and to resources.corwin.com/puzzlepiecephonics-gradeK for resources and ideas to deepen your students' learning throughout the week. Feel free to put your own spin on the routines, too. For daily lesson plans, see pages 96–103 of this Teacher's Guide.

TIPS FOR PHONEMIC AWARENESS	• Last week, students heard each segmented sound of a word and put the word back together. This week, they will be doing the opposite. Students will hear a complete word and segment the word into parts. • If you notice your students need additional practice, extend the activity with additional words.
TIPS FOR THE PUZZLE PIECE REVIEW	• This week on Days 1–3 you are introducing students to a new puzzle piece. Be sure to spend enough time introducing the piece so students understand their focus for that day. • Have students work with the same partner each day to build a word study relationship. • Students will likely notice that the *cow* piece and the *kick* piece represent the same sound. Let students know that this week when they hear the /k/ sound it will most likely be represented by the letter *k*. Let students know it is acceptable in everyday writing to represent the /k/ sound with the letter *c* or *k*. • The /x/ sound is not as common as the other consonant sounds that students have been learning. Explain to students that very few words begin with the letter *x*, and that is why the *mix* piece, which represents the letter *x*, has this sound and letter at the end.
TIPS FOR SUPPORTED BLENDING	• Follow the Supported Blending routine on page I-16 of the Introduction and hold students accountable for producing the initial sounds for each word. • Reblend lines if necessary.
TIPS FOR FORMATION	• Encourage students to circle the letter on the row that they feel they formed the best. Have them try to duplicate the letter. • Go around with a highlighter to help students who are struggling with their letters. • Have a station in your room with sand for students to practice forming their letters in. • If students are struggling with forming letters, relate the current letter to a previous formation. For example, if students are having a hard time forming the uppercase *O*, compare this to the formation of the uppercase *Q*.
TIPS FOR DICTATION	• If students are struggling to identify the initial letter or sound of a word, tell students to write the letter that says "/x/," "/k/," or "/ŏ/."

Preparing for Your Week

TIPS FOR SORTING

- This week students are sorting their pictures and words with three headers. On Days 1–3, students will be sorting with one header. Instruct students to place any unused picture and word cards and headers back into their word sort bags.
- On Day 2, if students can handle sorting both *Xx* and *Kk*, allow them to build off what they learned on Day 1. The same applies for Day 3.
- Take the time to visit with each student to make sure all are understanding the meaning of the picture.
- The sort contains words with authentic capitalization. Review the picture and word cards with students and go over this week's capitalized words.

TIPS FOR THE PRACTICE PIECES

- This Practice Piece time can be your opportunity to create fun, authentic experiences with letters.
  - **Xx:** Have students fill in an uppercase *X* and lowercase *x* with *x* stamps.
  - **Kk:** Have students fill in an uppercase *K* and lowercase *k* with kites.
  - **Oo:** Have students fill in an uppercase *O* and lowercase *o* with odd numbers.
  - Make it fun for your students using the supplies you have!

TIPS FOR FLUENCY

- This week students will read open-ended chants in which they can fill in the blank with their sort pictures. The chants are very repetitive and are meant to be interactive. Students will need support with the sight words in the chants.
- Students can illustrate other parts of the chants.
- Students can read their chants and couplets to a partner.
- Students can pull out pictures from their sort bags to fill in the blanks during the chants.
- Students may circle the letters of the week in each couplet.

TIPS FOR SPELLING CHECK

- Review the directions with students. They are writing the letter that represents the sound you dictate.
- Use teacher discretion when grading the Spelling Check.

Day 1

PHONEMIC AWARENESS: LISTEN

1. Give the directions. Say, "I am going to say a word. Your job is to break the word into individual sounds. For example, if I say '*bat*,' you say '/b/ /ă/ /t/.'"

2. Say the following words:

pop (/p/ /ŏ/ /p/)   bun (/b/ /ŭ/ /n/)   hit (/h/ /ĭ/ /t/)
moss (/m/ /ŏ/ /s/)   wag (/w/ /ă/ /g/)

THE BIG REVEAL

1. Hold up the *mix* puzzle piece and say, "This is the *mix* piece. It represents the letter *x*. The *mix* piece says '/x/ /x/ /x/' like at the end of the word *mix*. Bend your left arm at the elbow and pretend to hold a bowl. With your right hand, pretend to be mixing in the bowl. As you are mixing, say '/x/.' We will study this letter and sound all week. Let's make a list of words that have the *mix* sound in them" (record the words).

SUPPORTED BLENDING: PUTTING SOUNDS TOGETHER TO MAKE NEW WORDS

1. Follow the Supported Blending routine on page I-16 of the Introduction.

2. Display the following words on the board one line at a time. Facilitate a discussion about the blending line focus after each line.

3. Then display the weekly sight word.

mix	fox	fax	Discuss: final sound of /x/
x-ray	xylophone	box	Discuss: compare initial sounds /x/ in *x-ray* and /z/ in *xylophone*; final sound of /x/ in *box*

Sight Word: on

FORMATION: WRITING LETTERS

1. Have students turn to page 75 of the Learner's Notebook.

2. Model forming uppercase letter *X* and lowercase letter *x*.

Uppercase Formation	**Lowercase Formation**
Your pencil starts at the top line.	Your pencil starts at the middle line.
Form a slanted line all the way down to the bottom line, right.	Form a slanted line all the way down to the bottom line, right.
Pick your pencil up.	Pick your pencil up.
Your pencil starts at the top line, to the right.	Your pencil starts at the middle line, to the right.
Form a slanted line all the way down to the bottom line, left.	Form a slanted line all the way down to the bottom line, left.
Pick your pencil up.	Pick your pencil up.

3. Assist students in forming two lines of uppercase *X*s.

4. Assist students in forming two lines of lowercase *x*s.

Day 1 (Continued)

**PRACTICE:
COMPLETE
YOUR WORK ON
YOUR OWN**

1. Have students turn to page 73 of the Learner's Notebook.

2. Instruct students to tear out the sort and complete the following Practice Pieces: Quick Color, Careful Cut, and Sorting With Combined Picture and Word Cards (see further directions on pages I-37, I-38, and I-25 of the Introduction).

3. Instruct students that they are only using the *mix* header and words with the letter *x*.

4. Circulate as students work, which usually takes fifteen minutes, and coach as needed.

**FLUENCY:
READING LIKE
YOU'RE SPEAKING**

1. Have students turn to page 15 in the Fluency Notebook.

2. Have students read one or more of the following chants: "Mix," "Kick," and "Log."

3. Circulate and listen to students read or gather a small group of students who need additional support.

PHONEMIC AWARENESS: LISTEN

1. Give the directions. Say, "I am going to say a word. Your job is to break the word into individual sounds. For example, if I say 'bat,' you say '/b/ /ă/ /t/.'"

2. Say the following words:

> **cod (/k/ /ŏ/ /d/)**   **tack (/t/ /ă/ /k/)**   **Jim (/j/ /ĭ/ /m/)**
> **rot (/r/ /ŏ/ /t/)**   **wed (/w/ /ĕ/ /d/)**

THE BIG REVEAL

1. Say, "Yesterday we learned the *mix* piece. It represents the letter *x*. The *mix* piece says '/x/ /x/ /x/' like at the end of the word *mix*. Let's all do the motion for the *mix* piece together."

2. Hold up the *kick* puzzle piece and say, "This is the *kick* piece. It represents the letter *k*. The *kick* piece says '/k/ /k/ /k/' like at the beginning and the end of the word *kick*. Pretend you are kicking a ball by moving your foot from front to back and say '/k/.' We will study this letter and sound all week. Let's make a list of words that have the *kick* sound in them" (record the words).

SUPPORTED BLENDING: PUTTING SOUNDS TOGETHER TO MAKE NEW WORDS

1. Follow the Supported Blending routine on page I-16 of the Introduction.

2. Display the following words on the board one line at a time. Facilitate a discussion about the blending line focus after each line.

3. Then display the weekly sight word.

| kick | kiss | kite | Discuss: initial sound of /k/ |
| kid | Kim | kit | Discuss: initial sound of /k/; capital *K* in the name *Kim* |

Sight Word: on

FORMATION: WRITING LETTERS

1. Have students turn to page 76 of the Learner's Notebook.

2. Model forming uppercase letter *K* and lowercase letter *k*.

Uppercase Formation

Your pencil starts at the top line.

Form a straight line down to the bottom line.

Pick your pencil up.

Your pencil starts at the middle line.

Form a slanted line all the way to the top line, right.

Pick your pencil up.

Your pencil starts at the middle line.

Form a slanted line all the way down to the bottom line, right.

Pick your pencil up.

Lowercase Formation

Your pencil starts at the top line.

Form a straight line down to the bottom line.

Pick your pencil up.

Your pencil starts just below the middle line.

Form a slanted line to between the middle and top lines, right.

Pick your pencil up.

Your pencil starts just below the middle line.

Form a slanted line all the way down to the bottom line, right.

Pick your pencil up.

3. Assist students in forming two lines of uppercase *K*s.

4. Assist students in forming two lines of lowercase *k*s.

Day 2 (Continued)

SORT: WHAT IS YOUR FOCUS PATTERN?	**1.** Have students take out their bag of pictures (created on Day 1) and follow the Sorting With Combined Picture and Word Cards routine on page I-25 of the Introduction. **2.** Instruct students that they are only using the *kick* header and words with the letter *k*.
PRACTICE: COMPLETE YOUR WORK ON YOUR OWN	**1.** Students will follow the Grab and Write routine on page I-44 of the Introduction. **2.** Circulate as students work, which usually takes fifteen minutes, and coach as needed.
FLUENCY: READING LIKE YOU'RE SPEAKING	**1.** Have students turn to page 15 in the Fluency Notebook. **2.** Have students read one or more of the following chants: "Mix," "Kick," and "Log." **3.** Circulate and listen to students read or gather a small group of students who need additional support.

Day 3

PHONEMIC AWARENESS: LISTEN

1. Give the directions. Say, "I am going to say a word. Your job is to break the word into individual sounds. For example, if I say '*bat*,' you say '/b/ /ă/ /t/.'"

2. Say the following words:

nap (/n/ /ă/ /p/)   lit (/l/ /ĭ/ /t/)   rock (/r/ /ŏ/ /k/)
Ben (/b/ /ĕ/ /n/)   pug (/p/ /ŭ/ /g/)

THE BIG REVEAL

1. Say, "On Day 1, we learned the *mix* piece. It represents the letter *x*. The *mix* piece says '/x/ /x/ /x/' like at the end of the word *mix*. Let's all do the motion for the *mix* piece together."

2. Say, "Yesterday, we learned the *kick* piece. It represents the letter *k*. The *kick* piece says '/k/ /k/ /k/' like at the beginning and the end of the word *kick*. Let's all do the motion for the *kick* piece together."

3. Hold up the *log* puzzle piece and say, "This is the *log* piece. It represents the letter *o*. The *log* piece says '/ŏ/ /ŏ/ /ŏ/' like in the middle of the word *log*. Pretend to be a frog on a log, bounce up and down, and say '/ŏ/.' We will study this letter and sound all week. Let's make a list of words that have the *log* sound in them" (record the words).

SUPPORTED BLENDING: PUTTING SOUNDS TOGETHER TO MAKE NEW WORDS

1. Follow the Supported Blending routine on page I-16 of the Introduction.

2. Display the following words on the board one line at a time. Facilitate a discussion about the blending line focus after each line.

3. Then display the weekly sight word.

| odd | otter | off | Discuss: initial sound of /ŏ/ |
| octopus | ostrich | October | Discuss: initial sound of /ŏ/; capital *O* in the month *October* |

Sight Word: on

FORMATION: WRITING LETTERS

1. Have students turn to page 77 of the Learner's Notebook.

2. Model forming uppercase letter *O* and lowercase letter *o*.

Uppercase Formation	**Lowercase Formation**
Your pencil starts at the top line.	Your pencil starts at the middle line.
Form an oval that touches the bottom line and comes back up to the top line.	Form a circle that touches the bottom line and comes back up to the middle line.
Pick your pencil up.	Pick your pencil up.

3. Assist students in forming two lines of uppercase *O*s.

4. Assist students in forming two lines of lowercase *o*s.

SORT: WHAT IS YOUR FOCUS PATTERN?

1. Have students take out their bag of pictures (created on Day 1) and follow the Sorting With Combined Picture and Word Cards routine on page I-25 of the Introduction.

2. Instruct students that they are only using the *log* header and words with the letter *o*.

Day 3 (Continued)

PRACTICE: COMPLETE YOUR WORK ON YOUR OWN

1. Have students turn to page 78 in the Learner's Notebook.

2. Students will complete the Letter Matrix routine found on page I-45 of the Introduction.

3. Circulate as students work, which usually takes fifteen minutes, and coach as needed.

FLUENCY: READING LIKE YOU'RE SPEAKING

1. Have students turn to page 15 in the Fluency Notebook.

2. Have students read one or more of the following chants: "Mix," "Kick," and "Log."

3. Circulate and listen to students read or gather a small group of students who need additional support.

Day 4

PHONEMIC AWARENESS:
LISTEN

1. Give the directions. Say, "I am going to say a word. Your job is to break the word into individual sounds. For example, if I say '*bat*,' you say '/b/ /ă/ /t/.'"

2. Say the following words:

dot (/d/ /ŏ/ /t/)   fix (/f/ /ĭ/ /x/)   jet (/j/ /ĕ/ /t/)
kid (/k/ /ĭ/ /d/)   will (/w/ /ĭ/ /l/)

PUZZLE PIECE REVIEW

1. Say, "When I point to the piece, you tell me its name" (*mix, kick, log*).

2. Say, "When I point to the piece, you tell me its sound" (/x/, /k/, /ŏ/).

3. Say, "When I point to the piece, you tell me its spelling" (*x, k, o*).

4. Say, "Write the spellings in the air with your finger" (students will form the letters *x, k,* and *o*).

SUPPORTED BLENDING:
PUTTING SOUNDS TOGETHER TO MAKE NEW WORDS

1. Follow the Supported Blending routine on page I-16 of the Introduction.

2. Display the following words on the board one line at a time. Facilitate a discussion about the blending line focus after each line.

3. Then display the weekly sight word.

fix	mix	kicks	Discuss: initial sound of /k/; short vowel –*cks* mimics /x/
otter	kangaroo	fox	Discuss: initial or final sounds of /ŏ/, /k/, and /x/
October	olive	six	Discuss: initial or final sounds of /ŏ/ and /x/

Sight Word: **on**

DICTATION:
STRETCH OUT YOUR WORDS

1. Have students turn to page 79 of the Learner's Notebook.

2. Follow the Dictation routine on page I-21 of the Introduction to dictate the following words:

    I. box   2. otter   3. kangaroo   4. October   5. kid

    Sight Word: **on**

3. Hold students accountable for recording the initial sound in each word in their Learner's Notebook. For word 1, *box,* hold students accountable for the final sound /x/.

SORT: WHAT IS YOUR FOCUS PATTERN?

1. Have students take out their bag of pictures and words (created on Day 1) and follow the Sorting With Combined Picture and Word Cards routine on page I-25 of the Introduction.

PRACTICE:
COMPLETE YOUR WORK ON YOUR OWN

1. Have students complete the following Practice Pieces: Glue Words (on page I-41 of the Introduction) and Fluency Drill (on page I-46 of the Introduction).

2. Circulate as students work, which usually takes fifteen minutes, and coach as needed.

FLUENCY:
READING LIKE YOU'RE SPEAKING

1. Have students turn to page 15 in the Fluency Notebook.

2. Have students read one or more of the following chants: "Mix," "Kick," and "Log."

3. Circulate and listen to students read or gather a small group of students who need additional support.

Day 5

PHONEMIC AWARENESS: LISTEN

1. Give the directions. Say, "I am going to say a word. Your job is to break the word into individual sounds. For example, if I say '*bat*,' you say '/b/ /ă/ /t/.'"

2. Say the following words:

pot (/p/ /ŏ/ /t/)   Max (/m/ /ă/ /x/)   yell (/y/ /ĕ/ /l/)

bid (/b/ /ĭ/ /d/)   got (/g/ /ŏ/ /t/)

REVIEW PATTERNS OF THE WEEK

1. Say, "Find a partner."

2. Say, "Tell your partner the names of this week's pieces" (*mix, kick, log*).

3. Say, "Tell your partner the sounds of this week's pieces" (/x/, /k/, /ŏ/).

4. Say, "Tell your partner the spellings of this week's pieces" (*x, k, o*).

5. Say, "Write the spellings on your partner's back with your finger" (students will form the letters *x, k,* and *o*).

SPELLING CHECK

1. Follow the Spelling Check routine on page I-34 of the Introduction.

2. Have students turn to page 81 of the Learner's Notebook.

3. Say, "Write the letter that represents the sound you hear."

4. Dictate the following sounds (repeat the sound if needed):

1. /ŏ/
2. /k/
3. /x/
4. /ŏ/
5. /k/

Sight Word: on

LABELING THE ROOM

1. Label the classroom with things found from this week's sort.

HANDWRITING CHECK

1. Have students turn to page 82 in the Learner's Notebook.

2. Model and have students form the following letters:

1. Three uppercase *X*s
2. Three lowercase *x*s
3. Three uppercase *K*s
4. Three lowercase *k*s
5. Three uppercase *O*s
6. Three lowercase *o*s

WEEKLY CELEBRATION

1. Display the celebratory message: "On to the next! You learned the *mix, kick,* and *log* puzzle pieces!"

2. Encourage students to work together to read the message.

3. Have students copy the message onto their weekly certificate (see resources .corwin.com/puzzlepiecephonics-gradeK) and place it somewhere to take home.

Preparing for Your Week

Resources

PUZZLE PIECES

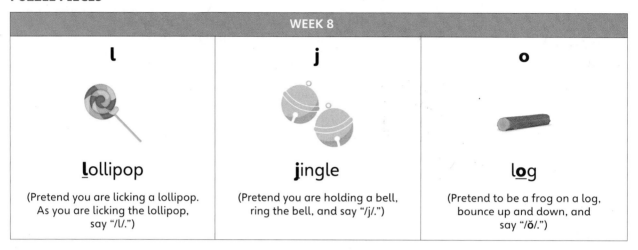

WEEK 8		
l	**j**	**o**
lollipop	**j**ingle	l**o**g
(Pretend you are licking a lollipop. As you are licking the lollipop, say "/l/.")	(Pretend you are holding a bell, ring the bell, and say "/j/.")	(Pretend to be a frog on a log, bounce up and down, and say "/ŏ/.")

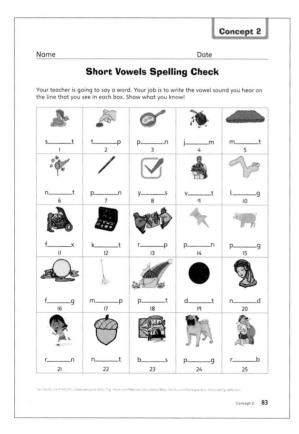

PREASSESSMENT DIRECTIONS

Complete this assessment any day(s) during Concept 2, Week 8. Instruct students to turn to **page 83 in the Learner's Notebook**. Tell students that you will use the results to form word study groups (see Tips for Scoring on page 105) and set goals. If necessary, you can split up the rows and complete different parts of the assessment on different days. When giving this assessment, go row by row in saying the word in the picture. Students are *not* guessing what the picture is. You tell them the word. Explain to students that they should fill in the blank with the short vowel sound they hear.

Lollipop: istock.com/PandaVector; Jingle: istock.com/LeshkaSmok; Log: istock.com/bennyb

Preparing for Your Week

PREASSESSMENT: SHORT VOWELS SPELLING CHECK

ANSWER KEY				
l. sat	2. tap	3. pan	4. jam	5. ,mat
6. net	7. pen	8. yes	9. vet	l0. leg
ll. fix	l2. kit	l3. rip	l4. pin	l5. pig
l6. fog	l7. mop	l8. pot	l9. dot	20. nod
2l. run	22. nut	23. bus	24. pug	25. rub

Yes: istock.com/S-S-S; Pin: istock.com/jane_Kelly; Pig: istock.com/Nadzeya_Dzivakova; Mop: istock.com/mhatzapa; Run: istock.com/graphic-bee

EVALUATING THE ASSESSMENT:
WHAT TO LOOK FOR

- One-to-one sound correspondence
- Knowledge of short vowels

TIPS FOR SCORING

The first row contains words with short vowel *a*. The second row contains words with short vowel *e*. The third row contains words with short vowel *i*. The fourth row contains words with short vowel *o*. The fifth row contains words with short vowel *u*.

This assessment is to be used to group your students and understand their needs. Each word is worth one point. For each correctly spelled word, students earn one point. Add up their points to see their total score.

- If students earn 0–15 points, they will be working with Group 1 words.
- If students earn 16–25 points, they will be working with Group 2 words.

This is a guide to get you started, but use teacher discretion when placing your students in groups. Remember, these groups are flexible and can change each week if necessary. See the key above for words and answers.

Preparing for Your Week

CORRESPONDING *LEARNER'S NOTEBOOK* PAGES

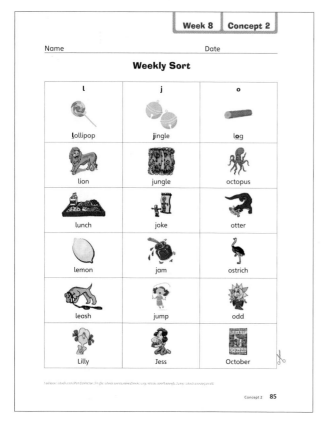

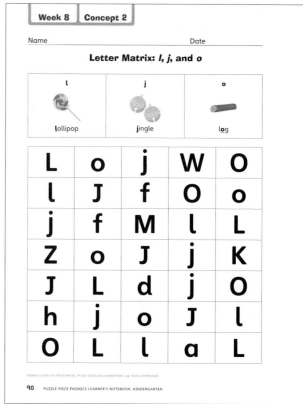

Preparing for Your Week

CORRESPONDING *FLUENCY NOTEBOOK PAGES*

Lollipop

l l l Lollipop!
l l l Lollipop!

_____

licks the lollipop.

_____

licks the lollipop.

l l l Lollipop!
l l l Lollipop!

_____

licks the lollipop.

_____

licks the lollipop.

l l l Lollipop!
l l l Lollipop!

Lollipop: istock.com/PandaVector

Jingle

j j j Jingle!
j j j Jingle!

The _____

can jingle!

The _____

can jingle!

j j j Jingle!
j j j Jingle!

The _____

can jingle!

The _____

can jingle!

j j j Jingle!
j j j Jingle!

Jingle: istock.com/LeshkaSmok

Log

o o o Log!
o o o Log!

A(n) _____

is hiding in the log!

A(n) _____

is hiding in the log!

o o o Log!
o o o Log!

A(n) _____

is hiding in the log!

A(n) _____

is hiding in the log!

o o o Log!
o o o Log!

Log: istock.com/bennyb

Ll

Lucy put mommy's lipstick on her lips.

Lucy is lucky that lipstick won't stick!

Jj

In the jungle, Jamie jumps rope.

Jumping 100 times is her hope!

Repeat: istock.com/pijama61

Oo

Oh no! My dog is lost in the fog.

Hurray! I found him next to the bog.

Preparing for Your Week

Tips for Management and Differentiation

Refer to this section and to resources.corwin.com/puzzlepiecephonics-gradeK for resources and ideas to deepen your students' learning throughout the week. Feel free to put your own spin on the routines, too. For daily lesson plans, see pages 110–116 of this Teacher's Guide.

TIPS FOR PHONEMIC AWARENESS	• Students will continue to hear a complete word and segment the word into parts. • If you notice your students need additional practice, extend the activity with more words.
TIPS FOR THE PUZZLE PIECE REVIEW	• This week on Days 1–2 you are introducing students to a new puzzle piece. Be sure to spend enough time introducing the piece so students understand their focus for that day. • Have students work with the same partner each day to build a word study relationship.
TIPS FOR SUPPORTED BLENDING	• Follow the Supported Blending routine and hold students accountable for producing the initial sounds for each word. • Reblend lines if necessary. • This late in Concept 2, students have learned many short vowel and consonant sounds. If you feel comfortable, encourage students to blend the words without your Supported Blending guidance.
TIPS FOR FORMATION	• Encourage students to circle the letter on the row that they feel they formed the best. Have them try to duplicate the letter. • Go around with a highlighter to help students who are struggling with their letters. • Have a station in your room with sand for students to practice forming their letters in.
TIPS FOR DICTATION	• If students are struggling to identify the initial sound of a word, isolate the sound for students and tell them to record that specific sound.
TIPS FOR SORTING	• This week students are sorting their pictures and words with three headers. On Days 1–2, students will only be sorting with two headers. Instruct students to place any unused picture and word cards and headers back into their word sort bags. • On Day 2, if students can handle sorting *Ll*, *Jj*, and *Oo*, allow them to build off what they learned last week and on Day 1. • The sort contains words with authentic capitalization. Review the picture and word cards with students and go over this week's capitalized words.

TIPS FOR THE PRACTICE PIECES	• This Practice Piece time can be your opportunity to create fun, authentic experiences with letters.
	  • **Ll:** Have students fill in an uppercase *L* and lowercase *l* with licorice.
	  • **Jj:** Have students fill in an uppercase *J* and lowercase *j* with jelly beans.
	  • **Oo:** Have students fill in an uppercase *O* and lowercase *o* with odd numbers.
	  • Make it fun for your students using the supplies you have!

Preparing for Your Week

TIPS FOR FLUENCY

- This week students will read open-ended chants in which they can fill in the blank with their sort pictures. The chants are very repetitive and are meant to be interactive. Students will need support with the sight words in the chants.
- Students can illustrate other parts of the chants.
- Students can read their chants and couplets to a partner.
- Students can pull out pictures from their sort bags to fill in the blanks during the chants.
- Students may circle the letters of the week in each couplet.

TIPS FOR SPELLING CHECK

- Review the directions with students. They are writing the letter that represents the sound you dictate.
- Use teacher discretion when grading the Spelling Check.

PHONEMIC AWARENESS: LISTEN

1. Give the directions. Say, "I am going to say a word. Your job is to break the word into individual sounds. For example, if I say '*bat*,' you say '/b/ /ă/ /t/.'"

2. Say the following words:

lab (/l/ /ă/ /b/)   fib (/f/ /ĭ/ /b/)   tell (/t/ /ĕ/ /l/)

dot (/d/ /ŏ/ /t/)   Jen (/j/ /ĕ/ /n/)

THE BIG REVEAL

1. Hold up the *lollipop* puzzle piece and say, "This is the *lollipop* piece. It represents the letter *l*. The *lollipop* piece says '/l/ /l/ /l/' like at the beginning of the word *lollipop*. Pretend you are licking a lollipop. As you are licking the lollipop, say '/l/.' We will study this letter and sound all week. Let's make a list of words that have the *lollipop* sound in them" (record the words).

SUPPORTED BLENDING: PUTTING SOUNDS TOGETHER TO MAKE NEW WORDS

1. Follow the Supported Blending routine on page I-16 of the Introduction.

2. Display the following words on the board one line at a time. Facilitate a discussion about the blending line focus after each line.

3. Then display the weekly sight word.

lollipop	lunch	lemon	Discuss: initial sound of /l/
lid	lot	lab	Discuss: initial sound of /l/
otter	Oliver	box	Discuss: review of sounds from previous weeks; capital *O* in the name *Oliver*

Sight Word: no

FORMATION: WRITING LETTERS

1. Have students turn to page 87 of the Learner's Notebook.

2. Model forming uppercase letter *L* and lowercase letter *l*.

Uppercase Formation

Your pencil starts at the top line.

Form a straight line all the way down to the bottom line.

Pick your pencil up.

Your pencil starts at the bottom line.

Form a straight, horizontal line to the right.

Pick your pencil up.

Lowercase Formation

Your pencil starts at the top line.

Form a straight line all the way down to the bottom line.

Pick your pencil up.

3. Assist students in forming two lines of uppercase *L*s.

4. Assist students in forming two lines of lowercase *l*s.

PRACTICE: COMPLETE YOUR WORK ON YOUR OWN

1. Have students turn to page 85 of the Learner's Notebook.

2. Instruct students to tear out the sort and complete the following Practice Pieces: Quick Color, Careful Cut, and Sorting With Combined Picture and Word Cards (see further directions on pages I-37, I-38, and I-25 of the Introduction).

3. Instruct students that they are only using the *lollipop* and *log* headers and words with the letters *l* and *o*.

4. Circulate as students work, which usually takes fifteen minutes, and coach as needed.

FLUENCY: READING LIKE YOU'RE SPEAKING

1. Have students turn to page 17 in the Fluency Notebook.

2. Have students read one or more of the following chants: "Lollipop," "Jingle," and "Log."

3. Circulate and listen to students read or gather a small group of students who need additional support.

Day 2

PHONEMIC AWARENESS: LISTEN

1. Give the directions. Say, "I am going to say a word. Your job is to break the word into individual sounds. For example, if I say '*bat*,' you say '/b/ /ă/ /t/.'"

2. Say the following words:

lot (/l/ /ŏ/ /t/)   Jill (/j/ /ĭ/ /l/)   met (/m/ /ĕ/ /t/)
bop (/b/ /ŏ/ /p/)   fun (/f/ /ŭ/ /n/)

THE BIG REVEAL

1. Say, "Yesterday we learned the *lollipop* piece. It represents the letter *l*. The *lollipop* piece says '/l/ /l/ /l/' like at the beginning of the word *lollipop*. Let's all do the motion for the *lollipop* piece together."

2. Hold up the *jingle* puzzle piece and say, "This is the *jingle* piece. It represents the letter *j*. The *jingle* piece says '/j/ /j/ /j/' like at the beginning of the word *jingle*. Pretend you are holding a bell, ring the bell, and say '/j/.' We will study this letter and sound all week. Let's make a list of words that have the *jingle* sound in them" (record the words).

SUPPORTED BLENDING: PUTTING SOUNDS TOGETHER TO MAKE NEW WORDS

1. Follow the Supported Blending routine on page I-16 of the Introduction.

2. Display the following words on the board one line at a time. Facilitate a discussion about the blending line focus after each line.

3. Then display the weekly sight word.

jingle	joke	jump	Discuss: initial sound of /j/
jam	jig	jet	Discuss: initial sound of /j/
ostrich	kite	Ken	Discuss: review of sounds from previous weeks; capital *K* in the name *Ken*

Sight Word: no

FORMATION: WRITING LETTERS

1. Have students turn to page 88 of the Learner's Notebook.

2. Model forming uppercase letter *J* and lowercase letter *j*.

Uppercase Formation	**Lowercase Formation**
Your pencil starts at the top line.	Your pencil starts at the middle line.
Form a straight line down to just above the bottom line.	Form a straight line down underneath the bottom line.
Then, curve your line as it touches the bottom line and extend the curve up to the left.	Then, curve your line as it goes below the bottom line and extend the curve up to the left.
Pick your pencil up.	Pick your pencil up.
Your pencil starts at the top line, to the left.	Your pencil starts halfway between the top line and the middle line.
Form a straight, horizontal line to the right.	Make a dot.
Pick your pencil up.	Pick your pencil up.

3. Assist students in forming two lines of uppercase *J*s.

4. Assist students in forming two lines of lowercase *j*s.

SORT: WHAT IS YOUR FOCUS PATTERN?

1. Have students take out their bag of pictures (created on Day 1) and follow the Sorting With Combined Picture and Word Cards routine on page I-25 of the Introduction.

2. Instruct students that they are only using the *jingle* and *log* headers and words with the letters *j* and *o*.

PRACTICE: COMPLETE YOUR WORK ON YOUR OWN

1. Students will follow the Grab and Write routine on page I-44 of the Introduction.

2. Circulate as students work, which usually takes fifteen minutes, and coach as needed.

FLUENCY: READING LIKE YOU'RE SPEAKING

1. Have students turn to page 17 in the Fluency Notebook.

2. Have students read one or more of the following chants: "Lollipop," "Jingle," and "Log."

3. Circulate and listen to students read or gather a small group of students who need additional support.

Day 3

PHONEMIC AWARENESS: LISTEN

1. Give the directions. Say, "I am going to say a word. Your job is to break the word into individual sounds. For example, if I say '*bat*,' you say '/b/ /ă/ /t/.'"

2. Say the following words:

mum (/m/ /ŭ/ /m/)   tip (/t/ /ĭ/ /p/)   led (/l/ /ĕ/ /d/)
cut (/k/ /ŭ/ /t/)   sad (/s/ /ă/ /d/)

PUZZLE PIECE REVIEW

1. Say, "When I point to the piece, you tell me its name" (*lollipop, jingle, log*).

2. Say, "When I point to the piece, you tell me its sound" (/l/, /j/, /ŏ/).

3. Say, "When I point to the piece, you tell me its spelling" (*l, j, o*).

4. Say, "Write the spellings in the air with your finger" (students will form the letters *l, j,* and *o*).

SUPPORTED BLENDING: PUTTING SOUNDS TOGETHER TO MAKE NEW WORDS

1. Follow the Supported Blending routine on page I-16 of the Introduction.

2. Display the following words on the board one line at a time. Facilitate a discussion about the blending line focus after each line.

3. Then display the weekly sight word.

log	jog	dog	Discuss: word family –*og* and the sound of /ŏg/
leash	jungle	octopus	Discuss: initial sounds of /l/, /j/, and /ŏ/
Lilly	Jess	Oliver	Discuss: initial sounds of /l/, /j/, and /ŏ/; capital letters *L, J,* and *O* for the names *Lilly, Jess,* and *Oliver*

Sight Word: no

DICTATION: STRETCH OUT YOUR WORDS

1. Have students turn to page 89 of the Learner's Notebook.

2. Follow the Dictation routine on page I-21 of the Introduction to dictate the following words:

l. olive   2. jitters   3. lovely   4. Lilly   5. learn

Sight Word: no

3. Hold students accountable for recording the initial sound in each word in their Learner's Notebook.

SORT: WHAT IS YOUR FOCUS PATTERN?

1. Have students take out their bag of pictures (created on Day 1) and follow the Sorting With Combined Picture and Word Cards routine on page I-25 of the Introduction.

PRACTICE: COMPLETE YOUR WORK ON YOUR OWN

1. Have students turn to page 90 in the Learner's Notebook.

2. Students will complete the Letter Matrix routine found on page I-45 of the Introduction.

3. Circulate as students work, which usually takes fifteen minutes, and coach as needed.

FLUENCY: READING LIKE YOU'RE SPEAKING

1. Have students turn to page 17 in the Fluency Notebook.

2. Have students read one or more of the following chants: "Lollipop," "Jingle," and "Log."

3. Circulate and listen to students read or gather a small group of students who need additional support.

PHONEMIC AWARENESS: LISTEN

1. Give the directions. Say, "I am going to say a word. Your job is to break the word into individual sounds. For example, if I say '*bat*,' you say '/b/ /ă/ /t/.'"

2. Say the following words:

yum (/y/ /ŭ/ /m/)   mad (/m/ /ă/ /d/)   lid (/l/ /ĭ/ /d/)
fix (/f/ /ĭ/ /x/)   red (/r/ /ĕ/ /d/)

PUZZLE PIECE REVIEW

1. Say, "When I point to the piece, you tell me its name" (*lollipop, jingle, log*).

2. Say, "When I point to the piece, you tell me its sound" (/l/, /j/, /ŏ/).

3. Say, "When I point to the piece, you tell me its spelling" (*l, j, o*).

4. Say, "Write the spellings in the air with your finger" (students will form the letters *l, j,* and *o*).

SUPPORTED BLENDING: PUTTING SOUNDS TOGETHER TO MAKE NEW WORDS

1. Follow the Supported Blending routine on page I-16 of the Introduction.

2. Display the following words on the board one line at a time. Facilitate a discussion about the blending line focus after each line.

3. Then display the weekly sight word.

jot	lot	got	Discuss: word family *–ot* and the sound of /ŏt/
jump	lump	dump	Discuss: word family *–ump* and the sound of /ŭmp/
Jax	kit	lox	Discuss: review of sounds from previous weeks; capital *J* in the name *Jax*

Sight Word: no

DICTATION: STRETCH OUT YOUR WORDS

1. Have students turn to page 91 of the Learner's Notebook.

2. Follow the Dictation routine on page I-21 of the Introduction to dictate the following words:

I. lemon 2. jolly 3. ostrich 4. Jess 5. leash

Sight Word: no

3. Hold students accountable for recording the initial sound in each word in their Learner's Notebook.

SORT: WHAT IS YOUR FOCUS PATTERN?

1. Have students take out their bag of pictures and words (created on Day 1) and follow the Sorting With Combined Picture and Word Cards routine on page I-25 of the Introduction.

PRACTICE: COMPLETE YOUR WORK ON YOUR OWN

1. Have students complete the following Practice Pieces: Glue Words (on page I-41 of the Introduction) and Fluency Drill (on page I-46 of the Introduction).

2. Circulate as students work, which usually takes fifteen minutes, and coach as needed.

FLUENCY: READING LIKE YOU'RE SPEAKING

1. Have students turn to page 17 in the Fluency Notebook.

2. Have students read one or more of the following chants: "Lollipop," "Jingle," and "Log."

3. Circulate and listen to students read or gather a small group of students who need additional support.

Day 5

PHONEMIC AWARENESS: LISTEN

1. Give the directions. Say, "I am going to say a word. Your job is to break the word into individual sounds. For example, if I say 'bat,' you say '/b/ /ă/ /t/.'"

2. Say the following words:

lock (/l/ /ŏ/ /k/)   him (/h/ /ĭ/ /m/)   box (/b/ /ŏ/ /x/)
gel (/j/ /ĕ/ /l/)   tap (/t/ /ă/ /p/)

REVIEW PATTERNS OF THE WEEK

1. Say, "Find a partner."

2. Say, "Tell your partner the names of this week's pieces" (*lollipop, jingle, log*).

3. Say, "Tell your partner the sounds of this week's pieces" (/l/, /j/, /ŏ/).

4. Say, "Tell your partner the spellings of this week's pieces" (*l, j, o*).

5. Say, "Write the spellings on your partner's back with your finger" (students will form the letters *l, j,* and *o*).

SPELLING CHECK

1. Follow the Spelling Check routine on page I-34 of the Introduction.

2. Have students turn to page 93 of the Learner's Notebook.

3. Say, "Write the letter that represents the sound you hear."

4. Dictate the following sounds (repeat the sound if needed):

1. /ŏ/
2. /l/
3. /j/
4. /x/
5. /k/

Sight Word: no

LABELING THE ROOM

1. Label the classroom with things found from this week's sort.

HANDWRITING CHECK

1. Have students turn to page 94 in the Learner's Notebook.

2. Model and have students form the following letters:

1. Three uppercase *L*s
2. Three lowercase *l*s
3. Three uppercase *J*s
4. Three lowercase *j*s
5. Three uppercase *O*s
6. Three lowercase *o*s

WEEKLY CELEBRATION

1. Display the celebratory message: "Learners, look out! You learned the *lollipop, jingle,* and *log* puzzle pieces!"

2. Encourage students to work together to read the message.

3. Have students copy the message onto their weekly certificate (see resources .corwin.com/puzzlepiecephonics-gradeK) and place it somewhere to take home.

Preparing for Your Week

Resources

PUZZLE PIECES

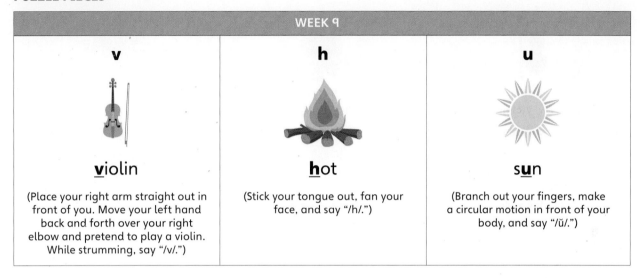

WEEK 9

v — **v**iolin
(Place your right arm straight out in front of you. Move your left hand back and forth over your right elbow and pretend to play a violin. While strumming, say "/v/.")

h — **h**ot
(Stick your tongue out, fan your face, and say "/h/.")

u — s**u**n
(Branch out your fingers, make a circular motion in front of your body, and say "/ŭ/.")

CORRESPONDING *LEARNER'S NOTEBOOK PAGES*

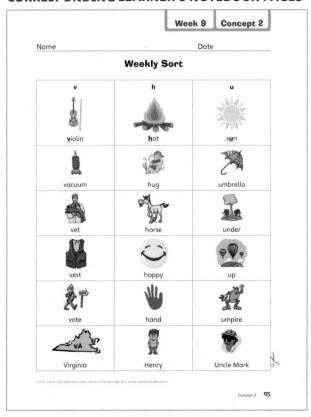

Week 9 | Concept 2

Name _____ Date _____

Weekly Sort

v	h	u
violin	hot	sun
vacuum	hug	umbrella
vet	horse	under
vest	happy	up
vote	hand	umpire
Virginia	Henry	Uncle Mark

Concept 2   95

Week 9 | Concept 2

Name _____ Date _____

Letter Matrix: *v, h,* and *u*

v	h	u
violin	hot	sun

V	u	v	R	H
s	U	f	u	v
h	B	V	k	h
x	H	z	U	D
U	v	h	t	u
Y	V	H	u	U
H	h	A	v	V

100   PUZZLE PIECE PHONICS LEARNER'S NOTEBOOK, KINDERGARTEN

Violin: istock.com/TopVectors; Hot: istock.com/terdpong2; Sun: istock.com/StudioBarcelona

Preparing for Your Week

CORRESPONDING *FLUENCY NOTEBOOK PAGES*

Violin

v v v Violin!

v v v Violin!

_____

plays the violin.

_____

plays the violin.

v v v Violin!

v v v Violin!

_____

plays the violin.

_____

plays the violin.

v v v Violin!

v v v Violin!

Violin: istock.com/TopVectors

Hot

h h h Hot!

h h h Hot!

Hot! Hot!

_____ is hot!

Hot! Hot!

_____ is hot!

h h h Hot!

h h h Hot!

Hot! Hot!

_____ is hot!

Hot! Hot!

_____ is hot!

h h h Hot!

h h h Hot!

Hot: istock.com/terdpong2

Sun

u u u Sun!

u u u Sun!

A(n) _____

is under the sun.

A(n) _____

is under the sun.

u u u Sun!

u u u Sun!

A(n) _____

is under the sun.

A(n) _____

is under the sun.

u u u Sun!

u u u Sun!

Sun: istock.com/StudioBarcelona

Vv

Vroom, vroom! Vicky veers the van to the right.

Vroom, vroom! The van vanishes out of sight!

Hh

"Help! I hurt my arm!" Harry gasped.

He hurried to the hospital to get a cast.

Uu

Run, run! I hit the ball to the sun!

The umpire says I'm out, but it was still fun!

Preparing for Your Week

Tips for Management and Differentiation

Refer to this section and to resources.corwin.com/puzzlepiecephonics-gradeK for resources and ideas to deepen your students' learning throughout the week. Feel free to put your own spin on the routines, too. For daily lesson plans, see pages 121–128 of this Teacher's Guide.

TIPS FOR PHONEMIC AWARENESS	• Students will listen to a word and count how many sounds are in that word. In order to count the number of phonemes, they will need to hear the word, break the word into phonemes, and count how many phonemes they heard. • If you notice your students need additional practice, extend the activity with more words. • Students may need to hear the word multiple times to hear the phonemes, then count them. Repeat any words as needed. • Have students hold up a finger for each phoneme they hear. • You may want to make "phoneme counters" for students. You can assemble these counters by taking a piece of yarn and adding beads to the yarn. Tie the yarn off at each end so the beads cannot slip off. When students hear a different phoneme, they will move the bead in order to count all of the sounds in a given word.
TIPS FOR THE PUZZLE PIECE REVIEW	• This week on Days 1–3 you are introducing students to a new puzzle piece. Be sure to spend enough time introducing the piece so students understand their focus for that day. • Have students work with the same partner each day to build a word study relationship.
TIPS FOR SUPPORTED BLENDING	• Follow the Supported Blending routine on page I-16 of the Introduction and hold students accountable for producing the initial sounds for each word. • Reblend lines if necessary. • This late in Concept 2, students have learned many short vowel and consonant sounds. If you feel comfortable, encourage students to blend the words without your Supported Blending guidance.
TIPS FOR FORMATION	• Encourage students to circle the letter on the row that they feel they formed the best. Have them try to duplicate the letter. • Go around with a highlighter to help students who are struggling with their letters. • Have a station in your room with sand for students to practice forming their letters in.
TIPS FOR DICTATION	• If students are struggling to identify the initial letter or sound of a word, tell students to write the letter that says "/v/," "/h/," or "/ŭ/."

(Continued)

Preparing for Your Week

TIPS FOR SORTING

- This week students are sorting their pictures and words with the three headers. On Days 1–3, students will only be sorting with one header. Instruct students to place any unused picture and word cards and headers back into their word sort bags.
- On Day 2, if students can handle sorting both *Vv* and *Hh*, allow them to build off what they learned on Day 1. The same applies for Day 3.
- The sort contains words with authentic capitalization. Review the picture and word cards with students and go over this week's capitalized words.

TIPS FOR THE PRACTICE PIECES

- This Practice Piece time can be your opportunity to create fun, authentic experiences with letters.
  - **Vv:** Have students fill in an uppercase *V* and lowercase *v* with Velcro.
  - **Hh:** Have students fill in an uppercase *H* and lowercase *h* with hearts.
  - **Uu:** Have students fill in an uppercase *U* and lowercase *u* with up arrows.
  - Make it fun for your students using the supplies you have!

TIPS FOR FLUENCY

- This week students will read open-ended chants in which they can fill in the blank with their sort pictures. The chants are very repetitive and are meant to be interactive. Students will need support with the sight words in the chants.
- Students can illustrate other parts of the chants.
- Students can read their chants and couplets to a partner.
- Students can pull out pictures from their sort bags to fill in the blanks during the chants.
- Students may circle the letters of the week in each couplet.

TIPS FOR SPELLING CHECK

- Review the directions with students. They are writing the letter that represents the sound you dictate.
- Use teacher discretion when grading the Spelling Check.

PHONEMIC AWARENESS: LISTEN	**1.** Give the directions. Say. "I am going to say a word. Your job is to tell me how many sounds are in that word. In order to count the sounds, you need to break the word into its individual parts. For example, if I say '*bat*,' you say '/b/ /ă/ /t/—three sounds!'"

2. Say the following words:

hug (3)   Tom (3)   clap (4)   add (2)   right (3)   punt (4)   hi (2)   slip (4) |
| **THE BIG REVEAL** | **1.** Hold up the *violin* puzzle piece and say, "This is the *violin* piece. It represents the letter *v*. The *violin* piece says '/v/ /v/ /v/' like at the beginning of the word *violin*. Place your right arm straight out in front of you. Move your left hand back and forth over your right elbow and pretend to play a violin. While strumming, say '/v/.' We will study this letter and sound all week. Let's make a list of words that have the *violin* sound in them" (record the words). |
| **SUPPORTED BLENDING: PUTTING SOUNDS TOGETHER TO MAKE NEW WORDS** | **1.** Follow the Supported Blending routine on page I-16 of the Introduction.

2. Display the following words on the board one line at a time. Facilitate a discussion about the blending line focus after each line.

3. Then display the weekly sight word.

violin	vet	vest	Discuss: initial sound of /v/
vacuum	vote	valley	Discuss: initial sound of /v/

Sight Word: up |
| **FORMATION: WRITING LETTERS** | **1.** Have students turn to page 97 of the Learner's Notebook.

2. Model forming uppercase letter *V* and lowercase letter *v*.

Uppercase Formation	**Lowercase Formation**
Your pencil starts at the top line.	Your pencil starts at the middle line.
Form a diagonal line to the bottom line, right.	Form a diagonal line to the bottom line, right.
Pick your pencil up.	Pick your pencil up.
Your pencil starts at the top line, to the right.	Your pencil starts at the middle line, to the right.
Form a diagonal line to the bottom line, left.	Form a diagonal line to the bottom line, left.
Pick your pencil up.	Pick your pencil up.

3. Assist students in forming two lines of uppercase *V*s.

4. Assist students in forming two lines of lowercase *v*s. |

(Continued)

Day 1 (Continued)

PRACTICE: COMPLETE YOUR WORK ON YOUR OWN	**1.** Have students turn to page 95 of the Learner's Notebook.
	2. Instruct students to tear out the sort and complete the following Practice Pieces: Quick Color, Careful Cut, and Sorting With Combined Picture and Word Cards (see further directions on pages I-37, I-38, and I-25 of the Introduction).
	3. Instruct students that they are only using the *violin* header and words with the letter *v*.
	4. Circulate as students work, which usually takes fifteen minutes, and coach as needed.
FLUENCY: READING LIKE YOU'RE SPEAKING	**1.** Have students turn to page 19 in the Fluency Notebook.
	2. Have students read one or more of the following chants: "Violin," "Hot," and "Sun."
	3. Circulate and listen to students read or gather a small group of students who need additional support.

PHONEMIC AWARENESS: LISTEN

1. Give the directions. Say, "I am going to say a word. Your job is to tell me how many sounds are in that word. In order to count the sounds, you need to break the word into its individual parts. For example, if I say '*bat*,' you say '/b/ /ă/ /t/—three sounds!'"

2. Say the following words:

mop (3)   by (2)   crib (4)   sit (3)   tell (3)   skip (4)   if (2)   ton (3)

THE BIG REVEAL

1. Say, "Yesterday we learned the *violin* piece. It represents the letter *v*. The *violin* piece says '/v/ /v/ /v/' like at the beginning of the word *violin*. Let's all do the motion for the *violin* piece together."

2. Hold up the *hot* puzzle piece and say, "This is the *hot* piece. It represents the letter *h*. The *hot* piece says '/h/ /h/ /h/' like at the beginning of the word *hot*. Stick your tongue out, fan your face, and say '/h/.' We will study this letter and sound all week. Let's make a list of words that have the *hot* sound in them" (record the words).

SUPPORTED BLENDING: PUTTING SOUNDS TOGETHER TO MAKE NEW WORDS

1. Follow the Supported Blending routine on page I-16 of the Introduction.

2. Display the following words on the board one line at a time. Facilitate a discussion about the blending line focus after each line.

3. Then display the weekly sight word.

| hot | hug | head | Discuss: initial sound of /h/ |
| happy | horse | hand | Discuss: initial sound of /h/ |

Sight Word: up

FORMATION: WRITING LETTERS

1. Have students turn to page 98 of the Learner's Notebook.

2. Model forming uppercase letter *H* and lowercase letter *h*.

Uppercase Formation	**Lowercase Formation**
Your pencil starts at the top line.	Your pencil starts at the top line.
Form a straight line down to the bottom line.	Form a straight line down to the bottom line.
Pick your pencil up.	Pick your pencil up.
Your pencil starts at the top line, to the right.	Your pencil starts just below the middle line.
Form a straight line down to the bottom line.	Form a hump all the way down to the bottom line.
Pick your pencil up.	Pick your pencil up.
Your pencil starts at the middle line.	
Form a straight line connecting the two straight lines.	
Pick your pencil up.	

3. Assist students in forming two lines of uppercase *H*s.

4. Assist students in forming two lines of lowercase *h*s.

(Continued)

Day 2 (Continued)

SORT: WHAT IS YOUR FOCUS PATTERN?

1. Have students take out their bag of pictures (created on Day 1) and follow the Sorting With Combined Picture and Word Cards routine on page I-25 of the Introduction.

2. Instruct students that they are only using the *hot* header and words with the letter *h*.

PRACTICE: COMPLETE YOUR WORK ON YOUR OWN

1. Students will follow the Grab and Write routine on page I-44 of the Introduction.

2. Circulate as students work, which usually takes fifteen minutes, and coach as needed.

FLUENCY: READING LIKE YOU'RE SPEAKING

1. Have students turn to page 19 in the Fluency Notebook.

2. Have students read one or more of the following chants: "Violin," "Hot," and "Sun."

3. Circulate and listen to students read or gather a small group of students who need additional support.

PHONEMIC AWARENESS: LISTEN

1. Give the directions. Say, "I am going to say a word. Your job is to tell me how many sounds are in that word. In order to count the sounds, you need to break the word into its individual parts. For example, if I say 'bat,' you say '/b/ /ă/ /t/—three sounds!'"

2. Say the following words:

sleep (4)   cup (3)   list (4)   I (1)   egg (2)   rip (3)   club (4)   elk (3)

THE BIG REVEAL

1. Say, "On Day 1, we learned the *violin* piece. It represents the letter *v*. The *violin* piece says '/v/ /v/ /v/' like at the beginning of the word *violin*. Let's all do the motion for the *violin* piece together."

2. Say, "Yesterday, we learned the *hot* piece. It represents the letter *h*. The *hot* piece says '/h/ /h/ /h/' like at the beginning of the word *hot*. Let's all do the motion for the *hot* piece together."

3. Hold up the *sun* puzzle piece and say, "This is the *sun* piece. It represents the letter *u*. The *sun* piece says '/ŭ/ /ŭ/ /ŭ/' like in the middle of the word *sun*. Branch out your fingers, make a circular motion in front of your body, and say '/ŭ/.' We will study this letter and sound all week. Let's make a list of words that have the *sun* sound in them" (record the words).

SUPPORTED BLENDING: PUTTING SOUNDS TOGETHER TO MAKE NEW WORDS

1. Follow the Supported Blending routine on page I-16 of the Introduction.

2. Display the following words on the board one line at a time. Facilitate a discussion about the blending line focus after each line.

3. Then display the weekly sight word.

under	umpire	up	Discuss: initial sound of /ŭ/
umbrella	undo	untie	Discuss: initial sound of /ŭ/

Sight Word: up

FORMATION: WRITING LETTERS

1. Have students turn to page 99 of the Learner's Notebook.

2. Model forming uppercase letter *U* and lowercase letter *u*.

Uppercase Formation	**Lowercase Formation**
Your pencil starts at the top line.	Your pencil starts at the middle line.
Form a straight line down to just above the bottom line.	Form a straight line down to just above the bottom line.
Curve the line while it touches the bottom line and extend the line back up to the top line.	Curve the line while it touches the bottom line and extend the line back up to the middle line.
Pick your pencil up.	Form a straight line down to the bottom line, on the right.
	Pick your pencil up.

3. Assist students in forming two lines of uppercase *U*s.

4. Assist students in forming two lines of lowercase *u*s.

(Continued)

Day 3 (Continued)

SORT: WHAT IS YOUR FOCUS PATTERN?

1. Have students take out their bag of pictures (created on Day 1) and follow the Sorting With Combined Picture and Word Cards routine on page I-25 of the Introduction.

2. Instruct students that they are only using the *sun* header and words with the letter *u*.

PRACTICE: COMPLETE YOUR WORK ON YOUR OWN

1. Have students turn to page 100 in the Learner's Notebook.

2. Students will complete the Letter Matrix routine found on page I-45 of the Introduction.

3. Circulate as students work, which usually takes fifteen minutes, and coach as needed.

FLUENCY: READING LIKE YOU'RE SPEAKING

1. Have students turn to page 19 in the Fluency Notebook.

2. Have students read one or more of the following chants: "Violin," "Hot," and "Sun."

3. Circulate and listen to students read or gather a small group of students who need additional support.

PHONEMIC AWARENESS: LISTEN

1. Give the directions. Say, "I am going to say a word. Your job is to tell me how many sounds are in that word. In order to count the sounds, you need to break the word into its individual parts. For example, if I say '*bat*,' you say '/b/ /ă/ /t/—three sounds!'"

2. Say the following words:

flip (4)   up (2)   met (3)   sun (3)   a (1)   job (3)   maid (3)   black (4)

PUZZLE PIECE REVIEW

1. Say, "When I point to the piece, you tell me its name" (*violin, hot, sun*).

2. Say, "When I point to the piece, you tell me its sound" (/v/, /h/, /ŭ/).

3. Say, "When I point to the piece, you tell me its spelling" (*v, h, u*).

4. Say, "Write the spellings in the air with your finger" (students will form the letters *v, h,* and *u*).

SUPPORTED BLENDING: PUTTING SOUNDS TOGETHER TO MAKE NEW WORDS

1. Follow the Supported Blending routine on page I-16 of the Introduction.

2. Display the following words on the board one line at a time. Facilitate a discussion about the blending line focus after each line.

3. Then display the weekly sight word.

van	hand	band	Discuss: vowel sound of /ă/
horse	voice	umbrella	Discuss: initial sounds of /h/, /v/, and /ŭ/
Uncle Tim	Henry	Virginia	Discuss: initial sounds of /ŭ/, /h/, and /v/; capital *U, T, H,* and *V* in the names *Uncle Tim, Henry,* and *Virginia*

Sight Word: up

DICTATION: STRETCH OUT YOUR WORDS

1. Have students turn to page 101 of the Learner's Notebook.

2. Follow the Dictation routine on page I-21 of the Introduction to dictate the following words:

1. vest   2. under   3. happy   4. hug   5. vote

Sight Word: up

3. Hold students accountable for recording the initial sound in each word in their Learner's Notebook.

SORT: WHAT IS YOUR FOCUS PATTERN?

1. Have students take out their bag of pictures and words (created on Day 1) and follow the Sorting With Combined Picture and Word Cards routine on page I-25 of the Introduction.

PRACTICE: COMPLETE YOUR WORK ON YOUR OWN

1. Have students complete the following Practice Pieces: Glue Words (on page I-41 of the Introduction) and Fluency Drill (on page I-46 of the Introduction).

2. Circulate as students work, which usually takes fifteen minutes, and coach as needed.

FLUENCY: READING LIKE YOU'RE SPEAKING

1. Have students turn to page 19 in the Fluency Notebook.

2. Have students read one or more of the following chants: "Violin," "Hot," and "Sun."

3. Circulate and listen to students read or gather a small group of students who need additional support.

Day 5

PHONEMIC AWARENESS: LISTEN

1. Give the directions. Say, "I am going to say a word. Your job is to tell me how many sounds are in that word. In order to count the sounds, you need to break the word into its individual parts. For example, if I say '*bat*,' you say '/b/ /ă/ /t/—three sounds!'"

2. Say the following words:

tin (3)   go (2)   smell (4)   jack (3)   speed (4)   math (3)   oak (2)   net (3)

REVIEW PATTERNS OF THE WEEK

1. Say, "Find a partner."

2. Say, "Tell your partner the names of this week's pieces" (*violin, hot, sun*).

3. Say, "Tell your partner the sounds of this week's pieces" (/v/, /h/, /ŭ/).

4. Say, "Tell your partner the spellings of this week's pieces" (*v, h, u*).

5. Say, "Write the spellings on your partner's back with your finger" (students will form the letters *v, h,* and *u*).

SPELLING CHECK

1. Follow the Spelling Check routine on page I-34 of the Introduction.

2. Have students turn to page 103 of the Learner's Notebook.

3. Say, "Write the letter that represents the sound you hear."

4. Dictate the following sounds (repeat the sound if needed):

I. /v/

2. /ŭ/

3. /h/

4. /v/

5. /ŭ/

Sight Word: up

LABELING THE ROOM

1. Label the classroom with things found from this week's sort.

HANDWRITING CHECK

1. Have students turn to page 104 in the Learner's Notebook.

2. Model and have students form the following letters:

1. Three uppercase *V*s

2. Three lowercase *v*s

3. Three uppercase *H*s

4. Three lowercase *h*s

5. Three uppercase *U*s

6. Three lowercase *u*s

WEEKLY CELEBRATION

1. Display the celebratory message: "Hip hip hooray! You learned the *violin, hot,* and *sun* puzzle pieces!"

2. Encourage students to work together to read the message.

3. Have students copy the message onto their weekly certificate (see resources .corwin.com/puzzlepiecephonics-gradeK) and place it somewhere to take home.

Preparing for Your Week

Resources

PUZZLE PIECES

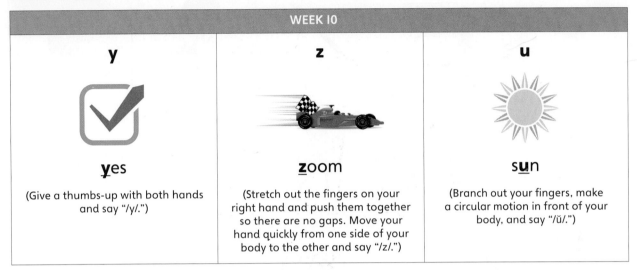

WEEK 10		
y	**z**	**u**
yes	**z**oom	s**u**n
(Give a thumbs-up with both hands and say "/y/.")	(Stretch out the fingers on your right hand and push them together so there are no gaps. Move your hand quickly from one side of your body to the other and say "/z/.")	(Branch out your fingers, make a circular motion in front of your body, and say "/ŭ/.")

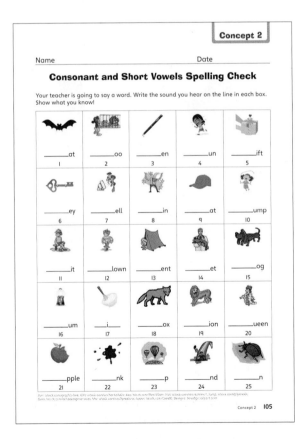

POSTASSESSMENT DIRECTIONS

The following postassessment assesses students' mastery of consonants and short vowels. This is the first postassessment of the year, and it will be used as a tool to identify which patterns students have mastered and which patterns students need to be retaught. It is also useful to evaluate students' ability to apply knowledge of multiple spelling patterns at a time. Students will continue to work with consonants and short vowels throughout the year. You can give this postassessment on any day or days during the last week of Concept 2. You can split up the rows and do parts on different days. Do what works for your class. When you are ready to give students this postassessment, have them turn to **page 105 in the Learner's Notebook**. Let students know that they are expected to do their best on this postassessment and they will continue to learn consonants and short vowels throughout all of kindergarten.

When giving this assessment, go row by row in saying the word represented by the picture. Students do not guess what the picture is.

Yes: istock.com/S-S-S; Zoom: istock.com/funnybank; Sun: istock.com/StudioBarcelona

Preparing for Your Week

POSTASSESSMENT: CONSONANT AND SHORT VOWELS SPELLING CHECK

ANSWER KEY				
1. bat	2. zoo	3. pen	4. run	5. gift
6. key	7. yell	8. win	9. hat	10. jump
11. sit	12. clown	13. tent	14. vet	15. dog
16. gum	17. mix	18. fox	19. lion	20. queen
21. apple	22. ink	23. up	24. end	25. on

Run: istock.com/graphic-bee; Gift: istock.com/UrchenkoJulia; Key: istock.com/DavidGoh; Hat: istock.com/stevezmina1;
Jump: istock.com/pijama61; Gum: istock.com/elinedesignservices; Mix: istock.com/vasilyevalara; Apple: istock.com/CandO_Designs; Ink: clipart.com

EVALUATING THE ASSESSMENT:
WHAT TO LOOK FOR

- One-to-one letter–sound correspondence
- Knowledge of consonants
- Knowledge of short vowels
- Knowledge of initial sounds
- Knowledge of final sound /x/

TIPS FOR SCORING

Rows 1–4 contain words that need the initial consonant sound to be filled in (with exception to the final sound of /x/ in word 17). Row 5 contains words that need the initial short vowel sound to be filled in.

Each letter/sound is worth one point. For each correctly spelled word, students earn one point. To show mastery of consonants and short vowels, students must show 80 percent mastery or correctly spell twenty out of twenty-five words phonetically.

Use teacher discretion when reviewing. If students use the incorrect spelling to represent the /k/ sound, you may count their answer as correct if they use the letter *c* or *k*.

Preparing for Your Week

CORRESPONDING *LEARNER'S NOTEBOOK PAGES*

Preparing for Your Week

CORRESPONDING *FLUENCY NOTEBOOK PAGES*

Yes	**Zoom**	**Sun**

y y y Yes!
y y y Yes!

Can I have a(n)

_____?

Yes!

Can I have a(n)

_____?

Yes!

y y y Yes!
y y y Yes!

Can I have a(n)

_____?

Yes!

Can I have a(n)

_____?

Yes!

y y y Yes!
y y y Yes!

z z z Zoom!
z z z Zoom!

Zoom, zoom!

_____ is

zooming!

Zoom, zoom!

_____ is

zooming!

z z z Zoom!
z z z Zoom!

Zoom, zoom!

_____ is

zooming!

Zoom, zoom!

_____ is

zooming!

z z z Zoom!
z z z Zoom!

u u u Sun!
u u u Sun!

A(n) _____

is under the sun.

A(n) _____

is under the sun.

u u u Sun!
u u u Sun!

A(n) _____

is under the sun.

A(n) _____

is under the sun.

u u u Sun!
u u u Sun!

Yes: istock.com/S-S-S

Zoom: istock.com/funnybank

Sun: istock.com/StudioBarcelona

Yy	**Zz**	**Uu**

"Yum, yum, yippee! These yams taste good."

"Yes, they do!" yelled Mom. "I told you they would!"

Zack saw a black and white striped zebra at the zoo.

Zoe saw chimpanzees, lizards, and grizzly bears too.

Run, run! I hit the ball to the sun!

The umpire says I'm out, but it was still fun!

Preparing for Your Week

Tips for Management and Differentiation

Refer to this section and to resources.corwin.com/puzzlepiecephonics-gradeK for resources and ideas to deepen your students' learning throughout the week. Feel free to put your own spin on the routines, too. For daily lesson plans, see pages 135–141 of this Teacher's Guide.

TIPS FOR PHONEMIC AWARENESS	• Students will continue to listen to a word and count how many sounds are in that word. In order to count the number of phonemes, they will need to hear the word, break the word into phonemes, and count how many phonemes they heard. • If you notice your students need additional practice, extend the activity with more words. • Students may need to hear the word multiple times to hear the phonemes, then count them. Repeat any words as needed. • Have students hold up a finger for each phoneme they hear. • You may want to make "phoneme counters" for students. You can assemble these counters by taking a piece of yarn and adding beads to the yarn. Tie the yarn off at each end so the beads cannot slip off. When students hear a different phoneme, they will move the bead in order to count all of the sounds in a given word.
TIPS FOR THE PUZZLE PIECE REVIEW	• This week on Days 1–2 you are introducing students to a new puzzle piece. Be sure to spend enough time introducing the piece so students understand their focus for that day. • Have students work with the same partner each day to build a word study relationship. • Celebrate students' success! Tell students that these are the last two consonant pieces they will be introduced to. Have a consonant celebration with students! Each student can dress up as his or her favorite consonant. For example, students can dress up as a bee to represent the *bee* (/b/) puzzle piece.
TIPS FOR SUPPORTED BLENDING	• Follow the Supported Blending routine and hold students accountable for producing the initial sounds for each word. • Reblend lines if necessary. • This late in Concept 2, students have learned many short vowel and consonant sounds. If you feel comfortable, encourage students to blend the words without your Supported Blending guidance.
TIPS FOR FORMATION	• Encourage students to circle the letter on the row that they feel they formed the best. Have them try to duplicate the letter. • Go around with a highlighter to help students who are struggling with their letters. • Have a station in your room with sand for students to practice forming their letters in.
TIPS FOR DICTATION	• If students are struggling to identify the initial sound of a word, isolate the sound for students and tell them to record that specific sound.

(Continued)

Preparing for Your Week

TIPS FOR SORTING

- This week students are sorting their pictures and words with the three headers. On Days 1–2, students will only be sorting with two headers. Instruct students to place any unused picture and word cards and headers back into their word sort bags.
- On Day 2, if students can handle sorting *Yy, Zz,* and *Uu,* allow them to build off what they learned last week and on Day 1.
- The sort contains words with authentic capitalization. Review the picture and word cards with students and go over this week's capitalized words.

TIPS FOR THE PRACTICE PIECES

- This Practice Piece time can be your opportunity to create fun, authentic experiences with letters.
  - **Yy:** Have students fill in an uppercase *Y* and lowercase *y* with yarn.
  - **Zz:** Have students fill in an uppercase *Z* and lowercase *z* with zeros.
  - **Uu:** Have students fill in an uppercase *U* and lowercase *u* with up arrows.
  - Make it fun for your students using the supplies you have!

TIPS FOR FLUENCY

- This week students will read open-ended chants in which they can fill in the blank with their sort pictures. The chants are very repetitive and are meant to be interactive. Students will need support with the sight words in the chants.
- Students can illustrate other parts of the chants.
- Students can read their chants and couplets to a partner.
- Students can pull out pictures from their sort bags to fill in the blanks during the poems.
- Students may circle the letters of the week in each couplet.

TIPS FOR SPELLING CHECK

- Review the directions with students. They are writing the letter that represents the sound you dictate.
- Use teacher discretion when grading the Spelling Check.

PHONEMIC AWARENESS: LISTEN

1. Give the directions. Say, "I am going to say a word. Your job is to tell me how many sounds are in that word. In order to count the sounds, you need to break the word into its individual parts. For example, if I say '*bat*,' you say '/b/ /ă/ /t/—three sounds!'"

2. Say the following words:

tie (2)   lip (3)   slam (4)   sun (3)   if (2)   yet (3)   in (2)   skip (4)

THE BIG REVEAL

1. Hold up the *yes* puzzle piece and say, "This is the *yes* piece. It represents the letter *y*. The *yes* piece says '/y/ /y/ /y/' like at the beginning of the word *yes*. Give a thumbs-up with both hands and say '/y/.' We will study this letter and sound all week. Let's make a list of words that have the *yes* sound in them" (record the words).

SUPPORTED BLENDING: PUTTING SOUNDS TOGETHER TO MAKE NEW WORDS

1. Follow the Supported Blending routine on page I-16 of the Introduction.

2. Display the following words on the board one line at a time. Facilitate a discussion about the blending line focus after each line.

3. Then display the weekly sight word.

yes	yak	yarn	Discuss: initial sound of /y/
yet	yo-yo	yuck	Discuss: initial sound of /y/
happy	vest	under	Discuss: review of sounds from previous weeks

Sight Word: us

FORMATION: WRITING LETTERS

1. Have students turn to page 109 of the Learner's Notebook.

2. Model forming uppercase letter *Y* and lowercase letter *y*.

Uppercase Formation

Your pencil starts at the top line.

Form a diagonal line to the middle line, right.

Pick your pencil up.

Your pencil starts at the top line, to the right.

Form a diagonal line to the middle line, left.

Pick your pencil up.

Your pencil starts at the middle line.

Form a straight line down to the bottom line.

Pick your pencil up.

Lowercase Formation

Your pencil starts at the middle line.

Form a diagonal line to the bottom line, right.

Pick your pencil up.

Your pencil starts at the middle line, to the right.

Form a diagonal line underneath the bottom line, left.

Pick your pencil up.

3. Assist students in forming two lines of uppercase *Y*s.

4. Assist students in forming two lines of lowercase *y*s.

(Continued)

Day 1 (Continued)

PRACTICE: COMPLETE YOUR WORK ON YOUR OWN

1. Have students turn to page 107 of the Learner's Notebook.

2. Instruct students to tear out the sort and complete the following Practice Pieces: Quick Color, Careful Cut, and Sorting With Combined Picture and Word Cards (see further directions on pages I-37, I-38, and I-25 of the Introduction).

3. Instruct students that they are only using the *yes* and *sun* headers and words with the letters *y* and *u*.

4. Circulate as students work, which usually takes fifteen minutes, and coach as needed.

FLUENCY: READING LIKE YOU'RE SPEAKING

1. Have students turn to page 21 in the Fluency Notebook.

2. Have students read one or more of the following chants: "Yes," "Zoom," and "Sun."

3. Circulate and listen to students read or gather a small group of students who need additional support.

PHONEMIC AWARENESS: LISTEN

1. Give the directions. Say, "I am going to say a word. Your job is to tell me how many sounds are in that word. In order to count the sounds, you need to break the word into its individual parts. For example, if I say '*bat*,' you say '/b/ /ă/ /t/—three sounds!'"

2. Say the following words:

cat (3)   no (2)   dot (3)   gut (3)   tent (4)   jump (4)   met (3)   bee (2)

THE BIG REVEAL

1. Say, "Yesterday we learned the *yes* piece. It represents the letter *y*. The *yes* piece says '/y/ /y/ /y/' like at the beginning of the word *yes*. Let's all do the motion for the *yes* piece together."

2. Hold up the *zoom* puzzle piece and say, "This is the *zoom* piece. It represents the letter *z*. The *zoom* piece says '/z/ /z/ /z/' like at the beginning of the word *zoom*. Stretch out the fingers on your right hand and push them together so there are no gaps. Move your hand quickly from one side of your body to the other and say '/z/.' We will study this letter and sound all week. Let's make a list of words that have the *zoom* sound in them" (record the words).

SUPPORTED BLENDING: PUTTING SOUNDS TOGETHER TO MAKE NEW WORDS

1. Follow the Supported Blending routine on page I-16 of the Introduction.

2. Display the following words on the board one line at a time. Facilitate a discussion about the blending line focus after each line.

3. Then display the weekly sight word.

zoom	zip	zoo	Discuss: initial sound of /z/
zig	zag	zit	Discuss: initial sound of /z/
vet	help	vest	Discuss: review of sounds from previous weeks

Sight Word: us

FORMATION: WRITING LETTERS

1. Have students turn to page 110 of the Learner's Notebook.

2. Model forming uppercase letter *Z* and lowercase letter *z*.

Uppercase Formation	Lowercase Formation
Your pencil starts at the top line.	Your pencil starts at the middle line.
Form a straight, horizontal line across the top line.	Form a straight, horizontal line across the middle line.
Form a diagonal line down to the bottom line, left.	Form a diagonal line down to the bottom line, left.
Form a straight, horizontal line across the bottom line, right.	Form a straight, horizontal line across the bottom line, right.
Pick your pencil up.	Pick your pencil up.

3. Assist students in forming two lines of uppercase *Z*s.

4. Assist students in forming two lines of lowercase *z*s.

SORT: WHAT IS YOUR FOCUS PATTERN?

1. Have students take out their bag of pictures (created on Day 1) and follow the Sorting With Combined Picture and Word Cards routine on page I-25 of the Introduction.

2. Instruct students that they are only using the *zoom* and *sun* headers and words with the letters *z* and *u*.

(Continued)

Day 2 (Continued)

PRACTICE: COMPLETE YOUR WORK ON YOUR OWN

1. Students will follow the Grab and Write routine on page I-44 of the Introduction.

2. Circulate as students work, which usually takes fifteen minutes, and coach as needed.

FLUENCY: READING LIKE YOU'RE SPEAKING

1. Have students turn to page 21 in the Fluency Notebook.

2. Have students read one or more of the following chants: "Yes," "Zoom," and "Sun."

3. Circulate and listen to students read or gather a small group of students who need additional support.

PHONEMIC AWARENESS: LISTEN

1. Give the directions. Say, "I am going to say a word. Your job is to tell me how many sounds are in that word. In order to count the sounds, you need to break the word into its individual parts. For example, if I say '*bat*,' you say '/b/ /ă/ /t/—three sounds!'"

2. Say the following words:

cub (3)   clot (4)   my (2)   a (1)   leg (3)   eat (2)   egg (2)   night (3)

PUZZLE PIECE REVIEW

1. Say, "When I point to the piece, you tell me its name" (*yes, zoom, sun*).

2. Say, "When I point to the piece, you tell me its sound" (/y/, /z/, /ŭ/).

3. Say, "When I point to the piece, you tell me its spelling" (*y, z, u*).

4. Say, "Write the spellings in the air with your finger" (students will form the letters *y*, *z*, and *u*).

SUPPORTED BLENDING: PUTTING SOUNDS TOGETHER TO MAKE NEW WORDS

1. Follow the Supported Blending routine on page I-16 of the Introduction.

2. Display the following words on the board one line at a time. Facilitate a discussion about the blending line focus after each line.

3. Then display the weekly sight word.

Zack	hack	back	Discuss: word family –*ack* and the sound of /ăck/; capital *Z* in the name *Zack*
yet	vet	set	Discuss: word family –*et* and the sound of /ĕt/
zip	zipper	zippers	Discuss: initial sound of /z/; root word *zip*

Sight Word: us

DICTATION: STRETCH OUT YOUR WORDS

1. Have students turn to page 111 of the Learner's Notebook.

2. Follow the Dictation routine on page I-21 of the Introduction to dictate the following words:

1. yarn   2. umpire   3. zipper   4. zoo   5. young

Sight Word: us

3. Hold students accountable for recording the initial sound in each word in their Learner's Notebook.

SORT: WHAT IS YOUR FOCUS PATTERN?

1. Have students take out their bag of pictures (created on Day 1) and follow the Sorting With Combined Picture and Word Cards routine on page I-25 of the Introduction.

PRACTICE: COMPLETE YOUR WORK ON YOUR OWN

1. Have students turn to page 112 in the Learner's Notebook.

2. Students will complete the Letter Matrix routine found on page I-45 of the Introduction.

3. Circulate as students work, which usually takes fifteen minutes, and coach as needed.

FLUENCY: READING LIKE YOU'RE SPEAKING

1. Have students turn to page 21 in the Fluency Notebook.

2. Have students read one or more of the following chants: "Yes," "Zoom," and "Sun."

3. Circulate and listen to students read or gather a small group of students who need additional support.

Day 4

PHONEMIC AWARENESS: LISTEN

1. Give the directions. Say, "I am going to say a word. Your job is to tell me how many sounds are in that word. In order to count the sounds, you need to break the word into its individual parts. For example, if I say '*bat*,' you say '/b/ /ă/ /t/—three sounds!'"

2. Say the following words:

dull (3)   to (2)   melt (4)   jazz (3)   hay (2)   fed (3)   sneak (4)   bit (3)

PUZZLE PIECE REVIEW

1. Say, "When I point to the piece, you tell me its name" (*yes, zoom, sun*).

2. Say, "When I point to the piece, you tell me its sound" (/y/, /z/, /ŭ/).

3. Say, "When I point to the piece, you tell me its spelling" (*y, z, u*).

4. Say, "Write the spellings in the air with your finger" (students will form the letters *y*, *z*, and *u*).

SUPPORTED BLENDING: PUTTING SOUNDS TOGETHER TO MAKE NEW WORDS

1. Follow the Supported Blending routine on page I-16 of the Introduction.

2. Display the following words on the board one line at a time. Facilitate a discussion about the blending line focus after each line.

3. Then display the weekly sight word.

zero	young	underneath	Discuss: initial sounds of /z/, /y/, and /ŭ/
umbrella	zoo	yak	Discuss: initial sounds of /ŭ/, /z/, and /y/
happy	Uncle Henry	vote	Discuss: initial sounds of /h/, /ŭ/, and /v/; capital *U* and *H* for the name *Uncle Henry*

Sight Word: us

DICTATION: STRETCH OUT YOUR WORDS

1. Have students turn to page 113 of the Learner's Notebook.

2. Follow the Dictation routine on page I-21 of the Introduction to dictate the following words:

I. zip   2. yet   3. hug   4. vet   5. Zack

Sight Word: us

3. Hold students accountable for recording the initial sound in each word in their Learner's Notebook.

SORT: WHAT IS YOUR FOCUS PATTERN?

1. Have students take out their bag of pictures and words (created on Day 1) and follow the Sorting With Combined Picture and Word Cards routine on page I-25 of the Introduction.

PRACTICE: COMPLETE YOUR WORK ON YOUR OWN

1. Have students complete the following Practice Pieces: Glue Words (on page I-41 of the Introduction) and Fluency Drill (on page I-46 of the Introduction).

2. Circulate as students work, which usually takes fifteen minutes, and coach as needed.

FLUENCY: READING LIKE YOU'RE SPEAKING

1. Have students turn to page 21 in the Fluency Notebook.

2. Have students read one or more of the following chants: "Yes," "Zoom," and "Sun."

3. Circulate and listen to students read or gather a small group of students who need additional support.

PHONEMIC AWARENESS: LISTEN

1. Give the directions. Say, "I am going to say a word. Your job is to tell me how many sounds are in that word. In order to count the sounds, you need to break the word into its individual parts. For example, if I say '*bat*,' you say '/b/ /ă/ /t/—three sounds!'"

2. Say the following words:

run (3)   it (2)   less (3)   plug (4)   slid (4)   mutt (3)   ace (2)   knit (3)

REVIEW PATTERNS OF THE WEEK

1. Say, "Find a partner."

2. Say, "Tell your partner the names of this week's pieces" (*yes, zoom, sun*).

3. Say, "Tell your partner the sounds of this week's pieces" (/y/, /z/, /ŭ/).

4. Say, "Tell your partner the spellings of this week's pieces" (*y, z, u*).

5. Say, "Write the spellings on your partner's back with your finger" (students will form the letters *y, z,* and *u*).

SPELLING CHECK

1. Follow the Spelling Check routine on page I-34 of the Introduction.

2. Have students turn to page 115 of the Learner's Notebook.

3. Say, "Write the letter that represents the sound you hear."

4. Dictate the following sounds (repeat the sound if needed):

1. /z/
2. /ŭ/
3. /y/
4. /h/
5. /v/

Sight Word: us

LABELING THE ROOM

1. Label the classroom with things found from this week's sort.

HANDWRITING CHECK

1. Have students turn to page 116 in the Learner's Notebook.

2. Model and have students form the following letters:

1. Three uppercase *Y*s
2. Three lowercase *y*s
3. Three uppercase *Z*s
4. Three lowercase *z*s
5. Three uppercase *U*s
6. Three lowercase *u*s

WEEKLY CELEBRATION

1. Display the celebratory message: "Yes! You zoomed through and learned the *yes, zoom,* and *sun* puzzle pieces!"

2. Encourage students to work together to read the message.

3. Have students copy the message onto their weekly certificate (see resources .corwin.com/puzzlepiecephonics-gradeK) and place it somewhere to take home.

Concept 3 Overview:

Short Vowels

istock.com/alvarez

WHAT ARE SHORT VOWELS?

Short vowels are vowels that do not say their name. They are found in closed syllables, or syllables in which a short vowel is followed by a consonant.

GOALS FOR THE CONCEPT

Students will
- Identify and represent short vowels
- Identify and represent consonant sounds
- Read and write sight words
- Recognize that words are made of letters
- Build word study routines
- Develop reading fluency and comprehension

WEEKS FOR THIS CONCEPT

Week 1: Short Vowels (*a, e*)
Week 2: Short Vowels (*e, o*)
Week 3: Short Vowels (*o, i*)
Week 4: Short Vowels (*i, u*)
Week 5: Short Vowels (*u, a*)

Resources

PUZZLE PIECES

WEEK I	
a	**e**

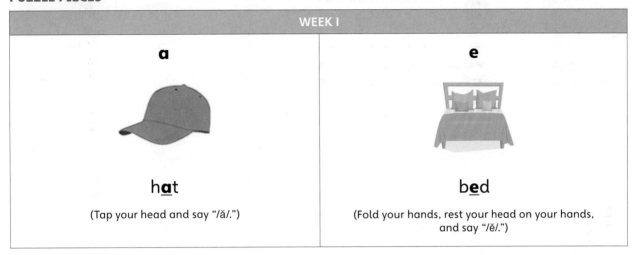

h<u>a</u>t	b<u>e</u>d
(Tap your head and say "/ă/.")	(Fold your hands, rest your head on your hands, and say "/ĕ/.")

Hat: istock.com/stevezmina1; Bed: istock.com/vasilyevalara

Preparing for Your Week

CORRESPONDING *LEARNER'S NOTEBOOK PAGES*

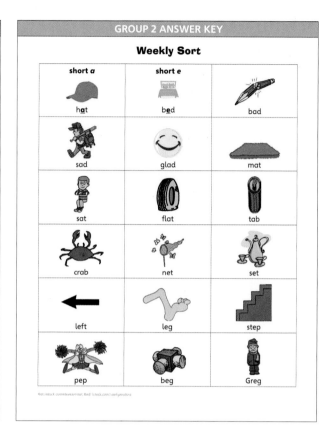

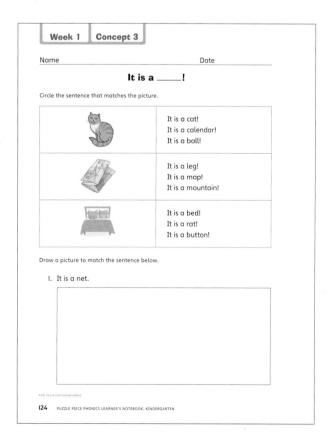

Preparing for Your Week

CORRESPONDING *FLUENCY NOTEBOOK PAGES*

Short *a*

Cat and Mat

That is a mat.
That is a cat.
The cat is on the mat.
The mat is on the cat.

Pam's Cat

Pam has a cat.
The cat naps on the mat.
The cat wakes up. He wants a snack.
Pam gives the cat a rat.
The cat is happy.
The cat gets back on his mat
to take a nap.

Cat: istock.com/luplupme

Short *e*

Bed and Sled

We get out of bed.
We get sleds.
We sled and sled.
Then, we get back
in bed.

Fred and Ted Sled

Fred and Ted get out their sleds!
They go up the path to the end.
Fred sits on his sled.
Ted sits on his sled.
The friends sled down the hill.
Then, they get up and go back
up the path.

Preparing for Your Week

Tips for Management and Differentiation

Refer to this section and to resources.corwin.com/puzzlepiecephonics-gradeK for resources and ideas to deepen your students' learning throughout the week. Feel free to put your own spin on the routines, too. For daily lesson plans, see pages 148–155 of this Teacher's Guide.

TIPS FOR PHONEMIC AWARENESS	• The focus for this week is changing the initial sound of the word read orally by the teacher. • If you notice your students need additional practice, extend the activity with more words. • Model with students how to change the initial sound of the word in their head. Walk them through the activity: "First, think of the word *cat*. Then, take the initial sound off (remove /k/), and you have the sound –*at*. Next, add the new initial sound /b/ to make the word *bat*."
TIPS FOR THE PUZZLE PIECE REVIEW	• Have students work with the same partner each day to build a word study relationship. • After you record the words from the Big Reveal on Day 1, leave up the word lists of short *a* and short *e*. Students can refer to these words throughout the week. • Remind students of why vowels are so important. Every word must have a vowel.
TIPS FOR BLENDING	• This is the first time your kindergarteners will be exposed to the Blending routine. Reblend lines if necessary—especially words with blends. • Use the Supported Blending routine for the sentence if your class needs additional support. • Hold students accountable for looking at the medial letter and producing the correct short vowel sound. Do not have students guess the sounds.
TIPS FOR DICTATION AND QUICK SWITCH	• This is the first time students will compete the Quick Switch routine. Model and complete the routine as a class until students are confident on their own. • If students are struggling to write the entire word during Dictation or Quick Switch, only hold them accountable for the medial (short vowel) sound.

TIPS FOR SORTING	• Model and positively reinforce the sorting routine repeatedly throughout the week. Students should see that you will consistently enforce the sorting routine this year!
	• Discuss the vocabulary words that appear in the sort. Vocabulary words include the following:
	  • Sort 1: *tab, gab, set, bet, beg, peg, pep, rep*
	  • Sort 2: *glad, flat, tab, set, left, beg, pep*

TIPS FOR THE PRACTICE PIECES	• This is the first week that students are sorting the entire sort on Day 1, and they are also being introduced to the Sorting With Separate Picture and Word Cards routine. If sorting takes an extended amount of time, that's okay; omit a Practice Piece. • Have students create a "Commonly Used Short Vowel Book." They can keep this book in their desk and write words with short vowels on each page. Their leveled books will have many common words that students will keep seeing. If they are having trouble with words, have them write the words in their "Commonly Used Short Vowel Book."

Preparing for Your Week

TIPS FOR FLUENCY

- This week students will read short story passages written to build reading stamina and fluency. There are two passages for each sorting group. One passage focuses on short *a*, and the other passage focuses on short *e*.
- Students can highlight words that contain short *a* or short *e* in the short stories.
- You can assign students fluency partners. Students will work together to achieve fluency with the short stories.
- Students can draw a picture that corresponds to the stories.
- Students may extend their stories after building their fluency.

TIPS FOR SPELLING CHECK

- From this week forward, students will be asked to record full words on the Spelling Check.
- Modify the routine as necessary for your class and, as always, use teacher discretion when grading.

THE PUZZLE PIECE FAMILY

Launch Concept 3: Short Vowels by following the Puzzle Piece Family routine found on page I-11 of the Introduction.

1. Show students the following words:

cat	mop
sip	crib
nut	fast
sad	log
yes	beg

2. Have students read the words with you.

3. Facilitate a discussion that leads them to discover the Puzzle Piece Family: Short Vowels.

PHONEMIC AWARENESS: LISTEN

1. Give the directions. Say, "I am going to say a word. Then, I am going to tell you to change the initial sound of that word to a different sound. Your job is to change the initial sound of the word in your brain, then say the new word. For example, if I say '*cat*, change the initial sound to /b/,' you say '*bat*.'"

2. Say the following words and sounds:

cat, /r/ (rat)   sad, /m/ (mad)   bag, /l/ (lag)   lap, /t/ (tap)   hat, /s/ (sat)

THE BIG REVEAL

1. Say, "This week we are going to start our short vowel word study. Let's say all of our short vowel sounds: '/ă/ /ĕ/ /ĭ/ /ŏ/ /ŭ/.' Great! This week we are going to take a closer look at two of our short vowels: short *a* and short *e*."

2. Hold up the *hat* puzzle piece and say, "This is the *hat* piece. It represents the letter *a*. The *hat* piece says '/ă/ /ă/ /ă/' like in the middle of the word *hat*. Tap your head and say '/ă/.' We will study this letter and sound all week. Let's make a list of words that have the *hat* sound in them" (record the words).

3. Hold up the *bed* puzzle piece and say, "This is the *bed* piece. It represents the letter *e*. The *bed* piece says '/ĕ/ /ĕ/ /ĕ/' like in the middle of the word *bed*. Fold your hands, rest your head on your hands, and say '/ĕ/.' We will study this letter and sound all week. Let's make a list of words that have the *bed* sound in them" (record the words).

BLENDING: PUTTING SOUNDS TOGETHER TO MAKE NEW WORDS

1. Follow the Blending routine on page I-17 of the Introduction.

2. Display the following words on the board one line at a time. Facilitate a discussion about the blending line focus after each line.

3. Then display the weekly sight words and sentence.

4. Discuss the examples of short vowels in the sentence.

hat	mat	sat	Discuss: medial sound of /ă/; final sound of /t/
bed	red	Ted	Discuss: medial sound of /ĕ/; final sound of /d/
bag	beg	peg	Discuss: medial sound of /ă/ or /ĕ/; final sound of /g/

Sight Words: can   is

Sentence: The hat is red.

DICTATION: STRETCH OUT YOUR WORDS

1. Have students turn to page 121 of the Learner's Notebook.

2. Follow the Dictation routine on page I-21 of the Introduction to dictate the following words.

    I. bag   2. red   3. mat

    Sight Word: is

3. If a student is struggling to write the full words, you can write the initial and final sounds and ask the student to record the vowel sound. Use Dictation as an informal pretest of students' knowledge of /ă/ and /ĕ/. Help students write the sight word and remind them this is a word they need to spell in a snap!

PRACTICE: COMPLETE YOUR WORK ON YOUR OWN

1. Have students turn to page 117 (Group 1) or 119 (Group 2) of the Learner's Notebook.

2. Instruct students to tear out the sort and complete the following Practice Pieces: Quick Color, Careful Cut, and Sorting With Separate Picture and Word Cards (see further directions on pages I-37, I-38, and I-26 of the Introduction).

3. Circulate as students work, which usually takes fifteen minutes, and coach as needed.

FLUENCY: READING LIKE YOU'RE SPEAKING

1. Have students turn to page 23 in the Fluency Notebook.

2. Have students read one or more of the following passages: "Cat and Mat," "Pam's Cat," "Bed and Sled," and "Fred and Ted Sled."

3. Circulate and listen to students read or gather a small group of students who need additional support.

Day 2

PHONEMIC AWARENESS: LISTEN

1. Give the directions. Say, "I am going to say a word. Then, I am going to tell you to change the initial sound of that word to a different sound. Your job is to change the initial sound of the word in your brain, then say the new word. For example, if I say '*cat*, change the initial sound to /b/,' you say '*bat*.'"

2. Say the following words and sounds:

led, /m/ (med)   pen, /k/ (Ken)   red, /s/ (said)   yes, /t/ (Tess)   pet, /l/ (let)

PUZZLE PIECE REVIEW

1. Say, "When I point to the piece, you tell me its name" (*hat, bed*).

2. Say, "When I point to the piece, you tell me its sound" (/ă/, /ĕ/).

3. Say, "When I point to the piece, you tell me its spelling" (*a, e*).

4. Say, "Write the spellings in the air with your finger" (students will form the letters *a* and *e*).

BLENDING: PUTTING SOUNDS TOGETHER TO MAKE NEW WORDS

1. Follow the Blending routine on page I-17 of the Introduction.

2. Display the following words on the board one line at a time. Facilitate a discussion about the blending line focus after each line.

3. Then display the weekly sight words and sentence.

4. Discuss the examples of short vowels in the sentence.

gab	tab	tap	Discuss: medial sound of /ă/
rep	pep	step	Discuss: medial sound of /ĕ/; final sound of /p/
rat	sat	flat	Discuss: medial sound of /ă/; final sound of /t/

Sight Words: can   is

Sentence: I can tap.

QUICK SWITCH: MANIPULATE YOUR WORDS

1. Have students turn to page 121 of the Learner's Notebook.

2. Follow the Quick Switch routine on page I-23 of the Introduction to dictate the following words:

bad → bed → bet → bat → rat

3. Support students as they learn this new routine. If a student is struggling to write the full words, you can write the initial and final sounds and ask the student to record the vowel sound.

SORT: WHAT IS YOUR FOCUS PATTERN?

1. Have students take out their bag of pictures and words (created on Day 1) and follow the Sorting With Separate Picture and Word Cards routine on page I-26 of the Introduction.

PRACTICE: COMPLETE YOUR WORK ON YOUR OWN

1. Students will follow the Read and Trade routine on page I-47 of the Introduction.

2. Circulate as students work, which usually takes fifteen minutes, and coach as needed.

FLUENCY: READING LIKE YOU'RE SPEAKING

1. Have students turn to page 23 in the Fluency Notebook.

2. Have students read one or more of the following passages: "Cat and Mat," "Pam's Cat," "Bed and Sled," and "Fred and Ted Sled."

3. Circulate and listen to students read or gather a small group of students who need additional support.

PHONEMIC AWARENESS: LISTEN	**1.** Give the directions. Say, "I am going to say a word. Then, I am going to tell you to change the initial sound of that word to a different sound. Your job is to change the initial sound of the word in your brain, then say the new word. For example, if I say '*cat*, change the initial sound to /b/,' you say '*bat*.'"
	2. Say the following words and sounds:

lad, /f/ (fad)   send, /b/ (bend)   rest, /p/ (pest)

tap, /g/ (gap)   dent, /l/ (lent)

PUZZLE PIECE REVIEW	**1.** Say, "When I point to the piece, you tell me its name" (*hat, bed*).
	2. Say, "When I point to the piece, you tell me its sound" (/ă/, /ĕ/).
	3. Say, "When I point to the piece, you tell me its spelling" (*a, e*).
	4. Say, "Write the spellings in the air with your finger" (students will form the letters *a* and *e*).

BLENDING: PUTTING SOUNDS TOGETHER TO MAKE NEW WORDS	**1.** Follow the Blending routine on page I-17 of the Introduction.
	2. Display the following words on the board one line at a time. Facilitate a discussion about the blending line focus after each line.
	3. Then display the weekly sight words and sentence.
	4. Discuss the examples of short vowels in the sentence.

bad	**sad**	**glad**	Discuss: medial sound of /ă/; final sound of /d/
net	**set**	**left**	Discuss: medial sound of /ĕ/; final sound of /t/
step	**sled**	**crab**	Discuss: medial sound of /ă/ or /ĕ/

Sight Words: can   is

Sentence: The cat is bad.

DICTATION: STRETCH OUT YOUR WORDS	**1.** Have students turn to page 122 of the Learner's Notebook.
	2. Follow the Dictation routine on page I-21 of the Introduction to dictate the following words:
	I. left 2. bad 3. set
	Sight Word: can
	3. Tell students to focus and record the medial sound they hear if they cannot encode the entire word during Dictation time.

SORT: WHAT IS YOUR FOCUS PATTERN?	**1.** Have students take out their bag of pictures and words (created on Day 1) and follow the Sorting With Separate Picture and Word Cards routine on page I-26 of the Introduction.

(Continued)

Day 3 (Continued)

PRACTICE: COMPLETE YOUR WORK ON YOUR OWN	**1.** Students will follow the Act It Out routine on page I-48 of the Introduction. **2.** Circulate as students work, which usually takes fifteen minutes, and coach as needed.
FLUENCY: READING LIKE YOU'RE SPEAKING	**1.** Have students turn to page 23 in the Fluency Notebook. **2.** Have students read one or more of the following passages: "Cat and Mat," "Pam's Cat," "Bed and Sled," and "Fred and Ted Sled." **3.** Circulate and listen to students read or gather a small group of students who need additional support.

PHONEMIC AWARENESS: LISTEN

1. Give the directions. Say, "I am going to say a word. Then, I am going to tell you to change the initial sound of that word to a different sound. Your job is to change the initial sound of the word in your brain, then say the new word. For example, if I say '*cat*, change the initial sound to /b/,' you say '*bat*.'"

2. Say the following words and sounds:

rent, /m/ (meant)   Sam, /r/ (ram)   yak, /t/ (tack)

Ned, /m/ (med)   pass, /m/ (mass)

PUZZLE PIECE REVIEW

1. Say, "When I point to the piece, you tell me its name" (*hat, bed*).

2. Say, "When I point to the piece, you tell me its sound" (/ă/, /ĕ/).

3. Say, "When I point to the piece, you tell me its spelling" (*a, e*).

4. Say, "Write the spellings in the air with your finger" (students will form the letters *a* and *e*).

BLENDING: PUTTING SOUNDS TOGETHER TO MAKE NEW WORDS

1. Follow the Blending routine on page I-17 of the Introduction.

2. Display the following words on the board one line at a time. Facilitate a discussion about the blending line focus after each line.

3. Then display the weekly sight words and sentence.

4. Discuss the examples of short vowels in the sentence.

met	mat	flat	Discuss: medial sound of /ă/ or /ĕ/; final sound of /t/
lad	glad	sled	Discuss: medial sound of /ă/ or /ĕ/; final sound of /d/
Greg	beg	bag	Discuss: medial sound of /ă/ or /ĕ/; final sound of /g/; capital G in the name *Greg*

Sight Words: can   is

Sentence: The sled is flat.

QUICK SWITCH: MANIPULATE YOUR WORDS

1. Have students turn to page 122 of the Learner's Notebook.

2. Follow the Quick Switch routine on page I-23 of the Introduction to dictate the following words:

leg → lag → rag → red → rad

3. Support students as they learn this new routine. Help students get from *rag* to *red* by identifying that both the medial and final sounds change. If a student is struggling to write the full words, you can write the initial and final sounds and ask the student to record the vowel sound.

SORT: WHAT IS YOUR FOCUS PATTERN?

1. Have students take out their bag of pictures and words (created on Day 1) and follow the Sorting With Separate Picture and Word Cards routine on page I-26 of the Introduction.

(Continued)

Day 4 (Continued)

PRACTICE: COMPLETE YOUR WORK ON YOUR OWN	**1.** Have students complete the following Practice Piece: Glue Words (on page I-41 of the Introduction). **2.** Circulate as students work, which usually takes fifteen minutes, and coach as needed.
FLUENCY: READING LIKE YOU'RE SPEAKING	**1.** Have students turn to page 23 in the Fluency Notebook. **2.** Have students read one or more of the following passages: "Cat and Mat," "Pam's Cat," "Bed and Sled," and "Fred and Ted Sled." **3.** Circulate and listen to students read or gather a small group of students who need additional support.

PHONEMIC AWARENESS: LISTEN

1. Give the directions. Say, "I am going to say a word. Then, I am going to tell you to change the initial sound of that word to a different sound. Your job is to change the initial sound of the word in your brain, then say the new word. For example, if I say, 'cat, change the initial sound to /b/,' you say 'bat.'"

2. Say the following words and sounds:

man, /t/ (tan)   hand, /s/ (sand)   pet, /n/ (net)
bed, /r/ (red)   hat, /p/ (pat)

REVIEW PATTERNS OF THE WEEK

1. Say, "Find a partner."

2. Say, "Tell your partner the names of this week's pieces" (*hat, bed*).

3. Say, "Tell your partner the sounds of this week's pieces" (/ă/, /ĕ/).

4. Say, "Tell your partner the spellings of this week's pieces" (*a, e*).

5. Say, "Write the spellings on your partner's back with your finger" (students will form the letters *a* and *e*).

SPELLING CHECK

1. Follow the Spelling Check routine on page I-34 of the Introduction.

2. Instruct students to sit in their word study groups and turn to page 123 of the Learner's Notebook.

3. Say, "I am going to say one word at a time to each group. Record the words as I say them to your group. Make sure you only record the words from your group."

4. Move back and forth between the groups and dictate the following words:

Words for Group I	Words for Group 2
I. bad	I. flat
2. sat	2. step
3. beg	3. sad
4. tab	4. crab
5. rep	5. left
Sentence: The rat is bad.	**Sentence: Step on the mat.**

WORD HUNT

1. Students will follow the Word Hunt routine on page I-55 of the Introduction.

2. Instruct students to search texts and the classroom for words with short *a* and short *e*.

COMPREHENSION CHECK

1. Have students turn to page 124 of the Learner's Notebook.

2. Students will follow the Comprehension Check routine on page I-36 of the Introduction.

3. Check students' work. Circled answers are as follows:

1. It is a cat!
2. It is a map!
3. It is a bed!

4. Students should have a picture of a net in the drawing box.

WEEKLY CELEBRATION

1. Display the celebratory message: "Not bad at all! You learned the *hat* and *bed* puzzle pieces!"

2. Encourage students to work together to read the message.

3. Have students copy the message onto their weekly certificate (see resources .corwin.com/puzzlepiecephonics-gradeK) and place it somewhere to take home.

Preparing for Your Week

Resources

PUZZLE PIECES

WEEK 2

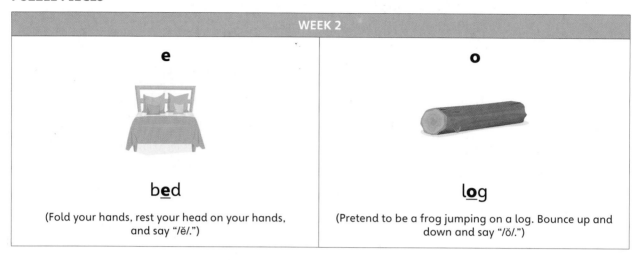

e	**o**
b**e**d	l**o**g
(Fold your hands, rest your head on your hands, and say "/ĕ/.")	(Pretend to be a frog jumping on a log. Bounce up and down and say "/ŏ/.")

Bed: istock.com/vasilyevalara; Log: istock.com/bennyb

Preparing for Your Week

CORRESPONDING *LEARNER'S NOTEBOOK PAGES*

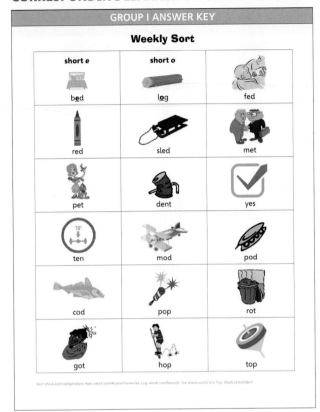

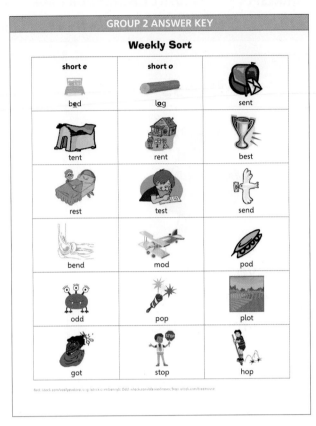

| Week 2 | Concept 3 |

Name _____ Date _____

I see the _____.

Circle the sentence that matches the picture.

(tent)	I see the turtle. I see the tent. I see the top.
(frog)	I see the frog. I see the fig. I see the fire station.
(stop sign)	I see the stop sign. I see the test. I see the soap.

Draw a picture to match the sentence below.

I. I see the sled.

Preparing for Your Week

CORRESPONDING _FLUENCY NOTEBOOK PAGES_

Short e

Dress

I have a dress.
The dress is red.
I like my new red dress.

My Present

Yes! Dad got me a present.
I got a new dress.
The dress is long and red.
The dress makes me feel happy.
When I wear the dress,
I feel my best!

Present: istock.com/TopVectors

Short o

Fox and Box

I see a fox.
I see a box.
I see a fox in a box.
The box has a fox in it.

The Fox's Walk

The fox went for a walk.
On the walk he saw a box.
The fox got into the box.
No one can see the fox.
The fox hid in the box!

Preparing for Your Week

Tips for Management and Differentiation

Refer to this section and to resources.corwin.com/puzzlepiecephonics-gradeK for resources and ideas to deepen your students' learning throughout the week. Feel free to put your own spin on the routines, too. For daily lesson plans, see pages 161–168 of this Teacher's Guide.

TIPS FOR PHONEMIC AWARENESS	• The focus for this week is changing the final sound of the word read orally by the teacher. If you notice your students need additional practice, extend the activity with more words. • Model with students how to change the final sound of the word in their head. Walk them through the activity: "First, think of the word *cat*. Then, take the final sound /t/ off *ca*. Next, add the new final sound /b/ to make the word *cab*." • The Phonemic Awareness activity may take a bit longer this week. Students are very familiar with changing initial sounds, but they may need more time to manipulate words in their head to change final sounds.
TIPS FOR THE PUZZLE PIECE REVIEW	• Have students work with the same partner each day to build a word study relationship. • After you record the words from the Big Reveal on Day 1, leave up the word list for short *o*. Remind students of your word list for short *e* that was created last week. • Remind students of why vowels are so important. Every word must have a vowel.
TIPS FOR BLENDING	• Reblend lines if necessary. • Use the Supported Blending routine for the sentence if your class needs help in reading the sentence. • Hold students accountable for looking at the medial letter and producing the correct short vowel sound. Do not have students guess the sounds.
TIPS FOR DICTATION AND QUICK SWITCH	• Students who are struggling with Quick Switch can have the teacher write the initial and final sounds on each line. When they hear the word, they will only need to focus on the medial sound.

TIPS FOR SORTING	• Model and positively reinforce the sorting routine repeatedly throughout the week. Students should see that you will consistently enforce the sorting routine this year!
	• Discuss the vocabulary words that appear in the sort. Vocabulary words include the following:
	   • Sort 1: *met, dent, mod, pod, cod, rot*
	   • Sort 2: *tent, rent, bend, mod, pod, odd, plot*

(Continued)

Preparing for Your Week

TIPS FOR THE PRACTICE PIECES

- This is the first concept in which students are sorting the entire sort on Day 1. They are also being introduced to the Sorting With Separate Picture and Word Cards routine. If sorting takes an extended amount of time, then you can omit a Practice Piece.
- Have students create a "Commonly Used Short Vowel Book." They can keep this book in their desk and write words with short vowels on each page. Their leveled books will have many common words that students will keep seeing. If they are having trouble with words, have them write the words in their "Commonly Used Short Vowel Book."

TIPS FOR FLUENCY

- Students can highlight words that contain short *e* or short *o* in the short stories.
- You can assign students fluency partners. Students will work together to achieve fluency with the short stories.
- Students can draw a picture that corresponds to the stories.
- Students may extend their stories after building their fluency.

Day 1

PHONEMIC AWARENESS: LISTEN

1. Give the directions. Say, "I am going to say a word. Then, I am going to tell you to change the final sound of that word to a different sound. Your job is to change the final sound of the word in your brain, then say the new word. For example, If I say 'cat, change the final sound to /b/,' you say 'cab.'"

2. Say the following words and sounds:

cat, /p/ (cap)   sad, /m/ (Sam)   bag, /d/ (bad)
lap, /b/ (lab)   hat, /v/ (have)

THE BIG REVEAL

1. Say, "This week we are going to continue our short vowel word study. Let's say all of our short vowel sounds: '/ă/ /ĕ/ /ĭ/ /ŏ/ /ŭ/.' Great! This week we are going to continue to study short vowel *e*. We will also take a closer look at another short vowel: *o*."

2. Hold up the *bed* puzzle piece and say, "You remember the *bed* piece. It represents the letter *e*. The *bed* piece says '/ĕ/ /ĕ/ /ĕ/' like in the middle of the word *bed*. Fold your hands, rest your head on your hands, and say '/ĕ/.' We will continue to study this letter and sound all week."

3. Hold up the *log* puzzle piece and say, "This is the *log* piece. It represents the letter *o*. The *log* piece says '/ŏ/ /ŏ/ /ŏ/' like in the middle of the word *log*. Pretend to be a frog on a log, bounce up and down, and say '/ŏ/.' We will study this letter and sound all week. Let's make a list of words that have the *log* sound in them" (record the words).

BLENDING: PUTTING SOUNDS TOGETHER TO MAKE NEW WORDS

1. Follow the Blending routine on page I-17 of the Introduction.

2. Display the following words on the board one line at a time. Facilitate a discussion about the blending line focus after each line.

3. Then display the weekly sight words and sentence.

4. Discuss the examples of short vowels in the sentence.

log	fog	dog	Discuss: medial sound of /ŏ/; final sound of /g/
bed	bend	friend	Discuss: medial sound of /ĕ/; discuss *friend* as a sight word students need to memorize
mod	pod	cod	Discuss: medial sound of /ŏ/; final sound of /d/

Sight Words: see   in

Sentence: I can see the bed.

DICTATION: STRETCH OUT YOUR WORDS

1. Have students turn to page 129 of the Learner's Notebook.

2. Follow the Dictation routine on page I-21 of the Introduction to dictate the following words:

l. pop   2. dent   3. got

Sight Word: in

3. Use Dictation as an informal pretest of students' knowledge of /ĕ/ and /ŏ/. Help students write the sight word and remind them this is a word they need to spell in a snap!

(Continued)

Day 1 (Continued)

PRACTICE: **COMPLETE** **YOUR WORK ON** **YOUR OWN**	**1.** Have students turn to page 125 (Group 1) or 127 (Group 2) of the Learner's Notebook. **2.** Instruct students to tear out the sort and complete the following Practice Pieces: Quick Color, Careful Cut, and Sorting With Separate Picture and Word Cards (see further directions on pages I-37, I-38, and I-26 of the Introduction). **3.** Circulate as students work, which usually takes fifteen minutes, and coach as needed.
FLUENCY: **READING LIKE** **YOU'RE SPEAKING**	**1.** Have students turn to page 24 in the Fluency Notebook. **2.** Have students read one or more of the following passages: "Dress," "My Present," "Fox and Box," and "The Fox's Walk." **3.** Circulate and listen to students read or gather a small group of students who need additional support.

Day 2

PHONEMIC AWARENESS: LISTEN

1. Give the directions. Say, "I am going to say a word. Then, I am going to tell you to change the final sound of that word to a different sound. Your job is to change the final sound of the word in your brain, then say the new word. For example, If I say 'cat, change the final sound to /b/,' you say 'cab.'"

2. Say the following words and sounds:

mop, /m/ (mom)   pod, /t/ (pot)   ten, /s/ (Tess)   rod, /n/ (Ron)   bet, /d/ (bed)

PUZZLE PIECE REVIEW

1. Say, When I point to the piece, you tell me its name" (*bed, log*).

2. Say, "When I point to the piece, you tell me its sound" (/ĕ/, /ŏ/).

3. Say, "When I point to the piece, you tell me its spelling" (*e, o*).

4. Say, "Write the spellings in the air with your finger" (students will form the letters *e* and *o*).

BLENDING: PUTTING SOUNDS TOGETHER TO MAKE NEW WORDS

1. Follow the Blending routine on page I-17 of the Introduction.

2. Display the following words on the board one line at a time. Facilitate a discussion about the blending line focus after each line.

3. Then display the weekly sight words and sentence.

4. Discuss the examples of short vowels in the sentence.

rest	best	test	Discuss: medial sound of /ĕ/; –*est* family
rot	got	plot	Discuss: medial sound of /ŏ/; –*ot* family
set	sent	tent	Discuss: medial sound of /ĕ/; help students use *set* to blend *sent* and *tent*

Sight Words: see   in

Sentence: The dog is in the tent.

QUICK SWITCH: MANIPULATE YOUR WORDS

1. Have students turn to page 129 of the Learner's Notebook.

2. Follow the Quick Switch routine on page I-23 of the Introduction to dictate the following words:

red → led → sled → let → best

3. Support students as they learn this new routine. Help students get from *let* to *best* by noticing that the initial and final sounds have changed. Help students stretch out the final consonant blend as a class. If a student is struggling to write the full words, you can write the initial and final sounds and ask the student to record the vowel sound.

SORT: WHAT IS YOUR FOCUS PATTERN?

1. Have students take out their bag of pictures and words (created on Day 1) and follow the Sorting With Separate Picture and Word Cards routine on page I-26 of the Introduction.

(Continued)

Day 2 (Continued)

PRACTICE: COMPLETE YOUR WORK ON YOUR OWN	**1.** Students will follow the Read and Trade routine on page I-47 of the Introduction.
	2. Circulate as students work, which usually takes fifteen minutes, and coach as needed.
FLUENCY: READING LIKE YOU'RE SPEAKING	**1.** Have students turn to page 24 in the Fluency Notebook.
	2. Have students read one or more of the following passages: "Dress," "My Present," "Fox and Box," and "The Fox's Walk."
	3. Circulate and listen to students read or gather a small group of students who need additional support.

PHONEMIC AWARENESS: LISTEN

1. Give the directions. Say, "I am going to say a word. Then, I am going to tell you to change the final sound of that word to a different sound. Your job is to change the final sound of the word in your brain, then say the new word. For example, If I say 'cat, change the final sound to /b/,' you say 'cab.'"

2. Say the following words and sounds:

moss, /p/ (mop)   tell, /d/ (Ted)   red, /p/ (rep)

top, /t/ (tot)   deck, /t/ (debt)

PUZZLE PIECE REVIEW

1. Say, "When I point to the piece, you tell me its name" (*bed, log*).

2. Say, "When I point to the piece, you tell me its sound" (/ĕ/, /ŏ/).

3. Say, "When I point to the piece, you tell me its spelling" (*e, o*).

4. Say, "Write the spellings in the air with your finger" (students will form the letters *e* and *o*).

BLENDING: PUTTING SOUNDS TOGETHER TO MAKE NEW WORDS

1. Follow the Blending routine on page I-17 of the Introduction.

2. Display the following words on the board one line at a time. Facilitate a discussion about the blending line focus after each line.

3. Then display the weekly sight words and sentence.

4. Discuss the examples of short vowels in the sentence.

pod	mod	odd	Discuss: medial sound of /ŏ/; –*od* family
bet	best	pest	Discuss: medial sound of /ĕ/; help students use *bet* to blend *best* and *pest*
hop	bop	stop	Discuss: medial sound of /ŏ/; –*op* family

Sight Words: see   in

Sentence: I hop on the bed.

DICTATION: STRETCH OUT YOUR WORDS

1. Have students turn to page 130 of the Learner's Notebook.

2. Follow the Dictation routine on page I-21 of the Introduction to dictate the following words:

I. sled   2. cod   3. rest

Sight Word: see

3. Tell students to focus and record the medial sound they hear if they cannot encode the entire word during Dictation time.

SORT: WHAT IS YOUR FOCUS PATTERN?

1. Have students take out their bag of pictures and words (created on Day 1) and follow the Sorting With Separate Picture and Word Cards routine on page I-26 of the Introduction.

PRACTICE: COMPLETE YOUR WORK ON YOUR OWN

1. Students will follow the Act It Out routine on page I-48 of the Introduction.

2. Circulate as students work, which usually takes fifteen minutes, and coach as needed.

FLUENCY: READING LIKE YOU'RE SPEAKING

1. Have students turn to page 24 in the Fluency Notebook.

2. Have students read one or more of the following passages: "Dress," "My Present," "Fox and Box," and "The Fox's Walk."

3. Circulate and listen to students read or gather a small group of students who need additional support.

Day 4

PHONEMIC AWARENESS: LISTEN	**1.** Give the directions. Say, "I am going to say a word. Then, I am going to tell you to change the final sound of that word to a different sound. Your job is to change the final sound of the word in your brain, then say the new word. For example, If I say 'cat, change the final sound to /b/,' you say 'cab.'"
	
	2. Say the following words and sounds:
	
	   med, /g/ (Meg) yell, /s/ (yes) pod, /p/ (pop)
	      got, /b/ (gob) deck, /n/ (den)

PUZZLE PIECE REVIEW 	**1.** Say, "When I point to the piece, you tell me its name" (*bed, log*). **2.** Say, "When I point to the piece, you tell me its sound" (/ĕ/, /ŏ/). **3.** Say, "When I point to the piece, you tell me its spelling" (*e, o*). **4.** Say, "Write the spellings in the air with your finger" (students will form the letters *e* and *o*).

BLENDING: PUTTING SOUNDS TOGETHER TO MAKE NEW WORDS	**1.** Follow the Blending routine on page I-17 of the Introduction. **2.** Display the following words on the board one line at a time. Facilitate a discussion about the blending line focus after each line. **3.** Then display the weekly sight words and sentence. **4.** Discuss the examples of short vowels in the sentence.

rep	crop	rap	Discuss: changes in the medial vowel
med	mod	mad	Discuss: changes in the medial vowel
bend	bond	band	Discuss: changes in the medial vowel

Sight Words: see in

Sentence: The band is mad.

QUICK SWITCH: MANIPULATE YOUR WORDS	**1.** Have students turn to page 130 of the Learner's Notebook. **2.** Follow the Quick Switch routine on page I-23 of the Introduction to dictate the following words: top → stop → tot → plot → pot **3.** Support students as they learn this new routine. Help students get from *stop* to *tot* by identifying that both the initial and final sounds have changed. If a student is struggling to write the full words, you can write the initial and final sounds and ask the student to record the vowel sound.

SORT: WHAT IS YOUR FOCUS PATTERN?	**1.** Have students take out their bag of pictures and words (created on Day 1) and follow the Sorting With Separate Picture and Word Cards routine on page I-26 of the Introduction.

**PRACTICE:
COMPLETE
YOUR WORK ON
YOUR OWN**

1. Have students complete the following Practice Piece: Glue Words (on page I-41 of the Introduction).

2. Circulate as students work, which usually takes fifteen minutes, and coach as needed.

**FLUENCY:
READING LIKE
YOU'RE SPEAKING**

1. Have students turn to page 24 in the Fluency Notebook.

2. Have students read one or more of the following passages: "Dress," "My Present," "Fox and Box," and "The Fox's Walk."

3. Circulate and listen to students read or gather a small group of students who need additional support.

PHONEMIC AWARENESS: LISTEN

1. Give the directions. Say, "I am going to say a word. Then, I am going to tell you to change the final sound of that word to a different sound. Your job is to change the final sound of the word in your brain, then say the new word. For example, If I say 'cat, change the final sound to /b/,' you say 'cab.'"

2. Say the following words and sounds:

taught, /d/ (Todd)   yep, /l/ (yell)   sock, /d/ (sod)
pot, /x/ (pox)   net, /k/ (neck)

REVIEW PATTERNS OF THE WEEK

1. Say, "Find a partner."

2. Say, "Tell your partner the names of this week's pieces" (*bed, log*).

3. Say, "Tell your partner the sounds of this week's pieces" (/ĕ/, /ŏ/).

4. Say, "Tell your partner the spellings of this week's pieces" (*e, o*).

5. Say, "Write the spellings on your partner's back with your finger" (students will form the letters *e* and *o*).

SPELLING CHECK

1. Follow the Spelling Check routine on page I-34 of the Introduction.

2. Instruct students to sit in their word study groups and turn to page 131 of the Learner's Notebook.

3. Say, "I am going to say one word at a time to each group. Record the words as I say them to your group. Make sure you only record the words from your group."

4. Move back and forth between the groups and dictate the following words:

Words for Group I	Words for Group 2
I. sled	I. sent
2. rot	2. pop
3. yes	3. bend
4. top	4. plot
5. red	5. best
Sentence: I see the bed.	**Sentence: I rest in bed.**

WORD HUNT

1. Students will follow the Word Hunt routine on page I-55 of the Introduction.

2. Instruct students to search texts and the classroom for words with short *e* and short *o*.

COMPREHENSION CHECK

1. Have students turn to page 132 of the Learner's Notebook.

2. Students will follow the Comprehension Check routine on page I-36 of the Introduction.

3. Check students' work. Circled answers are as follows:

1. I see the tent.
2. I see the frog.
3. I see the stop sign.

4. Students should have a picture of a sled.

WEEKLY CELEBRATION

1. Display the celebratory message: "Don't stop! You learned the *bed* and *log* puzzle pieces!"

2. Encourage students to work together to read the message.

3. Have students copy the message onto their weekly certificate (see resources.corwin .com/puzzlepiecephonics-gradeK) and place it somewhere to take home.

Preparing for Your Week

Resources

PUZZLE PIECES

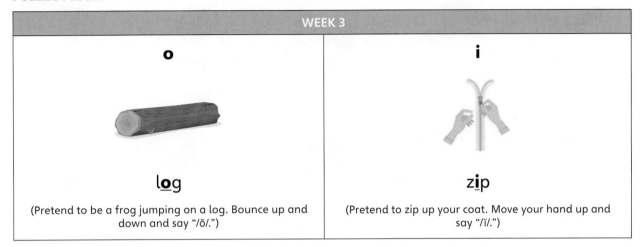

WEEK 3	
o	**i**
l**o**g	z**i**p
(Pretend to be a frog jumping on a log. Bounce up and down and say "/ŏ/.")	(Pretend to zip up your coat. Move your hand up and say "/ĭ/.")

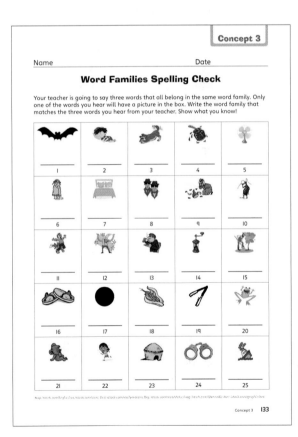

PREASSESSMENT DIRECTIONS

You can give the preassessment any day(s) during Concept 3, Week 3. You can split up the rows and do parts on different days. Do what works for your class.

Instruct students to turn to **page 133 in the Learner's Notebook**. Explain to students that they have not yet studied words with these spellings. This check will be used to see what they already know about word families. Tell students that you will use the results to form word study groups (see Tips for Scoring on page 171) and set goals.

When giving this assessment, go row by row in saying the group of words that all contain the same rime. The students will see a picture of the first word, but will listen to all three words and write the word family they hear. Students are *not* guessing what the picture is. You tell them the word and read the other two words in that word family. Students will only write the word family they hear in all three words. For example, after students hear *cat, mat, bat*, they will write *–at* in the box for that word family.

Log: istock.com/bennyb; Zip: istock.com/pe-art

Preparing for Your Week

PREASSESSMENT: WORD FAMILIES SPELLING CHECK

ANSWER KEY				
bat cat mat 1. -at	**nap** tap lap 2. -ap	**wag** nag tag 3. -ag	**jam** ham bam 4. -am	**fan** pan tan 5. -an
wet jet set 6. -et	**bed** fed red 7. -ed	**men** ten den 8. -en	**fell** well swell 9. -ell	**pest** best jest 10. -est
bit kit hit 11. -it	**win** grin bin 12. -in	**sip** tip zip 13. -ip	**mill** dill sill 14. -ill	**dig** fig big 15. -ig
flip-flop bop pop 16. -op	**dot** jot not 17. -ot	**cob** rob job 18. -ob	**tong** strong song 19. -ong	**frog** log smog 20. -og
cub hub sub 21. -ub	**run** pun nun 22. -un	**hut** gut but 23. -ut	**cuff** stuff huff 24. -uff	**sunk** junk dunk 25. -unk

Nap: istock.com/brgfx; Fan: istock.com/zzve; Bed: istock.com/vasilyevalara; Dig: istock.com/mutsMaks; Frog: istock.com/Glenne82; Run: istock.com/graphic-bee

Preparing for Your Week

EVALUATING THE ASSESSMENT:
WHAT TO LOOK FOR

- One-to-one sound correspondence
- Knowledge of consonants
- Knowledge of short vowels
- Knowledge of rime
- Recognizing that rhyming words contain the same rime

TIPS FOR SCORING

This assessment is to be used to group your students and understand their needs. The first row contains words with short vowel *a* families. The second row contains words with short vowel *e* families. The third row contains words with short vowel *i* families. The fourth row contains words with short vowel *o* families. The fifth row contains words with short vowel *u* families.

Each word family is worth one point. For each correctly spelled word family, students earn one point. Add up their points to see their total score.

- If students receive 0–15 points, they will be working with Group 1 words.
- If students received 16–25 points, they will be working with Group 2 words.

This is a guide to get you started, but use teacher discretion when placing your students in groups. Remember, these groups are flexible and can change each week if necessary. See the key above for words and answers.

Preparing for Your Week

CORRESPONDING *LEARNER'S NOTEBOOK PAGES*

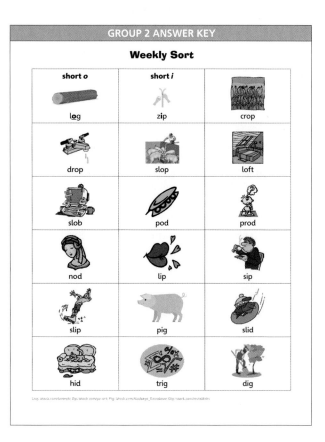

GROUP 1 ANSWER KEY

Weekly Sort

short *o*	short *i*	
log	zip	fog
dog	frog	hot
lot	plot	lob
mob	lip	sip
dip	pig	did
hid	big	dig

Log: istock.com/bennyb; Zip: istock.com/pt-art; Frog: istock.com/Glenn82; Hot: istock.com/birdpong2; Fire: istock.com/S-S-S; Pig: istock.com/Nadezya_Bolsakova; Dig: istock.com/mutuMaks

GROUP 2 ANSWER KEY

Weekly Sort

short *o*	short *i*	
log	zip	crop
drop	slop	loft
slob	pod	prod
nod	lip	sip
slip	pig	slid
hid	trig	dig

Log: istock.com/bennyb; Zip: istock.com/pt-art; Pig: istock.com/Nadezya_Bolsakova; Dig: istock.com/mutuMaks

---

Week 3	Concept 3

Name _____ Date _____

Can you _____?

Circle the sentence that matches the picture.

	Can you sip? Can you sit? Can you skip?
	Can you dog? Can you drag? Can you dig?
	Can you hip? Can you hop? Can you host?

Draw a picture to match the sentence below.

I. Do you see the fog?

Pig: istock.com/rusm; Bear/Sketch: istock.com/ski-article

Preparing for Your Week

CORRESPONDING *FLUENCY NOTEBOOK PAGES*

Short o

Moss

I can see moss.

I can see a log.

There is moss on the log.

The moss on the log is soft.

The Log in the Woods

There is a log in the woods.

The big log has green moss.

The moss grows on the log.

A frog likes to eat the moss on the log.

The frog is green just like the moss!

Short i

Pig

It is a pig.

Bill can see a pig.

The pig is pink.

Bill sees the pink pig.

Will and His Pig

The pig plays in his pen.

Will likes to play with his pet pig.

The pig plays in the mud. Will plays in the mud.

The pig gets messy. Will gets messy, too.

The pig and Will are covered in mud!

Preparing for Your Week

Tips for Management and Differentiation

Refer to this section and to resources.corwin.com/puzzzlepiecephonics-gradeK for resources and ideas to deepen your students' learning throughout the week. Feel free to put your own spin on the routines, too. For daily lesson plans, see pages 176–185 of this Teacher's Guide.

TIPS FOR PHONEMIC AWARENESS	• The focus for this week is changing the medial sound of the word read orally by the teacher. If you notice your students need additional practice, extend the activity with more words.
	• Model with students how to change the medial sound of the word in their head. Walk them through the activity: "First, think of the word *cat*. Then, take out the medial sound /a/ (*c___t*). Next, add the new medial sound /o/ to make the word *cot*."
	• The Phonemic Awareness activity may take a bit longer this week. Students are very familiar with changing initial sounds. They changed final sounds last week. This week they may need more time to manipulate words in their head to change medial sounds. If students are struggling, write the initial and final sounds on the board so they can see the sound that they need to change.
TIPS FOR THE PUZZLE PIECE REVIEW	• Have students work with the same partner each day to build a word study relationship.
	• After you record the words from the Big Reveal on Day 1, leave up the word list for short *i*. Remind students of your word list for short *o* that was created last week.
	• Remind students of why vowels are so important. Every word must have a vowel.
TIPS FOR BLENDING	• Reblend lines if necessary.
	• Use the Supported Blending routine for the sentence if your class needs help in reading the sentence.
	• Hold students accountable for looking at the medial letter and producing the correct short vowel sound. Do not have students guess the sounds.
TIPS FOR DICTATION AND QUICK SWITCH	• Students who are struggling with Quick Switch can have the teacher write the initial and final sounds on each line. When they hear the word, they will only need to focus on the medial sound.
TIPS FOR SORTING	• Model and positively reinforce the sorting routine repeatedly throughout the week. Students should see that you will consistently enforce the sorting routine this year!
	• Discuss the vocabulary words that appear in the sort. Vocabulary words include the following: • Sort 1: *fog, plot, lob, mob* • Sort 2: *crop, slop, loft, slob, pod, prod, nod, trig*

Preparing for Your Week

TIPS FOR THE PRACTICE PIECES

- This is the first concept in which students are sorting the entire sort on Day 1. They are also being introduced to the Sorting With Separate Picture and Word Cards routine. If sorting takes an extended amount of time, then you can omit a Practice Piece.
- Have students create a "Commonly Used Short Vowel Book." They can keep this book in their desk and write words with short vowels on each page. Their leveled books will have many common words that students will keep seeing. If they are having trouble with words, have them write the words in their "Commonly Used Short Vowel Book."

TIPS FOR FLUENCY

- Students can highlight words that contain short *o* or short *i* in the short stories.
- You can assign students fluency partners. Students will work together to achieve fluency with the short stories.
- Students can draw a picture that corresponds to the stories.
- Students may extend their stories after building their fluency.

Day 1

PHONEMIC AWARENESS: LISTEN

1. Give the directions. Say, "I am going to say a word. Then, I am going to tell you to change the medial sound of that word to a different sound. Your job is to change the medial sound of the word in your brain, then say the new word. For example, If I say '*set*, change the medial sound to /ă/,' you say '*sat*.'"

2. Say the following words and sounds:

hot, /ĭ/ (hit)   pet, /ă/ (pat)   dog, /ĭ/ (dig)   hem, /ă/ (ham)   lit, /ŏ/ (lot)

THE BIG REVEAL

1. Say, "This week we are going to continue our short vowel word study. Let's say all of our short vowel sounds: '/ă/ /ĕ/ /ĭ/ /ŏ/ /ŭ/.' Great! This week we are going to continue to study short vowel *o*. We will also take a closer look at another short vowel: *i*."

2. Hold up the *log* puzzle piece and say, "You remember the *log* piece. It represents the letter *o*. The *log* piece says '/ŏ/ /ŏ/ /ŏ/' like in the middle of the word *log*. Pretend to be a frog on a log, bounce up and down, and say '/ŏ/.' We will continue to study this letter and sound all week."

3. Hold up the *zip* puzzle piece and say, "This is the *zip* piece. It represents the letter *i*. The *zip* piece says '/ĭ/ /ĭ/ /ĭ/' like in the middle of the word *zip*. Pretend to zip up your coat. Move your hand up and say '/ĭ/.' We will study this letter and sound all week. Let's make a list of words that have the *zip* sound in them" (record the words).

BLENDING: PUTTING SOUNDS TOGETHER TO MAKE NEW WORDS

1. Follow the Blending routine on page I-17 of the Introduction.

2. Display the following words on the board one line at a time. Facilitate a discussion about the blending line focus after each line.

3. Then display the weekly sight words and sentence.

4. Discuss the examples of short vowels in the sentence.

log	mob	hot	Discuss: medial sound of /ŏ/
did	sip	pig	Discuss: medial sound of /ĭ/
lip	slip	loft	Discuss: medial sound of /ŏ/ or /ĭ/

Sight Words: to   you

Sentence: The pig is in his pen.

DICTATION: STRETCH OUT YOUR WORDS

1. Have students turn to page 139 of the Learner's Notebook.

2. Follow the Dictation routine on page I-21 of the Introduction to dictate the following words:

I. hot   2. lip   3. pig

Sight Word: you

3. Use Dictation as an informal pretest of students' knowledge of /ŏ/ and /ĭ/. Help students write the sight word and remind them this is a word they need to spell in a snap!

PRACTICE: COMPLETE YOUR WORK ON YOUR OWN	**1.** Have students turn to page 135 (Group 1) or 137 (Group 2) of the Learner's Notebook.
	2. Instruct students to tear out the sort and complete the following Practice Pieces: Quick Color, Careful Cut, and Sorting With Separate Picture and Word Cards (see further directions on pages I-37, I-38, and I-26 of the Introduction).
	3. Circulate as students work, which usually takes fifteen minutes, and coach as needed.
FLUENCY: READING LIKE YOU'RE SPEAKING	**1.** Have students turn to page 25 in the Fluency Notebook.
	2. Have students read one or more of the following passages: "Moss," "The Log in the Woods," "Pig," and "Will and His Pig."
	3. Circulate and listen to students read or gather a small group of students who need additional support.

Day 2

PHONEMIC AWARENESS: LISTEN	**1.** Give the directions. Say, "I am going to say a word. Then, I am going to tell you to change the medial sound of that word to a different sound. Your job is to change the medial sound of the word in your brain, then say the new word. For example, if I say '*set*, change the medial sound to /ă/,' you say '*sat*.'"
	2. Say the following words and sounds:
	mop, /ă/ (map) got, /ĕ/ (get) hop, /ĭ/ (hip) last, /ŏ/ (lost) met, /ă/ (mat)

PUZZLE PIECE REVIEW	**1.** Say, "When I point to the piece, you tell me its name" (*log, zip*).
	2. Say, "When I point to the piece, you tell me its sound" (/ŏ/, /ĭ/).
	3. Say, "When I point to the piece, you tell me its spelling" (*o, i*).
	4. Say, "Write the spellings in the air with your finger" (students will form the letters *o* and *i*).

BLENDING: PUTTING SOUNDS TOGETHER TO MAKE NEW WORDS	**1.** Follow the Blending routine on page I-17 of the Introduction.
	2. Display the following words on the board one line at a time. Facilitate a discussion about the blending line focus after each line.
	3. Then display the weekly sight words and sentence.
	4. Discuss the examples of short vowels in the sentence.

log	lot	lob	Discuss: medial sound of /ŏ/; changing final sound
nod	pod	sod	Discuss: medial sound of /ŏ/; changing initial sound
pit	spit	slit	Discuss: –*it* family

Sight Words: to   you

Sentence: The frog sat on the log.

QUICK SWITCH: MANIPULATE YOUR WORDS	**1.** Have students turn to page 139 of the Learner's Notebook.
	2. Follow the Quick Switch routine on page I-23 of the Introduction to dictate the following words:
	bid → lid → slid → sod → nod
	3. Support students as they learn this new routine. Help students get from *lid* to *slid* by stretching out the initial consonant blend as a class. Help students get from *slid* to *sod* by explaining that the initial and medial sound have both changed. If a student is struggling to write the full words, you can write the initial and final sounds and ask the student to record the vowel sound.

SORT: WHAT IS YOUR FOCUS PATTERN?	**1.** Have students take out their bag of pictures and words (created on Day 1) and follow the Sorting With Separate Picture and Word Cards routine on page I-26 of the Introduction.

PRACTICE: COMPLETE YOUR WORK ON YOUR OWN	**1.** Students will follow the Read and Trade routine on page I-47 of the Introduction. **2.** Circulate as students work, which usually takes fifteen minutes, and coach as needed.
FLUENCY: READING LIKE YOU'RE SPEAKING	**1.** Have students turn to page 25 in the Fluency Notebook. **2.** Have students read one or more of the following passages: "Moss," "The Log in the Woods," "Pig," and "Will and His Pig." **3.** Circulate and listen to students read or gather a small group of students who need additional support.

Day 3

PHONEMIC AWARENESS: LISTEN

1. Give the directions. Say, "I am going to say a word. Then, I am going to tell you to change the medial sound of that word to a different sound. Your job is to change the medial sound of the word in your brain, then say the new word. For example, if I say '*set*, change the medial sound to /ă/,' you say '*sat*.'"

2. Say the following words and sounds:

moss, /ă/ (mass)   tad, /ŏ/ (Todd)   red, /ĭ/ (rid)

pat, /ĕ/ (pet)   dock, /ĕ/ (deck)

PUZZLE PIECE REVIEW

1. Say, "When I point to the piece, you tell me its name" (*log, zip*).

2. Say, "When I point to the piece, you tell me its sound" (/ŏ/, /ĭ/).

3. Say, "When I point to the piece, you tell me its spelling" (*o, i*).

4. Say, "Write the spellings in the air with your finger" (students will form the letters *o* and *i*).

BLENDING: PUTTING SOUNDS TOGETHER TO MAKE NEW WORDS

1. Follow the Blending routine on page I-17 of the Introduction.

2. Display the following words on the board one line at a time. Facilitate a discussion about the blending line focus after each line.

3. Then display the weekly sight words and sentence.

4. Discuss the examples of short vowels in the sentence.

log	fog	hog	Discuss: –*og* family
hip	hid	hit	Discuss: medial sound of /ĭ/; changing final sound
moss	loss	gloss	Discuss: –*oss* family; point out the –*ss* spelling and explain that it also spells /s/

Sight Words: to   you

Sentence: You can see the moss.

DICTATION: STRETCH OUT YOUR WORDS

1. Have students turn to page 140 of the Learner's Notebook.

2. Follow the Dictation routine on page I-21 of the Introduction to dictate the following words:

I. hid   2. pod   3. slip

Sight Word: to

3. Tell students to focus and record the medial sound they hear if they cannot encode the entire word during Dictation time.

SORT: WHAT IS YOUR FOCUS PATTERN?

1. Have students take out their bag of pictures and words (created on Day 1) and follow the Sorting With Separate Picture and Word Cards routine on page I-26 of the Introduction.

PRACTICE: COMPLETE YOUR WORK ON YOUR OWN	**1.** Students will follow the Act It Out routine on page I-48 of the Introduction.
	2. Circulate as students work, which usually takes fifteen minutes, and coach as needed.
FLUENCY: READING LIKE YOU'RE SPEAKING	**1.** Have students turn to page 25 in the Fluency Notebook.
	2. Have students read one or more of the following passages: "Moss," "The Log in the Woods," "Pig," and "Will and His Pig."
	3. Circulate and listen to students read or gather a small group of students who need additional support.

Day 4

PHONEMIC AWARENESS: LISTEN

1. Give the directions. Say, "I am going to say a word. Then, I am going to tell you to change the medial sound of that word to a different sound. Your job is to change the medial sound of the word in your brain, then say the new word. For example, if I say '*set*, change the medial sound to /ă/,' you say '*sat*.'"

2. Say the following words and sounds:

    mad, /ĕ/ (med)   cat, /ĭ/ (kit)   pod, /ă/ (pad)   pit, /ŏ/ (pot)   lit, /ŏ/ (lot)

PUZZLE PIECE REVIEW

1. Say, "When I point to the piece, you tell me its name" (*log, zip*).

2. Say, "When I point to the piece, you tell me its sound" (/ŏ/, /ĭ/).

3. Say, "When I point to the piece, you tell me its spelling" (*o, i*).

4. Say, "Write the spellings in the air with your finger" (students will form the letters *o* and *i*).

BLENDING: PUTTING SOUNDS TOGETHER TO MAKE NEW WORDS

1. Follow the Blending routine on page I-17 of the Introduction.

2. Display the following words on the board one line at a time. Facilitate a discussion about the blending line focus after each line.

3. Then display the weekly sight words and sentence.

4. Discuss the examples of short vowels in the sentence.

did	dip	sip	Discuss: medial sound of /ĭ/
big	Bill	bit	Discuss: medial sound of /ĭ/; discuss the capital *B* in *Bill*
crop	drop	stop	Discuss: –*op* family; discuss the initial blends and reblend the line if necessary

Sight Words: to you

Sentence: Bill dropped the hot dogs!

QUICK SWITCH: MANIPULATE YOUR WORDS

1. Have students turn to page 140 of the Learner's Notebook.

2. Follow the Quick Switch routine on page I-23 of the Introduction to dictate the following words:

    lip → tip → hip → hop → hot

3. Support students as they learn this new routine. If a student is struggling to write the full words, you can write the initial and final sounds and ask the student to record the vowel sound.

SORT: WHAT IS YOUR FOCUS PATTERN?

1. Have students take out their bag of pictures and words (created on Day 1) and follow the Sorting With Separate Picture and Word Cards routine on page I-26 of the Introduction.

PRACTICE: COMPLETE YOUR WORK ON YOUR OWN

1. Have students complete the following Practice Piece: Glue Words (on page I-41 of the Introduction).

2. Circulate as students work, which usually takes fifteen minutes, and coach as needed.

**FLUENCY:
READING LIKE
YOU'RE SPEAKING**

1. Have students turn to page 25 in the Fluency Notebook.

2. Have students read one or more of the following passages: "Moss," "The Log in the Woods," "Pig," and "Will and His Pig."

3. Circulate and listen to students read or gather a small group of students who need additional support.

Day 5

PHONEMIC AWARENESS: LISTEN	**1.** Give the directions. Say, "I am going to say a word. Then, I am going to tell you to change the medial sound of that word to a different sound. Your job is to change the medial sound of the word in your brain, then say the new word. For example, if I say 'set, change the medial sound to /ă/,' you say 'sat.'"
	2. Say the following words and sounds:

fit, /ŏ/ (fought)   leg, /ŏ/ (log)   socks, /ĭ/ (six)   till, /ĕ/ (tell)   pod, /ă/ (pad)

REVIEW PATTERNS OF THE WEEK	**1.** Say, "Find a partner."
	2. Say, "Tell your partner the names of this week's pieces" (*log, zip*).
	3. Say, "Tell your partner the sounds of this week's pieces" (/ŏ/, /ĭ/).
	4. Say, "Tell your partner the spellings of this week's pieces" (*o, i*).
	5. Say, "Write the spellings on your partner's back with your finger" (students will form the letters *o* and *i*).
SPELLING CHECK	**1.** Follow the Spelling Check routine on page I-34 of the Introduction.
	2. Instruct students to sit in their word study groups and turn to page 141 of the Learner's Notebook.
	3. Say, "I am going to say one word at a time to each group. Record the words as I say them to your group. Make sure you only record the words from your group."
	4. Move back and forth between the groups and dictate the following words:

Words for Group 1	Words for Group 2
1. hid	1. slid
2. mob	2. crop
3. dig	3. dig
4. plot	4. loft
5. sip	5. slip
Sentence: You got the pig!	**Sentence: Get the pig to its pen.**

WORD HUNT	**1.** Students will follow the Word Hunt routine on page I-55 of the Introduction.
	2. Instruct students to search texts and the classroom for words with short *o* and short *i*.
COMPREHENSION CHECK	**1.** Have students turn to page 142 of the Learner's Notebook.
	2. Students will follow the Comprehension Check routine on page I-36 of the Introduction.
	3. Check students' work. Circled answers are as follows:
	1. Can you sip?
	2. Can you dig?
	3. Can you hop?
	4. Students should have a picture of fog.

WEEKLY CELEBRATION

1. Display the celebratory message: "It's a big win! You learned the *log* and *zip* puzzle pieces!"

2. Encourage students to work together to read the message.

3. Have students copy the message onto their weekly certificate (see resources .corwin.com/puzzlepiecephonics-gradeK) and place it somewhere to take home.

Preparing for Your Week

Resources

PUZZLE PIECES

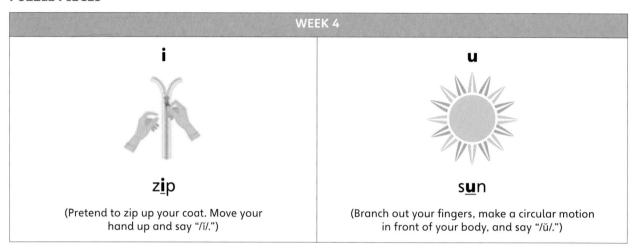

WEEK 4	
i	**u**
z**i**p	s**u**n
(Pretend to zip up your coat. Move your hand up and say "/ĭ/.")	(Branch out your fingers, make a circular motion in front of your body, and say "/ŭ/.")

Zip: istock.com/pe-art; Sun: istock.com/StudioBarcelona

Preparing for Your Week

CORRESPONDING *LEARNER'S NOTEBOOK PAGES*

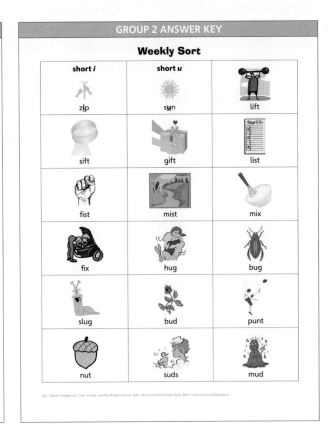

GROUP 1 ANSWER KEY

Weekly Sort

short *i*	short *u*	
zip	sun	fix
mix	six	kit
pit	slit	crib
skip	hug	bug
mug	bud	rut
nut	suds	mud

Zip: istock.com/pe-art. Sun: istock.com/StudioBarcelona. Mix: istock.com/vasilyevaliva

GROUP 2 ANSWER KEY

Weekly Sort

short *i*	short *u*	
zip	sun	lift
sift	gift	list
fist	mist	mix
fix	hug	bug
slug	bud	punt
nut	suds	mud

Zip: istock.com/pe-art. Sun: istock.com/StudioBarcelona. Gift: istock.com/orchenello. Mix: istock.com/vasilyevaliva

---

Week 4	Concept 3

Name _____ Date _____

The _____ is for the _____.

Circle the sentence that matches the picture.

	The bone is for the dog. The fish is for the cat.
	The pen is for the kid. The pin is for the bug.
	The cap is for the kit. The gift is for the girl.

Draw a picture to match the sentence below.

1. He went to the crib.

150   PUZZLE PIECE PHONICS LEARNER'S NOTEBOOK, KINDERGARTEN

Preparing for Your Week

CORRESPONDING *FLUENCY NOTEBOOK PAGES*

Short *i*

The Hill

Liz gets up the hill.

Bill gets up the hill.

Liz and Bill eat lunch.

They eat on top of the hill.

Liz and Bill

Liz and Bill skip up the hill.

They fixed a picnic lunch. They want to eat at the top of the hill.

Liz and Bill get to the top of the hill. They get out their lunch.

They eat six sandwiches and mugs of pop.

Liz and Bill get their fill and skip back down the hill.

Short *u*

The Bug

The frog hops by the bug.

The bug goes, "Buzz!"

The frog wants to eat.

The frog gets the bug.

Stuck in the Mud

The frog is in the mud.

The frog sees a bug.

The frog wants to eat the bug. He gets out his tongue.

He cannot get the bug! The frog is stuck!

The frog is stuck in the mud.

Preparing for Your Week

Tips for Management and Differentiation

Refer to this section and to resources.corwin.com/puzzlepiecephonics-gradeK for resources and ideas to deepen your students' learning throughout the week. Feel free to put your own spin on the routines, too. For daily lesson plans, see pages 190–198 of this Teacher's Guide.

TIPS FOR PHONEMIC AWARENESS	• Model with students how to change the various sounds of the words. • If you notice your students need additional practice, extend the activity with more words. • The Phonemic Awareness activity may take a bit longer this week. Students may need more time to change the medial and final sounds of words. On Days 4 and 5, students may need you to repeat the groups of words.
TIPS FOR THE PUZZLE PIECE REVIEW	• Have students work with the same partner each day to build a word study relationship. • After you record the words from the Big Reveal on Day 1, leave up the word list for short *u*. Remind students of your word list for short *i* that was created last week. • Remind students of why vowels are so important. Every word must have a vowel.
TIPS FOR BLENDING	• Reblend lines if necessary. • Use the Supported Blending routine for the sentence if your class needs help in reading the sentence. • Hold students accountable for looking at the medial letter and producing the correct short vowel sound. Do not have students guess the sounds.
TIPS FOR DICTATION AND QUICK SWITCH	• Students who are struggling with Quick Switch can have the teacher write the initial and final sounds on each line. When they hear the word, they will only need to focus on the medial sound.

TIPS FOR SORTING	• Model and positively reinforce the sorting routine repeatedly throughout the week. Students should see that you will consistently enforce the sorting routine this year!
	• Discuss the vocabulary words that appear in the sort. Vocabulary words include the following:
	  • Sort 1: *fix, mix, kit, pit, slit, mug, bud, suds, rut*
	  • Sort 2: *sift, fist, mist, mix, fix, slug, bud, suds, punt*

TIPS FOR THE PRACTICE PIECES	• This is the first concept in which students are sorting the entire sort on Day 1. They are also being introduced to the Sorting With Separate Picture and Word Cards routine. If sorting takes an extended amount of time, then you can omit a Practice Piece. • Have students create a "Commonly Used Short Vowel Book." They can keep this book in their desk and write words with short vowels on each page. Their leveled books will have many common words that students will keep seeing. If they are having trouble with words, have them write the words in their "Commonly Used Short Vowel Book."
TIPS FOR FLUENCY	• Students can highlight words that contain short *i* or short *u* in the short stories. • You can assign students fluency partners. Students will work together to achieve fluency with the short stories. • Students can draw a picture that corresponds to the stories. • Students may extend their stories after building their fluency.

Day 1

PHONEMIC AWARENESS: LISTEN

1. Give the directions. Say, "I am going to say a word. Then, I am going to tell you to change the initial sound of that word to a different sound. Your job is to change the initial sound of the word in your brain, then say the new word. For example, if I say '*mop*, change the initial sound to /t/,' you say '*top*.'"

2. Say the following words and sounds:

hot, /g/ (got)   pet, /l/ (let)   dog, /p/ (pog)   hem, /j/ (gem)   lit, /b/ (bit)

THE BIG REVEAL

1. Say, "This week we are going to continue our short vowel word study. Let's say all of our short vowel sounds: '/ă/ /ĕ/ /ĭ/ /ŏ/ /ŭ/.' Great! This week we are going to continue to study short vowel *i*. We will also take a closer look at another short vowel: *u*."

2. Hold up the *zip* puzzle piece and say, "You remember the *zip* piece. It represents the letter *i*. The *zip* piece says '/ĭ/ /ĭ/ /ĭ/' like in the middle of the word *zip*. Pretend to zip up your coat. Move your hand up and say '/ĭ/.' We will continue to study this letter and sound all week."

3. Hold up the *sun* puzzle piece and say, "This is the *sun* piece. It represents the letter *u*. The *sun* piece says '/ŭ/ /ŭ/ /ŭ/' like in the middle of the word *sun*. Branch out your fingers, make a circular motion in front of your body, and say '/ŭ/.' We will study this letter and sound all week. Let's make a list of words that have the *sun* sound in them" (record the words).

BLENDING: PUTTING SOUNDS TOGETHER TO MAKE NEW WORDS

1. Follow the Blending routine on page I-17 of the Introduction.

2. Display the following words on the board one line at a time. Facilitate a discussion about the blending line focus after each line.

3. Then display the weekly sight words and sentence.

4. Discuss the examples of short vowels in the sentence.

bug	nut	mud	Discuss: medial sound of /ŭ/
fix	pit	rib	Discuss: medial sound of /ĭ/
mug	lug	slug	Discuss: medial sound of /ŭ/; *–ug* family

Sight Words: for   go

Sentence: I have to go to the hut.

DICTATION: STRETCH OUT YOUR WORDS

1. Have students turn to page 147 of the Learner's Notebook.

2. Follow the Dictation routine on page I-21 of the Introduction to dictate the following words:

I. mud   2. pit   3. slug

Sight Word: go

3. Use Dictation as an informal pretest of students' knowledge of /ĭ/ and /ŭ/. Help students write the sight word and remind them this is a word they need to spell in a snap!

PRACTICE:
COMPLETE
YOUR WORK ON
YOUR OWN

1. Have students turn to page 143 (Group 1) or 145 (Group 2) of the Learner's Notebook.

2. Instruct students to tear out the sort and complete the following Practice Pieces: Quick Color, Careful Cut, and Sorting With Separate Picture and Word Cards (see further directions on pages I-37, I-38, and I-26 of the Introduction).

3. Circulate as students work, which usually takes fifteen minutes, and coach as needed.

FLUENCY:
READING LIKE
YOU'RE SPEAKING

1. Have students turn to page 26 in the Fluency Notebook.

2. Have students read one or more of the following passages: "The Hill," "Liz and Bill," "The Bug," and "Stuck in the Mud."

3. Circulate and listen to students read or gather a small group of students who need additional support.

Day 2

PHONEMIC AWARENESS: LISTEN

1. Give the directions. Say, "I am going to say a word. Then, I am going to tell you to change the medial sound of that word to a different sound. Your job is to change the medial sound of the word in your brain, then say the new word. For example, if I say '*set*, change the medial sound to /ă/,' you say '*sat*.'"

2. Say the following words and sounds:

gut, /ŏ/ (got)   beg, /ŭ/ (bug)   Jim, /ă/ (jam)   lit, /ĕ/ (let)   mess, /ă/ (mass)

PUZZLE PIECE REVIEW

1. Say, "When I point to the piece, you tell me its name" (*zip, sun*).

2. Say, "When I point to the piece, you tell me its sound" (/ĭ/, /ŭ/).

3. Say, "When I point to the piece, you tell me its spelling" (*i, u*).

4. Say, "Write the spellings in the air with your finger" (students will form the letters *i* and *u*).

BLENDING: PUTTING SOUNDS TOGETHER TO MAKE NEW WORDS

1. Follow the Blending routine on page I-17 of the Introduction.

2. Display the following words on the board one line at a time. Facilitate a discussion about the blending line focus after each line.

3. Then display the weekly sight words and sentence.

4. Discuss the examples of short vowels in the sentence.

rut	bud	suds	Discuss: medial sound of /ŭ/; discuss that the –s ending in *suds* means more than one
lit	sit	list	Discuss: medial sound of /ĭ/
lift	sift	gift	Discuss: medial sound of /ĭ/; –*ift* family

Sight Words: for go

Sentence: The gift is for Bill.

QUICK SWITCH: MANIPULATE YOUR WORDS

1. Have students turn to page 147 of the Learner's Notebook.

2. Follow the Quick Switch routine on page I-23 of the Introduction to dictate the following words:

bug → bud → mud → mid → lid

3. Support students as they learn this new routine. If a student is struggling to write the full words, you can write the initial and final sounds and ask the student to record the vowel sound.

SORT: WHAT IS YOUR FOCUS PATTERN?

1. Have students take out their bag of pictures and words (created on Day 1) and follow the Sorting With Separate Picture and Word Cards routine on page I-26 of the Introduction.

Day 2 (Continued)

PRACTICE: COMPLETE YOUR WORK ON YOUR OWN

1. Students will follow the Read and Trade routine on page I-47 of the Introduction.

2. Circulate as students work, which usually takes fifteen minutes, and coach as needed.

FLUENCY: READING LIKE YOU'RE SPEAKING

1. Have students turn to page 26 in the Fluency Notebook.

2. Have students read one or more of the following passages: "The Hill," "Liz and Bill," "The Bug," and "Stuck in the Mud."

3. Circulate and listen to students read or gather a small group of students who need additional support.

Day 3

PHONEMIC AWARENESS: LISTEN

1. Give the directions. Say, "I am going to say a word. Then, I am going to tell you to change the final sound of that word to a different sound. Your job is to change the final sound of the word in your brain, then say the new word. For example, if I say '*mat,* change the final sound to /p/,' you say '*map.*'"

2. Say the following words and sounds:

moss, /b/ (mob)   tad, /p/ (tap)   rub, /t/ (rut)   pat, /d/ (pad)   lick, /d/ (lid)

PUZZLE PIECE REVIEW

1. Say, "When I point to the piece, you tell me its name" (*zip, sun*).

2. Say, "When I point to the piece, you tell me its sound" (/ĭ/, /ŭ/).

3. Say, "When I point to the piece, you tell me its spelling" (*i, u*).

4. Say, "Write the spellings in the air with your finger" (students will form the letters *i* and *u*).

BLENDING: PUTTING SOUNDS TOGETHER TO MAKE NEW WORDS

1. Follow the Blending routine on page I-17 of the Introduction.

2. Display the following words on the board one line at a time. Facilitate a discussion about the blending line focus after each line.

3. Then display the weekly sight words and sentence.

4. Discuss the examples of short vowels in the sentence.

put	nut	punt	Discuss: medial sound of /ŭ/
mix	fix	tux	Discuss: medial sound of /ĭ/ and /ŭ/; final *x*
hut	hug	hub	Discuss: medial sound of /ŭ/; initial *h*

Sight Words: for   go

Sentence: Go get Jim in his crib.

DICTATION: STRETCH OUT YOUR WORDS

1. Have students turn to page 148 of the Learner's Notebook.

2. Follow the Dictation routine on page I-21 of the Introduction to dictate the following words:

I. fix   2. suds   3. crib

Sight Word: for

3. Tell students to focus and record the medial sound they hear if they cannot encode the entire word during Dictation time.

SORT: WHAT IS YOUR FOCUS PATTERN?

1. Have students take out their bag of pictures and words (created on Day 1) and follow the Sorting With Separate Picture and Word Cards routine on page I-26 of the Introduction.

PRACTICE: COMPLETE YOUR WORK ON YOUR OWN	**1.** Students will follow the Act It Out routine on page I-48 of the Introduction. **2.** Circulate as students work, which usually takes fifteen minutes, and coach as needed.
FLUENCY: READING LIKE YOU'RE SPEAKING	**1.** Have students turn to page 26 in the Fluency Notebook. **2.** Have students read one or more of the following passages: "The Hill," "Liz and Bill," "The Bug," and "Stuck in the Mud." **3.** Circulate and listen to students read or gather a small group of students who need additional support.

Day 4

PHONEMIC AWARENESS: LISTEN	**1.** Give the directions. Say, "I am going to say a group of words. Your job is to listen to the words and tell me what sound is the same in all of them (initial, medial, final). For example, if I say '*set, bed, den*,' you say 'medial sound /ĕ/.'"
	2. Say the following groups of words:
	mad, make, mop (initial sound /m/) mix, fox, Max (final sound /x/)
	got, gab, Gus (initial sound /g/) pit, bid, pill (medial sound /ĭ/)

PUZZLE PIECE REVIEW	**1.** Say, "When I point to the piece, you tell me its name" (*zip, sun*).
	2. Say, "When I point to the piece, you tell me its sound" (/ĭ/, /ŭ/).
	3. Say, "When I point to the piece, you tell me its spelling" (*i, u*).
	4. Say, "Write the spellings in the air with your finger" (students will form the letters *i* and *u*).

BLENDING: PUTTING SOUNDS TOGETHER TO MAKE NEW WORDS

1. Follow the Blending routine on page I-17 of the Introduction.

2. Display the following words on the board one line at a time. Facilitate a discussion about the blending line focus after each line.

3. Then display the weekly sight words and sentence.

4. Discuss the examples of short vowels in the sentence.

sip	**Kip**	**skip**	Discuss: medial sound of /ĭ/; discuss capital *K* in *Kip*
rut	**rust**	**ruff**	Discuss: medial sound of /ŭ/; discuss the double *f* in *ruff* and identify it as a spelling of /f/
bug	**hug**	**hugs**	Discuss: medial sound of /ŭ/; explain that the –*s* ending in *hugs* means more than one

Sight Words: for   go

Sentence: The pup can hug.

QUICK SWITCH: MANIPULATE YOUR WORDS	**1.** Have students turn to page 148 of the Learner's Notebook.
	2. Follow the Quick Switch routine on page I-23 of the Introduction to dictate the following words:
	lift → gift → gut → rut → rugs
	3. Support students as they learn this new routine. Help students get from *gift* to *gut* by identifying the change in the medial and final sound. Help students get from *rut* to *rugs* by writing the word *rug* and adding the -*s* ending, meaning more than one. If a student is struggling to write the full words, you can write the initial and final sounds and ask the student to record the vowel sound.

SORT: WHAT IS YOUR FOCUS PATTERN?	**1.** Have students take out their bag of pictures and words (created on Day 1) and follow the Sorting With Separate Picture and Word Cards routine on page I-26 of the Introduction.

Day 4 (Continued)

PRACTICE: COMPLETE YOUR WORK ON YOUR OWN	**1.** Have students complete the following Practice Piece: Glue Words (on page I-41 of the Introduction).
	2. Circulate as students work, which usually takes fifteen minutes, and coach as needed.
FLUENCY: READING LIKE YOU'RE SPEAKING	**1.** Have students turn to page 26 in the Fluency Notebook.
	2. Have students read one or more of the following passages: "The Hill," "Liz and Bill," "The Bug," and "Stuck in the Mud."
	3. Circulate and listen to students read or gather a small group of students who need additional support.

Day 5

PHONEMIC AWARENESS: LISTEN

1. Give the directions. Say, "I am going to say a group of words. Your job is to listen to the words and tell me what sound is the same in all of them (initial, medial, final). For example, if I say '*set, bed, den*,' you say 'medial sound /ĕ/.'"

2. Say the following groups of words:

lap, clip, cup (final sound /p/)   jot, Jim, jazz (initial sound /j/)
tap, cat, pass (medial sound /ă/)   miss, map, mug (initial sound /m/)

REVIEW PATTERNS OF THE WEEK

1. Say, "Find a partner."

2. Say, "Tell your partner the names of this week's pieces" (*zip, sun*).

3. Say, "Tell your partner the sound of this week's pieces" (/ĭ/, /ŭ/).

4. Say, "Tell your partner the spellings of this week's pieces" (*i, u*).

5. Say, "Write the spellings on your partner's back with your fingers" (students will form the letters *i* and *u*).

SPELLING CHECK

1. Follow the Spelling Check routine on page I-34 of the Introduction.

2. Instruct students to sit in their word study groups and turn to page 149 of the Learner's Notebook.

3. Say, "I am going to say one word at a time to each group. Record the words as I say them to your group. Make sure you only record the words from your group."

4. Move back and forth between the groups and dictate the following words:

Words for Group 1	**Words for Group 2**
1. six	1. mist
2. hug	2. bud
3. mud	3. fix
4. skip	4. punt
5. nut	5. slug
Sentence: Go get the mix!	**Sentence: The mix is for the bug.**

WORD HUNT

1. Students will follow the Word Hunt routine on page I-55 of the Introduction.

2. Instruct students to search texts and the classroom for words with short *i* and short *u*.

COMPREHENSION CHECK

1. Have students turn to page 150 of the Learner's Notebook.

2. Students will follow the Comprehension Check routine on page I-36 of the Introduction.

3. Check students' work. Circled answers are as follows:

1. The bone is for the dog.
2. The pen is for the kid.
3. The gift is for the girl.

4. Students should have a picture of a crib.

WEEKLY CELEBRATION

1. Display the celebratory message: "Lots of fun! You learned the *zip* and *sun* puzzle pieces!"

2. Encourage students to work together to read the message.

3. Have students copy the message onto their weekly certificate (see resources.corwin.com/puzzlepiecephonics-gradeK) and place it somewhere to take home.

Preparing for Your Week

Resources

PUZZLE PIECES

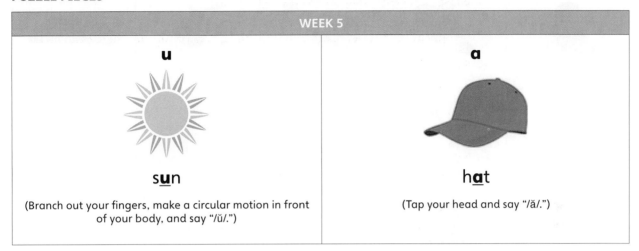

WEEK 5	
u	**a**
s<u>u</u>n	h<u>a</u>t
(Branch out your fingers, make a circular motion in front of your body, and say "/ŭ/.")	(Tap your head and say "/ă/.")

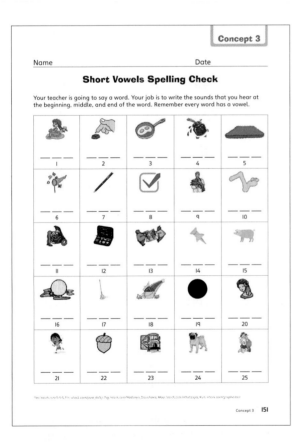

POSTASSESSMENT DIRECTIONS

This assessment is used to identify which consonant and short vowel sounds students can represent and which patterns students need to be retaught. It is also useful to evaluate students' ability to apply knowledge of all consonant and short vowel sounds. Students may be able to master a Spelling Check when there is a sound taught in isolation. However, they may struggle when asked to produce multiple sounds. This check is to primarily look for mastery of short vowel sounds, but will also check for students' mastery of consonant sounds.

You can give this postassessment any day during Concept 3, Week 5. You can split the rows and do parts on different days. Do what works for your class.

Instruct students to turn to **page 151 in the Learner's Notebook**.

Explain to students that they have studied all of the spellings in the words they will hear. The purpose of this check is to show what they know.

When giving this assessment, go row by row in saying the word represented by the picture. Students are not guessing what the picture is. You tell them the word.

Sun: istock.com/StudioBarcelona; Hat: istock.com/stevezmina1

Preparing for Your Week

POSTASSESSMENT: SHORT VOWELS SPELLING CHECK

ANSWER KEY				
1. sat	2. tap	3. pan	4. jam	5. mat
6. net	7. pen	8. yes	9. vet	10. leg
11. fix	12. kit	13. rip	14. pin	15. pig
16. fog	17. mop	18. pot	19. dot	20. nod
21. run	22. nut	23. bus	24. pug	25. rub

Yes: istock.com/S-S-S; Pin: istock.com/jane_Kelly; Pig: istock.com/Nadzeya_Dzivakova; Mop: istock.com/mhatzapa; Run: istock.com/graphic-bee

EVALUATING THE ASSESSMENT:
WHAT TO LOOK FOR

- One-to-one letter-sound correspondence
- Knowledge of consonants
- Knowledge of short vowels

TIPS FOR SCORING

Row 1 contains words with short vowel *a*. Row 2 contains words with short vowel *e*. Row 3 contains words with short vowel *i*. Row 4 contains words with short vowel *o*. Row 5 contains words with short vowel *u*. Have students write all of the sounds they hear in the word.

Each word is worth one point. For each correctly spelled word, students earn one point. To show mastery of consonants and short vowels, students must show 80 percent mastery or correctly spell twenty out of twenty-five words phonetically.

Use teacher discretion when reviewing. If students need to solely focus on the short vowel sound, only grade them on the medial sound they hear.

Preparing for Your Week

CORRESPONDING *LEARNER'S NOTEBOOK PAGES*

Preparing for Your Week

CORRESPONDING *FLUENCY NOTEBOOK PAGES*

Short *u*

Buzz

Buzz, buzz!

Buzz goes the bug.

Buzz the bug
wants a snack.

Buzz the bug
gets grass.

The Bug at Dusk

The bug is out at dusk.

It is dark. The bug lights up!

Buzz, buzz goes the bug!

The bug lights up the yard.

The bug passes the lamp. It lights up.

Buzz, buzz the bug goes into the
dark night.

Short *a*

Jan's Map

Jan is at camp.

Jan likes to go on
walks.

Jan has a map.

Jan's map helps her get
to the path.

Jan is on the path.

Jan and Dan at Camp

Jan is at camp.

Dan is at camp, too.

Jan and Dan use their map to get
to the path.

They walk on the path.
They walk over the grass.

Jan and Dan walk past the bog.
They walk all day long.

Jan and Dan get back to camp.
They are glad to be back.

Preparing for Your Week

Tips for Management and Differentiation

Refer to this section and to resources.corwin.com/puzzlepiecephonics-gradeK for resources and ideas to deepen your students' learning throughout the week. Feel free to put your own spin on the routines, too. For daily lesson plans, see pages 204–209 of this Teacher's Guide.

TIPS FOR PHONEMIC AWARENESS	• Model with students how to change the various sounds of the words. • If you notice your students need additional practice, extend the activity with more words. • The Phonemic Awareness activity may take a bit longer this week. Students may need more time to change the medial and final sounds of words. On Days 4 and 5, students may need you to repeat the groups of words.
TIPS FOR THE PUZZLE PIECE REVIEW	• Have students work with the same partner each day to build a word study relationship. • Remind students of your word lists for short *u* and short *a* that have already been created. • Remind students of why vowels are so important. Every word must have a vowel.
TIPS FOR BLENDING	• Reblend lines if necessary. • Use the Supported Blending routine for the sentence if your class needs help in reading the sentence. • Hold students accountable for looking at the medial letter and producing the correct short vowel sound. Do not have students guess the sounds.
TIPS FOR DICTATION AND QUICK SWITCH	• Students who are struggling with Quick Switch can have the teacher write the initial and final sounds on each line. When they hear the word, they will only need to focus on the medial sound.

TIPS FOR SORTING	• Model and positively reinforce the sorting routine repeatedly throughout the week. Students should see that you will consistently enforce the sorting routine this year!
	• Discuss the vocabulary words that appear in the sort. Vocabulary words include the following:
	  • Sort 1: *fuss, bunt, blub*
	  • Sort 2: *dusk, slump, rust, mask*

TIPS FOR THE PRACTICE PIECES	• This is the first concept in which students are sorting the entire sort on Day 1. They are also being introduced to the Sorting With Separate Picture and Word Cards routine. If sorting takes an extended amount of time, then you can omit a Practice Piece. • Have students create a "Commonly Used Short Vowel Book." They can keep this book in their desk and write words with short vowels on each page. Their leveled books will have many common words that students will keep seeing. If they are having trouble with words, have them write the words in their "Commonly Used Short Vowel Book."
TIPS FOR FLUENCY	• Students can highlight words that contain short *u* or short *a* in the short stories. • You can assign students fluency partners. Students will work together to achieve fluency with the short stories. • Students can draw a picture that corresponds to the stories. • Students may extend their stories after building their fluency.

Day 1

PHONEMIC AWARENESS: LISTEN

1. Give the directions. Say, "I am going to say a word. Then, I am going to tell you to change the initial sound of that word to a different sound. Your job is to change the initial sound of the word in your brain, then say the new word. For example, if I say '_mop_, change the initial sound to /t/,' you say '_top_.'"

2. Say the following words and sounds:

puck, /d/ (duck)   fin, /b/ (bin)   set, /p/ (pet)   hang, /f/ (fang)   top, /h/ (hop)

THE BIG REVEAL

1. Say, "This week we are going to continue our short vowel word study. Let's say all of our short vowel sounds: '/ă/ /ĕ/ /ĭ/ /ŏ/ /ŭ/.' Great! This week we are going to continue to study short vowel _u_. We will also take a closer look at another short vowel we looked at during the beginning of our short vowel concept: short vowel _a_."

2. Hold up the _sun_ puzzle piece and say, "You remember the _sun_ piece. It represents the letter _u_. The _sun_ piece says '/ŭ/ /ŭ/ /ŭ/' like in the middle of the word _sun_. Branch out your fingers, make a circular motion in front of your body, and say '/ŭ/.' We will continue to study this letter and sound all week."

3. Hold up the _hat_ puzzle piece and say, "You remember the _hat_ piece. It represents the letter _a_. The _hat_ piece says '/ă/ /ă/ /ă/' like in the middle of the word _hat_. Tap your head and say '/ă/.' We will continue to study this letter and sound all week."

BLENDING: PUTTING SOUNDS TOGETHER TO MAKE NEW WORDS

1. Follow the Blending routine on page I-17 of the Introduction.

2. Display the following words on the board one line at a time. Facilitate a discussion about the blending line focus after each line.

3. Then display the weekly sight words and sentence.

4. Discuss the examples of short vowels in the sentence.

tap	pat	past	Discuss: medial sound of /ă/
fun	run	must	Discuss: medial sound of /ŭ/
map	gas	Gus	Discuss: medial sound of /ă/ and /ŭ/; uppercase _g_ in _Gus_

Sight Words: or   if

Sentence: Gus got a big map.

DICTATION: STRETCH OUT YOUR WORDS

1. Have students turn to page 157 of the Learner's Notebook.

2. Follow the Dictation routine on page I-21 of the Introduction to dictate the following words:

I. tap   2. run   3. gas

Sight Word: or

3. Use Dictation as an informal pretest of students' knowledge of /ŭ/ and /ă/. Help students write the sight word and remind them this is a word they need to spell in a snap!

PRACTICE:
COMPLETE YOUR WORK ON YOUR OWN

1. Have students turn to page 153 (Group 1) or 155 (Group 2) of the Learner's Notebook.

2. Instruct students to tear out the sort and complete the following Practice Pieces: Quick Color, Careful Cut, and Sorting With Separate Picture and Word Cards (see further directions on pages I-37, I-38, and I-26 of the Introduction).

3. Circulate as students work, which usually takes fifteen minutes, and coach as needed.

FLUENCY:
READING LIKE YOU'RE SPEAKING

1. Have students turn to page 27 in the Fluency Notebook.

2. Have students read one or more of the following passages: "Buzz," "The Bug at Dusk," "Jan's Map," and "Jan and Dan at Camp."

3. Circulate and listen to students read or gather a small group of students who need additional support.

Day 2

PHONEMIC AWARENESS: LISTEN

1. Give the directions. Say, "I am going to say a word. Then, I am going to tell you to change the medial sound of that word to a different sound. Your job is to change the medial sound of the word in your brain, then say the new word. For example, if I say '*set*, change the medial sound to /ă/,' you say '*sat*.'"

2. Say the following words and sounds:

punt, /ă/ (pant)   hip, /ŏ/ (hop)   got, /ĕ/ (get)
head, /ă/ (had)   and pop, /ŭ/ (pup)

PUZZLE PIECE REVIEW

1. Say, "When I point to the piece, you tell me its name" (*sun, hat*).

2. Say, "When I point to the piece, you tell me its sound" (/ŭ/, /ă/).

3. Say, "When I point to the piece, you tell me its spelling" (*u, a*).

4. Say, "Write the spellings in the air with your finger" (students will form the letters *u* and *a*).

BLENDING: PUTTING SOUNDS TOGETHER TO MAKE NEW WORDS

1. Follow the Blending routine on page I-17 of the Introduction.

2. Display the following words on the board one line at a time. Facilitate a discussion about the blending line focus after each line.

3. Then display the weekly sight words and sentence.

4. Discuss the examples of short vowels in the sentence.

bust	must	rust	Discuss: –*ust* word family
lamp	camp	ramp	Discuss: –*amp* word family
fuss	pass	grass	Discuss: doubled consonant *s* as a spelling of /s/

Sight Words: or   if

Sentence: Pass the gift to Pam or Sam.

QUICK SWITCH: MANIPULATE YOUR WORDS

1. Have students turn to page 157 of the Learner's Notebook.

2. Follow the Quick Switch routine on page I-23 of the Introduction to dictate the following words:

tan → ran → fan → fun → run

3. Support students as they learn this new routine. If a student is struggling to write the full words, you can write the initial and final sounds and ask the student to record the vowel sound.

SORT: WHAT IS YOUR FOCUS PATTERN?

1. Have students take out their bag of pictures and words (created on Day 1) and follow the Sorting With Separate Picture and Word Cards routine on page I-26 of the Introduction.

PRACTICE: COMPLETE YOUR WORK ON YOUR OWN

1. Students will follow the Read and Trade routine on page I-47 of the Introduction.

2. Circulate as students work, which usually takes fifteen minutes, and coach as needed.

FLUENCY: READING LIKE YOU'RE SPEAKING

1. Have students turn to page 27 in the Fluency Notebook.

2. Have students read one or more of the following passages: "Buzz," "The Bug at Dusk," "Jan's Map," and "Jan and Dan at Camp."

3. Circulate and listen to students read or gather a small group of students who need additional support.

PHONEMIC AWARENESS: LISTEN	**1.** Give the directions. Say, "I am going to say a word. Then, I am going to tell you to change the final sound of that word to a different sound. Your job is to change the final sound of the word in your brain, then say the new word. For example, if I say '*mat,* change the final sound to /p/,' you say '*map.*'"
	2. Say the following words and sounds:
	hop, /t/ (hot) lid, /m/ (limb) run, /b/ (rub) lad, /p/ (lap) hen, /m/ (hem)

PUZZLE PIECE REVIEW	**1.** Say, "When I point to the piece, you tell me its name" (*sun, hat*).
	2. Say, "When I point to the piece, you tell me its sound" (/ŭ/, /ă/).
	3. Say, "When I point to the piece, you tell me its spelling" (*u, a*).
	4. Say, "Write the spellings in the air with your finger" (students will form the letters *u* and *a*).

BLENDING: PUTTING SOUNDS TOGETHER TO MAKE NEW WORDS	**1.** Follow the Blending routine on page I-17 of the Introduction.
	2. Display the following words on the board one line at a time. Facilitate a discussion about the blending line focus after each line.
	3. Then display the weekly sight words and sentence.
	4. Discuss the examples of short vowels in the sentence.

dump	lump	slump	Discuss: –*ump* word family
last	past	cast	Discuss: –*ast* word family
musk	mask	task	Discuss: –*sk* consonant blend

Sight Words: or if

Sentence: If the sun is up, it is past six.

DICTATION: STRETCH OUT YOUR WORDS	**1.** Have students turn to page 158 of the Learner's Notebook.
	2. Follow the Dictation routine on page I-21 of the Introduction to dictate the following words:
	1. must 2. past 3. bump
	Sight Word: if
	3. Tell students to focus and record the medial sound they hear if they cannot encode the entire word during Dictation time.

SORT: WHAT IS YOUR FOCUS PATTERN?	**1.** Have students take out their bag of pictures and words (created on Day 1) and follow the Sorting With Separate Picture and Word Cards routine on page I-26 of the Introduction.

PRACTICE: COMPLETE YOUR WORK ON YOUR OWN	**1.** Students will follow the Act It Out routine on page I-48 of the Introduction.
	2. Circulate as students work, which usually takes fifteen minutes, and coach as needed.

FLUENCY: READING LIKE YOU'RE SPEAKING	**1.** Have students turn to page 27 in the Fluency Notebook.
	2. Have students read one or more of the following passages: "Buzz," "The Bug at Dusk," "Jan's Map," and "Jan and Dan at Camp."
	3. Circulate and listen to students read or gather a small group of students who need additional support.

Day 4

PHONEMIC AWARENESS: LISTEN

1. Give the directions. Say, "I am going to say a group of words. Your job is to listen to the words and tell me what sound is the same in all of them (initial, medial, final). For example, if I say 'set, bed, den,' you say 'medial sound /ĕ/.'"

2. Say the following groups of words:

**hog, hip, head (initial sound /h/)   gut, hug, tux (medial sound /ŭ/)
live, lost, let (initial sound /l/)   bid, mud, Fred (final sound /d/)**

PUZZLE PIECE REVIEW

1. Say, "When I point to the piece, you tell me its name" (*sun, hat*).

2. Say, "When I point to the piece, you tell me its sound" (/ŭ/, /ă/).

3. Say, "When I point to the piece, you tell me its spelling" (*u, a*).

4. Say, "Write the spellings in the air with your finger" (students will form the letters *u* and *a*).

BLENDING: PUTTING SOUNDS TOGETHER TO MAKE NEW WORDS

1. Follow the Blending routine on page I-17 of the Introduction.

2. Display the following words on the board one line at a time. Facilitate a discussion about the blending line focus after each line.

3. Then display the weekly sight words and sentence.

4. Discuss the examples of short vowels in the sentence.

tan	pan	pant	Discuss: contrast word endings –*an* and –*ant*
sun	bun	bunt	Discuss: contrast word endings –*un* and –*unt*
grass	pass	past	Discuss: medial sound of /ă/

Sight Words: or   if

Sentence: Run fast to get on the bus!

QUICK SWITCH: MANIPULATE YOUR WORDS

1. Have students turn to page 158 of the Learner's Notebook.

2. Follow the Quick Switch routine on page I-23 of the Introduction to dictate the following words:

mast → must → rust → run → ran

3. Support students as they learn this new routine. If a student is struggling to write the full words, you can write the initial and final sounds and ask the student to record the vowel sound.

SORT: WHAT IS YOUR FOCUS PATTERN?

1. Have students take out their bag of pictures and words (created on Day 1) and follow the Sorting With Separate Picture and Word Cards routine on page I-26 of the Introduction.

PRACTICE: COMPLETE YOUR WORK ON YOUR OWN

1. Have students complete the following Practice Piece: Glue Words (on page I-41 of the Introduction).

2. Circulate as students work, which usually takes fifteen minutes, and coach as needed.

FLUENCY: READING LIKE YOU'RE SPEAKING

1. Have students turn to page 27 in the Fluency Notebook.

2. Have students read one or more of the following passages: "Buzz," "The Bug at Dusk," "Jan's Map," and "Jan and Dan at Camp."

3. Circulate and listen to students read or gather a small group of students who need additional support.

Day 5

PHONEMIC AWARENESS: LISTEN	**1.** Give the directions. Say, "I am going to say a group of words. Your job is to listen to the words and tell me what sound is the same in all of them (initial, medial, final). For example, if I say 'set, bed, den,' you say 'medial sound /ĕ/.'"

2. Say the following groups of words:

hop, got, clock (medial sound /ŏ/)   him, jam, hem (final sound /m/)
dip, sip, fin (medial sound /ĭ/)   pop, pill, put (initial sound /p/)

REVIEW PATTERNS OF THE WEEK

1. Say, "Find a partner."

2. Say, "Tell your partner the names of this week's pieces" (*sun, hat*).

3. Say, "Tell your partner the sounds of this week's pieces" (/ŭ/, /ă/).

4. Say, "Tell your partner the spellings of this week's pieces" (*u, a*).

5. Say, "Write the spellings on your partner's back with your finger" (students will form the letters *u* and *a*).

SPELLING CHECK

1. Follow the Spelling Check routine on page I-34 of the Introduction.

2. Instruct students to sit in their word study groups and turn to page 159 of the Learner's Notebook.

3. Say, "I am going to say one word at a time to each group. Record the words as I say them to your group. Make sure you only record the words from your group."

4. Move back and forth between the groups and dictate the following words:

Words for Group 1	**Words for Group 2**
1. bus	1. lamp
2. pass	2. grass
3. tap	3. bump
4. must	4. dusk
5. map	5. task
Sentence: We can go on the bus.	**Sentence: If you go to camp, you will have fun!**

WORD HUNT

1. Students will follow the Word Hunt routine on page I-55 of the Introduction.

2. Instruct students to search texts and the classroom for words with short *u* and short *a*.

COMPREHENSION CHECK

1. Have students turn to page 160 of the Learner's Notebook.

2. Students will follow the Comprehension Check routine on page I-36 of the Introduction.

3. Check students' work. Circled answers are as follows:

1. What if the bus was full?

2. What if the camp was hot?

3. What if the slug was small?

4. Students should have a picture of a boy being last.

WEEKLY CELEBRATION

1. Display the celebratory message: "We had a blast! You learned the *sun* and *hat* puzzle pieces!"

2. Encourage students to work together to read the message.

3. Have students copy the message onto their weekly certificate (see resources .corwin.com/puzzlepiecephonics-gradeK) and place it somewhere to take home.

Concept 4 Overview:

Short *a* Families

istock.com/vgajic

WHAT ARE WORD FAMILIES?

Students have learned all of their consonant and short vowel sounds. It is time for them to use their knowledge of consonants and short vowels to read and create words on their own. By being introduced to word families—words that have the same rime (vowel and any final consonants)—students will see comparisons and differences in words. They will use their knowledge of short *a* word families to manipulate and recall words.

GOALS FOR THE CONCEPT

Students will

- Identify and represent short vowels
- Identify and represent consonant sounds
- Read and write sight words
- Recognize that words with the same rime rhyme
- Manipulate words in order to create a new word
- Develop reading fluency and comprehension

WEEKS FOR THIS CONCEPT

Week 1: Short *a* Families (*–at, –ap, –ag*)
Week 2: Short *a* Families (*–am, –an, –and*)

Preparing for Your Week

Resources

PUZZLE PIECES

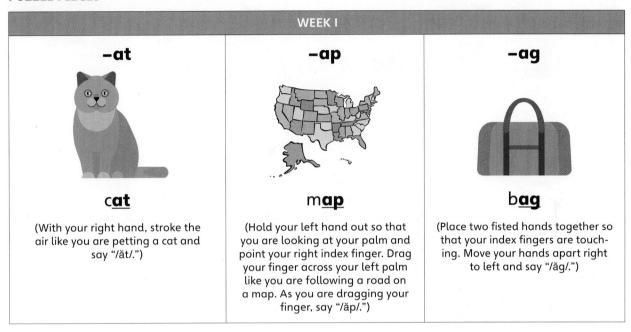

WEEK I		
–at	**–ap**	**–ag**
c**at**	m**ap**	b**ag**
(With your right hand, stroke the air like you are petting a cat and say "/ăt/.")	(Hold your left hand out so that you are looking at your palm and point your right index finger. Drag your finger across your left palm like you are following a road on a map. As you are dragging your finger, say "/ăp/.")	(Place two fisted hands together so that your index fingers are touching. Move your hands apart right to left and say "/ăg/.")

Cat: istock.com/Nadzeya_Dzivakova; Map: istock.com/Irma Burns; Bag: istock.com/missbobit

Preparing for Your Week

CORRESPONDING *LEARNER'S NOTEBOOK PAGES*

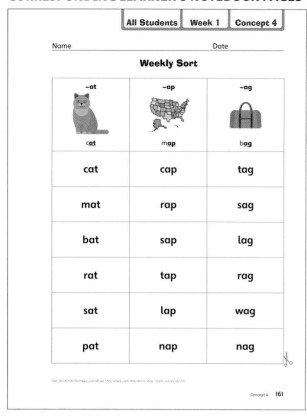

| All Students | Week 1 | Concept 4 |

Name _____ Date _____

Weekly Sort

–at	–ap	–ag
c**at**	m**ap**	b**ag**
cat	cap	tag
mat	rap	sag
bat	sap	lag
rat	tap	rag
sat	lap	wag
pat	nap	nag

Concept 4   161

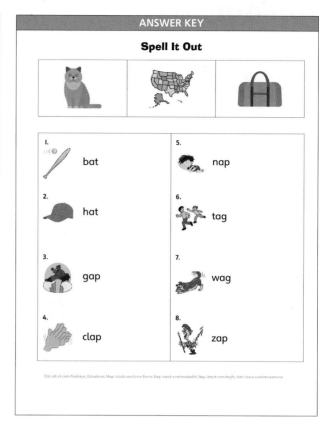

ANSWER KEY

Spell It Out

1.		5.	
	bat		nap
2.		6.	
	hat		tag
3.		7.	
	gap		wag
4.		8.	
	clap		zap

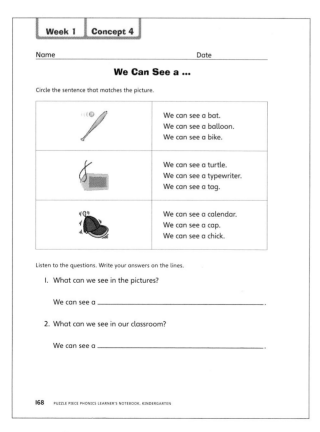

| Week 1 | Concept 4 |

Name _____ Date _____

We Can See a …

Circle the sentence that matches the picture.

	We can see a bat. We can see a balloon. We can see a bike.
	We can see a turtle. We can see a typewriter. We can see a tag.
	We can see a calendar. We can see a cap. We can see a chick.

Listen to the questions. Write your answers on the lines.

1. What can we see in the pictures?

   We can see a _____ .

2. What can we see in our classroom?

   We can see a _____ .

168   PUZZLE PIECE PHONICS LEARNER'S NOTEBOOK, KINDERGARTEN

CORRESPONDING *FLUENCY NOTEBOOK PAGES*

Cat and Rat

A cat! A cat!

A cat sits on the mat.

A rat! A rat!

A rat runs by the mat.

The cat! The cat!

The cat runs after the rat.

The rat! The rat!

The rat runs away from the cat.

The cat! The cat!

The cat can't find the rat!

The rat! The rat!

He will take a nap.

What Is That Tap?

Tap. Tap. Tap. What is that?

"What is tapping?" asked Pat.

Tap. Tap. Tap. What is that?

"Could it be a bat?" asked Pat.

Tap. Tap. Tap. What is that?

"Maybe it's my cat," thought Pat.

Tap. Tap. Tap. What is that?

"Perhaps it is a rat," said Pat.

Tap. Tap. Tap. What is that?

"It has to be my flag," said Pat.

Tap. Tap. Tap. WHAT IS THAT?

"I can't take it anymore!" yelled Pat.

Tap. Tap. Tap. Tap. Tap. Tap.

Pat opened the door and let out a laugh.

Turns out it was his friend, Matt.

That tap, tap, tap was just Matt.

Preparing for Your Week

Tips for Management and Differentiation

Refer to this section and to resources.corwin.com/puzzlepiecephonics-gradeK for resources and ideas to deepen your students' learning throughout the week. Feel free to put your own spin on the routines, too. For daily lesson plans, see pages 215–222 of this Teacher's Guide.

TIPS FOR PHONEMIC AWARENESS	• The focus for this week is listening for rhyming words. • If you notice your students need additional practice, extend the activity with more words. • Students are instructed to give a thumbs-up if the words rhyme or a thumbs-down if the words do not rhyme. You may substitute any motions for the activity. • If the two words rhyme, prompt students to verbally give you an additional word that rhymes. If the two words do not rhyme, prompt students to think of a word that rhymes with each.
TIPS FOR THE PUZZLE PIECE REVIEW	• Point out to students the two pieces that they have already learned that make up the word family piece. For example, when teaching the *–at* piece, point to the *hat* piece /ă/ and the *type* piece /t/. Explain to students that the *cat* piece takes both of those sounds and puts them on one piece to represent the *–at* family.
TIPS FOR BLENDING	• Reblend lines if necessary—especially words with blends and endings. • Remind students that the purpose of this concept is for them to use the words and spellings they know to assist them in spelling words they do not know. For example, if students can spell and identify the word *nap*, they can use that knowledge to blend and identify the word *snap*.
TIPS FOR DICTATION AND QUICK SWITCH	• If time permits, complete a Quick Switch word chain with the *–ag* family. • Students who are struggling with Quick Switch can write the rime (word family) on each line. When they hear the word, they will only need to focus on the initial sound.
TIPS FOR SORTING	• Model and positively reinforce the Sorting With Words routine repeatedly throughout the week. • Discuss the vocabulary words that appear in the sort. Vocabulary words include the following: • *bat, rap, sap, sag, lag, rag, nag*
TIPS FOR THE PRACTICE PIECES	• Support students with the vocabulary words for this week. They may need assistance in drawing the pictures.
TIPS FOR FLUENCY	• This week students will read poems with words in the short *a* families. When students reach mastery with the daily poem, they can revisit poems from prior weeks. • Students can highlight words within the short *a* families in the daily poems. • Students can participate in a "Fluency Celebration." Call on students who feel prepared to present a particular poem in front of the class. Other students can follow along in the Fluency Notebook. • There is space to have students illustrate the text underneath the poems. After students have mastered their fluency, have them illustrate to show comprehension.

THE PUZZLE PIECE FAMILY

Launch Concept 4: Short *a* Families by following the Puzzle Piece Family routine on page I-11 of the Introduction.

1. Show students the following words:

sat	Pam
fan	tag
pad	ran
band	bag
tap	tad

2. Have students read the words with you. Underline the vowel and final consonant(s) in each word.

3. Facilitate a discussion that leads them to discover the Puzzle Piece Family: Short *a* Families.

PHONEMIC AWARENESS: LISTEN

1. Give the directions. Say, "I am going to say two words. Your job is to tell me if the two words rhyme. Give me a thumbs-up if the words are rhyming words and a thumbs-down if the words are not rhyming words."

2. Say the following pairs of words:

trap, cap (yes)   rat, can (no)   tag, pat (no)   tag, rag (yes)
hat, bat (yes)

THE BIG REVEAL

1. Say, "Let's say all of our short vowel sounds." Lead students in saying "/ă/ /ĕ/ /ĭ/ /ŏ/ /ŭ/." Then say, "This week will be taking a closer look at short vowel *a*. We will be focusing on three short *a* families."

2. Hold up the *cat* puzzle piece and say, "This is the *cat* piece. It represents the short *a* family –at. The *cat* piece says '/ăt/ /ăt/ /ăt/' like at the end of the word *cat*. With your right hand, stroke the air like you are petting a cat and say '/ăt/.' Let's make a list of words that have the *cat* sound in them" (record the words).

3. Hold up the *map* puzzle piece and say, "This is the *map* piece. It represents the short *a* family –ap. The *map* piece says '/ăp/ /ăp/ /ăp/' like at the end of the word *map*. Hold your left hand out so that you are looking at your palm and point your right index finger. Drag your finger across your left palm like you are following a road on a map. As you are dragging your finger, say '/ăp/.' Let's make a list of words that have the *map* sound in them" (record the words).

4. Hold up the *bag* puzzle piece and say, "This is the *bag* piece. It represents the short *a* family –ag. The *bag* piece says '/ăg/ /ăg/ /ăg/' like at the end of the word *bag*. Place two fisted hands together so that your index fingers are touching. Move your hands apart right to left and say '/ăg/.' Let's make a list of words that have the *bag* sound in them" (record the words).

(Continued)

Day 1 (Continued)

BLENDING:
PUTTING SOUNDS
TOGETHER TO
MAKE NEW WORDS

1. Follow the Blending routine on page I-17 of the Introduction.

2. Display the following words on the board one line at a time. Facilitate a discussion about the blending line focus after each line.

3. Then display the weekly sight words and sentence.

4. Discuss the word with the short *a* family found in the sentence.

cat	mat	bat	Discuss: –*at* family
map	tap	rap	Discuss: –*ap* family
bag	tag	wag	Discuss: –*ag* family

Sight Words: we and

Sentence: We see a cat.

DICTATION:
STRETCH OUT
YOUR WORDS

1. Have students turn to page 163 of the Learner's Notebook.

2. Follow the Dictation routine on page I-21 of the Introduction to dictate the following words:

   1. cap 2. lag 3. rat

   Sight Word: and

3. Use Dictation as an informal pretest of students' knowledge of short *a* families. Help students write the sight word and remind them this is a word they need to spell in a snap!

PRACTICE:
COMPLETE
YOUR WORK ON
YOUR OWN

1. Have students turn to page 161 of the Learner's Notebook (Group 1 and Group 2 have the same sort this week).

2. Instruct students to tear out the sort and complete the following Practice Pieces: Quick Color, Careful Cut, Highlighter Hunt, and Sorting With Words (see further directions on pages I-37, I-38, I-43, and I-27 of the Introduction).

3. Circulate as students work, which usually takes fifteen minutes, and coach as needed.

FLUENCY:
READING LIKE
YOU'RE SPEAKING

1. Have students turn to page 28 in the Fluency Notebook.

2. Have students read one or more of the following poems: "Cat and Rat" and "What Is That Tap?"

3. Circulate and listen to students read or gather a small group of students who need additional support.

PHONEMIC AWARENESS: LISTEN

1. Give the directions. Say, "I am going to say two words. Your job is to tell me if the two words rhyme. Give me a thumbs-up if the words are rhyming words and a thumbs-down if the words are not rhyming words."

2. Say the following pairs of words:

Jan, cat (no)   fat, mat (yes)   tag, tan (no)   sad, bad (yes)   map, fan (no)

PUZZLE PIECE REVIEW

1. Say, "When I point to the piece, you tell me its name" (*cat, map, bag*).

2. Say, "When I point to the piece, you tell me its sound" (/ăt/, /ăp/, /ăg/).

3. Say, "When I point to the piece, you tell me its spelling" (*–at, –ap, –ag*).

4. Say, "Write the spellings in the air with your finger" (students will form the letters *–at, –ap,* and *–ag*).

BLENDING: PUTTING SOUNDS TOGETHER TO MAKE NEW WORDS

1. Follow the Blending routine on page I-17 of the Introduction.

2. Display the following words on the board one line at a time. Facilitate a discussion about the blending line focus after each line.

3. Then display the weekly sight words and sentence.

4. Ask students what they notice about the words in each column (all have same initial sound). Discuss the words with the short *a* family found in the sentence.

rat	sat	Nat	Discuss: *–at* family; capital *N* in *Nat* (name)
rap	sap	nap	Discuss: *–ap* family
rag	sag	nag	Discuss: *–ag* family

Sight Words: we   and

Sentence: Nat and I sat.

QUICK SWITCH: MANIPULATE YOUR WORDS

1. Have students turn to page 163 of the Learner's Notebook.

2. Follow the Quick Switch routine on page I-23 of the Introduction to dictate the following words:

map → tap → rap → lap → nap

3. Review the *–ap* family with students.

SORT: WHAT IS YOUR FOCUS PATTERN?

1. Have students take out their bag of words (created on Day 1) and follow the Sorting With Words routine on page I-27 of the Introduction.

PRACTICE: COMPLETE YOUR WORK ON YOUR OWN

1. Students will follow the Read and Trade routine on page I-47 of the Introduction.

2. Circulate as students work, which usually takes fifteen minutes, and coach as needed.

FLUENCY: READING LIKE YOU'RE SPEAKING

1. Have students turn to page 28 in the Fluency Notebook.

2. Have students read one or more of the following poems: "Cat and Rat" and "What Is That Tap?"

3. Circulate and listen to students read or gather a small group of students who need additional support.

Day 3

PHONEMIC AWARENESS: LISTEN

1. Give the directions. Say, "I am going to say two words. Your job is to tell me if the two words rhyme. Give me a thumbs-up if the words are rhyming words and a thumbs-down if the words are not rhyming words."

2. Say the following pairs of words:

sat, sad (no)   cap, rap (yes)   tan, span (yes)
tad, mad (yes)   Sam, pant (no)

PUZZLE PIECE REVIEW

1. Say, "When I point to the piece, you tell me its name" (*cat, map, bag*).

2. Say, "When I point to the piece, you tell me its sound" (/ăt/, /ăp/, /ăg/).

3. Say, "When I point to the piece, you tell me its spelling" (–at, –ap, –ag).

4. Say, "Write the spellings in the air with your finger" (students will form the letters –at, –ap, and –ag).

BLENDING: PUTTING SOUNDS TOGETHER TO MAKE NEW WORDS

1. Follow the Blending routine on page I-17 of the Introduction.

2. Display the following words on the board one line at a time. Facilitate a discussion about the blending line focus after each line.

3. Then display the weekly sight words and sentence.

4. Discuss the words with the short *a* family found in the sentence.

lap	slap	clap	Discuss: –ap family; compare and contrast *slap* and *clap* with *lap*
rag	brag	drag	Discuss: –ag family; compare and contrast *brag* and *drag* with *rag*
rat	brat	sprat	Discuss: –at family; compare and contrast *brat* and *sprat* with *rat*

Sight Words: we   and

Sentence: Is that a rat?

DICTATION: STRETCH OUT YOUR WORDS

1. Have students turn to page 164 of the Learner's Notebook.

2. Follow the Dictation routine on page I-21 of the Introduction to dictate the following words:

I. tag   2. lap   3. sat

Sight Word: we

3. To enrich students working above grade level, change out the words *lap* and *sat* to *slap* and *spat*. Encourage them to tap out all of the sounds in these words.

SORT: WHAT IS YOUR FOCUS PATTERN?

1. Have students take out their bag of words (created on Day 1) and follow the Sorting With Words routine on page I-27 of the Introduction.

**PRACTICE:
COMPLETE
YOUR WORK ON
YOUR OWN**

1. Have students turn to page 165 in the Learner's Notebook.

2. Students will complete the Spell It Out routine on page I-49 of the Introduction.

3. Circulate as students work, which usually takes fifteen minutes, and coach as needed.

**FLUENCY:
READING LIKE
YOU'RE SPEAKING**

1. Have students turn to page 28 in the Fluency Notebook.

2. Have students read one or more of the following poems: "Cat and Rat" and "What Is That Tap?"

3. Circulate and listen to students read or gather a small group of students who need additional support.

Day 4

PHONEMIC AWARENESS: LISTEN

1. Give the directions. Say, "I am going to say two words. Your job is to tell me if the two words rhyme. Give me a thumbs-up if the words are rhyming words and a thumbs-down if the words are not rhyming words."

2. Say the following pairs of words:

dad, rad (yes)   map, rag (no)   land, sand (yes)
wag, mad (no)   last, pat (no)

PUZZLE PIECE REVIEW

1. Say, "When I point to the piece, you tell me its name" (*cat, map, bag*).

2. Say, "When I point to the piece, you tell me its sound" (/ăt/, /ăp/, /ăg/).

3. Say, "When I point to the piece, you tell me its spelling" (–at, –ap, –ag).

4. Say, "Write the spellings in the air with your finger" (students will form the letters –at, –ap, and –ag).

BLENDING: PUTTING SOUNDS TOGETHER TO MAKE NEW WORDS

1. Follow the Blending routine on page I-17 of the Introduction.

2. Display the following words on the board one line at a time. Facilitate a discussion about the blending line focus after each line.

3. Then display the weekly sight words and sentence.

4. Discuss the plural words in the sentence. Talk about the –s at the end that makes the noun mean "more than one."

sat	spat	mats	Discuss: –at family; –s meaning "more than one"
nap	snap	caps	Discuss: –ap family; –s meaning "more than one"
lag	flag	tags	Discuss: –ag family; –s meaning "more than one"

Sight Words: we   and

Sentence: I like naps and flags.

QUICK SWITCH: MANIPULATE YOUR WORDS

1. Have students turn to page 164 of the Learner's Notebook.

2. Follow the Quick Switch routine on page I-23 of the Introduction to dictate the following words:

bat → pat → sat → rat → mat

3. Review the –at family with students.

SORT: WHAT IS YOUR FOCUS PATTERN?

1. Have students take out their bag of words (created on Day 1) and follow the Sorting With Words routine on page I-27 of the Introduction.

PRACTICE: COMPLETE YOUR WORK ON YOUR OWN

1. Have students complete the following Practice Piece: Glue, Draw a Picture (on page I-50 of the Introduction).

2. Circulate as students work, which usually takes fifteen minutes, and coach as needed.

FLUENCY: READING LIKE YOU'RE SPEAKING

1. Have students turn to page 28 in the Fluency Notebook.

2. Have students read one or more of the following poems: "Cat and Rat" and "What Is That Tap?"

3. Circulate and listen to students read or gather a small group of students who need additional support.

PHONEMIC AWARENESS: LISTEN

1. Give the directions. Say, "I am going to say two words. Your job is to tell me if the two words rhyme. Give me a thumbs-up if the words are rhyming words and a thumbs-down if the words are not rhyming words."

2. Say the following pairs of words:

tan, rad (no)   had, tad (yes)   dab, lab (yes)   can, pan (yes)   fad, pat (no)

REVIEW PATTERNS OF THE WEEK

1. Say, "Find a partner."

2. Say, "Tell your partner the names of this week's pieces" (*cat, map, bag*).

3. Say, "Tell your partner the sounds of this week's pieces" (/ăt/, /ăp/, /ăg/).

4. Say, "Tell your partner the spellings of this week's pieces" (*-at, -ap, -ag*).

5. Say, "Write the spellings on your partner's back with your finger" (students will form the letters *-at, -ap,* and *-ag*).

SPELLING CHECK

1. Follow the Spelling Check routine on page I-34 of the Introduction.

2. Instruct students to turn to page 167 of the Learner's Notebook.

3. Say, "I am going to say one word at a time. Record the words as I say them."

4. Dictate the following words:

Words for the Spelling Check

1. cap
2. rag
3. sat
4. rap
5. tag

Sentence: We see a bat.

WORD HUNT

1. Students will follow the Word Hunt routine on page I-55 of the Introduction.

2. Instruct students to search texts and the classroom for words within the short *a* families.

COMPREHENSION CHECK

1. Have students turn to page 168 of the Learner's Notebook.

2. Students will follow the Comprehension Check routine on page I-36 of the Introduction.

3. Check students' work. Circled answers are as follows:

   1. We can see a bat.

   2. We can see a tag.

   3. We can see a cap.

4. Possible written responses include the following:

   1. We can see a _____. (*bat, tag, cap*).

   2. We can see a _____. (Students may fill in the blank with anything they can see in the classroom.)

(Continued)

Day 5 (Continued)

WEEKLY CELEBRATION

1. Display the celebratory message: "That is how you do it! You learned the *cat, map,* and *bag* puzzle pieces!"

2. Encourage students to work together to read the message.

3. Have students copy the message onto their weekly certificate (see resources.corwin.com/puzzlepiecephonics-gradeK) and place it somewhere to take home.

Preparing for Your Week

Resources

PUZZLE PIECES

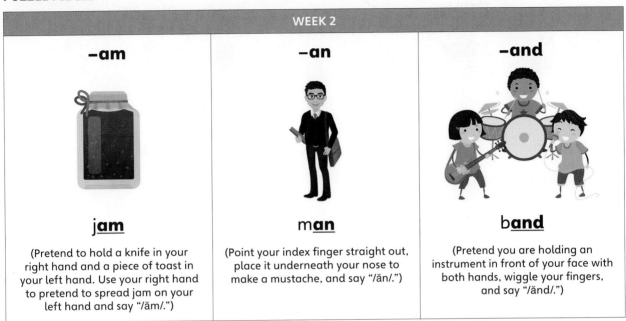

WEEK 2		
–am	**–an**	**–and**
j**am**	m**an**	b**and**
(Pretend to hold a knife in your right hand and a piece of toast in your left hand. Use your right hand to pretend to spread jam on your left hand and say "/ăm/.")	(Point your index finger straight out, place it underneath your nose to make a mustache, and say "/ăn/.")	(Pretend you are holding an instrument in front of your face with both hands, wiggle your fingers, and say "/ănd/.")

Jam: istock.com/muzzza; Man: istock.com/rafyfane; Band: istock.com/lenm

Preparing for Your Week

CORRESPONDING *LEARNER'S NOTEBOOK PAGES*

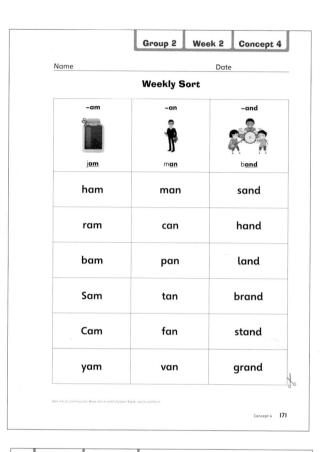

| Group 1 | Week 2 | Concept 4 |

Name _____ Date _____

Weekly Sort

–at cat	–ap map	–ag bag
cat	cap	tag
mat	rap	sag
bat	sap	lag
rat	tap	rag
sat	lap	wag
pat	nap	nag

Cat: istock.com/hocksya_0Livelovek; Map: istock.com/bubaone; Bag: istock.com/jcsmilly

Concept 4   169

| Group 2 | Week 2 | Concept 4 |

Name _____ Date _____

Weekly Sort

–am jam	–an man	–and band
ham	man	sand
ram	can	hand
bam	pan	land
Sam	tan	brand
Cam	fan	stand
yam	van	grand

Jam: istock.com/vvvita; Man: istock.com/cfarias; Band: istock.com/flisak

Concept 4   171

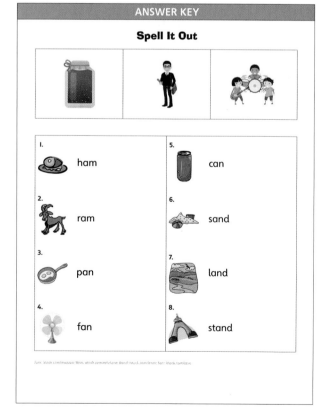

| ANSWER KEY |

Spell It Out

1.	ham	5.	can
2.	ram	6.	sand
3.	pan	7.	land
4.	fan	8.	stand

Jam: istock.com/vvvita; Man: istock.com/cfarias; Band: istock.com/flisak; Fan: istock.com/zava

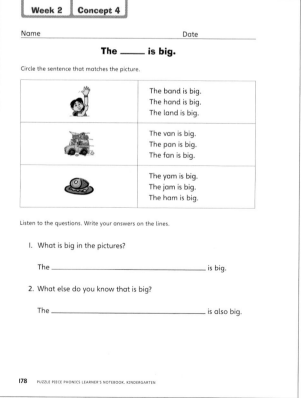

| Week 2 | Concept 4 |

Name _____ Date _____

The _____ is big.

Circle the sentence that matches the picture.

	The band is big. The hand is big. The land is big.
	The van is big. The pan is big. The fan is big.
	The yam is big. The jam is big. The ham is big.

Listen to the questions. Write your answers on the lines.

1. What is big in the pictures?

   The _____ is big.

2. What else do you know that is big?

   The _____ is also big.

Preparing for Your Week

CORRESPONDING *FLUENCY NOTEBOOK PAGES*

Tag!

"Tag—you're it!" said Jan.
"Tag—you're it!" said Stan.

"Tag—you're it!" shouted Cam.
"Tag—you're it!" shouted Sam.

"Tag—you're it!" yelled Pat.
"Tag—you're it!" yelled Matt.

We played tag.
We ran and ran.
Then we sat.
Then we napped.

Sounds

Crack! That's the bat.
Sam hit the ball.
He runs all the bases—
Gets home without a fall!

Splat! That's the pancake
Flipping in the pan.
Dad cooks up breakfast
For me and my sister, Jan.

Bam! That's the drum
Playing with the band.
They march through the town.
They are very grand.

Crash! That's the wave
Rising to the sand.
The water hits our stuff—
We go up, inland!

Preparing for Your Week

Tips for Management and Differentiation

Refer to this section and to resources.corwin.com/puzzlepiecephonics-gradeK for resources and ideas to deepen your students' learning throughout the week. Feel free to put your own spin on the routines, too. For daily lesson plans, see pages 228–234 of this Teacher's Guide.

TIPS FOR PHONEMIC AWARENESS	• The focus for this week is changing the initial sound of a word to make two rhyming words. • If you notice your students need additional practice, extend the activity with more words.
TIPS FOR THE PUZZLE PIECE REVIEW	• All students will be introduced to three new short *a* family puzzle pieces this week. However, if students did not master the *–at, –ap,* and *–ag* families from last week, they will be sorting and completing their Practice Pieces using last week's sort. Students who mastered the *–at, –ap,* and *–ag* families will move on to sorting with the *–am, –an,* and *–and* families this week. • Point out to students the two or three pieces that they have already learned that make up the word family piece. For example, when teaching the *–am* piece, point to the *hat* piece /ă/ and the *mop* piece /m/. Explain to students that the *jam* piece takes both of those sounds and puts them on one piece to represent the *–am* family.
TIPS FOR BLENDING	• Follow the Blending routine and hold students accountable for producing all sounds for each word. Although some students are sorting with last week's sort, all students will blend the same lines. These students will be exposed to the new short *a* families, but are not expected to master them. Line 3 is a review of the short *a* families taught last week. • Remind students that the purpose of this concept is for them to use the words and spellings they know to assist them in spelling words they do not know. For example, if students can spell and identify the word *can*, they can use that knowledge to blend and identify the word *scan*. • Students will blend words with the *st* consonant blend. You can introduce the *stop* puzzle piece before blending.
TIPS FOR DICTATION AND QUICK SWITCH	• If time permits, complete a Quick Switch word chain with the *–and* family. • Students who are struggling with Quick Switch can write the rime (word family) on each line. When they hear the word, they will only need to focus on the initial sound. • If the majority of your students are still working with last week's sort, you can repeat the Dictation and Quick Switch lessons from Concept 4, Week 1.
TIPS FOR SORTING	• Model and positively reinforce the Sorting With Words routine repeatedly throughout the week. • Discuss the vocabulary words that appear in the Group 2 sort. Vocabulary words include the following: • *ram, bam, yam, pan, tan, van, brand, grand*

Preparing for Your Week

TIPS FOR THE PRACTICE PIECES

- Support students with the vocabulary words for this week. They may need assistance in drawing the pictures.

TIPS FOR FLUENCY

- This week students will read poems with words in the short *a* families. When students reach mastery with the daily poem, they can revisit poems from prior weeks.
- Students can highlight words within the short *a* families in the daily poems.
- Students can participate in a "Fluency Celebration." Call on students who feel prepared to present a particular poem in front of the class. Other students can follow along in the Fluency Notebook.
- There is space to have students illustrate the text underneath the poems. After students have mastered their fluency, have them illustrate to show comprehension.

Day 1

PHONEMIC AWARENESS: LISTEN

1. Give the directions. Say, "I am going to say a word. Then I am going to ask you to change the initial sound. Your job is to listen to the word, change the initial sound, and say the two rhyming words. For example, if I say '*bad*, change the initial sound to /r/,' you say '*rad*.' Then, you say the two rhyming words: '*bad, rad*.'"

2. Say the following words and sounds:

> cat, /r/ (rat)   sad, /m/ (mad)   bag, /l/ (lag)   lap, /t/ (tap)   hat, /s/ (sat)

THE BIG REVEAL

1. Say, "Last week we learned the short *a* families of *-at*, *-ap*, and *-ag*. When I point to the puzzle piece, you say the family." Lead students in recognizing all the short *a* families from last week.

2. Say, "This week we will continue to study short *a* families. You will be introduced to three new families: *-am*, *-an*, and *-and*."

3. Hold up the *jam* puzzle piece and say, "This is the *jam* piece. It represents the short *a* family *-am*. The *jam* piece says '/ăm/ /ăm/ /ăm/' like at the end of the word *jam*. Pretend to hold a knife in your right hand and a piece of toast in your left hand. Use your right hand to pretend to spread jam on your left hand and say '/ăm/.' Let's make a list of words that have the *jam* sound in them" (record the words).

4. Hold up the *man* puzzle piece and say, "This is the *man* piece. It represents the short *a* family *-an*. The *man* piece says '/ăn/ /ăn/ /ăn/' like at the end of the word *man*. Point your index finger straight out, place it underneath your nose to make a mustache, and say '/ăn/.' Let's make a list of words that have the *man* sound in them" (record the words).

5. Hold up the *band* puzzle piece and say, "This is the *band* piece. It represents the short *a* family *-and*. The *band* piece says '/ănd/ /ănd/ /ănd/' like at the end of the word *band*. Pretend you are holding an instrument in front of your face with both hands, wiggle your fingers, and say '/ănd/.' Let's make a list of words that have the *band* sound in them" (record the words).

BLENDING: PUTTING SOUNDS TOGETHER TO MAKE NEW WORDS

1. Follow the Blending routine on page I-17 of the Introduction.

2. Display the following words on the board one line at a time. Facilitate a discussion about the blending line focus after each line.

3. Then display the weekly sight words and sentence.

4. Discuss the word within the short *a* family found in the sentence.

ham	tan	hand	Discuss: *-am*, *-an*, and *-and* families
bam	can	sand	Discuss: *-am*, *-an*, and *-and* families
bag	rap	flat	Discuss: review of word families from last week

Sight Words: big   the

Sentence: The band is big.

DICTATION: STRETCH OUT YOUR WORDS

1. Have students turn to page 173 of the Learner's Notebook.

2. Follow the Dictation routine on page I-21 of the Introduction to dictate the following words:

> l. can   2. ham   3. band
>
> Sight Word: big

DICTATION: STRETCH OUT YOUR WORDS (Continued)	**3.** Use Dictation as an informal pretest of students' knowledge of this week's short *a* families. For students who are continuing to study Concept 4, Week 1 words, encourage them to sound out the words for Dictation as best they can.
PRACTICE: COMPLETE YOUR WORK ON YOUR OWN	**1.** Have students turn to page 169 (Group 1) or page 171 (Group 2) of the Learner's Notebook. **2.** Instruct students to tear out the sort and complete the following Practice Pieces: Quick Color, Careful Cut, Highlighter Hunt, and Sorting With Words (see further directions on pages I-37, I-38, I-43, and I-27 of the Introduction). **3.** Circulate as students work, which usually takes fifteen minutes, and coach as needed.
FLUENCY: READING LIKE YOU'RE SPEAKING	**1.** Have students turn to page 29 in the Fluency Notebook. **2.** Have students read one or more of the following poems: "Tag!" and "Sounds." **3.** Circulate and listen to students read or gather a small group of students who need additional support.

Day 2

PHONEMIC AWARENESS: LISTEN

1. Give the directions. Say, "I am going to say a word. Then I am going to ask you to change the initial sound. Your job is to listen to the word, change the initial sound, and say the two rhyming words. For example, if I say 'bad, change the initial sound to /r/,' you say 'rad.' Then, you say the two rhyming words: 'bad, rad.'"

2. Say the following words and sounds:

sand, /b/ (band)   ran, /t/ (tan)   lad, /t/ (tad)
Sam, /b/ (bam)   dab, /f/ (fab)

PUZZLE PIECE REVIEW

1. Say, "When I point to the piece, you tell me its name" (*jam, man, band*).

2. Say, "When I point to the piece, you tell me its sound" (/ăm/, /ăn/, /ănd/).

3. Say, "When I point to the piece, you tell me its spelling" (*–am, –an, –and*).

4. Say, "Write the spellings in the air with your finger" (students will form the letters *–am, –an,* and *–and*).

BLENDING: PUTTING SOUNDS TOGETHER TO MAKE NEW WORDS

1. Follow the Blending routine on page I-17 of the Introduction.

2. Display the following words on the board one line at a time. Facilitate a discussion about the blending line focus after each line.

3. Then display the weekly sight words and sentence.

4. Discuss the short *a* family words found in the sentence.

ban	band	bands	Discuss: how the spellings of the words build off of each other; *–s* meaning "more than one"
pan	Pam	ran	Discuss: medial sound of /ă/; capital *P* in *Pam* (name)
brag	snap	stat	Discuss: review of word families from last week

Sight Words: big   the

Sentence: The man is by the sand.

QUICK SWITCH: MANIPULATE YOUR WORDS

1. Have students turn to page 173 of the Learner's Notebook.

2. Follow the Quick Switch routine on page I-23 of the Introduction to dictate the following words:

ham → ram → Sam → bam → yam

3. Review the *–am* family with students. Discuss the capital *S* in the word *Sam*. Explain to students that this word is capitalized because it is the name of a person.

SORT: WHAT IS YOUR FOCUS PATTERN?

1. Have students take out their bag of words (created on Day 1) and follow the Sorting With Words routine on page I-27 of the Introduction.

PRACTICE: COMPLETE YOUR WORK ON YOUR OWN

1. Students will follow the Read and Trade routine on page I-47 of the Introduction.

2. Circulate as students work, which usually takes fifteen minutes, and coach as needed.

FLUENCY: READING LIKE YOU'RE SPEAKING

1. Have students turn to page 29 in the Fluency Notebook.

2. Have students read one or more of the following poems: "Tag!" and "Sounds."

3. Circulate and listen to students read or gather a small group of students who need additional support.

PHONEMIC AWARENESS: LISTEN

1. Give the directions. Say, "I am going to say a word. Then I am going to ask you to change the initial sound. Your job is to listen to the word, change the initial sound, and say the two rhyming words. For example, if I say '*bad*, change the initial sound to /r/,' you say '*rad*.' Then, you say the two rhyming words: '*bad, rad*.'"

2. Say the following words and sounds:

ram, /k/ (Cam) ban, /p/ (pan) ham, /p/ (Pam)
Sam, /b/ (bam) dab, /f/ (fab)

PUZZLE PIECE REVIEW

1. Say, "When I point to the piece, you tell me its name" (*jam, man, band*).

2. Say, "When I point to the piece, you tell me its sound" (/ăm/, /ăn/, /ănd/).

3. Say, "When I point to the piece, you tell me its spelling" (–*am*, –*an*, –*and*).

4. Say, "Write the spellings in the air with your finger" (students will form the letters –*am*, –*an*, and –*and*).

BLENDING: PUTTING SOUNDS TOGETHER TO MAKE NEW WORDS

1. Follow the Blending routine on page I-17 of the Introduction.

2. Display the following words on the board one line at a time. Facilitate a discussion about the blending line focus after each line.

3. Then display the weekly sight words and sentence.

4. Discuss the adjective (*big*) in the sentence. Discuss with students what kind of cat they are visualizing while they read.

pan	span	scan	Discuss: how to use knowledge of one word on the line to read or spell the next
grand	stand	brand	Discuss: –*and* family
swag	slap	scrap	Discuss: review of word families from last week

Sight Words: big   the
Sentence: Pam has a big cat.

DICTATION: STRETCH OUT YOUR WORDS

1. Have students turn to page 174 of the Learner's Notebook.

2. Follow the Dictation routine on page I-21 of the Introduction to dictate the following words:

1. bam   2. land   3. scan

Sight Word: the

3. For students who are continuing to study Concept 4, Week 1 words, encourage them to sound out the words for Dictation as best they can.

SORT: WHAT IS YOUR FOCUS PATTERN?

1. Have students take out their bag of words (created on Day 1) and follow the Sorting With Words routine on page I-27 of the Introduction.

PRACTICE: COMPLETE YOUR WORK ON YOUR OWN

1. Have students turn to page 175 in the Learner's Notebook.

2. Students will complete the Spell It Out routine on page I-49 of the Introduction.

3. Circulate as students work, which usually takes fifteen minutes, and coach as needed.

FLUENCY: READING LIKE YOU'RE SPEAKING

1. Have students turn to page 29 in the Fluency Notebook.

2. Have students read one or more of the following poems: "Tag!" and "Sounds."

3. Circulate and listen to students read or gather a small group of students who need additional support.

Day 4

PHONEMIC AWARENESS: LISTEN

1. Give the directions. Say, "I am going to say a word. Then I am going to ask you to change the initial sound. Your job is to listen to the word, change the initial sound, and say the two rhyming words. For example, if I say '*bad*, change the initial sound to /r/,' you say '*rad.*' Then, you say the two rhyming words: '*bad, rad.*'"

2. Say the following words and sounds:

    **band, /l/ (land)   tan, /r/ (ran)   tag, /s/ (sag)
    sand, /h/ (hand)   Pam, /j/ (jam)**

PUZZLE PIECE REVIEW

1. Say, "When I point to the piece, you tell me its name" (*jam, man, band*).

2. Say, "When I point to the piece, you tell me its sound" (/ăm/, /ăn/, /ănd/).

3. Say, "When I point to the piece, you tell me its spelling" (*–am, –an, –and*).

4. Say, "Write the spellings in the air with your finger" (students will form the letters *–am, –an,* and *–and*).

BLENDING: PUTTING SOUNDS TOGETHER TO MAKE NEW WORDS

1. Follow the Blending routine on page I-17 of the Introduction.

2. Display the following words on the board one line at a time. Facilitate a discussion about the blending line focus after each line.

3. Then display the weekly sight words and sentence.

4. Discuss the capital words in the sentence. Explain to students that *Stan* is capitalized because it is the beginning of the sentence and a name.

ran	can	can't	Discuss: *–an* family; contraction *can't* meaning "cannot"
brand	scam	Stan	Discuss: blends (*br, sc, st*); capital *S* in *Stan* (name)
nag	scat	splat	Discuss: review of word families from last week

Sight Words: **big   the**

Sentence: **Stan can tag Pam.**

QUICK SWITCH: MANIPULATE YOUR WORDS

1. Have students turn to page 174 of the Learner's Notebook.

2. Follow the Quick Switch routine on page I-23 of the Introduction to dictate the following words:

    ran → man → fan → can → scan

3. Review the *–an* family with students.

SORT: WHAT IS YOUR FOCUS PATTERN?

1. Have students take out their bag of words (created on Day 1) and follow the Sorting With Words routine on page I-27 of the Introduction.

PRACTICE: COMPLETE YOUR WORK ON YOUR OWN

1. Have students complete the following Practice Piece: Glue, Draw a Picture (on page I-50 of the Introduction).

2. Circulate as students work, which usually takes fifteen minutes, and coach as needed.

FLUENCY: READING LIKE YOU'RE SPEAKING

1. Have students turn to page 29 in the Fluency Notebook.

2. Have students read one or more of the following poems: "Tag!" and "Sounds."

3. Circulate and listen to students read or gather a small group of students who need additional support.

Day 5

PHONEMIC AWARENESS: LISTEN

1. Give the directions. Say, "I am going to say a word. Then I am going to ask you to change the initial sound. Your job is to listen to the word, change the initial sound, and say the two rhyming words. For example, if I say '*bad,* change the initial sound to /r/,' you say '*rad*.' Then, you say the two rhyming words: '*bad, rad*.'"

2. Say the following words and sounds:

> **hat, /b/ (bat)   pack, /t/ (tack)   land, /s/ (sand)**
> **bam, /l/ (lamb)   tad, /s/ (sad)**

REVIEW PATTERNS OF THE WEEK

1. Say, "Find a partner."

2. Say, "Tell your partner the names of this week's pieces" (*jam, man, band*).

3. Say, "Tell your partner the sounds of this week's pieces" (/ăm/, /ăn/, /ănd/).

4. Say, "Tell your partner the spellings of this week's pieces" (*–am, –an, –and*).

5. Say, "Write the spellings on your partner's back with your finger" (students will form the letters *–am, –an,* and *–and*).

SPELLING CHECK

1. Follow the Spelling Check routine on page I-34 of the Introduction.

2. Instruct students to sit in their word study groups and turn to page 177 of the Learner's Notebook.

3. Say, "I am going to say one word at a time to each group. Record the words as I say them to your group. Make sure you only record the words from your group."

4. Move back and forth between the groups and dictate the following words:

Words for Group I

1. lap
2. nag
3. rat
4. sap
5. lag

Sentence: I pat the cat.

Words for Group 2

1. land
2. ram
3. stand
4. fan
5. can

Sentence: The band is big.

WORD HUNT

1. Students will follow the Word Hunt routine on page I-55 of the Introduction.

2. Instruct students to search texts and the classroom for words within the short *a* families.

COMPREHENSION CHECK

1. Have students turn to page 178 of the Learner's Notebook.

2. Students will follow the Comprehension Check routine on page I-36 of the Introduction.

3. Check students' work. Circled answers are as follows:

1. The hand is big.

2. The van is big.

3. The ham is big.

4. Possible written responses include the following:

1. The _____ (*hand, van, ham*) is big.

2. The _____ is also big. (Use teacher discretion when grading. Students may fill in the blank with any item they feel is big.)

(Continued)

Day 5 (Continued)

WEEKLY CELEBRATION

1. Display the celebratory message: "Yes you can! You learned the *jam, man,* and *band* puzzle pieces!"

2. Encourage students to work together to read the message.

3. Have students copy the message onto their weekly certificate (see resources .corwin.com/puzzlepiecephonics-gradeK) and place it somewhere to take home.

Concept 5 Overview:

Short e Families

istock.com/FatCamera

WHAT ARE WORD FAMILIES?

The short *e* families concept builds on students' word family knowledge. With the last concept, students focused on short *a* families. Students should start to see words in chunks as the onset and rime. They will use their knowledge of consonants and short vowel *e* to master new words.

GOALS FOR THE CONCEPT

Students will
- Identify and represent short vowels
- Identify and represent consonant sounds
- Read and write sight words
- Recognize that words with the same rime rhyme
- Manipulate words in order to create a new word
- Develop reading fluency and comprehension

WEEKS FOR THIS CONCEPT

Week 1: Short *e* Families (*−et, −ed, −en*)
Week 2: Short *e* Families (*−ell, −eck, −est*)

Preparing for Your Week

Resources

PUZZLE PIECES

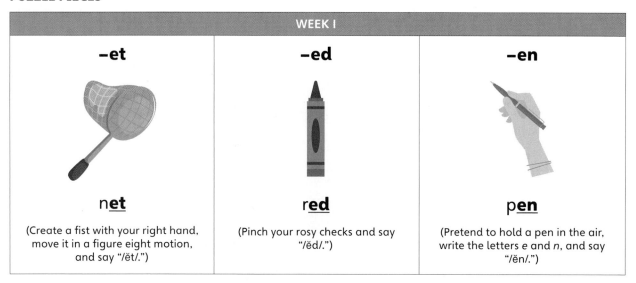

WEEK I		
–et	**–ed**	**–en**
n<u>et</u>	r<u>ed</u>	p<u>en</u>
(Create a fist with your right hand, move it in a figure eight motion, and say "/ĕt/.")	(Pinch your rosy checks and say "/ĕd/.")	(Pretend to hold a pen in the air, write the letters *e* and *n*, and say "/ĕn/.")

Net: istock.com/mocoo; Red: istock.com/MaksimYremenko; Pen: istock.com/pe-art

Preparing for Your Week

CORRESPONDING *LEARNER'S NOTEBOOK PAGES*

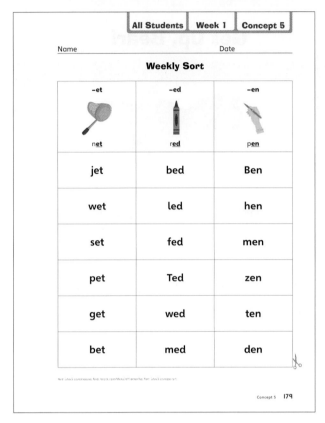

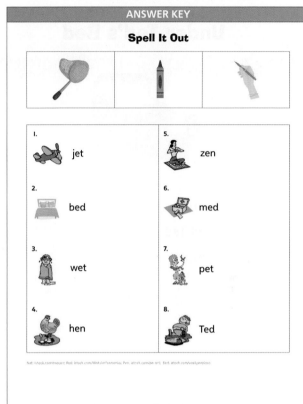

Preparing for Your Week

CORRESPONDING *FLUENCY NOTEBOOK PAGES*

Under Ted's Bed

"What is under your bed?"
Mom asked Ted.
"Not too much," Ted said.

"Just …
ten pens,
big red hens,
toy jets,
a cage for pets.
And …
Army men,
teddy bear Ben,
letters unsent,
a red circus tent."

"Not much?" Mom said.
"Not too much," said Ted.

Get Up, Bear!

Chick: Get up, Bear! Spring is here!
Bear: ZZZ!

Chick: Get up, Bear! Get out of bed!
Bear: ZZZZZZ!

Chick: Get up, Bear! Get out of your den!
Bear: ZZZZZZZZZ!

Chick: Get up, Bear! It's after ten!
Bear: ZZZZZZZZZZZZ!

Chick: Get up, Bear! Get up, get up, GET UP!
Bear: (growls) Noooooooo. It is comfy in my bed.

Chick: Get up, Bear! Come play and run!
Bear: Noooooo way, I must rest my head.

Chick: Get up, Bear! Spring is here!
Bear: Spring is here?

Chick: Yes, that's what I said!
Bear: Well, then, I'll get up.

Preparing for Your Week

Tips for Management and Differentiation

Refer to this section and to resources.corwin.com/puzzlepiecephonics-gradeK for resources and ideas to deepen your students' learning throughout the week. Feel free to put your own spin on the routines, too. For daily lesson plans, see pages 241–248 of this Teacher's Guide.

TIPS FOR PHONEMIC AWARENESS	• The focus for this week is listening for rhyming words. • If you notice your students need additional practice, extend the activity with more words. • Students are instructed to give a thumbs-up if the words rhyme or a thumbs-down if the words do not rhyme. You may substitute any motions for the activity. • If the two words rhyme, prompt students to verbally give you an additional word that rhymes. If the two words do not rhyme, prompt students to think of a word that rhymes with each.
TIPS FOR THE PUZZLE PIECE REVIEW	• Point out to students the two pieces that they have already learned that make up the word family piece. For example, when teaching the *–et* piece, point to the *bed* piece /ĕ/ and the *type* piece /t/. Explain to students that the *net* piece takes both of those sounds and puts them on one piece to represent the *–et* family.
TIPS FOR BLENDING	• Reblend lines if necessary. • Remind students that the purpose of this concept is for them to use the words and spellings they know to assist them in spelling words they do not know. For example, if students can spell and identify the word *led*, they can use that knowledge to blend and identify the word *sled*. • Students may need additional practice in reading words with the *ea* spelling of short *e* (*head, bread,* and *read*). These words will come up authentically in their reading. Create an oddballs poster for these words.
TIPS FOR DICTATION AND QUICK SWITCH	• If time permits, complete a Quick Switch word chain with the *–ed* and *–en* families. • Students who are struggling with Quick Switch can write the rime on each line. When they hear the word, they will only need to focus on the initial sound.
TIPS FOR SORTING	• Model and positively reinforce the Sorting With Words routine repeatedly throughout the week. • Discuss the vocabulary words that appear in the sort. Vocabulary words include the following: • *jet, set, bet, led, wed, med, hen, zen, den*

(Continued)

Preparing for Your Week

TIPS FOR THE PRACTICE PIECES

- Support students with the vocabulary words for this week. They may need assistance in drawing the pictures.

TIPS FOR FLUENCY

- Students can highlight words within the short *e* families in the daily poems.
- You can assign students fluency partners. Students will work together to achieve fluency with the daily poems.
- Students can participate in a "Fluency Celebration." Call on students who feel prepared to present a particular poem in front of the class. Other students can follow along in the Fluency Notebook.
- There is space to have students illustrate the text underneath the poems. After students have mastered their fluency, have them illustrate to show comprehension.
- "Get Up, Bear!" is written in parts. Students may act out the poem with a partner like a Reader's Theater script.

THE PUZZLE PIECE FAMILY

Launch Concept 5: Short *e* Families by following the Puzzle Piece Family routine on page I-11 of the Introduction.

1. Show students the following words:

ten	tell
red	Ted
bet	jet
deck	pen
rest	bent

2. Have students read the words with you. Underline the vowel and final consonant(s) in each word.

3. Facilitate a discussion that leads them to discover the Puzzle Piece Family: Short *e* Families.

PHONEMIC AWARENESS: LISTEN

1. Say, "I am going to say two words. Your job is to tell me if the two words rhyme. Give me a thumbs-up if the words are rhyming words and a thumbs-down if the words are not rhyming words."

2. Say the following pairs of words:

ten, den (yes)   get, bent (no)   hen, debt (no)
jet, set (yes)   bed, head (yes)

THE BIG REVEAL

1. Say, "Let's say all of our short vowel sounds." Lead students in saying "/ă/ /ĕ/ /ĭ/ /ŏ/ /ŭ/."

2. Say, "This week will be taking a closer look at short vowel *e*. We will be focusing on three short *e* families: *–et, –ed,* and *–en.*"

3. Hold up the *net* puzzle piece and say, "This is the *net* piece. It represents the short *e* family *–et*. The *net* piece says '/ĕt/ /ĕt/ /ĕt/' like at the end of the word *net*. Create a fist with your right hand, move it in a figure eight motion, and say '/ĕt/.' Let's make a list of words that have the *net* sound in them" (record the words).

4. Hold up the *red* puzzle piece and say, "This is the *red* piece. It represents the short *e* family *–ed*. The *red* piece says '/ĕd/ /ĕd/ /ĕd/' like at the end of the word *red*. Pinch your rosy cheeks and say '/ĕd/.' Let's make a list of words that have the *red* sound in them" (record the words).

5. Hold up the *pen* puzzle piece and say, "This is the *pen* piece. It represents the short *e* family *–en*. The *pen* piece says '/ĕn/ /ĕn/ /ĕn/' like at the end of the word *pen*. Pretend to hold a pen in the air, write the letters *e* and *n*, and say '/ĕn/.' Let's make a list of words that have the *pen* sound in them" (record the words).

(Continued)

BLENDING:
PUTTING SOUNDS
TOGETHER TO
MAKE NEW WORDS

1. Follow the Blending routine on page I-17 of the Introduction.

2. Display the following words on the board one line at a time. Facilitate a discussion about the blending line focus after each line.

3. Then display the weekly sight words and sentence.

4. Discuss the words that contain short _e_ families in the sentence.

net	set	let	Discuss: –_et_ word family
red	fed	bed	Discuss: –_ed_ word family
pen	hen	men	Discuss: –_en_ word family

Sight Words: ten   red

Sentence: The pen is red.

DICTATION:
STRETCH OUT
YOUR WORDS

1. Have students turn to page 181 of the Learner's Notebook.

2. Follow the Dictation routine on page I-21 of the Introduction to dictate the following words:

    I. met   2. hen   3. fed

    Sight Word: red

3. Use Dictation as an informal pretest of students' knowledge of this week's short _e_ families.

PRACTICE:
COMPLETE
YOUR WORK ON
YOUR OWN

1. Have students turn to page 179 of the Learner's Notebook.

2. Instruct students to tear out the sort and complete the following Practice Pieces: Quick Color, Careful Cut, Highlighter Hunt, and Sorting With Words (see further directions on pages I-37, I-38, I-43, and I-27 of the Introduction).

3. Circulate as students work, which usually takes fifteen minutes, and coach as needed.

FLUENCY:
READING LIKE
YOU'RE SPEAKING

1. Have students turn to page 30 in the Fluency Notebook.

2. Have students read one or more of the following poems: "Under Ted's Bed" and "Get Up, Bear!"

3. Circulate and listen to students read or gather a small group of students who need additional support.

PHONEMIC AWARENESS: LISTEN

1. Give the directions. Say, "I am going to say two words. Your job is to tell me if the two words rhyme. Give me a thumbs-up if the words are rhyming words and a thumbs-down if the words are not rhyming words."

2. Say the following pairs of words:

set, pen (no)   red, fed (yes)   men, pet (no)
Peg, leg (yes)   rent, pet (no)

PUZZLE PIECE REVIEW

1. Say, "When I point to the piece, you tell me its name" (*net, red, pen*).

2. Say, "When I point to the piece, you tell me its sound" (/ĕt/, /ĕd/, /ĕn/).

3. Say, "When I point to the piece, you tell me its spelling" (*–et, –ed, –en*).

4. Say, "Write the spellings in the air with your finger" (students will form the letters *–et, –ed,* and *–en*).

BLENDING: PUTTING SOUNDS TOGETHER TO MAKE NEW WORDS

1. Follow the Blending routine on page I-17 of the Introduction.

2. Display the following words on the board one line at a time. Facilitate a discussion about the blending line focus after each line.

3. Then display the weekly sight words and sentence.

4. Compare and contrast the words that contain short *e* families in the sentence. Discuss the *–s* in *hens* meaning "more than one."

pet	bet	get	Discuss: *–et* word family
med	wed	Ted	Discuss: *–ed* word family; discuss the uppercase *T* in *Ted*
den	ten	zen	Discuss: *–en* word family

Sight Word: ten   red

Sentence: We see ten pet hens.

QUICK SWITCH: MANIPULATE YOUR WORDS

1. Have students turn to page 181 of the Learner's Notebook.

2. Follow the Quick Switch routine on page I-23 of the Introduction to dictate the following words:

set → pet → bet → net → jet

3. Have students identify that all of today's Quick Switch words are in the *–et* family.

SORT: WHAT IS YOUR FOCUS PATTERN?

1. Have students take out their bag of words (created on Day 1) and follow the Sorting With Words routine on page I-27 of the Introduction.

PRACTICE: COMPLETE YOUR WORK ON YOUR OWN

1. Students will follow the Read and Trade routine on page I-47 of the Introduction.

2. Circulate as students work, which usually takes fifteen minutes, and coach as needed.

FLUENCY: READING LIKE YOU'RE SPEAKING

1. Have students turn to page 30 in the Fluency Notebook.

2. Have students read one or more of the following poems: "Under Ted's Bed" and "Get Up, Bear!"

3. Circulate and listen to students read or gather a small group of students who need additional support.

Day 3

PHONEMIC AWARENESS: LISTEN

1. Give the directions. Say, "I am going to say two words. Your job is to tell me if the two words rhyme. Give me a thumbs-up if the words are rhyming words and a thumbs-down if the words are not rhyming words."

2. Say the following pairs of words:

fell, felt (no)   Ted, wed (yes)   Ben, ten (yes)   yet, met (yes)   deck, dent (no)

PUZZLE PIECE REVIEW

1. Say, "When I point to the piece, you tell me its name" (_net, red, pen_).

2. Say, "When I point to the piece, you tell me its sound" (/ĕt/, /ĕd/, /ĕn/).

3. Say, "When I point to the piece, you tell me its spelling" (–_et_, –_ed_, –_en_).

4. Say, "Write the spellings in the air with your finger" (students will form the letters –_et_, –_ed_, and –_en_).

BLENDING: PUTTING SOUNDS TOGETHER TO MAKE NEW WORDS

1. Follow the Blending routine on page I-17 of the Introduction.

2. Display the following words on the board one line at a time. Facilitate a discussion about the blending line focus after each line.

3. Then display the weekly sight words and sentence.

4. Discuss the adjective (_red_) in the sentence. Discuss with students what kind of sled they are visualizing while they read.

let	led	sled	Discuss: vowel /ĕ/; help students use _led_ to blend _sled_
bet	Ben	bent	Discuss: vowel /ĕ/; help students use _Ben_ to blend _bent_
fed	red	Fred	Discuss: vowel /ĕ/; help students use _red_ to blend _Fred_

Sight Word: ten   red

Sentence: The sled is red.

DICTATION: STRETCH OUT YOUR WORDS

1. Have students turn to page 182 of the Learner's Notebook.

2. Follow the Dictation routine on page I-21 of the Introduction to dictate the following words:

   I. bet   2. wed   3. set

   Sight Word: ten

3. Have students identify the word family before recording each word. You can enrich students who need a challenge by dictating the additional word _went_.

SORT: WHAT IS YOUR FOCUS PATTERN?

1. Have students take out their bag of words (created on Day 1) and follow the Sorting With Words routine on page I-27 of the Introduction.

PRACTICE: COMPLETE YOUR WORK ON YOUR OWN

1. Have students turn to page 183 in the Learner Notebook.

2. Students will complete the Spell It Out routine on page I-49 of the Introduction.

3. Circulate as students work, which usually takes fifteen minutes, and coach as needed.

FLUENCY: READING LIKE YOU'RE SPEAKING

1. Have students turn to page 30 in the Fluency Notebook.

2. Have students read one or more of the following poems: "Under Ted's Bed" and "Get Up, Bear!"

3. Circulate and listen to students read or gather a small group of students who need additional support.

PHONEMIC AWARENESS: LISTEN

1. Give the directions. Say, "I am going to say two words. Your job is to tell me if the two words rhyme. Give me a thumbs-up if the words are rhyming words and a thumbs-down if the words are not rhyming words."

2. Say the following pairs of words:

Fred, said (yes)   best, bed (no)   lent, sent (yes)
Jess, let (no)   rest, head (no)

PUZZLE PIECE REVIEW

1. Say, "When I point to the piece, you tell me its name" (*net, red, pen*).

2. Say, "When I point to the piece, you tell me its sound" (/ĕt/, /ĕd/, /ĕn/).

3. Say, "When I point to the piece, you tell me its spelling" (*–et, –ed, –en*).

4. Say, "Write the spellings in the air with your finger" (students will form the letters *–et, –ed,* and *–en*).

BLENDING: PUTTING SOUNDS TOGETHER TO MAKE NEW WORDS

1. Follow the Blending routine on page I-17 of the Introduction.

2. Display the following words on the board one line at a time. Facilitate a discussion about the blending line focus after each line.

3. Then display the weekly sight words and sentence.

4. Discuss the plural words *bears* and *dens* in the sentence. Explain to students that adding the *–s* means "more than one."

den	ten	tens	Discuss: *–en* family; discuss the *–s* ending in *tens*
yet	pet	pets	Discuss: *–et* family; discuss the *–s* ending in *pets*
head	bread	read	Discuss: *–ead* family; explain that *ea* can be used to spell /ĕ/

Sight Words: ten   red

Sentence: Bears live in dens.

QUICK SWITCH: MANIPULATE YOUR WORDS

1. Have students turn to page 182 of the Learner's Notebook.

2. Follow the Quick Switch routine on page I-23 of the Introduction to dictate the following words:

let → bet → bed → Ben → pen

3. This Quick Switch chain includes all of the word families for the week. Help students hear all of the sounds in the words they are manipulating.

SORT: WHAT IS YOUR FOCUS PATTERN?

1. Have students take out their bag of words (created on Day 1) and follow the Sorting With Words routine on page I-27 of the Introduction.

PRACTICE: COMPLETE YOUR WORK ON YOUR OWN

1. Have students complete the following Practice Piece: Glue, Draw a Picture (on page I-50 of the Introduction).

2. Circulate as students work, which usually takes fifteen minutes, and coach as needed.

(Continued)

Day 4 (Continued)

**FLUENCY:
READING LIKE
YOU'RE SPEAKING**

1. Have students turn to page 30 in the Fluency Notebook.

2. Have students read one or more of the following poems: "Under Ted's Bed" and "Get Up, Bear!"

3. Circulate and listen to students read or gather a small group of students who need additional support.

PHONEMIC AWARENESS: LISTEN

1. Give the directions. Say, "I am going to say two words. Your job is to tell me if the two words rhyme. Give me a thumbs-up if the words are rhyming words and a thumbs-down if the words are not rhyming words."

2. Say the following pairs of words:

> fret, tech (no)   tell, smell (yes)   let, Brett (yes)
> lend, friend (yes)   sent, vet (no)

REVIEW PATTERNS OF THE WEEK

1. Say, "Find a partner."

2. Say, "Tell your partner the names of this week's pieces" (*net, red, pen*).

3. Say, "Tell your partner the sounds of this week's pieces" (/ĕt/, /ĕd/, /ĕn/).

4. Say, "Tell your partner the spellings of this week's pieces" (*–et, –ed, –en*).

5. Say, "Write the spellings on your partner's back with your finger" (students will form the letters *–et, –ed,* and *–en*).

SPELLING CHECK

1. Follow the Spelling Check routine on page I-34 of the Introduction.

2. Instruct students to turn to page 185 of the Learner's Notebook.

3. Say, "I am going to say one word at a time. Record the words as I say them."

4. Dictate the following words:

Words for the Spelling Check

l. fed
2. set
3. ten
4. med
5. den

Sentence: The hen is red.

WORD HUNT

1. Students will follow the Word Hunt routine on page I-55 of the Introduction.

2. Instruct students to search texts and the classroom for words within this week's short *e* families.

COMPREHENSION CHECK

1. Have students turn to page 186 of the Learner's Notebook.

2. Students will follow the Comprehension Check routine on page I-36 of the Introduction.

3. Check students' work. Circled answers are as follows:

1. The bed is red.

2. The hen is red.

3. The tent is red.

4. Possible written responses include the following:

1. The _____ (*bed, hen, tent*) is red.

2. The _____ is also red. (Use teacher discretion when grading. Students may fill in the blank with any item that is red.)

(Continued)

Day 5 (Continued)

WEEKLY CELEBRATION

1. Display the celebratory message: "You bet you can! You learned the *net, red,* and *pen* puzzle pieces!"

2. Encourage students to work together to read the message.

3. Have students copy the message onto their weekly certificate (see resources .corwin.com/puzzlepiecephonics-gradeK) and place it somewhere to take home.

Resources

PUZZLE PIECES

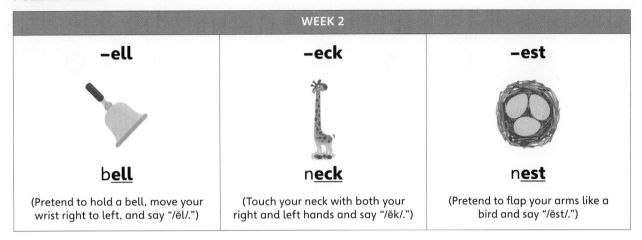

WEEK 2		
–ell	**–eck**	**–est**
b**ell**	n**eck**	n**est**
(Pretend to hold a bell, move your wrist right to left, and say "/ĕl/.")	(Touch your neck with both your right and left hands and say "/ĕk/.")	(Pretend to flap your arms like a bird and say "/ĕst/.")

Bell: istock.com/Quarta_; Neck: istock.com/passengerz; Nest: istock.com/StudioBarcelona

Preparing for Your Week

CORRESPONDING *LEARNER'S NOTEBOOK* PAGES

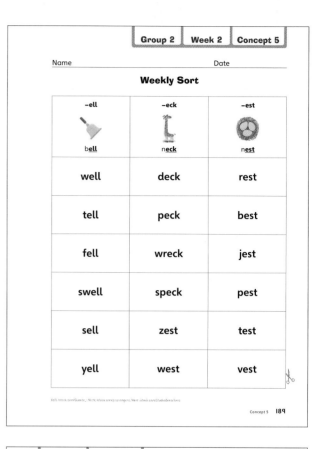

| Group 1 | Week 2 | Concept 5 |

Name _____ Date _____

Weekly Sort

–et	–ed	–en
n**et**	r**ed**	p**en**
jet	bed	Ben
wet	led	hen
set	fed	men
pet	Ted	zen
get	wed	ten
bet	med	den

Concept 5   187

| Group 2 | Week 2 | Concept 5 |

Name _____ Date _____

Weekly Sort

–ell	–eck	–est
b**ell**	n**eck**	n**est**
well	deck	rest
tell	peck	best
fell	wreck	jest
swell	speck	pest
sell	zest	test
yell	west	vest

Concept 5   189

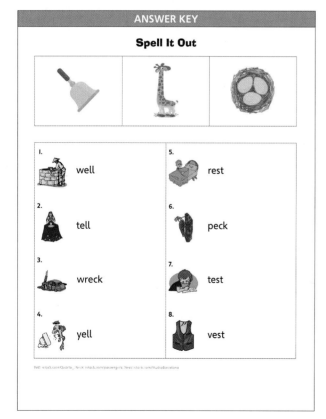

ANSWER KEY

Spell It Out

1. well	5. rest
2. tell	6. peck
3. wreck	7. test
4. yell	8. vest

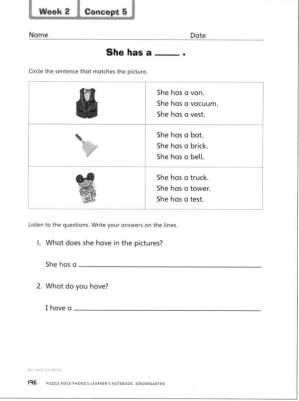

| Week 2 | Concept 5 |

Name _____ Date _____

She has a _____ .

Circle the sentence that matches the picture.

	She has a van. She has a vacuum. She has a vest.
	She has a bat. She has a brick. She has a bell.
	She has a truck. She has a tower. She has a test.

Listen to the questions. Write your answers on the lines.

1. What does she have in the pictures?

   She has a _____.

2. What do you have?

   I have a _____.

196   PUZZLE PIECE PHONICS LEARNER'S NOTEBOOK, KINDERGARTEN

Preparing for Your Week

CORRESPONDING *FLUENCY NOTEBOOK PAGES*

I Took My Test

I took my test.

I did my best.

I hope I did so well.

I took my test.

I did my best.

It's just too soon to tell!

I took my test.

I did my best.

I really know a lot.

I took my test.

I did my best.

A star is what I got!

Why Do Woodpeckers Peck?

Peck, peck. Peck, peck, peck.

Woodpecker is working hard

Pecking at that tree in my front yard.

Peck, peck. Peck, peck, peck.

Woodpecker is getting lunch!

He pecks for insects and larvae
to munch!

Peck, peck. Peck, peck, peck.

Woodpecker is making a nest!

In that dead tree cavity homes are
the best.

Peck, peck. Peck, peck, peck.

Woodpecker is hammering to talk!

He wants his mate to come back to
the flock.

Peck, peck, peck, peck, peck.

Woodpecker has had a busy day.

He pecks to eat, to sleep, and when
he has things to say.

Preparing for Your Week

Tips for Management and Differentiation

Refer to this section and to resources.corwin.com/puzzlepiecephonics-gradeK for resources and ideas to deepen your students' learning throughout the week. Feel free to put your own spin on the routines, too. For daily lesson plans, see pages 254–261 of this Teacher's Guide.

TIPS FOR PHONEMIC AWARENESS	• The focus for this week is changing the initial sound of a word to make two rhyming words. • If you notice your students need additional practice, extend the activity with more words.
TIPS FOR THE PUZZLE PIECE REVIEW	• All students will be introduced to three new short e family puzzle pieces this week. However, if students did not master the –et, –ed, and –en families from last week, they will be sorting and completing their Practice Pieces using last week's sort. Students who mastered the –et, –ed, and –en families will move on to sorting with the –ell, –eck, and –est families this week. • Point out to students the two or three pieces that they have already learned that make up the word family piece. For example, when teaching the –ell piece, point to the *bed* piece /ĕ/ and the *lollipop* piece /l/. Explain to students that the *bell* piece takes both of those sounds and puts them on one piece to represent the –ell family.
TIPS FOR BLENDING	• Follow the Blending routine and hold students accountable for producing all sounds for each word. Although some students are sorting with last week's sort, all students will blend the same lines. These students will be exposed to the new short e families, but are not expected to master them. Line 3 is a review of the short e families taught last week. • This week students will be exposed to the short vowel –ck spelling pattern. Up until this point, students have seen one letter and represented that one letter with one sound. With the short vowel –ck spelling pattern, students will learn that at times one sound is represented by multiple letters. You can briefly introduce and display the *clock* puzzle piece to show this sound spelling. Students are not expected to master this concept in one week. When blending, make sure to have two fingers under the spellings. This will show students that although there are multiple letters, they are only producing one sound. • Students will also be exposed to a vowel sound followed by a double consonant. Model to students that when they encounter the double consonant in their reading, they will not pronounce the sound twice. • Remind students that the purpose of this concept is for them to use the words and spellings they know to assist them in spelling words they do not know. For example, if students can spell and identify the word *peck*, they can use that knowledge to blend and identify the word *speck*.
TIPS FOR DICTATION AND QUICK SWITCH	• If time permits, complete a Quick Switch word chain with the –eck family. • Students who are struggling with Quick Switch can write the rime on each line. When they hear the word, they will only need to focus on the initial sound. • If the majority of your students are still working with last week's sort, you can repeat the Dictation and Quick Switch lessons from Concept 4, Week 1.

Preparing for Your Week

TIPS FOR SORTING	• Model and positively reinforce the Sorting With Words routine repeatedly throughout the week. • Discuss the vocabulary words that appear in the Group 2 sort. Vocabulary words include the following: • _swell, sell, deck, peck, wreck, speck, zest, jest, pest, vest_
TIPS FOR THE PRACTICE PIECES	• Support students with the vocabulary words for this week. They may need assistance in drawing the pictures.
TIPS FOR FLUENCY	• Students can highlight words within the short _e_ families in the daily poems. • You can assign students fluency partners. Students will work together to achieve fluency with the daily poems. • Students can participate in a "Fluency Celebration." Call on students who feel prepared to present a particular poem in front of the class. Other students can follow along in the Fluency Notebook.

Day 1

PHONEMIC AWARENESS: LISTEN

1. Give the directions. Say, "I am going to say a word. Then I am going to ask you to change the initial sound. Your job is to listen to the word, change the initial sound, and say the two rhyming words. For example, if I say 'bad, change the initial sound to /r/,' you say 'rad.' Then, you say the two rhyming words: 'bad, rad.'"

2. Say the following words and sounds:

bet, /n/ (net)　said, /m/ (med)　Ted, /l/ (led)　Jen, /t/ (ten)　get, /s/ (set)

THE BIG REVEAL

1. Say, "Last week we learned the short e families of –et, –ed, and –en. When I point to the piece, you say the family." Lead students in recognizing all the short e families from last week.

2. Say, "This week will continue to study short e families. You will be introduced to three new families: –ell, –eck, and –est."

3. Hold up the *bell* puzzle piece and say, "This is the *bell* piece. It represents the short e family –ell. The *bell* piece says '/ĕl/ /ĕl/ /ĕl/' like at the end of the word *bell*. Pretend to hold a bell, move your wrist right to left, and say '/ĕl/.' Let's make a list of words that have the *bell* sound in them" (record the words).

4. Hold up the *neck* puzzle piece and say, "This is the *neck* piece. It represents the short e family –eck. The neck piece says '/ĕk/ /ĕk/ /ĕk/' like at the end of the word *neck*. Touch your neck with both your right and left hands and say '/ĕk/.' Let's make a list of words that have the *neck* sound in them" (record the words).

5. Hold up the *nest* puzzle piece and say, "This is the *nest* piece. It represents the short e family –est. The *nest* piece says '/ĕst/ /ĕst/ /ĕst/' like at the end of the word *nest*. Pretend to flap your arms like a bird and say '/ĕst/.' Let's make a list of words that have the *nest* sound in them" (record the words).

BLENDING: PUTTING SOUNDS TOGETHER TO MAKE NEW WORDS

1. Follow the Blending routine on page I-17 of the Introduction.

2. Display the following words on the board one line at a time. Facilitate a discussion about the blending line focus after each line.

3. Then display the weekly sight words and sentence.

4. Discuss the word within the short e family found in the sentence.

bell	yell	nest	Discuss: –ell and –est word families; explain to students that double consonants make one sound
neck	deck	rest	Discuss: –eck and –est word families; explain to students that short vowel –ck makes one sound
set	wed	den	Discuss: review of word families from last week

Sight Words:　said　she

Sentence: We sat on the deck.

DICTATION:
STRETCH OUT
YOUR WORDS

1. Have students turn to page 191 of the Learner's Notebook.

2. Follow the Dictation routine on page I-21 of the Introduction to dictate the following words:

    I. yell   2. deck   3. rest

    Sight Word: said

3. Use Dictation as an informal pretest of students' knowledge of this week's short *e* families. For students who are continuing to study Concept 5, Week 1 words, encourage them to sound out the words for Dictation as best they can. Review the –*ll* and –*ck* patterns before dictating the words *yell* and *deck*.

PRACTICE:
COMPLETE
YOUR WORK ON
YOUR OWN

1. Have students turn to page 187 (Group 1) or page 189 (Group 2) of the Learner's Notebook.

2. Instruct students to tear out the sort and complete the following Practice Pieces: Quick Color, Careful Cut, Highlighter Hunt, and Sorting With Words (see further directions on pages I-37, I-38, I-43, and I-27 of the Introduction).

3. Circulate as students work, which usually takes fifteen minutes, and coach as needed.

FLUENCY:
READING LIKE
YOU'RE SPEAKING

1. Have students turn to page 31 in the Fluency Notebook.

2. Have students read one or more of the following poems: "I Took My Test" and "Why Do Woodpeckers Peck?"

3. Circulate and listen to students read or gather a small group of students who need additional support.

Day 2

PHONEMIC AWARENESS: LISTEN

1. Give the directions. Say, "I am going to say a word. Then I am going to ask you to change the initial sound. Your job is to listen to the word, change the initial sound, and say the two rhyming words. For example, if I say 'bad, change the initial sound to /r/,' you say 'rad.' Then, you say the two rhyming words: 'bad, rad.'"

2. Say the following words and sounds:

deck, /n/ (neck)   rest, /t/ (test)   med, /f/ (fed)
west, /v/ (vest)   fell, /y/ (yell)

PUZZLE PIECE REVIEW

1. Say, "When I point to the piece, you tell me its name" (*bell, neck, nest*).

2. Say, "When I point to the piece, you tell me its sound" (/ĕl/, /ĕk/, /ĕst/).

3. Say, "When I point to the piece, you tell me its spelling" (–ell, –eck, –est).

4. Say, "Write the spellings in the air with your finger" (students will form the letters –ell, –eck, and –est).

BLENDING: PUTTING SOUNDS TOGETHER TO MAKE NEW WORDS

1. Follow the Blending routine on page I-17 of the Introduction.

2. Display the following words on the board one line at a time. Facilitate a discussion about the blending line focus after each line.

3. Then display the weekly sight words and sentence.

4. Discuss the short *e* family words in the sentence.

sell	well	swell	Discuss: –*ell* word family
deck	peck	speck	Discuss: –*eck* word family
Ted	get	hen	Discuss: review of word families from last week

Sight Words: said she

Sentence: She has a red vest.

QUICK SWITCH: MANIPULATE YOUR WORDS

1. Have students turn to page 191 of the Learner's Notebook.

2. Follow the Quick Switch routine on page I-23 of the Introduction to dictate the following words:

well → tell → sell → fell → yell

3. Review the –*ell* word family with students. Remind them that the double *l* produces the /l/ sound.

SORT: WHAT IS YOUR FOCUS PATTERN?

1. Have students take out their bag of words (created on Day 1) and follow the Sorting With Words routine on page I-27 of the Introduction.

PRACTICE: COMPLETE YOUR WORK ON YOUR OWN

1. Students will follow the Read and Trade routine on page I-47 of the Introduction.

2. Circulate as students work, which usually takes fifteen minutes, and coach as needed.

FLUENCY: READING LIKE YOU'RE SPEAKING

1. Have students turn to page 31 in the Fluency Notebook.

2. Have students read one or more of the following poems: "I Took My Test" and "Why Do Woodpeckers Peck?"

3. Circulate and listen to students read or gather a small group of students who need additional support.

PHONEMIC AWARENESS: LISTEN

1. Give the directions. Say, "I am going to say a word. Then I am going to ask you to change the initial sound. Your job is to listen to the word, change the initial sound, and say the two rhyming words. For example, if I say '*bad*, change the initial sound to /r/,' you say '*rad*.' Then, you say the two rhyming words: '*bad, rad*.'"

2. Say the following words and sounds:

red, /b/ (bed)   tell, /w/ (well)   pest, /j/ (jest)
friend, /b/ (bend)   check, /d/ (deck)

PUZZLE PIECE REVIEW

1. Say, "When I point to the piece, you tell me its name" (*bell, neck, nest*).

2. Say, "When I point to the piece, you tell me its sound" (/ĕl/, /ĕk/, /ĕst/).

3. Say, "When I point to the piece, you tell me its spelling" (*–ell, –eck, –est*).

4. Say, "Write the spellings in the air with your finger" (students will form the letters *–ell, –eck,* and *–est*).

BLENDING: PUTTING SOUNDS TOGETHER TO MAKE NEW WORDS

1. Follow the Blending routine on page I-17 of the Introduction.

2. Display the following words on the board one line at a time. Facilitate a discussion about the blending line focus after each line.

3. Then display the weekly sight words and sentence.

4. Discuss the quotation marks in the sentence. Explain to students that the marks show someone (Ben) is speaking.

deck	wreck	specks	Discuss: *–eck* family; *–s* ending in *specks*
fell	jest	tests	Discuss: *–ell* and *–est* families; *–s* ending on *tests*
men	bet	bed	Discuss: review of word families from last week

Sight Words: said   she

Sentence: "I can see the nest," said Ben.

DICTATION: STRETCH OUT YOUR WORDS

1. Have students turn to page 192 of the Learner's Notebook.

2. Follow the Dictation routine on page I-21 of the Introduction to dictate the following words:

I. tell   2. zest   3. speck

Sight Word: she

3. For students who are continuing to study Concept 5, Week 1 words, encourage them to sound out the words for Dictation as best they can. Review the *–ll* and *–ck* patterns before dictating the words *tell* and *speck*.

SORT: WHAT IS YOUR FOCUS PATTERN?

1. Have students take out their bag of words (created on Day 1) and follow the Sorting With Words routine on page I-27 of the Introduction.

PRACTICE: COMPLETE YOUR WORK ON YOUR OWN

1. Have students turn to page 193 in the Learner's Notebook.

2. Students will complete the Spell It Out routine on page I-49 of the Introduction.

3. Circulate as students work, which usually takes fifteen minutes, and coach as needed.

(Continued)

Day 3 (Continued)

FLUENCY:
READING LIKE
YOU'RE SPEAKING

1. Have students turn to page 31 in the Fluency Notebook.

2. Have students read one or more of the following poems: "I Took My Test" and "Why Do Woodpeckers Peck?"

3. Circulate and listen to students read or gather a small group of students who need additional support.

PHONEMIC AWARENESS: LISTEN

1. Give the directions. Say, "I am going to say a word. Then I am going to ask you to change the initial sound. Your job is to listen to the word, change the initial sound, and say the two rhyming words. For example, if I say '*bad*, change the initial sound to /r/,' you say '*rad*.' Then, you will say the two rhyming words: '*bad, rad*.'"

2. Say the following words and sounds:

sent, /l/ (lent) debt, /y/ (yet) beg, /l/ (leg)
guest, /p/ (pest) rent, /d/ (dent)

PUZZLE PIECE REVIEW

1. Say, "When I point to the piece, you tell me its name" (*bell, neck, nest*).

2. Say, "When I point to the piece, you tell me its sound" (/ĕl/, /ĕk/, /ĕst/).

3. Say, "When I point to the piece, you tell me its spelling" (*–ell, –eck, –est*).

4. Say, "Write the spellings in the air with your finger" (students will form the letters *–ell, –eck*, and *–est*).

BLENDING: PUTTING SOUNDS TOGETHER TO MAKE NEW WORDS

1. Follow the Blending routine on page I-17 of the Introduction.

2. Display the following words on the board one line at a time. Facilitate a discussion about the blending line focus after each line.

3. Then display the weekly sight words and sentence.

4. Discuss the two rhyming words in the sentence (*best* and *test*).

best	bell	bells	Discuss: initial *b*; discuss the *–s* ending in *bells*
tell	test	tests	Discuss: initial *t*; discuss the *–s* ending in *tests*
well	west	wreck	Discuss: initial *w*; discuss that *wr* is a spelling of /r/

Sight Words: said she

Sentence: She did her best on the test.

QUICK SWITCH: MANIPULATE YOUR WORDS

1. Have students turn to page 192 of the Learner's Notebook.

2. Follow the Quick Switch routine on page I-23 of the Introduction to dictate the following words:

rest → best → jest → pest → test

3. Review the *–est* family with students.

SORT: WHAT IS YOUR FOCUS PATTERN?

1. Have students take out their bag of words (created on Day 1) and follow the Sorting With Words routine on page I-27 of the Introduction.

PRACTICE: COMPLETE YOUR WORK ON YOUR OWN

1. Have students complete the following Practice Piece: Glue, Draw a Picture (on page I-50 of the Introduction).

2. Circulate as students work, which usually takes fifteen minutes, and coach as needed.

FLUENCY: READING LIKE YOU'RE SPEAKING

1. Have students turn to page 31 in the Fluency Notebook.

2. Have students read one or more of the following poems: "I Took My Test" and "Why Do Woodpeckers Peck?"

3. Circulate and listen to students read or gather a small group of students who need additional support.

PHONEMIC AWARENESS: LISTEN	**1.** Give the directions. Say, "I am going to say a word. Then I am going to ask you to change the initial sound. Your job is to listen to the word, change the initial sound, and say the two rhyming words. For example, if I say '*bad*, change the initial sound to /r/,' you say '*rad*.' Then, you say the two rhyming words: '*bad, rad*.'"

2. Say the following words and sounds:

met, /b/ (bet)   wreck, /sp/ (speck)   best, /r/ (rest)
hem, /j/ (gem)   red, /h/ (head)

REVIEW PATTERNS OF THE WEEK

1. Say, "Find a partner."

2. Say, "Tell your partner the names of this week's pieces" (*bell, neck, nest*).

3. Say, "Tell your partner the sounds of this week's pieces" (/ĕl/, /ĕk/, /ĕst/).

4. Say, "Tell your partner the spellings of this week's pieces" (–*ell*, –*eck*, –*est*).

5. Say, "Write the spellings on your partner's back with your finger" (students will form the letters –*ell*, –*eck*, and –*est*).

SPELLING CHECK

1. Follow the Spelling Check routine on page I-34 of the Introduction.

2. Instruct students to sit in their word study groups and turn to page 195 of the Learner's Notebook.

3. Say, "I am going to say one word at a time to each group. Record the words as I say them to your group. Make sure you only record the words from your group."

4. Move back and forth between the groups and dictate the following words:

Words for Group I	**Words for Group 2**
1. jet	1. pest
2. med	2. deck
3. ten	3. swell
4. bet	4. vest
5. led	5. yell
Sentence: She is by the hens.	**Sentence: "I will pass the test," said Ted.**

WORD HUNT

1. Students will follow the Word Hunt routine on page I-55 of the Introduction.

2. Instruct students to search texts and the classroom for words within the short *e* families.

COMPREHENSION CHECK

1. Have students turn to page 196 of the Learner's Notebook.

2. Students will follow the Comprehension Check routine on page I-36 of the Introduction.

3. Check students' work. Circled answers are as follows:

   1. She has a vest.

   2. She has a bell.

   3. She has a test.

4. Possible written responses include the following:

   1. She has a _____. (*vest, bell, test*)

   2. I have a _____. (Use teacher discretion when grading. Students may fill in the blank with any item they have.)

WEEKLY CELEBRATION

1. Display the celebratory message: "You are the best! You learned the _bell, neck,_ and _nest_ puzzle pieces!"

2. Encourage students to work together to read the message.

3. Have students copy the message onto their weekly certificate (see resources .corwin.com/puzzlepiecephonics-gradeK) and place it somewhere to take home.

Concept 6 Overview:

Short *i* Families

istock.com/tatyana_tomsickova

WHAT ARE WORD FAMILIES?

This short *i* families concept builds on students' word family knowledge. During the last two concepts, students focused on short *a* and short *e* families. Students should start to see words in chunks as the onset and rime. They will use their knowledge of consonants and short vowel *i* to master new words.

GOALS FOR THE CONCEPT

Students will
*   Identify and represent short vowels
*   Identify and represent consonant sounds
*   Read and write sight words
*   Recognize that words with the same rime rhyme
*   Manipulate words in order to create a new word
*   Develop reading fluency and comprehension

WEEKS FOR THIS CONCEPT

Week 1: Short *i* Families (*–it, –in, –ip*)
Week 2: Short *i* Families (*–ick, –ill, –ig*)

Preparing for Your Week

Resources

PUZZLE PIECES

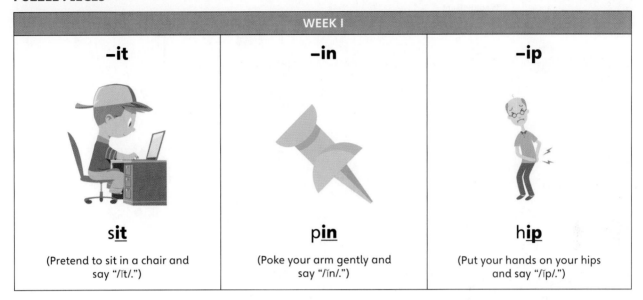

WEEK I		
–it	**–in**	**–ip**
s**it**	p**in**	h**ip**
(Pretend to sit in a chair and say "/ĭt/.")	(Poke your arm gently and say "/ĭn/.")	(Put your hands on your hips and say "/ĭp/.")

Sit: istock.com/pijama6l; Pin: istock.com/jane_Kelly; Hip: istock.com/MichikoDesign

Preparing for Your Week

CORRESPONDING _LEARNER'S NOTEBOOK_ PAGES

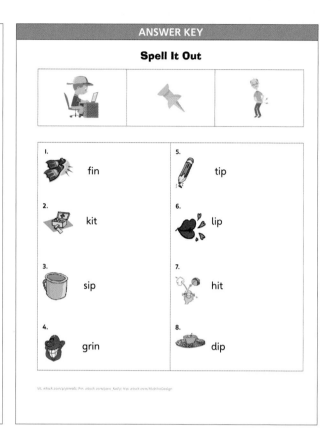

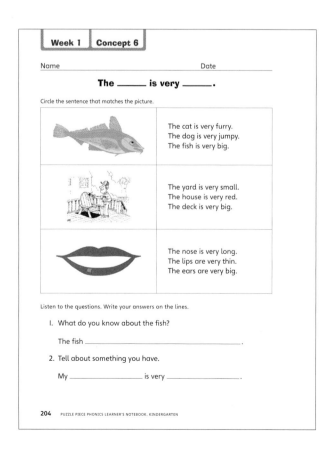

Preparing for Your Week

CORRESPONDING *FLUENCY NOTEBOOK PAGES*

Zip, Zip, STUCK

Zip, zip, STUCK.

"It will not go down,"

Kip says with a frown.

Zip, zip, STUCK.

"It's stuck for me too,"

says a friend named Sue.

Zip, zip, STUCK.

"That zipper won't budge,"

says teacher Mrs. Mudge.

Zip, zip, STUCK.

"What will I do?"

This zipper is like glue.

Zip, Zip, STUCK.

Mrs. Mudge gets a pin.

She pulls down with a grin.

Zip, Zip, OUT!

Kip is free!

The class is happy!

Fred and Frida Fish

Fred the fish has no fins.

He just sinks

    and sinks

        and sinks

to the bottom of the sea.

"Someone please help me!"

Frida fish sees Fred falling.

She just swims

    and swims

        and swims

to the bottom of the sea.

"Fred, don't worry—I am coming!"

Frida fish helps finless Fred.

He grabs onto her fin with his head.

Frida swims and pulls Fred all day.

Fred is thankful that now he can play!

Zip: istock.com/pe-art

Preparing for Your Week

Tips for Management and Differentiation

Refer to this section and to resources.corwin.com/puzzlepiecephonics-gradeK for resources and ideas to deepen your students' learning throughout the week. Feel free to put your own spin on the routines, too. For daily lesson plans, see pages 268–274 of this Teacher's Guide.

TIPS FOR PHONEMIC AWARENESS	• If you notice your students need additional practice, extend the activity with more words. • Students are instructed to give a thumbs-up if the words rhyme or a thumbs-down if the words do not rhyme. You may substitute any motions for the activity. • If the two words rhyme, prompt students to verbally give you an additional word that rhymes. If the two words do not rhyme, prompt students to think of a word that rhymes with each.
TIPS FOR THE PUZZLE PIECE REVIEW	• Last week, students learned the short _e_ families. Students may confuse the /ĕ/ sound with the /ĭ/ sound. When this occurs, have students tap out the word they are on and correspond the tapping with pointing to the puzzle pieces. • Point out to students the two pieces that they have already learned that make up the word family piece. For example, when teaching the _–it_ piece, point to the _zip_ piece /ĭ/ and the _type_ piece /t/. Explain to students that the _sit_ piece takes both of those sounds and puts them on one piece to represent the _–it_ family.
TIPS FOR BLENDING	• Reblend lines if necessary. • Remind students that the purpose of this concept is for them to use the words and spellings they know to assist them in spelling words they do not know. For example, if students can spell and identify the word _win_, they can use that knowledge to blend and identify the word _twin_. • Students may need additional practice in contrasting short vowel _e_ and short vowel _i_. If students are confusing the sounds, add an extra blending line of short _e_ words so they can blend, see, and hear the difference. • Students will blend digraphs and consonant blends this week. You can briefly introduce and display the _whale_ piece and the _shoe_ piece before blending on Day 2. On Day 4, introduce the _drum_ piece to students.
TIPS FOR DICTATION AND QUICK SWITCH	• If time permits, extend the Quick Switch activity to incorporate words from all short _i_ families. • Assist students who are struggling with Quick Switch by writing the rime on each line. When they hear the word, they will only need to focus on the initial sound.
TIPS FOR SORTING	• Model and positively reinforce the Sorting With Words routine repeatedly throughout the week. • Discuss the vocabulary words that appear in the sort. Vocabulary words include the following: • _wit, kit, lit, pit, pin, fin, bin, tin, grin, hip, tip, rip, sip, dip_

Preparing for Your Week

TIPS FOR THE PRACTICE PIECES

- Support students with the vocabulary words for this week. They may need assistance in drawing the pictures.

TIPS FOR FLUENCY

- Students can highlight words within the short *i* families in the daily poems.
- You can assign students fluency partners. Students will work together to achieve fluency with the daily poems.
- Students can participate in a "Fluency Celebration." Call on students who feel prepared to present a particular poem in front of the class. Other students can follow along in the Fluency Notebook.

THE PUZZLE PIECE FAMILY

Launch Concept 6: Short _i_ Families by following the Puzzle Piece Family routine on page I-11 of the Introduction.

1. Show students the following words:

wit	bin
lip	sick
gill	pig
grin	hit
dip	kick

2. Have students read the words with you. Underline the vowel and final consonant(s) in each word.

3. Facilitate a discussion that leads them to discover the Puzzle Piece Family: Short _i_ Families.

PHONEMIC AWARENESS: LISTEN

1. Give the directions. Say, "I am going to say two words. Your job is to tell me if the two words rhyme. Give me a thumbs-up if the words are rhyming words and a thumbs-down if the words are not rhyming words."

2. Say the following pairs of words:

tip, lip (yes) bin, zip (no) win, hit (no) grin, fin (yes) hip, dip (yes)

THE BIG REVEAL

1. Say, "Let's say all of our short vowel sounds." Lead students in saying "/ă/ /ĕ/ /ĭ/ /ŏ/ /ŭ/."

2. Say, "This week we will be taking a closer look at short vowel _i_. We will be focusing on three short _i_ families."

3. Hold up the _sit_ puzzle piece and say, "This is the _sit_ piece. It represents the short _i_ family –_it_. The _sit_ piece says '/ĭt/ /ĭt/ /ĭt/' like at the end of the word _sit_. Pretend to sit in a chair and say '/ĭt/.' Let's make a list of words that have the _sit_ sound in them" (record the words).

4. Hold up the _pin_ puzzle piece and say, "This is the _pin_ piece. It represents the short _i_ family –_in_. The _pin_ piece says '/ĭn/ /ĭn/ /ĭn/' like at the end of the word _pin_. Poke your arm gently and say '/ĭn/.' Let's make a list of words that have the _pin_ sound in them" (record the words).

5. Hold up the _hip_ puzzle piece and say, "This is the _hip_ piece. It represents the short _i_ family –_ip_. The _hip_ piece says '/ĭp/ /ĭp/ /ĭp/' like at the end of the word _hip_. Put your hands on your hips and say '/ĭp/.' Let's make a list of words that have the _hip_ sound in them" (record the words).

Day 1 (Continued)

BLENDING:
PUTTING SOUNDS
TOGETHER TO
MAKE NEW WORDS

1. Follow the Blending routine on page I-17 of the Introduction.

2. Display the following words on the board one line at a time. Facilitate a discussion about the blending line focus after each line.

3. Then display the weekly sight words and sentence.

4. Discuss the two words that contain short _i_ in the sentence. Identify the word _sit_ as part of the _-it_ family and help students blend the word _still_.

sit	hit	bit	Discuss: _-it_ word family
pin	fin	win	Discuss: _-in_ word family
hip	rip	sip	Discuss: _-ip_ word family

Sight Words: sit   very

Sentence: I sit very still at my desk.

DICTATION:
STRETCH OUT
YOUR WORDS

1. Have students turn to page 199 of the Learner's Notebook.

2. Follow the Dictation routine on page I-21 of the Introduction to dictate the following words:

　I. **pin**　2. **rip**　3. **bit**

　Sight Word: sit

3. Use Dictation as an informal pretest of students' knowledge of this week's short _i_ families.

PRACTICE:
COMPLETE
YOUR WORK ON
YOUR OWN

1. Have students turn to page 197 of the Learner's Notebook.

2. Instruct students to tear out the sort and complete the following Practice Pieces: Quick Color, Careful Cut, Highlighter Hunt, and Sorting With Words (see further directions on pages I-37, I-38, I-43, and I-27 of the Introduction).

3. Circulate as students work, which usually takes fifteen minutes, and coach as needed.

FLUENCY:
READING LIKE
YOU'RE SPEAKING

1. Have students turn to page 32 in the Fluency Notebook.

2. Have students read one or more of the following poems: "Zip, Zip, STUCK" and "Fred and Frida Fish."

3. Circulate and listen to students read or gather a small group of students who need additional support.

Day 2

PHONEMIC AWARENESS: LISTEN

1. Give the directions. Say, "I am going to say two words. Your job is to tell me if the two words rhyme. Give me a thumbs-up if the words are rhyming words and a thumbs-down if the words are not rhyming words."

2. Say the following pairs of words:

rip, wit (no)   sit, kit (yes)   fit, sick (no)   tin, bin (yes)   list, zip (no)

PUZZLE PIECE REVIEW

1. Say, "When I point to the piece, you tell me its name" (*sit, pin, hip*).

2. Say, "When I point to the piece, you tell me its sound" (/ĭt/, /ĭn/, /ĭp/).

3. Say, "When I point to the piece, you tell me its spelling" (*–it, –in, –ip*).

4. Say, "Write the spellings in the air with your finger" (students will form the letters *–it, –in,* and *–ip*).

BLENDING: PUTTING SOUNDS TOGETHER TO MAKE NEW WORDS

1. Follow the Blending routine on page I-17 of the Introduction.

2. Display the following words on the board one line at a time. Facilitate a discussion about the blending line focus after each line.

3. Then display the weekly sight words and sentence.

4. Discuss the two words that contain short *i* in the sentence. Identify the word *fin* as part of the *–in* family and help students blend the word *fish*.

wit	pit	kit	Discuss: *–it* word family
win	pin	kin	Discuss: *–in* word family
whip	pip	Kip	Discuss: *–ip* word family; the *wh* spelling of /w/ in *whip*; capital *K* in the name *Kip*

Sight Words: sit   very

Sentence: The fish had a red fin.

QUICK SWITCH: MANIPULATE YOUR WORDS

1. Have students turn to page 199 of the Learner's Notebook.

2. Follow the Quick Switch routine on page I-23 of the Introduction to dictate the following words:

hit → lit → lip → sip → zip

3. Have students change from the *–it* family to the *–ip* family.

SORT: WHAT IS YOUR FOCUS PATTERN?

1. Have students take out their bag of words (created on Day 1) and follow the Sorting With Words routine on page I-27 of the Introduction.

PRACTICE: COMPLETE YOUR WORK ON YOUR OWN

1. Students will follow the Read and Trade routine on page I-47 of the Introduction.

2. Circulate as students work, which usually takes fifteen minutes, and coach as needed.

FLUENCY: READING LIKE YOU'RE SPEAKING

1. Have students turn to page 32 in the Fluency Notebook.

2. Have students read one or more of the following poems: "Zip, Zip, STUCK" and "Fred and Frida Fish."

3. Circulate and listen to students read or gather a small group of students who need additional support.

PHONEMIC AWARENESS: LISTEN

1. Give the directions. Say, "I am going to say two words. Your job is to tell me if the two words rhyme. Give me a thumbs-up if the words are rhyming words and a thumbs-down if the words are not rhyming words."

2. Say the following pairs of words:

kit, lick (no)   **spit, hit** (yes)   **dip, grip** (yes)   **fin, win** (yes)   **bit, miss** (no)

PUZZLE PIECE REVIEW

1. Say, "When I point to the piece, you tell me its name" (*sit, pin, hip*).

2. Say, "When I point to the piece, you tell me its sound" (/ĭt/, /ĭn/, /ĭp/).

3. Say, "When I point to the piece, you tell me its spelling" (*–it, –in, –ip*).

4. Say, "Write the spellings in the air with your finger" (students will form the letters *–it, –in,* and *–ip*).

BLENDING: PUTTING SOUNDS TOGETHER TO MAKE NEW WORDS

1. Follow the Blending routine on page I-17 of the Introduction.

2. Display the following words on the board one line at a time. Facilitate a discussion about the blending line focus after each line.

3. Then display the weekly sight words and sentence.

4. Discuss the adjective (*happy*) in the sentence. Discuss with students what kind of cat they are visualizing while they read.

lit	hit	grit	Discuss: *–it* word family
tin	bin	grin	Discuss: *–in* word family
tip	rip	grip	Discuss: *–ip* word family; point out that all words in the last column begin with *gr–*

Sight Words: sit   very

Sentence: The cat had a very happy grin.

DICTATION: STRETCH OUT YOUR WORDS

1. Have students turn to page 200 of the Learner's Notebook.

2. Follow the Dictation routine on page I-21 of the Introduction to dictate the following words:

  I. zip   2. kit   3. grin

  Sight Word: very

3. The word *kit* includes the *k* spelling of /k/. Gently correct students if they use *c* to spell /k/.

SORT: WHAT IS YOUR FOCUS PATTERN?

1. Have students take out their bag of words (created on Day 1) and follow the Sorting With Words routine on page I-27 of the Introduction.

PRACTICE: COMPLETE YOUR WORK ON YOUR OWN

1. Have students turn to page 201 in the Learner's Notebook.

2. Students will complete the Spell It Out routine found on page I-49 of the Introduction.

3. Circulate as students work, which usually takes fifteen minutes, and coach as needed.

FLUENCY: READING LIKE YOU'RE SPEAKING

1. Have students turn to page 32 in the Fluency Notebook.

2. Have students read one or more of the following poems: "Zip, Zip, STUCK" and "Fred and Frida Fish."

3. Circulate and listen to students read or gather a small group of students who need additional support.

PHONEMIC AWARENESS: LISTEN

1. Give the directions. Say, "I am going to say two words. Your job is to tell me if the two words rhyme. Give me a thumbs-up if the words are rhyming words and a thumbs-down if the words are not rhyming words."

2. Say the following pairs of words:

mitt, pit (yes)   fib, flip (no)   crib, bib (yes)   lit, pig (no)   pill, fin (no)

PUZZLE PIECE REVIEW

1. Say, "When I point to the piece, you tell me its name" (_sit, pin, hip_).

2. Say, "When I point to the piece, you tell me its sound" (/ĭt/, /ĭn/, /ĭp/).

3. Say, "When I point to the piece, you tell me its spelling" (_–it, –in, –ip_).

4. Say, "Write the spellings in the air with your finger" (students will form the letters _–it, –in,_ and _–ip_).

BLENDING: PUTTING SOUNDS TOGETHER TO MAKE NEW WORDS

1. Follow the Blending routine on page I-17 of the Introduction.

2. Display the following words on the board one line at a time. Facilitate a discussion about the blending line focus after each line.

3. Then display the weekly sight words and sentence.

4. Help students identify the short _i_ family word found in the sentence. Identify the adjective _big_ and ask students what they are visualizing when they read.

tin	win	twin	Discuss: _–in_ word family
sip	lip	slip	Discuss: _–ip_ word family
dip	rip	drip	Discuss: _–ip_ word family; point out the initial consonant blends in the words in the last column

Sight Words: sit   very

Sentence: The rip was very big.

QUICK SWITCH: MANIPULATE YOUR WORDS

1. Have students turn to page 200 of the Learner's Notebook.

2. Follow the Quick Switch routine on page I-23 of the Introduction to dictate the following words:

fin → bin → tin → tip → hip

3. Words for this Quick Switch chain are in the _–in_ family and _–ip_ family. Help students get from _tin_ to _tip_.

SORT: WHAT IS YOUR FOCUS PATTERN?

1. Have students take out their bag of words (created on Day 1) and follow the Sorting With Words routine on page I-27 of the Introduction.

PRACTICE: COMPLETE YOUR WORK ON YOUR OWN

1. Have students complete the following Practice Piece: Glue, Draw a Picture (on page I-50 of the Introduction).

2. Circulate as students work, which usually takes fifteen minutes, and coach as needed.

FLUENCY: READING LIKE YOU'RE SPEAKING

1. Have students turn to page 32 in the Fluency Notebook.

2. Have students read one or more of the following poems: "Zip, Zip, STUCK" and "Fred and Frida Fish."

3. Circulate and listen to students read or gather a small group of students who need additional support.

PHONEMIC AWARENESS: LISTEN

1. Give the directions. Say, "I am going to say two words. Your job is to tell me if the two words rhyme. Give me a thumbs-up if the words are rhyming words and a thumbs-down if the words are not rhyming words."

2. Say the following pairs of words:

his, hip (no)   fit, kit (yes)   hint, lint (yes)   hid, did (yes)   lid, flip (no)

REVIEW PATTERNS OF THE WEEK

1. Say, "Find a partner."

2. Say, "Tell your partner the names of this week's pieces" (*sit, pin, hip*).

3. Say, "Tell your partner the sounds of this week's pieces" (/ĭt/, /ĭn/, /ĭp/).

4. Say, "Tell your partner the spellings of this week's pieces" (*–it, –in, –ip*).

5. Say, "Write the spellings on your partner's back with your fingers" (students will form the letters *–it, –in,* and *–ip*).

SPELLING CHECK

1. Follow the Spelling Check routine on page I-34 of the Introduction.

2. Instruct students to turn to page 203 of the Learner's Notebook.

3. Say, "I am going to say one word at a time. Record the words as I say them."

4. Dictate the following words:

Words for the Spelling Check

I. dip
2. win
3. pit
4. grin
5. lip

Sentence: His lips are very red.

WORD HUNT

1. Students will follow the Word Hunt routine on page I-55 of the Introduction.

2. Instruct students to search texts and the classroom for words within this week's short *i* families.

COMPREHENSION CHECK

1. Have students turn to page 204 of the Learner's Notebook.

2. Students will follow the Comprehension Check routine on page I-36 of the Introduction.

3. Check students' work. Circled answers are as follows:

1. The fish is very big.

2. The deck is very big.

3. The lips are very thin.

4. Possible written responses include the following:

1. The fish _____ (is very big; has spots; is purple and blue; any one response that is supported by the text or picture is correct).

2. My _____ is very _____ (students may fill in the blank with an adjective about anything they have).

(Continued)

Day 5 (Continued)

**WEEKLY
CELEBRATION**

1. Display the celebratory message: "It is a win! You learned the _sit, pin_, and _hip_ puzzle pieces!"

2. Encourage students to work together to read the message.

3. Have students copy the message onto their weekly certificate (see resources .corwin.com/puzzlepiecephonics-gradeK) and place it somewhere to take home.

Preparing for Your Week

Resources

PUZZLE PIECES

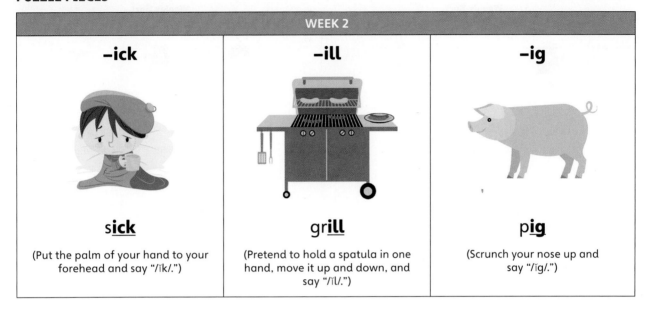

WEEK 2		
–ick	**–ill**	**–ig**
s**ick**	gr**ill**	p**ig**
(Put the palm of your hand to your forehead and say "/ĭk/.")	(Pretend to hold a spatula in one hand, move it up and down, and say "/ĭl/.")	(Scrunch your nose up and say "/ĭg/.")

Sick: istock.com/pijama61; Grill: istock.com/nicolecioe; Pig: istock.com/Nadzeya_Dzivakova

Preparing for Your Week

CORRESPONDING *LEARNER'S NOTEBOOK PAGES*

| Group 1 | Week 2 | Concept 6 |

Name _____ Date _____

Weekly Sort

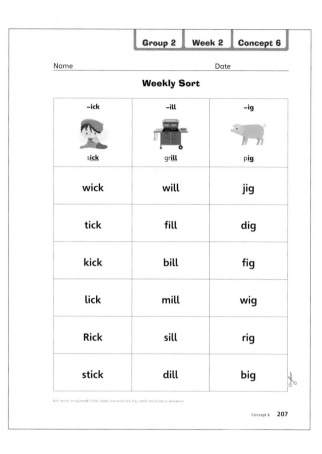

–it	–in	–ip
si**t**	p**in**	hi**p**
wit	fin	tip
kit	bin	lip
bit	tin	rip
hit	win	sip
lit	grin	zip
pit	lip	dip

Concept 6 **205**

| Group 2 | Week 2 | Concept 6 |

Name _____ Date _____

Weekly Sort

–ick	–ill	–ig
si**ck**	gr**ill**	p**ig**
wick	will	jig
tick	fill	dig
kick	bill	fig
lick	mill	wig
Rick	sill	rig
stick	dill	big

Concept 6 **207**

ANSWER KEY

Spell It Out

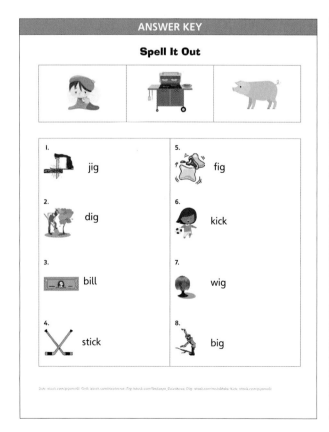

1. jig	5. fig
2. dig	6. kick
3. bill	7. wig
4. stick	8. big

| Week 2 | Concept 6 |

Name _____ Date _____

The _____ is as big as a _____!

Circle the sentence that matches the picture.

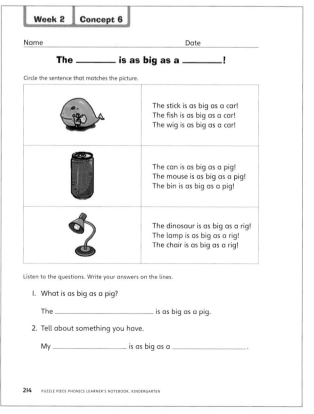

The stick is as big as a car!
The fish is as big as a car!
The wig is as big as a car!

The can is as big as a pig!
The mouse is as big as a pig!
The bin is as big as a pig!

The dinosaur is as big as a rig!
The lamp is as big as a rig!
The chair is as big as a rig!

Listen to the questions. Write your answers on the lines.

1. What is as big as a pig?

   The _____ is as big as a pig.

2. Tell about something you have.

   My _____ is as big as a _____.

214 PUZZLE PIECE PHONICS LEARNER'S NOTEBOOK, KINDERGARTEN

CORRESPONDING *FLUENCY NOTEBOOK PAGES*

Quick, Quick!

Quick, quick!
Give the ball a kick!

Quick, quick!
Give the lamp a wick!

Quick, quick!
Give the cone a lick!

Quick, quick!
Give the clock a tick!

Quick, quick!
Give the mail to Rick!

Quick, quick!
Give the dog a stick!

Quick, quick!

Give the _____

a(n) _____!

Summer Picnic

Come on over!
We're having a picnic.
It's a nice, hot summer day.
Get the sprinkler out to play!

Come on over!
We're firing up the grill.
We'll have food for all of you
On our big new barbeque!

Come on over!
We're scooping the ice cream.
Quick! It will drip—have a lick
Before the treat melts and sticks.

Come on over!
We're eating outside.
Bring your family and some friends.
The picnic will never end!

Quick: istock.com/Victor_Brave

Preparing for Your Week

Tips for Management and Differentiation

Refer to this section and to resources.corwin.com/puzzlepiecephonics-gradeK for resources and ideas to deepen your students' learning throughout the week. Feel free to put your own spin on the routines, too. For daily lesson plans, see pages 280–288 of this Teacher's Guide.

TIPS FOR PHONEMIC AWARENESS	• The focus for this week is changing the initial sound of a word to make two rhyming words. • If you notice your students need additional practice, extend the activity with more words.
TIPS FOR THE PUZZLE PIECE REVIEW	• All students will be introduced to three new short *i* family puzzle pieces this week. However, if students did not master the –*it*, –*in*, and –*ip* families from last week, they will be sorting and completing their Practice Pieces using last week's sort. Students who mastered the –*it*, –*in*, and –*ip* families will move on to sorting with the –*ick*, –*ill*, and –*ig* families this week. • Point out to students the two or three pieces that they have already learned that make up the word family piece. For example, when teaching the –*ig* piece, point to the *zip* piece /ĭ/ and the *gum* piece /g/. Explain to students that the *pig* piece takes both of those sounds and puts them on one piece to represent the –*ig* family.
TIPS FOR BLENDING	• Follow the Blending routine and hold students accountable for producing all sounds for each word. Although some students are sorting with last week's sort, all students will blend the same lines. These students will be exposed to the new short *i* families, but are not expected to master them. Line 3 is a review of the short *i* families taught last week. • Students have been introduced to the idea that two letters can be used to represent one sound. This week students will see another short vowel –*ck* family: –*ick*. Compare this family to the –*eck* family from Concept 5 and refer to the *clock* puzzle piece. • Students will also be exposed to a vowel sound followed by a double consonant. Model seeing the two consonants together and reading the sound only once. • Reblend lines if necessary. • Remind students that the purpose of this concept is for them to use the words and spellings they know to assist them in spelling words they do not know. For example, if students can spell and identify the word *fill*, they can use that knowledge to blend and identify the word *frill*.
TIPS FOR DICTATION AND QUICK SWITCH	• If time permits, extend the Quick Switch activity to use words from all families. • Students who are struggling with Quick Switch can write the rime on each line. When they hear the word, they will only need to focus on the initial sound. • If the majority of your students are still working with last week's sort, you can repeat the Dictation and Quick Switch lessons from Concept 6, Week 1.

Preparing for Your Week

TIPS FOR SORTING
- Model and positively reinforce the Sorting With Words routine repeatedly throughout the week.
- Discuss the vocabulary words that appear in the sort. Vocabulary words in the Group 2 sort include the following:
  - *wick, tick, bill, mill, sill, dill, jig, fig, wig, rig*

TIPS FOR THE PRACTICE PIECES
- Support students with the vocabulary words for this week. They may need assistance in drawing the pictures.

TIPS FOR FLUENCY
- Students can highlight words within the short *i* families in the daily poems.
- You can assign students fluency partners. Students will work together to achieve fluency with the daily poems.
- Students can participate in a "Fluency Celebration." Call on students who feel prepared to present a particular poem in front of the class. Other students can follow along in the Fluency Notebook.

Day 1

PHONEMIC AWARENESS: LISTEN

1. Give the directions. Say, "I am going to say a word. Then I am going to ask you to change the initial sound. Your job is to listen to the word, change the initial sound, and say the two rhyming words. For example, if I say '*bad*, change the initial sound to /r/,' you say '*rad*.' Then, you say the two rhyming words: '*bad, rad*.'"

2. Say the following words and sounds:

> sit, /b/ (bit)   bin, /t/ (tin)   lip, /s/ (sip)   wig, /f/ (fig)   mix, /s/ (six)

THE BIG REVEAL

1. Say, "Last week we learned the short *i* families of –*ip*, –*in*, and –*it*. When I point to the piece, you say the family." Lead students in recognizing all the short *i* families from last week.

2. Say, "This week we will continue to study short *i* families. You will be introduced to three new families: –*ick, –ill*, and *–ig*."

3. Hold up the *sick* puzzle piece and say, "This is the *sick* piece. It represents the short *i* family –*ick*. The *sick* piece says '/ĭk/ /ĭk/ /ĭk/' like at the end of the word *sick*. Put the palm of your hand to your forehead and say '/ĭk/.' Let's make a list of words that have the *sick* sound in them" (record the words).

4. Hold up the *grill* puzzle piece and say, "This is the *grill* piece. It represents the short *i* family –*ill*. The *grill* piece says '/ĭl/ /ĭl/ /ĭl/' like at the end of the word *grill*. Pretend to hold a spatula in one hand, move it up and down, and say '/ĭl/.' Let's make a list of words that have the *grill* sound in them" (record the words).

5. Hold up the *pig* puzzle piece and say, "This is the *pig* piece. It represents the short *i* family –*ig*. The *pig* piece says '/ĭg/ /ĭg/ /ĭg/' like at the end of the word *pig*. Scrunch your nose up and say '/ĭg/.' Let's make a list of words that have the *pig* sound in them" (record the words).

BLENDING: PUTTING SOUNDS TOGETHER TO MAKE NEW WORDS

1. Follow the Blending routine on page I-17 of the Introduction.

2. Display the following words on the board one line at a time. Facilitate a discussion about the blending line focus after each line.

3. Then display the weekly sight words and sentence.

4. Discuss the word within the short *i* family found in the sentence.

sick	grill	pig	Discuss: –*ick*, –*ill*, and –*ig* word families
kick	fill	dig	Discuss: –*ick*, –*ill*, and –*ig* word families
pit	lip	win	Discuss: review of word families from last week

Sight Words: six   as

Sentence: I was as sick as a dog.

DICTATION: STRETCH OUT YOUR WORDS

1. Have students turn to page 209 of the Learner's Notebook.

2. Follow the Dictation routine on page I-21 of the Introduction to dictate the following words:

> l. will   2. tick   3. big

> Sight Word: as

3. Use Dictation as an informal pretest of students' knowledge of this week's short *i* families. For students who are continuing to study Concept 6, Week 1 words, encourage them to sound out the words for Dictation as best they can. Assist students with the words *will* and *tick*. These words have multiple letters representing one sound.

**PRACTICE:
COMPLETE YOUR
WORK ON YOUR
OWN**

1. Have students turn to page 205 (Group 1) or page 207 (Group 2) of the Learner's Notebook.

2. Instruct students to tear out the sort and complete the following Practice Pieces: Quick Color, Careful Cut, Highlighter Hunt, and Sorting With Words (see further directions on pages I-37, I-38, I-43, and I-27 of the Introduction).

3. Circulate as students work, which usually takes fifteen minutes, and coach as needed.

**FLUENCY:
READING LIKE
YOU'RE SPEAKING**

1. Have students turn to page 33 in the Fluency Notebook.

2. Have students read one or more of the following poems: "Quick, Quick!" and "Summer Picnic."

3. Circulate and listen to students read or gather a small group of students who need additional support.

Day 2

PHONEMIC AWARENESS: LISTEN

1. Give the directions. Say, "I am going to say a word. Then I am going to ask you to change the initial sound. Your job is to listen to the word, change the initial sound, and say the two rhyming words. For example, if I say '*bad*, change the initial sound to /r/,' you say '*rad*.' Then, you say the two rhyming words: '*bad, rad*.'"

2. Say the following words and sounds:

> jig, /b/ (big)   mill, /s/ (sill)   lick, /n/ (Nick)   fill, /b/ (bill)   wig, /r/ (rig)

PUZZLE PIECE REVIEW

1. Say, "When I point to the piece, you tell me its name" (*sick, grill, pig*).

2. Say, "When I point to the piece, you tell me its sound" (/ĭk/, /ĭl/, /ĭg/).

3. Say, "When I point to the piece, you tell me its spelling" (*–ick, –ill, –ig*).

4. Say, "Write the spellings in the air with your finger" (students will form the letters *–ick, –ill,* and *–ig*).

BLENDING: PUTTING SOUNDS TOGETHER TO MAKE NEW WORDS

1. Follow the Blending routine on page I-17 of the Introduction.

2. Display the following words on the board one line at a time. Facilitate a discussion about the blending line focus after each line.

3. Then display the weekly sight words and sentence.

4. Discuss the short *i* family words found in the sentence.

wick	lick	tick	Discuss: *–ick* word family
mill	sill	dill	Discuss: *–ill* word family
bit	grin	zip	Discuss: review of word families from last week

Sight Words: six   as

Sentence: The six pigs ran up the hill.

QUICK SWITCH: MANIPULATE YOUR WORDS

1. Have students turn to page 209 of the Learner's Notebook.

2. Follow the Quick Switch routine on page I-23 of the Introduction to dictate the following words:

> wig → rig → dig → dill → fill

3. Review the *–ig* and *–ill* word families with students. Help students get from *dig* to *dill*.

SORT: WHAT IS YOUR FOCUS PATTERN?

1. Have students take out their bag of words (created on Day 1) and follow the Sorting With Words routine on page I-27 of the Introduction.

PRACTICE: COMPLETE YOUR WORK ON YOUR OWN

1. Students will follow the Read and Trade routine on page I-47 of the Introduction.

2. Circulate as students work, which usually takes fifteen minutes, and coach as needed.

FLUENCY: READING LIKE YOU'RE SPEAKING

1. Have students turn to page 33 in the Fluency Notebook.

2. Have students read one or more of the following poems: "Quick, Quick!" and "Summer Picnic."

3. Circulate and listen to students read or gather a small group of students who need additional support.

PHONEMIC AWARENESS: LISTEN

1. Give the directions. Say, "I am going to say a word. Then I am going to ask you to change the initial sound. Your job is to listen to the word, change the initial sound, and say the two rhyming words. For example, if I say '*bad*, change the initial sound to /r/,' you say '*rad*.' Then, you say the two rhyming words: '*bad, rad*.'"

2. Say the following words and sounds:

tick, /k/ (kick)   dill, /p/ (pill)   fig, /p/ (pig)   sick, /p/ (pick)   jig, /d/ (dig)

PUZZLE PIECE REVIEW

1. Say, "When I point to the piece, you tell me its name" (*sick, grill, pig*).

2. Say, "When I point to the piece, you tell me its sound" (/ĭk/, /ĭl/, /ĭg/).

3. Say, "When I point to the piece, you tell me its spelling" (–*ick*, –*ill*, –*ig*).

4. Say, "Write the spellings in the air with your finger" (students will form the letters –*ick*, –*ill*, and –*ig*).

BLENDING: PUTTING SOUNDS TOGETHER TO MAKE NEW WORDS

1. Follow the Blending routine on page I-17 of the Introduction.

2. Display the following words on the board one line at a time. Facilitate a discussion about the blending line focus after each line.

3. Then display the weekly sight words and sentence.

4. Identify the short *i* family words in the sentence. Identify the –*s* ending on *bricks* and explain to students that there is more than one brick.

wick	will	wig	Discuss: initial sound /w/
Bick	bill	big	Discuss: initial sound /b/; identify the capital *B* in the name *Bick*
kit	kin	Kip	Discuss: initial sound /k/; identify the capital *K* in the name *Kip*; review word families from last week

Sight Words: six   as

Sentence: Kip will get the bricks.

DICTATION: STRETCH OUT YOUR WORDS

1. Have students turn to page 210 of the Learner's Notebook.

2. Follow the Dictation routine on page I-21 of the Introduction to dictate the following words:

I. **dig**   2. **stick**   3. **mill**

Sight Word: six

3. For students who are continuing to study Week 1 words, encourage them to sound out the words for Dictation as best they can. Assist students with the words *stick* and *mill*. These words have multiple letters representing one sound.

SORT: WHAT IS YOUR FOCUS PATTERN?

1. Have students take out their bag of words (created on Day 1) and follow the Sorting With Words routine on page I-27 of the Introduction.

(Continued)

Day 3 (Continued)

PRACTICE: COMPLETE YOUR WORK ON YOUR OWN	**1.** Have students turn to page 211 in the Learner's Notebook.
	2. Students will complete the Spell It Out routine found on page I-49 of the Introduction.
	3. Circulate as students work, which usually takes fifteen minutes, and coach as needed.
FLUENCY: READING LIKE YOU'RE SPEAKING	**1.** Have students turn to page 33 in the Fluency Notebook.
	2. Have students read one or more of the following poems: "Quick, Quick!" and "Summer Picnic."
	3. Circulate and listen to students read or gather a small group of students who need additional support.

PHONEMIC AWARENESS: LISTEN

1. Give the directions. Say, "I am going to say a word. Then I am going to ask you to change the initial sound. Your job is to listen to the word, change the initial sound, and say the two rhyming words. For example, if I say '_bad_, change the initial sound to /r/,' you say '_rad._' Then, you say the two rhyming words: '_bad, rad._'"

2. Say the following groups of words:

lift, /g/ (gift)   lid, /r/ (rid)   list, /r/ (wrist)   mill, /h/ (hill)   sip, /t/ (tip)

PUZZLE PIECE REVIEW

1. Say, "When I point to the piece, you tell me its name" (_sick, grill, pig_).

2. Say, "When I point to the piece, you tell me its sound" (/ĭk/, /ĭl/, /ĭg/).

3. Say, "When I point to the piece, you tell me its spelling" (_–ick, –ill, –ig_).

4. Say, "Write the spellings in the air with your finger" (students will form the letters _–ick, –ill,_ and _–ig_).

BLENDING: PUTTING SOUNDS TOGETHER TO MAKE NEW WORDS

1. Follow the Blending routine on page I-17 of the Introduction.

2. Display the following words on the board one line at a time. Facilitate a discussion about the blending line focus after each line.

3. Then display the weekly sight words and sentence.

4. Discuss the short _i_ family words in the sentence. Explain to students that _Bill_ and _Rick_ are capitalized because they are names.

sick	**tick**	**stick**	Discuss: _–ick_ word family; help students use _tick_ to blend _stick_
fill	**rill**	**frill**	Discuss: _–ill_ word family; help students use _rill_ to blend _frill_
sip	**lip**	**slip**	Discuss: _–ip_ word family; help students use _lip_ to blend _slip_

Sight Words: six   as

Sentence: Bill kicked the ball to Rick.

QUICK SWITCH: MANIPULATE YOUR WORDS

1. Have students turn to page 210 of the Learner's Notebook.

2. Follow the Quick Switch routine on page I-23 of the Introduction to dictate the following words:

lick → tick → wick → will → grill

3. Review the _–ick_ and _–ill_ families with students. Help students get from _wick_ to _will_.

SORT: WHAT IS YOUR FOCUS PATTERN?

1. Have students take out their bag of words (created on Day 1) and follow the Sorting With Words routine on page I-27 of the Introduction.

PRACTICE: COMPLETE YOUR WORK ON YOUR OWN

1. Have students complete the following Practice Piece: Glue, Draw a Picture (on page I-50 of the Introduction).

2. Circulate as students work, which usually takes fifteen minutes, and coach as needed.

(Continued)

Day 4 (Continued)

**FLUENCY:
READING LIKE
YOU'RE SPEAKING**

1. Have students turn to page 33 in the Fluency Notebook.

2. Have students read one or more of the following poems: "Quick, Quick!" and "Summer Picnic."

3. Circulate and listen to students read or gather a small group of students who need additional support.

PHONEMIC AWARENESS: LISTEN	**1.** Give the directions. Say, "I am going to say a word. Then I am going to ask you to change the initial sound. Your job is to listen to the word, change the initial sound, and say the two rhyming words. For example, if I say '*bad*, change the initial sound to /r/,' you say '*rad*.' Then, you say the two rhyming words: '*bad, rad*.'"
	2. Say the following words and sounds:
	mix, /s/ (six) pick, /t/ (tick) bill, /s/ (sill) stick, /l/ (lick) hid, /d/ (did)
REVIEW PATTERNS OF THE WEEK	**1.** Say, "Find a partner."
	2. Say, "Tell your partner the names of this week's pieces" (*sick, grill, pig*).
	2. Say, "Tell your partner the sounds of this week's pieces" (/ĭk/, /ĭl/, /ĭg/).
	3. Say, "Tell your partner the spellings of this week's pieces" (*–ick, –ill, –ig*).
	4. Say, "Write the spellings on your partner's back with your finger" (students will form the letters *–ick, –ill*, and *–ig*).
SPELLING CHECK	**1.** Follow the Spelling Check routine on page I-34 of the Introduction.
	2. Instruct students to sit in their word study groups and turn to page 213 of the Learner's Notebook.
	3. Say, "I am going to say one word at a time to each group. Record the words as I say them to your group. Make sure you only record the words from your group."
	4. Move back and forth between the groups and dictate the following words:

Words for Group I	Words for Group 2
I. fin	I. lick
2. zip	2. dill
3. lit	3. rig
4. tin	4. fill
5. dip	5. stick
Sentence: I had six sips.	**Sentence: The stick is as big as a dog!**

WORD HUNT	**1.** Students will follow the Word Hunt routine on page I-55 of the Introduction.
	2. Instruct students to search texts and the classroom for words within the short *i* families.
COMPREHENSION CHECK	**1.** Have students turn to page 214 of the Learner's Notebook.
	2. Students will follow the Comprehension Check routine on page I-36 of the Introduction.
	3. Check students' work. Circled answers are as follows:
	1. The fish is as big as a car!
	2. The can is as big as a pig!
	3. The lamp is as big as a rig!
	4. Possible written responses include the following:
	1. The <u>can</u> is as big as a pig.
	2. My _____ is as big as a _____. Students may put any logical two words into the blanks. For example, "My chair is as big as a door!"

(Continued)

Day 5 (Continued)

**WEEKLY
CELEBRATION**

1. Display the celebratory message: "What a big win! You learned the _sick, grill,_ and _pig_ puzzle pieces!"

2. Encourage students to work together to read the message.

3. Have students copy the message onto their weekly certificate (see resources .corwin.com/puzzlepiecephonics-gradeK) and place it somewhere to take home.

Concept 7 Overview:

Short *o* Families

istock.com/monkeybusinessimages

WHAT ARE WORD FAMILIES?

This short *o* families concept builds on students' word family knowledge. During the last three concepts, students focused on short *a*, short *e*, and short *i* families. Students should be seeing words in chunks as the onset and rime. They will use their knowledge of consonants and short vowel *o* to master new words.

GOALS FOR THE CONCEPT

Students will
- Identify and represent short vowels
- Identify and represent consonant sounds
- Read and write sight words
- Recognize that words with the same rime rhyme
- Manipulate words in order to create a new word
- Develop reading fluency and comprehension

WEEKS FOR THIS CONCEPT

Week 1: Short *o* Families (*–op, –ot, –ob*)
Week 2: Short *o* Families (*–ong, –ock, –og*)

Preparing for Your Week

Resources

PUZZLE PIECES

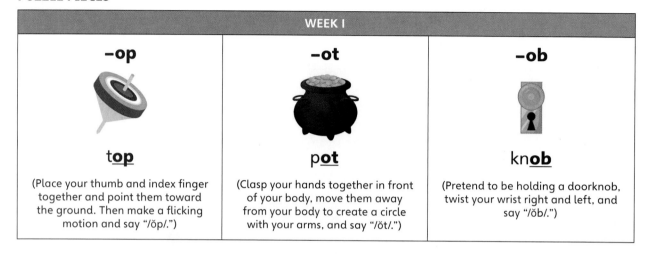

WEEK I		
–op	**–ot**	**–ob**
t**op**	p**ot**	kn**ob**
(Place your thumb and index finger together and point them toward the ground. Then make a flicking motion and say "/ŏp/.")	(Clasp your hands together in front of your body, move them away from your body to create a circle with your arms, and say "/ŏt/.")	(Pretend to be holding a doorknob, twist your wrist right and left, and say "/ŏb/.")

Top: istock.com/chdwh; Pot: istock.com/johnnylemonseed; Knob: istock.com/wektorygrafika

Preparing for Your Week

CORRESPONDING _LEARNER'S NOTEBOOK PAGES_

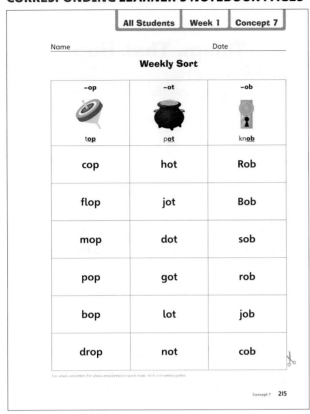

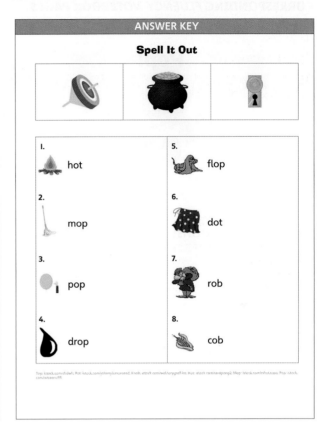

Preparing for Your Week

CORRESPONDING *FLUENCY NOTEBOOK PAGES*

Pop!

I got 10 balloons!

Pop!

Pop!

Pop!

Now I have 7.

I got 7 balloons!

Pop!

Pop!

Now I have 5.

I got 5 balloons!

Pop!

Now I have 4.

I got 4 balloons!

Pop!

Pop!

Now I have 2.

I got 2 balloons!

Pop!

Now I only have 1.

Things That Hop

I hop in the green grass.

I eat lots of carrots and like to hop fast.

I am a **bunny**!

I hop in the Outback.

I have strong legs and joeys in my sack.

I am a **kangaroo**!

I hop around the pond.

I catch flies with my long tongue.

I am a **frog**!

I hop in farmers' fields.

My green belly has my ears!

I am a **grasshopper**!

Preparing for Your Week

Tips for Management and Differentiation

Refer to this section and to resources.corwin.com/puzzlepiecephonics-gradeK for resources and ideas to deepen your students' learning throughout the week. Feel free to put your own spin on the routines, too. For daily lesson plans, see pages 294–300 of this Teacher's Guide.

TIPS FOR PHONEMIC AWARENESS	• If you notice your students need additional practice, extend the activity with more words. • Students are instructed to give a thumbs-up if the words rhyme or a thumbs-down if the words do not rhyme. You may substitute any motions for the activity. • If the two words rhyme, prompt students to verbally give you an additional word that rhymes. If the two words do not rhyme, prompt students to think of a word that rhymes with each.
TIPS FOR THE PUZZLE PIECE REVIEW	• Point out to students the two pieces that they have already learned that make up the word family piece. For example, when teaching the –ot piece, point to the *hot* piece /ŏ/ and the *type* piece /t/. Explain to students that the *pot* piece takes both of those sounds and puts them on one piece to represent the –ot family.
TIPS FOR BLENDING	• Reblend lines if necessary. • Remind students that the purpose of this concept is for them to use the words and spellings they know to assist them in spelling words they do not know. For example, if students can spell and identify the word *lot*, they can use that knowledge to blend and identify the word *plot*.
TIPS FOR DICTATION AND QUICK SWITCH	• If time permits, extend the Quick Switch activity to incorporate words from all short *o* families. • Assist students who are struggling with Quick Switch by writing the rime on each line. When they hear the word, they will only need to focus on the initial sound.
TIPS FOR SORTING	• Model and positively reinforce the Sorting With Words routine repeatedly throughout the week. • Discuss the vocabulary words that appear in the sort. Vocabulary words include the following: • *cop, flop, mop, bop, jot, dot, sob, rob, job, cob*
TIPS FOR THE PRACTICE PIECES	• Support students with the vocabulary words for this week. They may need assistance in drawing the pictures.
TIPS FOR FLUENCY	• Students can highlight words within the short *o* families in the daily poems. • You can assign students fluency partners. Students will work together to achieve fluency with the daily poems. • Students can participate in a "Fluency Celebration." Call on students who feel prepared to present a particular poem in front of the class. Other students can follow along in the Fluency Notebook. • "Things That Hop" is a "Who Am I?" poem. Read the poem to the students on the first day to see if they can use the context clues to figure out the animals that hop.

Day 1

THE PUZZLE PIECE FAMILY

Launch Concept 7: Short _o_ Families by following the Puzzle Piece Family routine on page I-11 of the Introduction.

1. Show students the following words:

top	clock
got	hog
drop	knob
cob	jog
long	lock

2. Have students read the words with you. Underline the vowel and final consonant(s) in each word.

3. Facilitate a discussion that leads them to discover the Puzzle Piece Family: Short _o_ Families.

PHONEMIC AWARENESS: LISTEN

1. Give the directions. Say, "I am going to say two words. Your job is to tell me if the two words rhyme. Give me a thumbs-up if the words are rhyming words and a thumbs-down if the words are not rhyming words."

2. Say the following pairs of words:

**pop, bop (yes) rob, got (no) drop, not (no)
job, knob (yes) jot, hot (yes)**

THE BIG REVEAL

1. Say, "Let's say all of our short vowel sounds." Lead students in saying "/ă/ /ĕ/ /ĭ/ /ŏ/ /ŭ/."

2. Say, "This week we will be taking a closer look at short vowel _o_. We will be focusing on three short _o_ families: –op, –ot, and –ob."

3. Hold up the _top_ puzzle piece and say, "This is the _top_ piece. It represents the short _o_ family –op. The _top_ piece says '/ŏp/ /ŏp/ /ŏp/' like at the end of the word _top_. Place your thumb and index finger together and point them toward the ground. Then make a flicking motion and say '/ŏp/.' Let's make a list of words that have the _top_ sound in them" (record the words).

4. Hold up the _pot_ puzzle piece and say, "This is the _pot_ piece. It represents the short _o_ family –ot. The _pot_ piece says '/ŏt/ /ŏt/ /ŏt/' like at the end of the word _pot_. Clasp your hands together in front of your body, move them away from your body to create a circle with your arms, and say '/ŏt/.' Let's make a list of words that have the _pot_ sound in them" (record the words).

5. Hold up the _knob_ puzzle piece and say, "This is the _knob_ piece. It represents the short _o_ family –ob. The _knob_ piece says '/ŏb/ /ŏb/ /ŏb/' like at the end of the word _knob_. Pretend to be holding a doorknob, twist your wrist right and left, and say '/ŏb/.' Let's make a list of words that have the _knob_ sound in them" (record the words).

Day 1 (Continued)

BLENDING:
PUTTING SOUNDS
TOGETHER TO
MAKE NEW WORDS

1. Follow the Blending routine on page I-17 of the Introduction.

2. Display the following words on the board one line at a time. Facilitate a discussion about the blending line focus after each line.

3. Then display the weekly sight words and sentence.

4. Discuss the words within the short *o* family found in the sentence.

top	**mop**	**pop**	Discuss: *–op* word family
pot	**hot**	**dot**	Discuss: *–ot* word family
knob	**job**	**cob**	Discuss: *–ob* word family; help students read the *kn–* spelling of /n/

Sight Words: not   off

Sentence: I got a lot of mops.

DICTATION:
STRETCH OUT
YOUR WORDS

1. Have students turn to page 217 of the Learner's Notebook.

2. Follow the Dictation routine on page I-21 of the Introduction to dictate the following words:

   I. top   2. hot   3. job

   Sight Word: off

3. Use Dictation as an informal pretest of students' knowledge of this week's short *o* families.

PRACTICE:
COMPLETE
YOUR WORK ON
YOUR OWN

1. Have students turn to page 215 of the Learner's Notebook.

2. Instruct students to tear out the sort and complete the following Practice Pieces: Quick Color, Careful Cut, Highlighter Hunt, and Sorting With Words (see further directions on pages I-37, I-38, I-43, and I-27 of the Introduction).

3. Circulate as students work, which usually takes fifteen minutes, and coach as needed.

FLUENCY:
READING LIKE
YOU'RE SPEAKING

1. Have students turn to page 34 in the Fluency Notebook.

2. Have students read one or more of the following poems: "Pop!" and "Things That Hop."

3. Circulate and listen to students read or gather a small group of students who need additional support.

Day 2

PHONEMIC AWARENESS: LISTEN	**1.** Give the directions. Say, "I am going to say two words. Your job is to tell me if the two words rhyme. Give me a thumbs-up if the words are rhyming words and a thumbs-down if the words are not rhyming words."
	2. Say the following pairs of words:
	<div align="center">not, pop (no) hot, pot (yes) lot, flop (no) dot, snot (yes) cob, mop (no)</div>
PUZZLE PIECE REVIEW	**1.** Say, "When I point to the piece, you tell me its name" (*top, pot, knob*).
	2. Say, "When I point to the piece, you tell me its sound" (/ŏp/, /ŏt/, /ŏb/).
	3. Say, "When I point to the piece, you tell me its spelling" (*–op, –ot, –ob*).
	4. Say, "Write the spellings in the air with your finger" (students will form the letters *–op, –ot,* and *–ob*).
BLENDING: PUTTING SOUNDS TOGETHER TO MAKE NEW WORDS	**1.** Follow the Blending routine on page I-17 of the Introduction.
	2. Display the following words on the board one line at a time. Facilitate a discussion about the blending line focus after each line.
	3. Then display the weekly sight words and sentence.
	4. Discuss the short *o* family words found in the sentence.

bop	drop	flop	Discuss: *–op* word family
not	got	lot	Discuss: *–ot* word family
rob	sob	Bob	Discuss: *–ob* word family; identify *Bob* as a name

Sight Words: not   off

Sentence: Bob went off to his job.

QUICK SWITCH: MANIPULATE YOUR WORDS	**1.** Have students turn to page 217 of the Learner's Notebook.
	2. Follow the Quick Switch routine on page I-23 of the Introduction to dictate the following words:
	<div align="center">top → bop → pop → pot → got</div>
	3. Review the *–op* and *–ot* families. Help students get from *pop* to *pot*.
SORT: WHAT IS YOUR FOCUS PATTERN?	**1.** Have students take out their bag of words (created on Day 1) and follow the Sorting With Words routine on page I-27 of the Introduction.
PRACTICE: COMPLETE YOUR WORK ON YOUR OWN	**1.** Students will follow the Read and Trade routine on page I-47 of the Introduction.
	2. Circulate as students work, which usually takes fifteen minutes, and coach as needed.
FLUENCY: READING LIKE YOU'RE SPEAKING	**1.** Have students turn to page 34 in the Fluency Notebook.
	2. Have students read one or more of the following poems: "Pop!" and "Things That Hop."
	3. Circulate and listen to students read or gather a small group of students who need additional support.

PHONEMIC AWARENESS: LISTEN

1. Give the directions. Say, "I am going to say two words. Your job is to tell me if the two words rhyme. Give me a thumbs-up if the words are rhyming words and a thumbs-down if the words are not rhyming words."

2. Say the following groups of words:

dot, pod (no)   flop, bop (yes)   Bob, sob (yes)
got, fought (yes)   sock, got (no)

PUZZLE PIECE REVIEW

1. Say, "When I point to the piece, you tell me its name" (*top, pot, knob*).

2. Say, "When I point to the piece, you tell me its sound" (/ŏp/, /ŏt/, /ŏb/).

3. Say, "When I point to the piece, you tell me its spelling" (*–op, –ot, –ob*).

4. Say, "Write the spellings in the air with your finger" (students will form the letters *–op, –ot,* and *–ob*).

BLENDING: PUTTING SOUNDS TOGETHER TO MAKE NEW WORDS

1. Follow the Blending routine on page I-17 of the Introduction.

2. Display the following words on the board one line at a time. Facilitate a discussion about the blending line focus after each line.

3. Then display the weekly sight words and sentence.

4. Discuss the short *o* family words found in the sentence. Ask students what they visualized while reading the sentence.

lop	hop	mop	Discuss: *–op* word family
lot	hot	mot	Discuss: *–ot* word family
lob	hob	mob	Discuss: *–ob* word family; point out that all words in each column begin with *the same consonant*

Sight Words: not   off

Sentence: She will not drop the cat.

DICTATION: STRETCH OUT YOUR WORDS

1. Have students turn to page 218 of the Learner's Notebook.

2. Follow the Dictation routine on page I-21 of the Introduction to dictate the following words:

I. dot   2. hop   3. sob

Sight Word: not

3. Discuss *sob* as a vocabulary word.

SORT: WHAT IS YOUR FOCUS PATTERN?

1. Have students take out their bag of words (created on Day 1) and follow the Sorting With Words routine on page I-27 of the Introduction.

PRACTICE: COMPLETE YOUR WORK ON YOUR OWN

1. Have students turn to page 219 in the Learner's Notebook.

2. Students will complete the Spell It Out routine on page I-49 of the Introduction.

3. Circulate as students work, which usually takes fifteen minutes, and coach as needed.

FLUENCY: READING LIKE YOU'RE SPEAKING

1. Have students turn to page 34 in the Fluency Notebook.

2. Have students read one or more of the following poems: "Pop!" and "Things That Hop."

3. Circulate and listen to students read or gather a small group of students who need additional support.

Day 4

PHONEMIC AWARENESS: LISTEN	**1.** Give the directions, Say, "I am going to say two words. Your job is to tell me if the two words rhyme. Give me a thumbs-up if the words are rhyming words and a thumbs-down if the words are not rhyming words."
	
	2. Say the following groups of words:
	
	    caught, hot (yes) pop, pot (no) fog, bog (yes)
	    song, lot (no) tot, tock (no)

PUZZLE PIECE REVIEW	**1.** Say, "When I point to the piece, you tell me its name" (_top, pot, knob_). **2.** Say, "When I point to the piece, you tell me its sound" (/ŏp/, /ŏt/, /ŏb/). **3.** Say, "When I point to the piece, you tell me its spelling" (–_op_, –_ot_, –_ob_). **4.** Say, "Write the spellings in the air with your finger" (students will form the letters –_op_, –_ot_, and –_ob_).
BLENDING: PUTTING SOUNDS TOGETHER TO MAKE NEW WORDS	**1.** Follow the Blending routine on page I-17 of the Introduction. **2.** Display the following words on the board one line at a time. Facilitate a discussion about the blending line focus after each line. **3.** Then display the weekly sight words and sentence. **4.** Discuss the short _o_ family word found in the sentence. Discuss who might be saying the sentence (a bus driver, a parent, etc.).

cop	crop	plop	Discuss: –_op_ word family
pot	lot	plot	Discuss: –_ot_ word family; help students use _lot_ to blend _plot_
gob	Bob	blob	Discuss: –_ob_ word family; identify the capital _B_ in _Bob_ and help students use _Bob_ to blend _blob_

Sight Words: not   off

Sentence: Do not get off the bus.

QUICK SWITCH: MANIPULATE YOUR WORDS	**1.** Have students turn to page 218 of the Learner's Notebook. **2.** Follow the Quick Switch routine on page I-23 of the Introduction to dictate the following words: **Rob → sob → job → jot → got** **3.** Review the –_ob_ family and –_ot_ family. Help students get from _job_ to _jot_.
SORT: WHAT IS YOUR FOCUS PATTERN?	**1.** Have students take out their bag of words (created on Day 1) and follow the Sorting With Words routine on page I-27 of the Introduction.
PRACTICE: COMPLETE YOUR WORK ON YOUR OWN	**1.** Have students complete the following Practice Piece: Glue, Draw a Picture (on page I-50 of the Introduction). **2.** Circulate as students work, which usually takes fifteen minutes, and coach as needed.
FLUENCY: READING LIKE YOU'RE SPEAKING	**1.** Have students turn to page 34 in the Fluency Notebook. **2.** Have students read one or more of the following poems: "Pop!" and "Things That Hop." **3.** Circulate and listen to students read or gather a small group of students who need additional support.

PHONEMIC AWARENESS: LISTEN

1. Give the directions. Say, "I am going to say two words. Your job is to tell me if the two words rhyme. Give me a thumbs-up if the words are rhyming words and a thumbs-down if the words are not rhyming words."

2. Say the following pairs of words:

> **bop, hot (no)   dot, got (yes)   lock, hawk (yes)
> cop, drop (yes)   Rob, Todd (no)**

REVIEW PATTERNS OF THE WEEK

1. Say, "Find a partner."

2. Say, "Tell your partner the names of this week's pieces" (*top, pot, knob*).

3. Say, "Tell your partner the sounds of this week's pieces" (/ŏp/, /ŏt/, /ŏb/).

4. Say, "Tell your partner the spellings of this week's pieces" (*–op, –ot, –ob*).

5. Say, "Write the spellings on your partner's back with your finger" (students will form the letters *–op, –ot,* and *–ob*).

SPELLING CHECK

1. Follow the Spelling Check routine on page I-34 of the Introduction.

2. Instruct students to turn to page 221 of the Learner's Notebook.

3. Say, "I am going to say one word at a time. Record the words as I say them."

4. Dictate the following words:

Words for the Spelling Check

1. pop
2. job
3. lot
4. not
5. mop

Sentence: Rob did not get a mop.

WORD HUNT

1. Students will follow the Word Hunt routine on page I-55 of the Introduction.

2. Instruct students to search texts and the classroom for words within this week's short *o* families.

COMPREHENSION CHECK

1. Have students turn to page 222 of the Learner's Notebook.

2. Students will follow the Comprehension Check routine on page I-36 of the Introduction.

3. Check students' work. Circled answers are as follows:

1. The pot is not full.
2. The dog is not white.
3. The mop is not lost.

(Continued)

Day 5 (Continued)

COMPREHENSION CHECK (Continued)

4. Possible written responses include the following:

1. The dog is _____ (not white; brown; long; any one response that is supported by the text or picture is correct).
2. My _____ (glass, plate, pot, dog, cat, hamster, mop, broom, vacuum) is not lost. (Students may also put any logical word(s) into the blank(s). For example, "My sock is not lost.")

WEEKLY CELEBRATION

1. Display the celebratory message: "A top-notch job! You learned the *top*, *pot*, and *knob* puzzle pieces!"

2. Encourage students to work together to read the message.

3. Have students copy the message onto their weekly certificate (see resources.corwin.com/puzzlepiecephonics-gradeK) and place it somewhere to take home.

Preparing for Your Week

Resources

PUZZLE PIECES

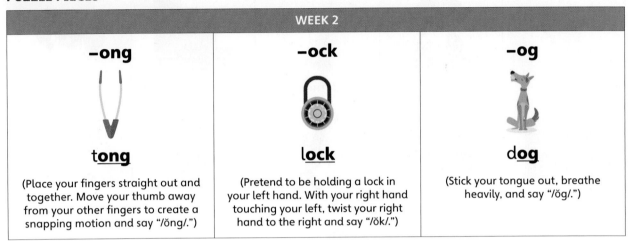

WEEK 2		
–ong	**–ock**	**–og**
t**ong**	l**ock**	d**og**
(Place your fingers straight out and together. Move your thumb away from your other fingers to create a snapping motion and say "/ŏng/.")	(Pretend to be holding a lock in your left hand. With your right hand touching your left, twist your right hand to the right and say "/ŏk/.")	(Stick your tongue out, breathe heavily, and say "/ŏg/.")

PREASSESSMENT DIRECTIONS

You can give the preassessment any day(s) during Concept 7, Week 2. You can split up the rows and do parts on different days. Do what works for your class.

Instruct students to turn to **page 223 in the Learner's Notebook**. Explain to students that they have not studied multiple short vowels within the same sort. Up to this point, students have only focused on one or two short vowels mixed per week. This check will be used to see how well they can already apply their knowledge of short vowels to spell new words. Tell students that you will use the results to form word study groups (see Tips for Scoring on page 302) and set goals.

When giving this assessment, go row by row in saying the word in the picture. Students are *not* guessing what the picture is. You tell them the word.

Tong: istock.com/adekvat; Lock: istock.com/luplupme; Dog: istock.com/TopVectors

Preparing for Your Week

PREASSESSMENT: MIXED VOWELS AND CONSONANTS SPELLING CHECK

ANSWER KEY				
I. clap	2. pup	3. mop	4. step	5. rip
6. mist	7. last	8. rust	9. lost	10. best
II. hem	12. mom	13. ram	14. slim	15. plum
16. fun	17. win	18. men	19. plan	20. non
21. glad	22. plug	23. sunk	24. send	25. pick

Mop: istock.com/mhatzapa; Fun: istock.com/graphic-bee

EVALUATING THE ASSESSMENT: WHAT TO LOOK FOR

- One-to-one sound correspondence
- Knowledge of consonants
- Knowledge of short vowels
- Knowledge of basic blends

TIPS FOR SCORING

This assessment is to be used to group your students and understand their needs. All rows contain mixed short vowels and consonants. Students will need to listen to the word and tap out the sounds they hear.

Each word is worth one point. For each correctly spelled word, students earn one point. Add up their points to see their total score.

- If students receive 0–14 points, they will be working with Group 1 words.
- If students receive 15–25 points, they will be working with Group 2 words.

This is a guide to get you started, but use teacher discretion when placing your students in groups. Remember, these groups are flexible and can change each week if necessary. See key above for answers.

Preparing for Your Week

CORRESPONDING *LEARNER'S NOTEBOOK PAGES*

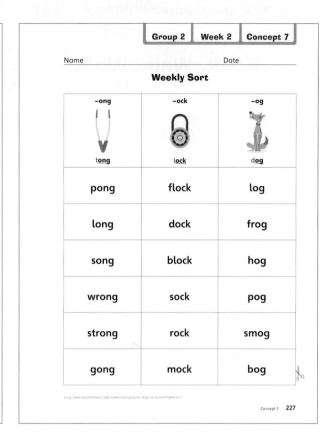

Group 1 | Week 2 | Concept 7

Name _____ Date _____

Weekly Sort

–op	–ot	–ob
t**op**	p**ot**	kn**ob**
cop	hot	Rob
flop	jot	Bob
mop	dot	sob
pop	got	rob
bop	lot	job
drop	not	cob

Concept 7 **225**

Group 2 | Week 2 | Concept 7

Name _____ Date _____

Weekly Sort

–ong	–ock	–og
t**ong**	l**ock**	d**og**
pong	flock	log
long	dock	frog
song	block	hog
wrong	sock	pog
strong	rock	smog
gong	mock	bog

Concept 7 **227**

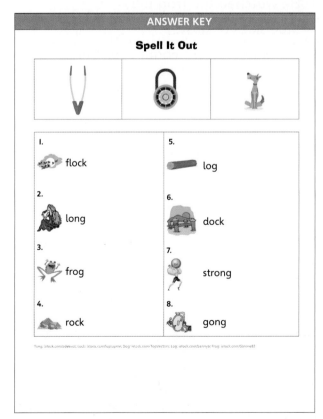

ANSWER KEY

Spell It Out

1. flock	5. log
2. long	6. dock
3. frog	7. strong
4. rock	8. gong

Tong: istock.com/adekvat; Lock: istock.com/luplupme; Dog: istock.com/TopVectors; Log: istock.com/bennyb; Frog: istock.com/Gonne83

Week 2 | Concept 7

Name _____ Date _____

The _____ got a _____.

Circle the sentence that matches the picture.

	The frog got a lily pad. The frog got a rock. The frog got a bug.
	The dog got a bone. The dog got a house. The dog got a pat.
	The hog got a nap. The hog got a carrot. The hog got a bath.

Listen to the questions. Write your answers on the lines.

1. What did the frog get?

   The frog got a _____

2. Tell about something you were given.

   I got a _____

234   PUZZLE PIECE PHONICS LEARNER'S NOTEBOOK, KINDERGARTEN

Preparing for Your Week

CORRESPONDING _FLUENCY NOTEBOOK PAGES_

Walk, Walk, Walk

Walk, walk, walk—
There's something in my sock!

Walk, walk, walk—
That something starts to talk!

Walk, walk, hop—
Turns out it was a frog!

Walk, walk, hop—
We hang out all day long.

Hop, hop, hop—
We head toward the pond.

Hop, hop, hop—
We have a special bond.

Frog and Fox

There once was a giant frog
who loved to hop on the log.
He jumped all day—
blue skies or gray.
He loved his home on the bog.

There once was a giant fox
who hid quietly by the rocks.
He watched the frog play—
blue skies or gray.
He waited for his chance to stalk.

One day the frog saw the fox.
He was scared, but they had a talk.
Frog asked fox to play.
The two played all day.
Frog learned even he could outfox.

Preparing for Your Week

Tips for Management and Differentiation

Refer to this section and to resources.corwin.com/puzzlepiecephonics-gradeK for resources and ideas to deepen your students' learning throughout the week. Feel free to put your own spin on the routines, too. For daily lesson plans, see pages 307–316 of this Teacher's Guide.

TIPS FOR PHONEMIC AWARENESS	• The focus for this week is changing the initial sound of a word to make two rhyming words. • If you notice your students need additional practice, extend the activity with more words.
TIPS FOR THE PUZZLE PIECE REVIEW	• All students will be introduced to three new short *o* family puzzle pieces this week. However, if students did not master the *–op, –ot,* and *–ob* families from last week, they will be sorting and completing their Practice Pieces using last week's sort. Students who mastered the *–op, –ot,* and *–ob* families will move on to sorting with the *–ong, –ock,* and *–og* families this week. • Point out to students the two or three pieces that they have already learned that make up the word family piece. For example, when teaching the *–og* piece, point to the *log* piece /ŏ/ and the *gum* piece /g/. Explain to students that the *dog* piece takes both of those sounds and puts them on one piece to represent the *–og* family.
TIPS FOR BLENDING	• Follow the Blending routine and hold students accountable for producing all sounds for each word. Although some students are sorting with last week's sort, all students will blend the same lines. These students will be exposed to the new short *o* families, but are not expected to master them. Line 3 is a review of the short *o* families taught last week. • Reblend lines if necessary. • Remind students that the purpose of this concept is for them to use the words and spellings they know to assist them in spelling words they do not know. For example, if students can spell and identify the word *bog*, they can use that knowledge to blend and identify the word *blog*. • Take a closer look at the *–og* and *–ong* families. When students are writing, they may omit the *n* in the *–ong* family. Hold students accountable for capturing this sound. • Students will blend words in the *–ock* family. Connect this word family to the *–eck* and *–ick* word families and refer to the *clock* piece.
TIPS FOR DICTATION AND QUICK SWITCH	• If time permits, extend the Quick Switch word chains to incorporate all families each day. • Students who are struggling with Quick Switch can write the rime on each line. When they hear the word, they will only need to focus on the initial sound. • If the majority of your students are still working with last week's sort, you can repeat the Dictation and Quick Switch lessons from Concept 7, Week 1.

(Continued)

Preparing for Your Week

TIPS FOR SORTING

- Model and positively reinforce the Sorting With Words routine repeatedly throughout the week.
- Discuss the vocabulary words that appear in the sort. Vocabulary words in the Group 2 sort include the following:
  - *tong, pong, wrong, strong, gong, flock, dock, mock, hog, pog, smog, bog*

TIPS FOR THE PRACTICE PIECES

- Support students with the vocabulary words for this week. They may need assistance in drawing the pictures.

TIPS FOR FLUENCY

- Students can highlight words within the short *o* families in the daily poems.
- You can assign students fluency partners. Students will work together to achieve fluency with the daily poems.
- Students can participate in a "Fluency Celebration." Call on students who feel prepared to present a particular poem in front of the class. Other students can follow along in the Fluency Notebook.

PHONEMIC AWARENESS: LISTEN

1. Give the directions. Say, "I am going to say a word. Then I am going to ask you to change the initial sound. Your job is to listen to the word, change the initial sound, and say the two rhyming words. For example, if I say '*bad*, change the initial sound to /r/,' you say '*rad*.' Then, you say the two rhyming words: '*bad, rad*.'"

2. Say the following words and sounds:

hot, /l/ (lot)   mop, /t/ (top)   moss, /t/ (toss)
rot, /f/ (fought)   sock, /l/ (lock)

THE BIG REVEAL

1. Say, "Last week we learned the short o families of *–op, –ot*, and *–ob*. When I point to the piece, you say the family." Lead students in recognizing all the short o families from last week.

2. Say, "This week we will continue to study short o families. You will be introduced to three new families: *–ong, –ock*, and *–og*."

3. Hold up the *tong* puzzle piece and say, "This is the *tong* piece. It represents the short o family *–ong*. The *tong* piece says '/ŏng/ /ŏng/ /ŏng/' like at the end of the word *tong*. Place your fingers straight out and together. Move your thumb away from your fingers to create a snapping motion and say '/ŏng/.' Let's make a list of words that have the *tong* sound in them" (record the words).

4. Hold up the *lock* puzzle piece and say, "This is the *lock* piece. It represents the short o family *–ock*. The *lock* piece says '/ŏk/ /ŏk/ /ŏk/' like at the end of the word *lock*. Pretend to be holding a lock in your left hand. With your right hand touching your left, twist your right hand to the right and say '/ŏk/.' Let's make a list of words that have the *lock* sound in them" (record the words).

5. Hold up the *dog* puzzle piece and say, "This is the *dog* piece. It represents the short o family *–og*. The *dog* piece says '/ŏg/ /ŏg/ /ŏg/' like at the end of the word *dog*. Stick your tongue out, breathe heavily, and say '/ŏg/.' Let's make a list of words that have the *dog* sound in them" (record the words).

BLENDING: PUTTING SOUNDS TOGETHER TO MAKE NEW WORDS

1. Follow the Blending routine on page I-17 of the Introduction.

2. Display the following words on the board one line at a time. Facilitate a discussion about the blending line focus after each line.

3. Then display the weekly sight words and sentence.

4. In the sentence, help students use context clues to read the word *bone*. Discuss the words within the short o families.

tong	lock	dog	Discuss: *–ong, –ock*, and *–og* word families
long	dock	hog	Discuss: *–ong, –ock*, and *–og* word families
drop	lot	job	Discuss: review of word families from last week

Sight Words: got   hot

Sentence: The dog's job is to get the bone.

(Continued)

DICTATION:
STRETCH OUT
YOUR WORDS

1. Have students turn to page 229 of the Learner's Notebook.

2. Follow the Dictation routine on page I-21 of the Introduction to dictate the following words:

    I. **long**   2. **dock**   3. **hog**

    Sight Word: got

3. Use Dictation words as an informal pretest. For students who are continuing to study Week 1 words, encourage them to sound out the words for Dictation as best they can.

PRACTICE:
COMPLETE
YOUR WORK ON
YOUR OWN

1. Have students turn to page 225 (Group 1) or page 227 (Group 2) of the Learner's Notebook.

2. Instruct students to tear out the sort and complete the following Practice Pieces: Quick Color, Careful Cut, Highlighter Hunt, and Sorting With Words (see further directions on pages I-37, I-38, I-43, and I-27 of the Introduction).

3. Circulate as students work, which usually takes fifteen minutes, and coach as needed.

FLUENCY:
READING LIKE
YOU'RE SPEAKING

1. Have students turn to page 35 in the Fluency Notebook.

2. Have students read one or more of the following poems: "Walk, Walk, Walk" and "Frog and Fox."

3. Circulate and listen to students read or gather a small group of students who need additional support.

PHONEMIC AWARENESS: LISTEN

1. Give the directions. Say, "I am going to say a word. Then I am going to ask you to change the initial sound. Your job is to listen to the word, change the initial sound, and say the two rhyming words. For example, if I say '*bad*, change the initial sound to /r/,' you say '*rad.*' Then, you say the two rhyming words: '*bad, rad.*'"

2. Say the following words and sounds:

bond, /p/ (pond)   hot, /g/ (got)   pod, /m/ (mod)
Bob, /r/ (rob)   pop, /h/ (hop)

PUZZLE PIECE REVIEW

1. Say, "When I point to the piece, you tell me its name" (*tong, lock, dog*).

2. Say, "When I point to the piece, you tell me its sound" (/ŏng/, /ŏk/, /ŏg/).

3. Say, "When I point to the piece, you tell me its spelling" (*-ong, -ock, -og*).

4. Say, "Write the spellings in the air with your finger" (students will form the letters *-ong, -ock,* and *-og*).

BLENDING: PUTTING SOUNDS TOGETHER TO MAKE NEW WORDS

1. Follow the Blending routine on page I-17 of the Introduction.

2. Display the following words on the board one line at a time. Facilitate a discussion about the blending line focus after each line.

3. Then display the weekly sight words and sentence.

4. Discuss the short *o* family words found in the sentence.

bog	smog	frog	Discuss: *-og* word family
song	wrong	gong	Discuss: *-ong* word family; help students read the *wr-* spelling of /r/ in *wrong*
flop	sob	dot	Discuss: review of word families from last week

Sight Words: got   hot
Sentence: **The frog got a big pad to sit on.**

QUICK SWITCH: MANIPULATE YOUR WORDS

1. Have students turn to page 229 of the Learner's Notebook.

2. Follow the Quick Switch routine on page I-23 of the Introduction to dictate the following words:

log → frog → dog → dock → block

3. Review the *-og* and *-ock* word families with students. Help students get from *dog* to *dock*.

SORT: WHAT IS YOUR FOCUS PATTERN?

1. Have students take out their bag of words (created on Day 1) and follow the Sorting With Words routine on page I-27 of the Introduction.

PRACTICE: COMPLETE YOUR WORK ON YOUR OWN

1. Students will follow the Read and Trade routine on page I-47 of the Introduction.

2. Circulate as students work, which usually takes fifteen minutes, and coach as needed.

(Continued)

Day 2 (Continued)

**FLUENCY:
READING LIKE
YOU'RE SPEAKING**

1. Have students turn to page 35 in the Fluency Notebook.

2. Have students read one or more of the following poems: "Walk, Walk, Walk" and "Frog and Fox."

3. Circulate and listen to students read or gather a small group of students who need additional support.

Day 3

PHONEMIC AWARENESS: LISTEN

1. Give the directions. Say, "I am going to say a word. Then I am going to ask you to change the initial sound. Your job is to listen to the word, change the initial sound, and say the two rhyming words. For example, if I say '*bad*, change the initial sound to /r/,' you say '*rad*.' Then, you say the two rhyming words: '*bad, rad*.'"

2. Say the following words and sounds:

mom, /t/ (Tom)   got, /p/ (pot)   toss, /l/ (loss)
tong, /l/ (long)   sock, /r/ (rock)

PUZZLE PIECE REVIEW

1. Say, "When I point to the piece, you tell me its name" (*tong, lock, dog*).

2. Say, "When I point to the piece, you tell me its sound" (/ŏng/, /ŏk/, /ŏg/).

3. Say, "When I point to the piece, you tell me its spelling" (*-ong, -ock, -og*).

4. Say, "Write the spellings in the air with your finger" (students will form the letters *-ong, -ock,* and *-og*).

BLENDING: PUTTING SOUNDS TOGETHER TO MAKE NEW WORDS

1. Follow the Blending routine on page I-17 of the Introduction.

2. Display the following words on the board one line at a time. Facilitate a discussion about the blending line focus after each line.

3. Then display the weekly sight words and sentence.

4. In the sentence, discuss the words within the short *o* families. Identify the exclamation mark and model for students how to read the sentence with excitement.

rock	block	mock	Discuss: *-ock* word family
wrong	pong	pog	Discuss: *-ong* and *-og* word families
rot	drop	job	Discuss: review word families from last week

Sight Words: got   hot
Sentence: Bob got the wrong socks!

DICTATION: STRETCH OUT YOUR WORDS

1. Have students turn to page 230 of the Learner's Notebook.

2. Follow the Dictation routine on page I-21 of the Introduction to dictate the following words:

l. rock   2. song   3. smog
Sight Word: hot

3. For students who are continuing to study Week 1 words, encourage them to sound out the words for Dictation as best they can.

SORT: WHAT IS YOUR FOCUS PATTERN?

1. Have students take out their bag of words (created on Day 1) and follow the Sorting With Words routine on page I-27 of the Introduction.

PRACTICE: COMPLETE YOUR WORK ON YOUR OWN

1. Have students turn to page 231 in the Learner's Notebook.

2. Students will complete the Spell It Out routine found on page I-49 of the Introduction.

3. Circulate as students work, which usually takes fifteen minutes, and coach as needed.

(Continued)

Day 3 (Continued)

**FLUENCY:
READING LIKE
YOU'RE SPEAKING**

1. Have students turn to page 35 in the Fluency Notebook.

2. Have students read one or more of the following poems: "Walk, Walk, Walk" and "Frog and Fox."

3. Circulate and listen to students read or gather a small group of students who need additional support.

PHONEMIC AWARENESS: LISTEN

1. Give the directions. Say, "I am going to say a word. Then I am going to ask you to change the initial sound. Your job is to listen to the word, change the initial sound, and say the two rhyming words. For example, if I say '*bad*, change the initial sound to /r/,' you say '*rad*.' Then, you say the two rhyming words: '*bad, rad*.'"

2. Say the following words and *sounds*:

rot, /k/ (cot)   hawk, /t/ (tock)   dog, /f/ (fog)

dot, /h/ (hot)   Dom, /n/ (nom)

PUZZLE PIECE REVIEW

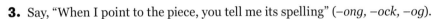

1. Say, "When I point to the piece, you tell me its name" (*tong, lock, dog*).

2. Say, "When I point to the piece, you tell me its sound" (/ŏng/, /ŏk/, /ŏg/).

3. Say, "When I point to the piece, you tell me its spelling" (*–ong, –ock, –og*).

4. Say, "Write the spellings in the air with your finger" (students will form the letters *–ong, –ock,* and *–og*).

BLENDING: PUTTING SOUNDS TOGETHER TO MAKE NEW WORDS

1. Follow the Blending routine on page I-17 of the Introduction.

2. Display the following words on the board one line at a time. Facilitate a discussion about the blending line focus after each line.

3. Then display the weekly sight words and sentence.

4. Discuss the capital *R* in *Rob* in the sentence. Explain to students that *Rob* is capitalized because it is a name and it is the first word in a sentence.

flock	block	smock	Discuss: *–ock* word family
smog	blog	strong	Discuss: *–og* and *–ong* word families
blob	slot	plop	Discuss: review word families from last week

Sight Words: got   hot

Sentence: **Rob was hot by the dock.**

QUICK SWITCH: MANIPULATE YOUR WORDS

1. Have students turn to page 230 of the Learner's Notebook.

2. Follow the Quick Switch routine on page I-23 of the Introduction to dictate the following words:

block → lock → long → song → strong

3. Review the *–ock* and *–ong* word families with students. Help students get from *lock* to *long*.

SORT: WHAT IS YOUR FOCUS PATTERN?

1. Have students take out their bag of words (created on Day 1) and follow the Sorting With Words routine on page I-27 of the Introduction.

PRACTICE: COMPLETE YOUR WORK ON YOUR OWN

1. Have students complete the following Practice Piece: Glue, Draw a Picture (on page I-50 of the Introduction).

2. Circulate as students work, which usually takes fifteen minutes, and coach as needed.

(Continued)

Day 4 (Continued)

**FLUENCY:
READING LIKE
YOU'RE SPEAKING**

1. Have students turn to page 35 in the Fluency Notebook.

2. Have students read one or more of the following poems: "Walk, Walk, Walk" and "Frog and Fox."

3. Circulate and listen to students read or gather a small group of students who need additional support.

PHONEMIC AWARENESS: LISTEN

1. Give the directions. Say, "I am going to say a word. Then I am going to ask you to change the initial sound. Your job is to listen to the word, change the initial sound, and say the two rhyming words. For example, if I say '*bad*, change the initial sound to /r/,' you say '*rad.*' Then, you say the two rhyming words: '*bad, rad.*'"

2. Say the following words and sounds:

**lot, /j/ (jot)   mock, /d/ (dock)   bond, /p/ (pond)
fog, /b/ (bog)   rod, /p/ (pod)**

REVIEW PATTERNS OF THE WEEK

1. Say, "Find a partner."

2. Say, "Tell your partner the names of this week's pieces" (*tong, lock, dog*).

3. Say, "Tell your partner the sounds of this week's pieces" (/ŏng/, /ŏk/, /ŏg/).

4. Say, "Tell your partner the spellings of this week's pieces" (*–ong, –ock, –og*).

5. Say, "Write the spellings on your partner's back with your finger" (students will form the letters *–ong, –ock,* and *–og*).

SPELLING CHECK

1. Follow the Spelling Check routine on page I-34 of the Introduction.

2. Instruct students to sit in their word study groups and turn to page 233 of the Learner's Notebook.

3. Say, "I am going to say one word at a time to each group. Record the words as I say them to your group. Make sure you only record the words from your group."

4. Move back and forth between the groups and dictate the following words:

Words for Group 1	Words for Group 2
1. flop	1. block
2. dot	2. frog
3. job	3. long
4. cop	4. rock
5. rob	5. smog
Sentence: I got the mop.	**Sentence: The strong man can pick up the rock.**

WORD HUNT

1. Students will follow the Word Hunt routine on page I-55 of the Introduction.

2. Instruct students to search texts and the classroom for words within the short *o* families.

COMPREHENSION CHECK

1. Have students turn to page 234 of the Learner's Notebook.

2. Students will follow the Comprehension Check routine on page I-36 of the Introduction.

3. Check students' work. Circled answers are as follows:

1. The frog got a bug.
2. The dog got a pat.
3. The hog got a nap.

4. Possible written responses include the following:

1. The frog got a <u>bug</u>.
2. I got a _____. (Students may put any logical word in the blank. For example, "I got a baseball.")

(Continued)

Day 5 (Continued)

WEEKLY CELEBRATION

1. Display the celebratory message: "You rock! You learned the _tong, lock,_ and _dog_ puzzle pieces!"

2. Encourage students to work together to read the message.

3. Have students copy the message onto their weekly certificate (see resources.corwin .com/puzzlepiecephonics-gradeK) and place it somewhere to take home.

Concept 8 Overview:

Short _u_ Families

WHAT ARE WORD FAMILIES?

This short _u_ families concept builds on students' word family knowledge. During the last four concepts, students focused on short _a_, short _e_, short _i_, and short _o_ families. Students should be seeing words in chunks as the onset and rime. They will use their knowledge of consonants and short vowel _u_ to master new words.

GOALS FOR THE CONCEPT

Students will
- Identify and represent short vowels
- Identify and represent consonant sounds
- Read and write sight words
- Recognize that words with the same rime rhyme
- Manipulate words in order to create a new word
- Develop reading fluency and comprehension

WEEKS FOR THIS CONCEPT

Week 1: Short _u_ Families (_–ub, –un, –ut_)
Week 2: Short _u_ Families (_–uff, –uck, –unk_)

istock.com/Weedezign

Preparing for Your Week

Resources

PUZZLE PIECES

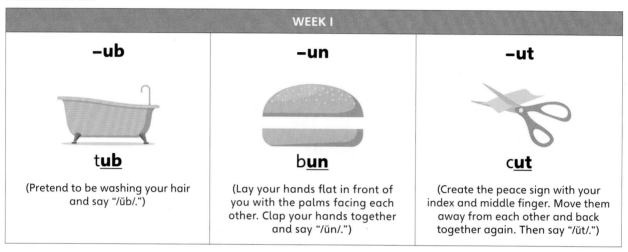

WEEK I		
–ub	**–un**	**–ut**
t**ub**	b**un**	c**ut**
(Pretend to be washing your hair and say "/ŭb/.")	(Lay your hands flat in front of you with the palms facing each other. Clap your hands together and say "/ŭn/.")	(Create the peace sign with your index and middle finger. Move them away from each other and back together again. Then say "/ŭt/.")

Tub: istock.com/Photoplotnikov; Bun: istock.com/Photoplotnikov; Cut: istock.com/Janista

Preparing for Your Week

CORRESPONDING *LEARNER'S NOTEBOOK PAGES*

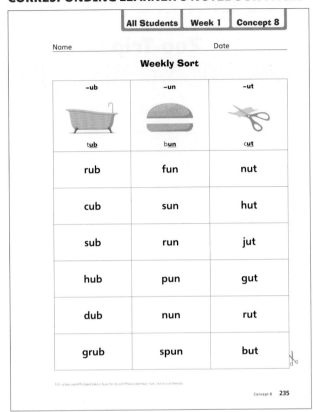

| All Students | Week 1 | Concept 8 |

Name _____ Date _____

Weekly Sort

–ub	–un	–ut
t**ub**	b**un**	c**ut**
rub	fun	nut
cub	sun	hut
sub	run	jut
hub	pun	gut
dub	nun	rut
grub	spun	but

Concept 8 235

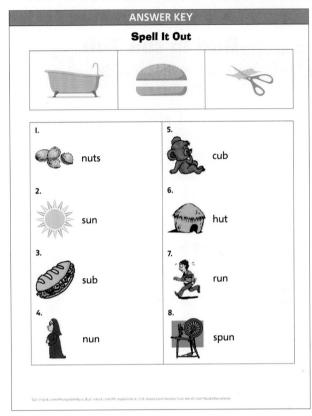

ANSWER KEY

Spell It Out

1. nuts
2. sun
3. sub
4. nun
5. cub
6. hut
7. run
8. spun

| Week 1 | Concept 8 |

Name _____ Date _____

The _____ ran to the _____ .

Circle the sentence that matches the picture.

	The pup ran to the tree. The pup ran to the grass. The pup ran to the hut.
	The kids ran to the bus. The kids ran to the tub. The kids ran to the net.
	The mom ran to the camp. The mom ran to the truck. The mom ran to the mud.

Listen to the questions. Write your answers on the lines.

1. Who ran to the bus?

   The _____ ran to the bus.

2. Where have you run?

   I ran to the _____ .

242   PUZZLE PIECE PHONICS LEARNER'S NOTEBOOK, KINDERGARTEN

Preparing for Your Week

CORRESPONDING *FLUENCY NOTEBOOK* PAGES

Bud in the Tub

Bud is in the tub.

Bud is covered in suds!

Rub a dub dub—

Bud soaks in the tub.

Bud is in the tub.

Suds are over the tub.

Rub a dub dub—

We can't see Bud!

Bud is in the tub.

There are too many suds!

Rub a dub dub—

Oh! There is Bud!

Bud is in the tub.

Bud pops and pops the suds.

Rub a dub dub—

Bud is out of the tub.

Zoo Trip

Our class went on a trip to the zoo.

We had fun the whole day through:

First, we visited the monkey huts.

We saw gorillas beating their guts!

Next, we went to the baby bear cubs.

We saw their moms giving back rubs!

Then, we had a break to eat lunch.

We had subs and chips for a crunch.

After lunch, we checked out the spider hub.

We saw webs spun to capture their grub.

Our whole class enjoyed and had fun.

We loved our zoo trip in the sun!

Preparing for Your Week

Tips for Management and Differentiation

Refer to this section and to resources.corwin.com/puzzlepiecephonics-gradeK for resources and ideas to deepen your students' learning throughout the week. Feel free to put your own spin on the routines, too. For daily lesson plans, see pages 322–330 of this Teacher's Guide.

TIPS FOR PHONEMIC AWARENESS	• If you notice your students need additional practice, extend the activity with more words. • Students are instructed to give a thumbs-up if the words rhyme or a thumbs-down if the words do not rhyme. You may substitute any motions for the activity. • If the two words rhyme, prompt students to verbally give you an additional word that rhymes. If the two words do not rhyme, prompt students to think of a word that rhymes with each.
TIPS FOR THE PUZZLE PIECE REVIEW	• Have students work with the same partner each day to build a word study relationship. • Point out to students the two pieces that they have already learned that make up the word family piece. For example, when teaching the *–ut* piece, point to the *sun* piece /ŭ/ and the *type* piece /t/. Explain to students that the *cut* piece takes both of those sounds and puts them on one piece to represent the *–ut* family.
TIPS FOR BLENDING	• Reblend lines if necessary. • Remind students that the purpose of this concept is for them to use the words and spellings they know to assist them in spelling words they do not know. For example, if students can spell and identify the word *sub*, they can use that knowledge to blend and identify the word *stub*. • When reading the two sight words of the week to students, explain that the word *run* is a verb (an action word) and the word *ran* is the past tense of the word *run*.
TIPS FOR DICTATION AND QUICK SWITCH	• If time permits, extend the Quick Switch activity to incorporate words from all short *u* families. • Assist students who are struggling with Quick Switch by writing the rime on each line. When they hear the word, they will only need to focus on the initial sound.
TIPS FOR SORTING	• Model and positively reinforce the Sorting With Words routine repeatedly throughout the week. • Discuss the vocabulary words that appear in the sort. Vocabulary words include the following: • *tub, rub, cub, sub, hub, dub, grub, bun, pun, nun, spun, jut, gut, rut*
TIPS FOR THE PRACTICE PIECES	• Support students with the vocabulary words for this week. They may need assistance in drawing the pictures.
TIPS FOR FLUENCY	• Students can highlight words within the short *u* families in the daily poems. • You can assign students fluency partners. Students will work together to achieve fluency with the daily poems. • Students can participate in a "Fluency Celebration." Call on students who feel prepared to present a particular poem in front of the class. Other students can follow along in the Fluency Notebook.

Day 1

THE PUZZLE PIECE FAMILY

Launch Concept 8: Short _u_ Families by following the Puzzle Piece Family routine on page I-11 of the Introduction.

1. Show students the following words:

tub	sun
rut	spun
truck	junk
fluff	sub
pun	but

2. Have students read the words with you. Underline the vowel and final consonant(s) in each word.

3. Facilitate a discussion that leads them to discover the Puzzle Piece Family: Short _u_ Families.

PHONEMIC AWARENESS: LISTEN

1. Give the directions. Say, "I am going to say two words. Your job is to tell me if the two words rhyme. Give me a thumbs-up if the words are rhyming words and a thumbs-down if the words are not rhyming words."

2. Say the following pairs of words:

cub, sub (yes)   gut, hub (no)   sun, rut (no)   pun, nun (yes)   cut, hut (yes)

THE BIG REVEAL

1. Say, "Let's say all of our short vowel sounds." Lead students in saying "/ă/ /ĕ/ /ĭ/ /ŏ/ /ŭ/."

2. Say, "This week we will be taking a closer look at short vowel _u_. We will be focusing on three short _u_ families: *–ub, –un,* and *–ut*."

3. Hold up the *tub* puzzle piece and say, "This is the *tub* piece. It represents the short _u_ family *–ub*. The *tub* piece says '/ŭb/ /ŭb/ /ŭb/' like at the end of the word *tub*. Pretend to be washing your hair and say '/ŭb/.' Let's make a list of words that have the *tub* sound in them" (record the words).

4. Hold up the *bun* puzzle piece and say, "This is the *bun* piece. It represents the short _u_ family *–un*. The *bun* piece says '/ŭn/ /ŭn/ /ŭn/' like at the end of the word *bun*. Lay your hands flat in front of you with the palms facing each other. Clap your hands together and say '/ŭn/.' Let's make a list of words that have the *bun* sound in them" (record the words).

5. Hold up the *cut* puzzle piece and say, "This is the *cut* piece. It represents the short _u_ family *–ut*. The *cut* piece says '/ŭt/ /ŭt/ /ŭt/' like at the end of the word *cut*. Create the peace sign with your index and middle finger. Move them away from each other and back together again. Then say '/ŭt/.' Let's make a list of words that have the *cut* sound in them" (record the words).

BLENDING: PUTTING SOUNDS TOGETHER TO MAKE NEW WORDS

1. Follow the Blending routine on page I-17 of the Introduction.

2. Display the following words on the board one line at a time. Facilitate a discussion about the blending line focus after each line.

3. Then display the weekly sight words and sentence.

4. Discuss the word within the short *u* family found in the sentence.

tub	sub	cub	Discuss: *–ub* word family
bun	fun	sun	Discuss: *–un* word family
cut	nut	but	Discuss: *–ut* word family

Sight Words: run   ran

Sentence: The cub ran to his mom.

DICTATION: STRETCH OUT YOUR WORDS

1. Have students turn to page 237 of the Learner's Notebook.

2. Follow the Dictation routine on page I-21 of the Introduction to dictate the following words:

I. sub   2. fun   3. nut

Sight Word: run

3. Use Dictation as an informal pretest of students' knowledge of this week's short *u* families.

PRACTICE: COMPLETE YOUR WORK ON YOUR OWN

1. Have students turn to page 235 of the Learner's Notebook.

2. Instruct students to tear out the sort and complete the following Practice Pieces: Quick Color, Careful Cut, Highlighter Hunt, and Sorting With Words (see further directions on pages I-37, I-38, I-43, and I-27 of the Introduction).

3. Circulate as students work, which usually takes fifteen minutes, and coach as needed.

FLUENCY: READING LIKE YOU'RE SPEAKING

1. Have students turn to page 36 in the Fluency Notebook.

2. Have students read one or more of the following poems: "Bud in the Tub" and "Zoo Trip."

3. Circulate and listen to students read or gather a small group of students who need additional support.

Day 2

PHONEMIC AWARENESS: LISTEN

1. Give the directions. Say, "I am going to say two words. Your job is to tell me if the two words rhyme. Give me a thumbs-up if the words are rhyming words and a thumbs-down if the words are not rhyming words."

2. Say the following pairs of words:

**buff, bun (no)   junk, punk (yes)   nut, spun (no)
pun, sun (yes)   duck, hunt (no)**

PUZZLE PIECE REVIEW

1. Say, "When I point to the piece, you tell me its name" (_tub, bun, cut_).

2. Say, "When I point to the piece, you tell me its sound" (/ŭb/, /ŭn/, /ŭt/).

3. Say, "When I point to the piece, you tell me its spelling (–ub, –un, –ut).

4. Say, "Write the spellings in the air with your finger" (students will form the letters –ub, –un, and –ut).

BLENDING: PUTTING SOUNDS TOGETHER TO MAKE NEW WORDS

1. Follow the Blending routine on page I-17 of the Introduction.

2. Display the following words on the board one line at a time. Facilitate a discussion about the blending line focus after each line.

3. Then display the weekly sight words and sentence.

4. Discuss the short _u_ family word found in the sentence. Have students identify the sight word in the sentence (_ran_) and identify that this sentence happened in the past.

hub	**dub**	**grub**	Discuss: –ub word family
pun	**nun**	**spun**	Discuss: –un word family
gut	**rut**	**jut**	Discuss: –ut word family

Sight Words: run   ran

Sentence: The man ran into the hut.

QUICK SWITCH: MANIPULATE YOUR WORDS

1. Have students turn to page 237 of the Learner's Notebook.

2. Follow the Quick Switch routine on page I-23 of the Introduction to dictate the following words:

hub → cub → sub → sun → run

3. Review the –ub and –un families. Help students get from _sub_ to _sun_.

SORT: WHAT IS YOUR FOCUS PATTERN?

1. Have students take out their bag of words (created on Day 1) and follow the Sorting With Words routine on page I-27 of the Introduction.

PRACTICE: COMPLETE YOUR WORK ON YOUR OWN

1. Students will follow the Read and Trade routine on page I-47 of the Introduction.

2. Circulate as students work, which usually takes fifteen minutes, and coach as needed.

FLUENCY: READING LIKE YOU'RE SPEAKING

1. Have students turn to page 36 in the Fluency Notebook.

2. Have students read one or more of the following poems: "Bud in the Tub" and "Zoo Trip."

- Circulate and listen to students read or gather a small group of students who need additional support.

Day 3

PHONEMIC AWARENESS: LISTEN

1. Give the directions. Say, "I am going to say two words. Your job is to tell me if the two words rhyme. Give me a thumbs-up if the words are rhyming words and a thumbs-down if the words are not rhyming words."

2. Say the following pairs of words:

grub, but (no) puck, luck (yes) cub, rub (yes)
gut, jut (yes) lunch, but (no)

PUZZLE PIECE REVIEW

1. Say, "When I point to the piece, you tell me its name" (_tub, bun, cut_).

2. Say, "When I point to the piece, you tell me its sound" (/ŭb/, /ŭn/, /ŭt/).

3. Say, "When I point to the piece, you tell me its spelling" (–_ub_, –_un_, –_ut_).

4. Say, "Write the spellings in the air with your finger" (students will form the letters –_ub_, –_un_, and –_ut_).

BLENDING: PUTTING SOUNDS TOGETHER TO MAKE NEW WORDS

1. Follow the Blending routine on page I-17 of the Introduction.

2. Display the following words on the board one line at a time. Facilitate a discussion about the blending line focus after each line.

3. Then display the weekly sight words and sentence.

4. Discuss the action words in the sentence (_ran_ and _stubbed_). Ask students how they would feel if they completed these actions.

sub	tub	stub	Discuss: –_ub_ word family; help students read the _st_– consonant blend in _stub_
sun	pun	spun	Discuss: –_un_ word family; help students read the _sp_– consonant blend in _spun_
tut	rut	strut	Discuss: –_ut_ word family; help students read the _str_– consonant blend in _strut_

Sight Words: run   ran

Sentence: I ran and stubbed my toe!

DICTATION: STRETCH OUT YOUR WORDS

1. Have students turn to page 238 of the Learner's Notebook.

2. Follow the Dictation routine on page I-21 of the Introduction to dictate the following words:

1. but   2. tub   3. sun

Sight Word: ran

3. You can extend Dictation by incorporating the words _stub_, _stun_, and _strut_ as a challenge.

SORT: WHAT IS YOUR FOCUS PATTERN?

1. Have students take out their bag of words (created on Day 1) and follow the Sorting With Words routine on page I-27 of the Introduction.

(Continued)

Day 3 (Continued)

PRACTICE: **COMPLETE** **YOUR WORK ON** **YOUR OWN**	**1.** Have students turn to page 239 in the Learner's Notebook. **2.** Students will complete the Spell It Out routine found on page I-49 of the Introduction. **3.** Circulate as students work, which usually takes fifteen minutes, and coach as needed.
FLUENCY: **READING LIKE** **YOU'RE SPEAKING**	**1.** Have students turn to page 36 in the Fluency Notebook. **2.** Have students read one or more of the following poems: "Bud in the Tub" and "Zoo Trip." **3.** Circulate and listen to students read or gather a small group of students who need additional support.

PHONEMIC AWARENESS: LISTEN	**1.** Give the directions. Say, "I am going to say two words. Your job is to tell me if the two words rhyme. Give me a thumbs-up if the words are rhyming words and a thumbs-down if the words are not rhyming words."
	2. Say the following pairs of words:

hunt, bunt (yes)   nun, rut (no)   trunk, dunk (yes)
rub, fun (no)   grub, spun (no)

PUZZLE PIECE REVIEW	**1.** Say, "When I point to the piece, you tell me its name" (*tub, bun, cut*).
	2. Say, "When I point to the piece, you tell me its sound" (/ŭb/, /ŭn/, /ŭt/).
	3. Say, "When I point to the piece, you tell me its spelling" (*–ub, –un, –ut*).
	4. Say, "Write the spellings in the air with your finger" (students will form the letters *–ub, –un,* and *–ut*).

BLENDING: PUTTING SOUNDS TOGETHER TO MAKE NEW WORDS	**1.** Follow the Blending routine on page I-17 of the Introduction.
	2. Display the following words on the board one line at a time. Facilitate a discussion about the blending line focus after each line.
	3. Then display the weekly sight words and sentence.
	4. Discuss the vocabulary word *grub* and ask students what type of *grub* they enjoy eating.

rub	**run**	**rut**	Discuss: review the short *u* word families; identify the initial consonant in each word
sub	**sun**	**strut**	Discuss: review the short *u* word families; identify the initial consonant in each word
hub	**nun**	**hut**	Discuss: review the short *u* word families; identify the initial consonant in each word

Sight Words: run   ran

Sentence: We ran to grab some grub.

QUICK SWITCH: MANIPULATE YOUR WORDS	**1.** Have students turn to page 238 of the Learner's Notebook.
	2. Follow the Quick Switch routine on page I-23 of the Introduction to dictate the following words:

nun → bun → run → rut → jut

	3. Review the *–un* and *–ut* families. Help students get from *run* to *rut*.
SORT: WHAT IS YOUR FOCUS PATTERN?	**1.** Have students take out their bag of words (created on Day 1) and follow the Sorting With Words routine on page I-27 of the Introduction.
PRACTICE: COMPLETE YOUR WORK ON YOUR OWN	**1.** Have students complete the following Practice Piece: Glue, Draw a Picture (on page I-50 of the Introduction).
	2. Circulate as students work, which usually takes fifteen minutes, and coach as needed.

(Continued)

Day 4 (Continued)

FLUENCY: READING LIKE YOU'RE SPEAKING

1. Have students turn to page 36 in the Fluency Notebook.

2. Have students read one or more of the following poems: "Bud in the Tub" and "Zoo Trip."

3. Circulate and listen to students read or gather a small group of students who need additional support.

PHONEMIC AWARENESS: LISTEN

1. Give the directions. Say, "I am going to say two words. Your job is to tell me if the two words rhyme. Give me a thumbs-up if the words are rhyming words and a thumbs-down if the words are not rhyming words."

2. Say the following pairs of words:

dub, but (no)   punt, hunt (yes)   fun, run (yes)
tuck, buck (yes)   gut, dub (no)

REVIEW PATTERNS OF THE WEEK

1. Say, "Find a partner."

2. Say, "Tell your partner the names of this week's pieces" (*tub, bun, cut*).

2. Say, "Tell your partner the sounds of this week's pieces" (/ŭb/, /ŭn/, /ŭt/).

3. Say, "Tell your partner the spellings of this week's pieces" (*–ub, –un, –ut*).

4. Say, "Write the spellings on your partner's back with your finger" (students will form the letters *–ub, –un,* and *–ut*).

SPELLING CHECK

1. Follow the Spelling Check routine on page I-34 of the Introduction.

2. Instruct students to turn to page 241 of the Learner's Notebook.

3. Say, "I am going to say one word at a time. Record the words as I say them."

4. Dictate the following words:

Words for the Spelling Check

l. sub
2. fun
3. but
4. spun
5. rub

Sentence: We ran to get a sub.

WORD HUNT

1. Students will follow the Word Hunt routine on page I-55 of the Introduction.

2. Instruct students to search texts and the classroom for words within this week's short *u* families.

COMPREHENSION CHECK

1. Have students turn to page 242 of the Learner's Notebook.

2. Students will follow the Comprehension Check routine on page I-36 of the Introduction.

3. Check students' work. Circled answers are as follows:

1. The pup ran to the hut.

2. The kids ran to the bus.

3. The mom ran to the mud.

4. Possible written responses include the following:

1. The kids ran to the bus.

2. I ran to the _____. (Students may put any logical word in the blank. For example, "I ran to the playground.")

(Continued)

Day 5 (Continued)

**WEEKLY
CELEBRATION**

1. Display the celebratory message: "What good fun! You learned the *tub, bun,* and *cut* puzzle pieces!"

2. Encourage students to work together to read the message.

3. Have students copy the message onto their weekly certificate (see resources .corwin.com/puzzlepiecephonics-gradeK) and place it somewhere to take home.

Preparing for Your Week

Resources

PUZZLE PIECES

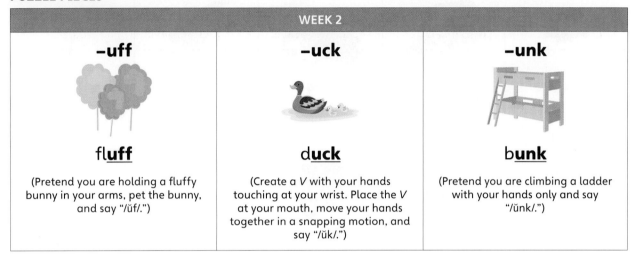

WEEK 2		
–uff	**–uck**	**–unk**
fl**uff**	d**uck**	b**unk**
(Pretend you are holding a fluffy bunny in your arms, pet the bunny, and say "/ŭf/.")	(Create a *V* with your hands touching at your wrist. Place the *V* at your mouth, move your hands together in a snapping motion, and say "/ŭk/.")	(Pretend you are climbing a ladder with your hands only and say "/ŭnk/.")

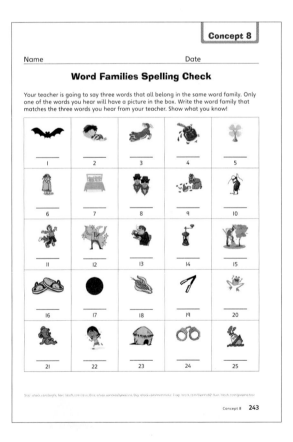

POSTASSESSMENT DIRECTIONS

This assessment is used to identify which word families students can represent and which patterns students need to be retaught. It is also useful to evaluate students' ability to apply knowledge of all consonant and short vowel sounds. Students may be able to master a Spelling Check when there is a sound taught in isolation. However, they may struggle when asked to produce multiple sounds. This check is to primarily look for mastery of word families.

You can give this postassessment any day during Concept 8, Week 2. You can split the rows and do parts on different days. Do what works for your class.

Instruct students to turn to **page 243 in the Learner's Notebook**. Explain to students that they have studied all of the spellings in the words they will hear. The purpose of this check is to show what they know.

When giving this assessment, go row by row in saying the word represented by the picture. Then say the other two words in the word family. Students are not guessing what the picture is. You tell them the word and read the other two words in that word family. Students will only write the word family they hear in all three words. For example, after students hear *cat, mat, bat*, they will write *–at* in the box for that word family.

Fluff: istock.com/djvstock; Duck: istock.com/graphic-bee; Bunk: istock.com/keko-ka

Preparing for Your Week

POSTASSESSMENT: WORD FAMILIES SPELLING CHECK

ANSWER KEY				
bat cat mat 1. –at	**_nap_** tap lap 2. –ap	**_wag_** nag tag 3. –ag	**_jam_** ham bam 4. –am	**_fan_** pan tan 5. –an
wet jet set 6. –et	**_bed_** fed red 7. –ed	**_men_** ten den 8. –en	**_fell_** well swell 9. –ell	**_pest_** best jest 10. –est
bit kit hit 11. –it	**_win_** grin bin 12. –in	**_sip_** tip zip 13. –ip	**_mill_** dill sill 14. –ill	**_dig_** fig big 15. –ig
flop bop pop 16. –op	**_dot_** jot not 17. –ot	**_cob_** rob job 18. –ob	**_tong_** strong song 19. –ong	**_frog_** log smog 20. –og
cub hub sub 21. –ub	**_run_** pun nun 22. –un	**_hut_** gut but 23. –ut	**_cuff_** stuff huff 24. –uff	**_sunk_** junk dunk 25. –unk

Nap: istock.com/brgfx; Fan: istock.com/zzve; Bed: istock.com/vasilyevalara; Dig: istock.com/mutsMaks; Frog: istock.com/Glenne82; Run: istock.com/graphic-bee

Preparing for Your Week

EVALUATING THE ASSESSMENT: WHAT TO LOOK FOR

- One-to-one sound correspondence
- Knowledge of consonants
- Knowledge of short vowels
- Knowledge of basic blends
- Knowledge of rime
- Recognizing that rhyming words contain the same rime

TIPS FOR SCORING

Row 1 contains words within short vowel *a* families. Row 2 contains words within short vowel *e* families. Row 3 contains words with short vowel *i* families. Row 4 contains words with short vowel *o* families. Row 5 contains words with short vowel *u* families. Have students write the word families they hear.

Each rime is worth one point. For each correctly spelled rime, students earn one point. To show mastery of word families, students must show 80 percent mastery or correctly phonetically spell twenty out of twenty-five rimes.

Use teacher discretion when grading.

Preparing for Your Week

CORRESPONDING _LEARNER'S NOTEBOOK_ PAGES

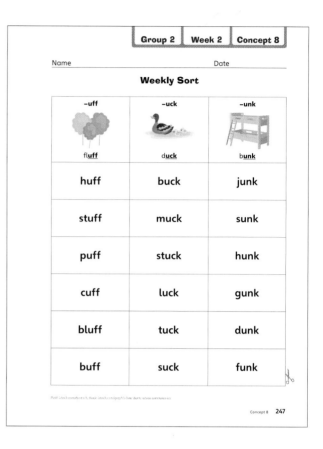

Group 1 | Week 2 | Concept 8

Name _____ Date _____

Weekly Sort

–ub	–un	–ut
t**ub**	b**un**	c**ut**
rub	fun	nut
cub	sun	hut
sub	run	jut
hub	pun	gut
dub	nun	rut
grub	spun	but

Concept 8   245

Group 2 | Week 2 | Concept 8

Name _____ Date _____

Weekly Sort

–uff	–uck	–unk
fl**uff**	d**uck**	b**unk**
huff	buck	junk
stuff	muck	sunk
puff	stuck	hunk
cuff	luck	gunk
bluff	tuck	dunk
buff	suck	funk

Concept 8   247

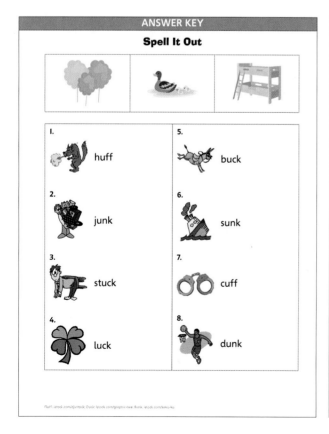

ANSWER KEY

Spell It Out

1. huff
2. junk
3. stuck
4. luck
5. buck
6. sunk
7. cuff
8. dunk

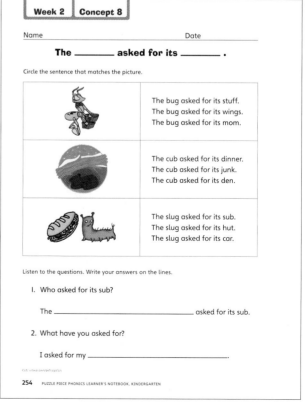

Week 2 | Concept 8

Name _____ Date _____

The _____ asked for its _____ .

Circle the sentence that matches the picture.

The bug asked for its stuff.
The bug asked for its wings.
The bug asked for its mom.

The cub asked for its dinner.
The cub asked for its junk.
The cub asked for its den.

The slug asked for its sub.
The slug asked for its hut.
The slug asked for its car.

Listen to the questions. Write your answers on the lines.

1. Who asked for its sub?

   The _____ asked for its sub.

2. What have you asked for?

   I asked for my _____

254   PUZZLE PIECE PHONICS LEARNER'S NOTEBOOK, KINDERGARTEN

Preparing for Your Week

CORRESPONDING _FLUENCY NOTEBOOK PAGES_

I'll Huff and I'll Puff!

Big, Bad Wolf: I'll HUFF and I'll PUFF and I'll blow down all your stuff!

Little Pig: Oh no, don't waste your time. You don't want this stuff of mine.

Big, Bad Wolf: I'll HUFF and I'll PUFF and I'll blow down all your stuff!

Little Pig: That's not smart—it'll make a mess.

I can give you the stuff that's best!

Big, Bad Wolf: I'll HUFF and I'll PUFF and I'll blow down all your stuff!

Little Pig: You really don't want to push your luck.

I'll give you stuff that's worth a buck.

Big, Bad Wolf: I'll HUFF and I'll PUFF and I'll blow down all your stuff!

Little Pig: Really, Mr. Wolf, let's move on.

It's time for you to be gone!

Big, Bad Wolf: I'll HUFF and I'll PUFF and …

(_Little Pig closes door_)

Little Pig: Goodbye, Wolf, I've had enough!

Ode to My Lucky Penny

Lucky penny, lucky penny,

I love you.

Lucky penny, lucky penny,

I found you.

I saw you glimmer in the sun.

I picked you up—you were the one!

Lucky penny, lucky penny,

I love you.

Lucky penny, lucky penny,

you helped me through.

I was taking a math test.

With your luck, I did my best!

Lucky penny, lucky penny,

you bring luck.

Lucky penny, lucky penny,

99 more, I'd have a buck!

Preparing for Your Week

Tips for Management and Differentiation

Refer to this section and to resources.corwin.com/puzzlepiecephonics-gradeK for resources and ideas to deepen your students' learning throughout the week. Feel free to put your own spin on the routines, too. For daily lesson plans, see pages 338–347 of this Teacher's Guide.

TIPS FOR PHONEMIC AWARENESS

- The focus for this week is changing the initial sound of a word to make two rhyming words.
- If you notice your students need additional practice, extend the activity with more words.

TIPS FOR THE PUZZLE PIECE REVIEW

- All students will be introduced to three new short _u_ family puzzle pieces this week. However, if students did not master the –_ub_, –_un_, and –_ut_ families from last week, they will be sorting and completing their Practice Pieces using last week's sort. Students who mastered the –_ub_, –_un_, and –_ut_ families will move on to sorting with the –_uff_, –_uck_, and –_unk_ families this week.
- Point out to students the two or three pieces that they have already learned that make up the word family piece. For example, when teaching the –_uff_ piece, point to the _sun_ piece /ŭ/ and the _fan_ piece /f/. Explain to students that the _fluff_ piece takes both of those sounds and puts them on one piece to represent the –_uff_ family.

TIPS FOR BLENDING

- Follow the Blending routine and hold students accountable for producing all sounds for each word. Although some students are sorting with last week's sort, all students will blend the same lines. These students will be exposed to the new short _u_ families, but are not expected to master them. Line 3 is a review of the short _u_ families taught last week.
- Reblend lines if necessary.
- Remind students that the purpose of this concept is for them to use the words and spellings they know to assist them in spelling words they do not know. For example, if students can spell and identify the word _puck_, they can use that knowledge to blend and identify the word _pluck_.
- Take a closer look at the –_uck_ and –_unk_ families. When students are writing, they may omit the _n_ in the –_unk_ family. Hold students accountable for capturing this sound.
- Students will blend words in the –_uck_ family. Connect this to the other short vowel –_ck_ word families and display the _clock_ piece.

TIPS FOR DICTATION AND QUICK SWITCH

- If time permits, extend the Quick Switch word chains to incorporate all families each day.
- Students who are struggling with Quick Switch can write the rime on each line. When they hear the word, they will only need to focus on the initial sound.
- If the majority of your students are still working with last week's sort, you can repeat the Dictation and Quick Switch lessons from Concept 8, Week 1.

Preparing for Your Week

TIPS FOR SORTING

- Model and positively reinforce the Sorting With Words routine repeatedly throughout the week.
- Discuss the vocabulary words that appear in the sort. Vocabulary words in the Group 2 sort include the following:
  - *fluff, huff, puff, cuff, bluff, buff, buck, muck, tuck, suck, junk, sunk, hunk, gunk, dunk, funk*

TIPS FOR THE PRACTICE PIECES

- Support students with the vocabulary words for this week. They may need assistance in drawing the pictures.

TIPS FOR FLUENCY

- Students can highlight words within the short *u* families in the daily poems.
- You can assign students fluency partners. Students will work together to achieve fluency with the daily poems.
- Students can participate in a "Fluency Celebration." Call on students who feel prepared to present a particular poem in front of the class. Other students can follow along in the Fluency Notebook.
- Both poems present challenges for students this week. You can partner students to work on and above grade level. Students who need more support can read the repetitive part of the Big, Bad Wolf in "I'll Huff and I'll Puff!"

Day 1

PHONEMIC AWARENESS: LISTEN

1. Give the directions. Say, "I am going to say a word. Then I am going to ask you to change the initial sound. Your job is to listen to the word, change the initial sound, and say the two rhyming words. For example, if I say '_bad_, change the initial sound to /r/,' you say '_rad_.' Then, you say the two rhyming words: '_bad, rad_.'"

2. Say the following words and sounds:

hut, /m/ (mutt)   rough, /t/ (tough)   sunk, /h/ (hunk)
luck, /t/ (tuck)   puff, /k/ (cuff)

THE BIG REVEAL

1. Say, "Last week we learned the short _u_ families of –_ub_, –_un_, and –_ut_. When I point to the piece, you say the family." Lead students in recognizing all the short _u_ families from last week.

2. Say, "This week we will continue to study short _u_ families. You will be introduced to three new families: –_uff_, –_uck_, and –_unk_."

3. Hold up the _fluff_ puzzle piece and say, "This is the _fluff_ piece. It represents the short _u_ family –_uff_. The _fluff_ piece says '/ŭf/ /ŭf/ /ŭf/' like at the end of the word _fluff_. Pretend you are holding a fluffy bunny in your arms, pet the bunny, and say '/ŭf/.' Let's make a list of words that have the _fluff_ sound in them" (record the words).

4. Hold up the _duck_ puzzle piece and say, "This is the _duck_ piece. It represents the short _u_ family –_uck_. The _duck_ piece says '/ŭk/ /ŭk/ /ŭk/' like at the end of the word _duck_. Create a _V_ with your hands touching at your wrist. Place the _V_ at your mouth, move your hands together in a snapping motion, and say '/ŭk/.' Let's make a list of words that have the _duck_ sound in them" (record the words).

5. Hold up the _bunk_ puzzle piece and say, "This is the _bunk_ piece. It represents the short _u_ family –_unk_. The _bunk_ piece says '/ŭnk/ /ŭnk/ /ŭnk/' like at the end of the word _bunk_. Pretend you are climbing a ladder with your hands only and say '/ŭnk/.' Let's make a list of words that have the _bunk_ sound in them" (record the words).

BLENDING: PUTTING SOUNDS TOGETHER TO MAKE NEW WORDS

1. Follow the Blending routine on page I-17 of the Introduction.

2. Display the following words on the board one line at a time. Facilitate a discussion about the blending line focus after each line.

3. Then display the weekly sight words and sentence.

4. Discuss the words within the short _u_ families found in the sentence.

fluff	duck	bunk	Discuss: –_uff_, –_uck_, and –_unk_ word families
cuff	buck	junk	Discuss: –_uff_, –_uck_, and –_unk_ word families
hub	spun	hut	Discuss: review of word families from last week

Sight Words: its   ask

Sentence: The duck fluffed its wings.

DICTATION:
STRETCH OUT
YOUR WORDS

1. Have students turn to page 249 of the Learner's Notebook.

2. Follow the Dictation routine on page I-21 of the Introduction to dictate the following words:

I. bunk   2. junk   3. fluff

Sight Word: ask

3. Use Dictation words as an informal pretest. For students who are continuing to study Week 1 words, encourage them to sound out the words for Dictation as best they can. Assist students in doubling the consonant in the word *fluff*.

PRACTICE:
COMPLETE
YOUR WORK ON
YOUR OWN

1. Have students turn to page 245 (Group 1) or page 247 (Group 2) of the Learner's Notebook.

2. Instruct students to tear out the sort and complete the following Practice Pieces: Quick Color, Careful Cut, Highlighter Hunt, and Sorting With Words (see further directions on pages I-37, I-38, I-43, and I-27 of the Introduction).

3. Circulate as students work, which usually takes fifteen minutes, and coach as needed.

FLUENCY:
READING LIKE
YOU'RE SPEAKING

1. Have students turn to page 37 in the Fluency Notebook.

2. Have students read one or more of the following poems: "I'll Huff and I'll Puff!" and "Ode to My Lucky Penny."

3. Circulate and listen to students read or gather a small group of students who need additional support.

PHONEMIC AWARENESS: LISTEN

1. Give the directions. Say, "I am going to say a word. Then I am going to ask you to change the initial sound. Your job is to listen to the word, change the initial sound, and say the two rhyming words. For example, if I say '_bad_, change the initial sound to /r/,' you say '_rad_.' Then, you say the two rhyming words: '_bad, rad_.'"

2. Say the following words and sounds:

run, /p/ (pun)   dunk, /g/ (gunk)   Gus, /f/ (fuss)
duck, /p/ (puck)   junk, /f/ (funk)

PUZZLE PIECE REVIEW

1. Say, "When I point to the piece, you tell me its name" (_fluff, duck, bunk_).

2. Say, "When I point to the piece, you tell me its sound" (/ŭf/, /ŭk/, ŭnk/).

3. Say, "When I point to the piece, you tell me its spelling" (–_uff, –uck, –unk_).

4. Say, "Write the spellings in the air with your finger" (students will form the letters –_uff, –uck,_ and –_unk_).

BLENDING: PUTTING SOUNDS TOGETHER TO MAKE NEW WORDS

1. Follow the Blending routine on page I-17 of the Introduction.

2. Display the following words on the board one line at a time. Facilitate a discussion about the blending line focus after each line.

3. Then display the weekly sight words and sentence.

4. Discuss the short _u_ family words found in the sentence.

suck	tuck	stuck	Discuss: –_uck_ word family; discuss the similar initial consonants
sunk	stunk	trunk	Discuss: –_unk_ word family; discuss the similar initial consonants
run	cub	nut	Discuss: review of word families from last week

Sight Words: its   ask

Sentence: The cub had to ask for the nut.

QUICK SWITCH: MANIPULATE YOUR WORDS

1. Have students turn to page 249 of the Learner's Notebook.

2. Follow the Quick Switch routine on page I-23 of the Introduction to dictate the following words:

buff → bluff → luck → tuck → truck

3. Review the –_uff_ and –_uck_ word families with students. Help students get from _bluff_ to _luck_.

SORT: WHAT IS YOUR FOCUS PATTERN?

1. Have students take out their bag of words (created on Day 1) and follow the Sorting With Words routine on page I-27 of the Introduction.

PRACTICE: COMPLETE YOUR WORK ON YOUR OWN

1. Students will follow the Read and Trade routine on page I-47 of the Introduction.

2. Circulate as students work, which usually takes fifteen minutes, and coach as needed.

**FLUENCY:
READING LIKE
YOU'RE SPEAKING**

1. Have students turn to page 37 in the Fluency Notebook.

2. Have students read one or more of the following poems: "I'll Huff and I'll Puff!" and "Ode to My Lucky Penny."

3. Circulate and listen to students read or gather a small group of students who need additional support.

Day 3

PHONEMIC AWARENESS: LISTEN

1. Give the directions. Say, "I am going to say a word. Then I am going to ask you to change the initial sound. Your job is to listen to the word, change the initial sound, and say the two rhyming words. For example, if I say '*bad*, change the initial sound to /r/,' you say '*rad*.' Then, you say the two rhyming words: '*bad, rad*.'"

2. Say the following words and sounds:

runt, /p/ (punt)   but, /n/ (nut)   suck, /m/ (muck)
fun, /s/ (sun)   lug, /r/ (rug)

PUZZLE PIECE REVIEW

1. Say, "When I point to the piece, you tell me its name" (*fluff, duck, bunk*).

2. Say, "When I point to the piece, you tell me its sound" (/ŭf/, /ŭk/, ŭnk/).

3. Say, "When I point to the piece, you tell me its spelling" (*–uff, –uck, –unk*).

4. Say, "Write the spellings in the air with your finger" (students will form the letters *–uff, –uck,* and *–unk*).

BLENDING: PUTTING SOUNDS TOGETHER TO MAKE NEW WORDS

1. Follow the Blending routine on page I-17 of the Introduction.

2. Display the following words on the board one line at a time. Facilitate a discussion about the blending line focus after each line.

3. Then display the weekly sight words and sentence.

4. Discuss the capital *L* in *Lund*. Remind students that names are capitalized.

buff	bluff	stuff	Discuss: *–uff* word family
buck	bunk	bunks	Discuss: *–uck* and *–unk* word families; explain that the *s* ending on *bunks* means "more than one"
rub	run	rut	Discuss: review word families from last week

Sight Words: its   ask
Sentence: **Ms. Lund asked the class to study.**

DICTATION: STRETCH OUT YOUR WORDS

1. Have students turn to page 250 of the Learner's Notebook.

2. Follow the Dictation routine on page I-21 of the Introduction to dictate the following words:

l. stuff   2. dunk   3. luck

Sight Word: its

3. For students who are continuing to study Week 1 words, encourage them to sound out the words for Dictation as best they can. Assist students in recording the consonant blend and double *f* in *stuff*.

SORT: WHAT IS YOUR FOCUS PATTERN?

1. Have students take out their bag of words (created on Day 1) and follow the Sorting With Words routine on page I-27 of the Introduction.

PRACTICE: COMPLETE YOUR WORK ON YOUR OWN

1. Have students turn to page 251 in the Learner's Notebook.

2. Students will complete the Spell It Out routine on page I-49 of the Introduction.

3. Circulate as students work, which usually takes fifteen minutes, and coach as needed.

**FLUENCY:
READING LIKE
YOU'RE SPEAKING**

1. Have students turn to page 37 in the Fluency Notebook.

2. Have students read one or more of the following poems: "I'll Huff and I'll Puff!" and "Ode to My Lucky Penny."

3. Circulate and listen to students read or gather a small group of students who need additional support.

Day 4

PHONEMIC AWARENESS: LISTEN

1. Give the directions. Say, "I am going to say a word. Then I am going to ask you to change the initial sound. Your job is to listen to the word, change the initial sound, and say the two rhyming words. For example, if I say '*bad*, change the initial sound to /r/,' you say '*rad*.' Then, you say the two rhyming words: '*bad, rad*.'"

2. Say the following words and sounds:

bunt, /h/ (hunt)   sub, /t/ (tub)   dug, /l/ (lug)
sunk, /h/ (hunk)   puff, /h/ (huff)

PUZZLE PIECE REVIEW

1. Say, "When I point to the piece, you tell me its name" (*fluff, duck, bunk*).

2. Say, "When I point to the piece, you tell me its sound" (/ŭf/, /ŭk/, /ŭnk/).

3. Say, "When I point to the piece, you tell me its spelling" (*–uff, –uck, –unk*).

4. Say, "Write the spellings in the air with your finger" (students will form the letters *–uff, –uck,* and *–unk*).

BLENDING: PUTTING SOUNDS TOGETHER TO MAKE NEW WORDS

1. Follow the Blending routine on page I-17 of the Introduction.

2. Display the following words on the board one line at a time. Facilitate a discussion about the blending line focus after each line.

3. Then display the weekly sight words and sentence.

4. Identify the short *u* family word in the sentence. Ask students what they visualize when reading the sentence.

stuff	stuck	sunk	Discuss: initial consonant *s*; identify the word family in each word
puff	puck	plunk	Discuss: initial consonant *p*; identify the word family in each word
fun	gut	grub	Discuss: review word families from last week

Sight Words: its   ask

Sentence: The hog stuck its belly out.

QUICK SWITCH: MANIPULATE YOUR WORDS

1. Have students turn to page 250 of the Learner's Notebook.

2. Follow the Quick Switch routine on page I-23 of the Introduction to dictate the following words:

muck → buck → bunk → sunk → stunk

3. Review the *–uck* and *–unk* word families with students. Help students get from *buck* to *bunk*.

SORT: WHAT IS YOUR FOCUS PATTERN?

1. Have students take out their bag of words (created on Day 1) and follow the Sorting With Words routine on page I-27 of the Introduction.

PRACTICE: COMPLETE YOUR WORK ON YOUR OWN

1. Have students complete the following Practice Piece: Glue, Draw a Picture (on page I-50 of the Introduction).

2. Circulate as students work, which usually takes fifteen minutes, and coach as needed.

FLUENCY: READING LIKE YOU'RE SPEAKING

1. Have students turn to page 37 in the Fluency Notebook.

2. Have students read one or more of the following poems: "I'll Huff and I'll Puff!" and "Ode to My Lucky Penny."

3. Circulate and listen to students read or gather a small group of students who need additional support.

Day 5

PHONEMIC AWARENESS: LISTEN	**1.** Give the directions. Say, "I am going to say a word. Then I am going to ask you to change the initial sound. Your job is to listen to the word, change the initial sound, and say the two rhyming words. For example, if I say '*bad*, change the initial sound to /r/,' you say '*rad*.' Then, you say the two rhyming words: '*bad, rad*.'"

2. Say the following words and sounds:

sud, /b/ (bud)　　muck, /d/ (duck)　　fuss, /m/ (muss)

bug, /p/ (pug)　　just, /r/ (rust)

REVIEW PATTERNS OF THE WEEK	**1.** Say, "Find a partner."

2. Say, "Tell your partner the name of this week's pieces" (*fluff, duck, bunk*).

3. Say, "Tell your partner the sound of this week's pieces" (/ŭf/, /ŭk/, /ŭnk/).

4. Say, "Tell your partner the spellings of this week's pieces" (–*uff*, –*uck*, –*unk*).

5. Say, "Write the spellings on your partner's back with your finger" (students will form the letters –*uff*, –*uck*, and –*unk*).

SPELLING CHECK	**1.** Follow the Spelling Check routine on page I-34 of the Introduction.

2. Instruct students to sit in their word study groups and turn to page 253 of the Learner's Notebook.

3. Say, "I am going to say one word at a time to each group. Record the words as I say them to your group. Make sure you only record the words from your group."

4. Move back and forth between the groups and dictate the following words:

Words for Group 1	**Words for Group 2**
1. hub	1. funk
2. jut	2. bluff
3. run	3. stuck
4. dub	4. dunk
5. spun	5. buck
Sentence: The duck got its grub.	**Sentence: The bus got its back end stuck in the mud.**

WORD HUNT	**1.** Students will follow the Word Hunt routine on page I-55 of the Introduction.

2. Instruct students to search texts and the classroom for words within the short *u* families.

COMPREHENSION CHECK

1. Have students turn to page 254 of the Learner's Notebook.

2. Students will follow the Comprehension Check routine on page I-36 of the Introduction.

3. Check students' work. Circled answers are as follows:

1. The bug asked for its stuff.
2. The cub asked for its den.
3. The slug asked for its sub.

4. Possible written responses include the following:

1. The slug asked for its sub.
2. I asked for my _____. (Students may put any logical word in the blank. For example, "I asked for my pencil.")

WEEKLY CELEBRATION

1. Display the celebratory message: "Slam dunk! You learned the _fluff, duck,_ and _bunk_ puzzle pieces!"

2. Encourage students to work together to read the message.

3. Have students copy the message onto their weekly certificate (see resources .corwin.com/puzzlepiecephonics-gradeK) and place it somewhere to take home.

Concept 9 Overview:

Mixed Short Vowel Review

WHAT ARE SHORT VOWELS?

Students have been studying short vowel families for the past ten weeks. At this point in the year, they should be very familiar and comfortable with short vowels! However, they have not studied more than one short vowel at the same time since Concept 3. In Concept 9, students will need to recall all of the short vowel sounds in order to read and write words with similar consonant sounds but different vowel sounds.

GOALS FOR THE CONCEPT

Students will
- Identify and represent short vowels
- Identify and represent consonant sounds
- Read and write sight words
- Manipulate words in order to create a new word
- Develop reading fluency and comprehension

WEEKS FOR THIS CONCEPT

Week 1: Mixed Short Vowel Review
(–ap, –ep, –ip, –op, –up)
Week 2: Mixed Short Vowel Review
(–am, –em, –im, –om, –um)
Week 3: Mixed Short Vowel Review
(–an, –en, –in, –on, –un)
Week 4: Mixed Short Vowel Review
(–ast, –est, –ist, –ost, –ust)

Preparing for Your Week

Resources

PUZZLE PIECES

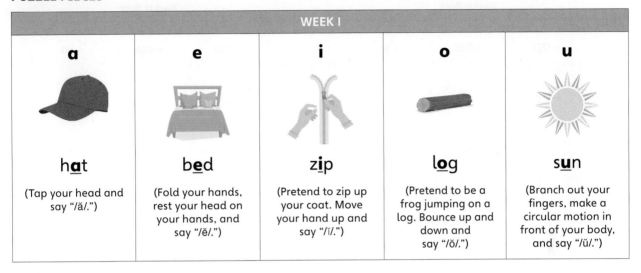

WEEK 1				
a	**e**	**i**	**o**	**u**
h**a**t	b**e**d	z**i**p	l**o**g	s**u**n
(Tap your head and say "/ă/.")	(Fold your hands, rest your head on your hands, and say "/ĕ/.")	(Pretend to zip up your coat. Move your hand up and say "/ĭ/.")	(Pretend to be a frog jumping on a log. Bounce up and down and say "/ŏ/.")	(Branch out your fingers, make a circular motion in front of your body, and say "/ŭ/.")

Hat: istock.com/stevezmina1; Bed: istock.com/vasilyevalara; Zip: istock.com/pe-art; Log: istock.com/bennyb; Sun: istock.com/StudioBarcelona

Preparing for Your Week

CORRESPONDING *LEARNER'S NOTEBOOK PAGES*

Group 1 | Week 1 | Concept 9

Name _____ Date _____

Weekly Sort

–ap	–ep	–ip
–op	–up	cup
map	step	lip
tap	stop	skip
clap	mop	trip
hop	pup	flap

Concept 9 **255**

Group 2 | Week 1 | Concept 9

Name _____ Date _____

Weekly Sort

–ap	–ep	–ip
–op	–up	pup
zap	step	cup
trap	strep	slip
clap	top	snip
plop	flop	drip

Concept 9 **257**

Week 1 | Concept 9

Name _____ Date _____

A Mess!

Circle the sentence that matches the picture.

	The pup hops up! The pig hops up! The pest hops up!
	He skips the cup. He tips the cup. He breaks the cup.
	Get a map for the mess. Get a mom for the mess. Get a mop for the mess.

Use the text to answer the questions.

1. How does the pup make a mess? The pup _____ .

2. Why do the people get a mop? A mop can _____ .

Preparing for Your Week

CORRESPONDING *FLUENCY NOTEBOOK PAGES*

Hopscotch

Skip, step,

Skip, step,

Skip, step,

STOMP!

Playing Hopscotch.

Jump up—

WHOMP!

Skip, step,

Skip, step,

Skip, step,

STOP!

Playing Hopscotch.

I'm at the—

TOP!

The Perfect Pup

I want a pup

with ears that flop

and paws that plop

and a tongue that slops.

I want a pup

who fetches sticks

and gives big licks

and does good tricks.

I want a pup

to be my pet.

We haven't met.

Can I have him yet?

Preparing for Your Week

Tips for Management and Differentiation

Refer to this section and to resources.corwin.com/puzzlepiecephonics-gradeK for resources and ideas to deepen your students' learning throughout the week. Feel free to put your own spin on the routines, too. For daily lesson plans, see pages 354–362 of this Teacher's Guide.

TIPS FOR PHONEMIC AWARENESS	• The focus for this week is segmenting words. • If you notice your students need additional practice, extend the activity with more words.
TIPS FOR THE PUZZLE PIECE REVIEW	• Students will review all of the short vowel pieces this week. You should review the names, sounds, and spellings of the focus puzzle pieces every day. • Spend more time on any vowels your students may be mixing up or struggling to identify.
TIPS FOR BLENDING	• If your students master words that end in *p* early in the week, then you can blend words similar to those for Day 4 earlier. On the other hand, if your students are still struggling to read words with mixed vowels by Day 4, then you can have them continue to blend words from their sorts. • Both of the sight words this week are question words. Your students may need additional practice with these words to understand how they are used and ways to start sentences that answer how and why questions. Give students time to answer the question with a partner, move around to music, and then answer the same question (or a different question) with a new partner.
TIPS FOR DICTATION AND QUICK SWITCH	• This is the first week students will record a sentence with Dictation. Say the sentence slowly and model how to use resources around the room for support (the puzzle pieces, a word wall, etc.). If some students need additional scaffolding, you can write parts of the sentence in highlighter and encourage them to trace over your writing. • Support your students as much as necessary so they feel successful. You can complete the routine as a class or have students check their work after each letter, if necessary.

TIPS FOR SORTING	• Model and positively reinforce the sorting routine repeatedly throughout the week.
	• Discuss the vocabulary words that appear in the sort. Vocabulary words include the following:
	   • Sort 1: *mop, flap*
	   • Sort 2: *zap, plop, strep, flop, snip*

Preparing for Your Week

TIPS FOR THE PRACTICE PIECES

- Teach students how to complete Create a Puzzle Piece. You may need to create class puzzle pieces and allow students to share the work of coloring them in this week, since it is the first time students have seen this Practice Piece.
- Students can complete Color-Code Writing this week by making all of the words with short *a* one color, all of the words with short *e* another color, and so on. They can add other words with each vowel sound to their list as well.
- Students may need support with Super Sentences, as this is their first time completing this activity. You can teach the routine by writing some sentences as a whole class. Then release responsibility as students are ready.

TIPS FOR FLUENCY

- This week students will read poems ending in a short vowel plus *p*. When students reach mastery with the daily poems, they can revisit poems from last week.
- Students can highlight words with a short vowel plus *p*.
- You can assign students fluency partners. Students will work together to achieve fluency with the daily poems.
- Students can participate in a "Fluency Celebration." Call on students who feel prepared to present a particular poem in front of the class. Other students can follow along in the Fluency Notebook.

Day 1

THE PUZZLE PIECE FAMILY

Launch Concept 9: Mixed Short Vowel Review by following the Puzzle Piece Family routine on page I-11 of the Introduction.

1. Show students the following words:

cap	lost
cop	ham
cup	hem
last	pin
list	pan

2. Have students read the words with you. Underline the vowel in each word.

3. Facilitate a discussion that leads them to discover the Puzzle Piece Family: Short Vowels.

PHONEMIC AWARENESS: LISTEN

1. Give the directions. Say, "I am going to say a word. I want you to tell me the sounds in the word. So if I say 'map, you say '/m/ /ă/ /p/.'"

2. Say the following words:

tap   step   lip   hip   hop   mop   top   tip   sip   sap

THE BIG REVEAL

1. Say, "We have been studying short vowel families. We know all of our short vowel sounds very well! We're now ready to mix up all of the short vowels and read and write words with /ă/, /ĕ/, /ĭ/, /ŏ/, and /ŭ/. Let's review our short vowel pieces."

2. Say, "This is the *hat* puzzle piece. It represents the letter *a*. The hat piece says /ă/ like in the middle of the word *hat*. Let's do the motion of the *hat* piece. Good!"

3. Say, "This is the *bed* puzzle piece. It represents the letter *e*. The bed piece says /ĕ/ like in the middle of the word *bed*. Let's do the motion of the *bed* piece. Good!"

4. Say, "This is the *zip* puzzle piece. It represents the letter *i*. The *zip* piece says /ĭ/ like in the middle of the word *zip*. Let's do the motion of the *zip* piece. Good!"

5. Say, "This is the *log* puzzle piece. It represents the letter *o*. The log piece says /ŏ/ like in the middle of the word *log*. Let's do the motion of the *log* piece. Good!"

6. Say, "This is the *sun* puzzle piece. It represents the letter *u*. The sun piece says /ŭ/ like in the middle of the word *sun*. Let's do the motion of the *sun* piece. Good!"

BLENDING: PUTTING SOUNDS TOGETHER TO MAKE NEW WORDS

1. Follow the Blending routine on page I-17 of the Introduction.

2. Display the following words on the board one line at a time. Facilitate a discussion about the blending line focus after each line.

3. Then display the weekly sight words and sentence.

4. Discuss the question mark in the sentence and model reading with intonation and answering a *why* question.

BLENDING: PUTTING SOUNDS TOGETHER TO MAKE NEW WORDS (Continued)	mop	stop	step	Discuss: compare and contrast the –*op* family words with *step*
	tap	clap	cup	Discuss: compare and contrast the –*ap* family words with *cup*
	tip	skip	sup	Discuss: compare and contrast the –*ip* family words with *sup*

Sight Words: how   why

Sentence: Why did you clap?

DICTATION:
STRETCH OUT
YOUR WORDS

1. Have students turn to page 259 of the Learner's Notebook.

2. Follow the Dictation routine on page I-21 of the Introduction to dictate the following words:

l. tap   2. map   3. hop   4. mop

Sight Word: how

Sentence: The cup is big.

3. Use Dictation as an informal pretest of students' knowledge of mixed short vowels. Help students write the sight word and repeat the sentence as many times as needed.

PRACTICE:
COMPLETE
YOUR WORK ON
YOUR OWN

1. Have students turn to page 255 (Group 1) or 257 (Group 2) of the Learner's Notebook.

2. Instruct students to tear out the sort and complete the following Practice Pieces: Quick Color, Careful Cut, Highlighter Hunt, and Sorting With Words (see further directions on pages I-37, I-38, I-43, and I-27 of the Introduction).

3. Circulate as students work, which usually takes fifteen minutes, and coach as needed.

FLUENCY: READING
LIKE YOU'RE
SPEAKING

1. Have students turn to page 38 in the Fluency Notebook.

2. Have students read one or more of the following poems: "Hopscotch" and "The Perfect Pup."

3. Circulate and listen to students read or gather a small group of students who need additional support.

Day 2

PHONEMIC AWARENESS: LISTEN

1. Give the directions. Say, "I am going to say a word. I want you to tell me the sounds in the word. So if I say '*map*,' you say '/m/ /ă/ /p/.'"

2. Say the following words:

pop   pup   cup   tip   nip   nap   drop   drip   hop   step

PUZZLE PIECE REVIEW

1. Say, "When I point to the piece, you tell me its name" (*hat, bed, zip, log, sun*).

2. Say, "When I point to the piece, you tell me its sound" (/ă/, /ĕ/, /ĭ/, /ŏ/, /ŭ/).

3. Say, "When I point to the piece, you tell me its spelling" (*a, e, i, o, u*).

4. Say, "Write the spellings in the air with your finger" (students will form the letters *a, e, i, o,* and *u*).

BLENDING: PUTTING SOUNDS TOGETHER TO MAKE NEW WORDS

1. Follow the Blending routine on page I-17 of the Introduction.

2. Display the following words on the board one line at a time. Facilitate a discussion about the blending line focus after each line.

3. Then display the weekly sight words and sentence.

4. Discuss the question mark in the sentence and model reading with intonation and answering a *how* question.

flap	flip	flop	Discuss: *fl* blend as initial sound; *p* as final sound; contrast short vowel medial sounds
sip	step	stop	Discuss: *s* or *st* blend as initial sound; *p* as final sound; contrast short vowel medial sounds
pup	pop	pep	Discuss: *p* as initial sound; *p* as final sound; contrast short vowel medial sounds

Sight Words: how   why

Sentence: How did it pop?

QUICK SWITCH: MANIPULATE YOUR WORDS

1. Have students turn to page 259 of the Learner's Notebook.

2. Follow the Quick Switch routine on page I-23 of the Introduction to dictate the following words:

map → tap → tip → hip → hop

3. Help students segment words and identify whether the vowel or consonant sound is changing.

SORT: WHAT IS YOUR FOCUS PATTERN?

1. Have students take out their bag of words (created on Day 1) and follow the Sorting With Words routine on page I-27 of the Introduction.

PRACTICE: COMPLETE YOUR WORK ON YOUR OWN

1. Students will follow the Create a Puzzle Piece routine on page I-51 of the Introduction.

2. Circulate as students work, which usually takes fifteen minutes, and coach as needed.

FLUENCY: READING LIKE YOU'RE SPEAKING

1. Have students turn to page 38 in the Fluency Notebook.

2. Have students read one or more of the following poems: "Hopscotch" and "The Perfect Pup."

3. Circulate and listen to students read or gather a small group of students who need additional support.

Day 3

PHONEMIC AWARENESS: LISTEN	**1.** Give the directions. Say, "I am going to say a word. I want you to tell me the sounds in the word. So if I say '*map*,' you say '/m/ /ă/ /p/.'"
	2. Say the following words:
	clip clap clop cup cap nap flap flip flop top
PUZZLE PIECE REVIEW	**1.** Say, "When I point to the piece, you tell me its name" (*hat, bed, zip, log, sun*).
	2. Say, "When I point to the piece, you tell me its sound" (/ă/, /ĕ/, /ĭ/, /ŏ/, /ŭ/).
	3. Say, "When I point to the piece, you tell me its spelling" (*a, e, i, o, u*).
	4. Say, "Write the spellings in the air with your finger" (students will form the letters *a, e, i, o*, and *u*).
BLENDING: PUTTING SOUNDS TOGETHER TO MAKE NEW WORDS	**1.** Follow the Blending routine on page I-17 of the Introduction.
	2. Display the following words on the board one line at a time. Facilitate a discussion about the blending line focus after each line.
	3. Then display the weekly sight words and sentence.
	4. Discuss the question mark in the sentence and model reading with intonation and answering a *why* question.
	tap hop cup Discuss: mix of consonant and short vowel sounds
	lip stop flap Discuss: blends found in *stop* and *flap*
	step pup mop Discuss: blend found in *step*
	Sight Words: how why
	Sentence: Why did the pup stop?
DICTATION: STRETCH OUT YOUR WORDS	**1.** Have students turn to page 260 of the Learner's Notebook.
	2. Follow the Dictation routine on page I-21 of the Introduction to dictate the following words:
	I. step 2. hop 3. tip 4. flap
	Sight Word: why
	Sentence: I can skip.
	3. Help students segment the words and reference puzzle pieces as necessary.
SORT: WHAT IS YOUR FOCUS PATTERN?	**1.** Have students take out their bag of words (created on Day 1) and follow the Sorting With Words routine on page I-27 of the Introduction.
PRACTICE: COMPLETE YOUR WORK ON YOUR OWN	**1.** Students will complete the Color-Code Writing routine on page I-52 of the Introduction.
	2. Circulate as students work, which usually takes fifteen minutes, and coach as needed.

FLUENCY:
READING LIKE
YOU'RE SPEAKING

1. Have students turn to page 38 in the Fluency Notebook.

2. Have students read one or more of the following poems: "Hopscotch" and "The Perfect Pup."

3. Circulate and listen to students read or gather a small group of students who need additional support.

Day 4

PHONEMIC AWARENESS: LISTEN

1. Give the directions. Say, "I am going to say a word. Your job is to tell me the vowel sound you hear in the word. Do the motion of the sound you hear. So if I say '*skip*,' you do the motion of the *zip* piece."

2. Say the following words:

clap   top   drop   step   lip   cup   pup   map   hip   flap

PUZZLE PIECE REVIEW

1. Say, "When I point to the piece, you tell me its name" (*hat, bed, zip, log, sun*).

2. Say, "When I point to the piece, you tell me its sound" (/ă/, /ĕ/, /ĭ/, /ŏ/, /ŭ/).

3. Say, "When I point to the piece, you tell me its spelling" (*a, e, i, o, u*).

4. Say, "Write the spellings in the air with your finger" (students will form the letters *a, e, i, o,* and *u*).

BLENDING: PUTTING SOUNDS TOGETHER TO MAKE NEW WORDS

1. Follow the Blending routine on page I-17 of the Introduction.

2. Display the following words on the board one line at a time. Facilitate a discussion about the blending line focus after each line.

3. Then display the weekly sight words and sentence.

4. Discuss the question mark in the sentence and model reading with intonation and answering a *how* question.

flap	**flip**	**flick**	Discuss: contrast word families
step	**stop**	**stock**	Discuss: contrast word families
pop	**pup**	**puff**	Discuss: contrast word families

Sight Words: how   why

Sentence: How did it flip?

QUICK SWITCH: MANIPULATE YOUR WORDS

1. Have students turn to page 260 of the Learner's Notebook.

2. Follow the Quick Switch routine on page I-23 of the Introduction to dictate the following words:

pup → puck → pack → tack → tap

3. Help students get from *pup* to *puck* by reviewing the *–uck* family. Help students get from *puck* to *pack* by identifying the change in vowel sound and by relating the *–ack* family to the *–uck* family.

SORT: WHAT IS YOUR FOCUS PATTERN?

1. Have students take out their bag of words (created on Day 1) and follow the Sorting With Words routine on page I-27 of the Introduction.

PRACTICE: COMPLETE YOUR WORK ON YOUR OWN

1. Have students complete the following Practice Pieces: Glue, Draw a Picture and Super Sentences (on pages I-50 and I-53 of the Introduction).

2. Circulate as students work, which usually takes fifteen minutes, and coach as needed.

FLUENCY: READING LIKE YOU'RE SPEAKING

1. Have students turn to page 38 in the Fluency Notebook.

2. Have students read one or more of the following poems: "Hopscotch" and "The Perfect Pup."

3. Circulate and listen to students read or gather a small group of students who need additional support.

PHONEMIC AWARENESS: LISTEN	**1.** Give the directions. Say, "I am going to say a word. Your job is to tell me the vowel sound you hear in the word. Do the motion of the sound you hear. So if I say 'skip,' you do the motion of the *zip* piece."
	2. Say the following words:

rap rip hop pup stop step cup flop drip flap

REVIEW PATTERNS OF THE WEEK	**1.** Say, "Find a partner."
	2. Say, "Tell your partner the names of this week's pieces" (*hat, bed, zip, log, sun*).
	3. Say, "Tell your partner the sounds of this week's pieces" (/ă/, /ĕ/, /ĭ/, /ŏ/, /ŭ/)
	4. Say, "Tell your partner the spellings of this week's pieces" (*a, e, i, o, u*).
	5. Say, "Write the spellings on your partner's back with your finger" (students will form the letters a, e, *i, o, u*).

SPELLING CHECK	**1.** Follow the Spelling Check routine on page I-34 of the Introduction.
	2. Instruct students to sit in their word study groups and turn to page 261 of the Learner's Notebook.
	3. Say, "I am going to say one word at a time to each group. Record the words as I say them to your group. Make sure you only record the words from your group."
	4. Move back and forth between the groups and dictate the following words:

Words for Group 1

1. tap
2. pup
3. step
4. lip
5. mop

Sentence: I can hop up.

Words for Group 2

1. flop
2. zap
3. slip
4. cup
5. step

Sentence: The trap is set up.

WORD HUNT	**1.** Students will follow the Word Hunt routine on page I-55 of the Introduction.
	2. Instruct students to search texts and the classroom for words with short vowels.

COMPREHENSION CHECK	**1.** Have students turn to page 262 of the Learner's Notebook.
	2. Students will follow the Comprehension Check routine on page I-36 of the Introduction.
	3. Check students' work. Circled answers are as follows:

1. The pup hops up!
2. He tips the cup.
3. Get a mop for the mess.

4. Possible written responses include the following:

1. The pup hops up. The pup tips the cup. The pup breaks the cup. (Students may put any logical word or phrase in the blank.)
2. A mop can _____. (Students may put any logical word or phrase into the blank. For example, "A mop can make the floors sparkle.")

(Continued)

Day 5 (Continued)

WEEKLY CELEBRATION

1. Display the celebratory message: "Hip hip hooray! You are mastering the *hat, bed, zip, log,* and *sun* pieces!"

2. Encourage students to work together to read the message.

3. Have students copy the message onto their weekly certificate (see resources .corwin.com/puzzlepiecephonics-gradeK) and place it somewhere to take home.

Preparing for Your Week

Resources

PUZZLE PIECES

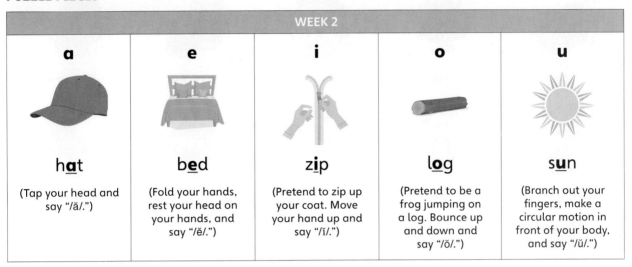

WEEK 2				
a	**e**	**i**	**o**	**u**
h**a**t	b**e**d	z**i**p	l**o**g	s**u**n
(Tap your head and say "/ă/.")	(Fold your hands, rest your head on your hands, and say "/ĕ/.")	(Pretend to zip up your coat. Move your hand up and say "/ĭ/.")	(Pretend to be a frog jumping on a log. Bounce up and down and say "/ŏ/.")	(Branch out your fingers, make a circular motion in front of your body, and say "/ŭ/.")

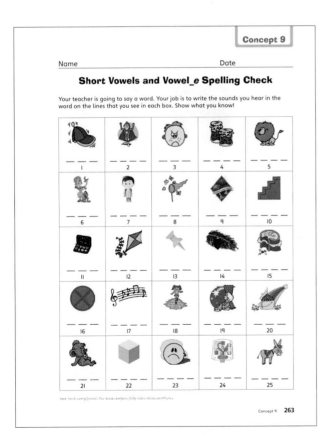

PREASSESSMENT DIRECTIONS

You can give this preassessment any day(s) during Concept 9, Week 2. You can split up the rows and do parts on different days. Do what works for your class.

Instruct students to turn to **page 263 in the Learner's Notebook**.

Explain to students that they have not yet studied words with these spellings. This check will be used to see what they already know about vowel_*e*. Tell students that you will use the results to form word study groups (see Tips for Scoring on page 364) and set goals.

When giving this assessment, go row by row in saying the words that go along with the picture. Students are *not* guessing what the picture is.

Hat: istock.com/stevezmina1; Bed: istock.com/vasilyevalara; Zip: istock.com/pe-art; Log: istock.com/bennyb; Sun: istock.com/StudioBarcelona

Preparing for Your Week

PREASSESSMENT: SHORT VOWELS AND VOWEL_e SPELLING CHECK

ANSWER KEY				
1. cap	2. cape	3. mad	4. made	5. mane
6. pet	7. Pete	8. net	9. eve	10. step
11. kit	12. kite	13. pin	14. pine	15. bite
16. not	17. note	18. hop	19. hope	20. pot
21. cub	22. cube	23. fuss	24. fuse	25. mule

Pete: istock.com/pijama6l; Pin: istock.com/jane_Kelly; Cube: istock.com/Physicx

EVALUATING THE ASSESSMENT: WHAT TO LOOK FOR

- Knowledge of consonants
- Knowledge of short vowels
- Knowledge of vowel_e
- Knowledge of basic blends

TIPS FOR SCORING

This assessment is to be used to group your students and understand their needs. Each row contains words with either a short vowel or a long vowel that is represented by the vowel_e spelling pattern. All of the long vowel (vowel_e) words can be found in columns 2, 4, and 5.

For each correctly spelled word, students earn one point. Add up their points to see their total score.

- If students receive 0–14 points, they will be working with Group 1 words.
- If students receive 15–25 points, they will be working with Group 2 words.

This is a guide to get you started, but use teacher discretion when placing your students in groups. Remember, these groups are flexible and can change each week if necessary. See the key above for answers.

Preparing for Your Week

CORRESPONDING *LEARNER'S NOTEBOOK PAGES*

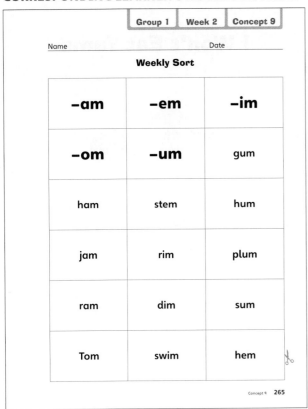

| Group 1 | Week 2 | Concept 9 |

Name _____   Date _____

Weekly Sort

-am	-em	-im
-om	-um	gum
ham	stem	hum
jam	rim	plum
ram	dim	sum
Tom	swim	hem

Concept 9   **265**

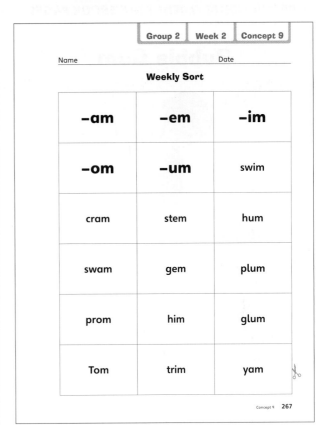

| Group 2 | Week 2 | Concept 9 |

Name _____   Date _____

Weekly Sort

-am	-em	-im
-om	-um	swim
cram	stem	hum
swam	gem	plum
prom	him	glum
Tom	trim	yam

Concept 9   **267**

| Week 2 | Concept 9 |

Name _____   Date _____

What Is for Lunch?

Circle the sentence that matches the picture.

	Dad will have ham. Dad will have a ram. Dad will have hum.
	Mom will have gum. Mom will have ham. Mom will have jam.
	Bud will have a stem. Bud will have a gum. Bud will have a plum.

Use the text to answer the questions.

1. What will Dad have for lunch? Dad will have _____.

2. What do you have? I have a _____.

Preparing for Your Week

CORRESPONDING *FLUENCY NOTEBOOK PAGES*

Bubble Gum

Bubble gum,

Bubble gum,

Pop, pop, pop!

Crack and snap,

Just like that!

Bubble gum,

Bubble gum,

Yum, yum, yum!

Chomp and crunch,

After lunch!

I Won't Eat Yams

I won't eat yams.

No way,

No how!

Don't you try to make me, now!

I'll eat jam and ham.

I'll eat plums and gum.

I'll eat clams and spam.

I'll even eat scum!

But I won't eat yams.

No how,

No way!

Take those yucky yams away!

Preparing for Your Week

Tips for Management and Differentiation

Refer to this section and to resources.corwin.com/puzzlepiecephonics-gradeK for resources and ideas to deepen your students' learning throughout the week. Feel free to put your own spin on the routines, too. For daily lesson plans, see pages 368–375 of this Teacher's Guide.

TIPS FOR PHONEMIC AWARENESS	• The focus for this week is segmenting words. • If you notice your students need additional practice, extend the activity with more words.
TIPS FOR THE PUZZLE PIECE REVIEW	• Students will review all of the short vowel pieces this week. • Spend more time on any vowels your students may be mixing up or struggling to identify.
TIPS FOR BLENDING	• Like last week, both of the sight words this week are question words. Your students may need additional practice with these words to understand how they are used and ways to start sentences that answer *what* and *who* questions. You can post sentence starters and orally pose *what* and *who* questions. Give students time to answer the question with a partner, move around to music, then answer the same question (or a different question) with a new partner. • Students will blend a word with the *tr* consonant blend on Day 2. You can briefly introduce and display the *truck* puzzle piece before blending.
TIPS FOR DICTATION AND QUICK SWITCH	• Continue to support students as they learn to record sentences during Dictation. Say the sentence slowly and model how to use resources around the room for support (the puzzle pieces, a word wall, etc.). If some students need additional scaffolding, you can write parts of the sentence in highlighter and encourage them to trace over your writing. • Support your students as much as necessary so they feel successful. You can complete the routine as a class or have students check their work after each letter, if necessary.

TIPS FOR SORTING	• Model and positively reinforce the sorting routine repeatedly throughout the week.
	• Discuss the vocabulary words that appear in the sort. Vocabulary words include the following:
	   • Sort 1: *jam, ham, stem, rim, dim, hum, plum, sum, hem*
	   • Sort 2: *cram, swam, prom, stem, gem, trim, hum, plum, glum, yam*

TIPS FOR THE PRACTICE PIECES	• Review the routines for Create a Puzzle Piece, Color-Code Writing, and Super Sentences as necessary. You can complete the routines as a class if students still need additional support before working independently. • There are many vocabulary words this week. You can use independent practice time to help students working with Sort 2 to define and apply their vocabulary words.
TIPS FOR FLUENCY	• This week students will read poems with various short vowels. • Students can highlight words with a short vowel plus *m*. • You can assign students fluency partners. Students will work together to achieve fluency with the daily poems. • Students can participate in a "Fluency Celebration." Call on students who feel prepared to present a particular poem in front of the class. Other students can follow along in the Fluency Notebook.

PHONEMIC AWARENESS: LISTEN

1. Give the directions. Say, "I am going to say a word. I want you to tell me the sounds in the word. So if I say '*map*,' you say '/m/ /ă/ /p/.'"

2. Say the following words:

> flap mop map clap clop flip cup lip skip step

THE BIG REVEAL

1. Say, "Remember that we now know our short vowels very well and are ready to mix them up! This week we will again read and write words with /ă/, /ĕ/, /ĭ/, /ŏ/, and /ŭ/. Let's review our short vowel pieces."

2. Say, "This is the *hat* puzzle piece. It represents the letter *a*. The *hat* piece says '/ă/' like in the middle of the word *hat*. Let's do the motion of the *hat* piece. Good!"

3. Say, "This is the *bed* puzzle piece. It represents the letter *e*. The *bed* piece says '/ĕ/' like in the middle of the word *bed*. Let's do the motion of the *bed* piece. Good!"

4. Say, "This is the *zip* puzzle piece. It represents the letter *i*. The *zip* piece says '/ĭ/' like in the middle of the word *zip*. Let's do the motion of the *zip* piece. Good!"

5. Say, "This is the *log* puzzle piece. It represents the letter *o*. The *log* piece says '/ŏ/' like in the middle of the word *log*. Let's do the motion of the *log* piece. Good!"

6. Say, "This is the *sun* puzzle piece. It represents the letter *u*. The *sun* piece says '/ŭ/' like in the middle of the word *sun*. Let's do the motion of the *sun* piece. Good!"

BLENDING: PUTTING SOUNDS TOGETHER TO MAKE NEW WORDS

1. Follow the Blending routine on page I-17 of the Introduction.

2. Display the following words on the board one line at a time. Facilitate a discussion about the blending line focus after each line.

3. Then display the weekly sight words and sentence.

4. Discuss the question mark in the sentence and model reading with intonation and answering a *who* question.

jam	ram	rim	Discuss: compare and contrast the *–am* family words with *rim*
gum	hum	Tom	Discuss: compare and contrast the *–um* family words with *Tom*; capital *T* in the name *Tom*
hem	stem	swim	Discuss: compare and contrast the *–em* family words with *swim*

Sight Words: what who

Sentence: Who can swim?

DICTATION: STRETCH OUT YOUR WORDS

1. Have students turn to page 269 of the Learner's Notebook.

2. Follow the Dictation routine on page I-21 of the Introduction to dictate the following words:

> I. hum 2. sum 3. ham 4. jam

> **Sight Word: what**

> **Sentence: Tom can swim.**

3. Use Dictation as an informal pretest of students' knowledge of this week's mixed vowels.

PRACTICE:
COMPLETE
YOUR WORK ON
YOUR OWN

1. Have students turn to page 265 (Group 1) or page 267 (Group 2) of the Learner's Notebook.

2. Instruct students to tear out the sort and complete the following Practice Pieces: Quick Color, Careful Cut, Highlighter Hunt, and Sorting With Words (see further directions on pages I-37, I-38, I-43, and I-27 of the Introduction).

3. Circulate as students work, which usually takes fifteen minutes, and coach as needed.

FLUENCY:
READING LIKE
YOU'RE SPEAKING

1. Have students turn to page 39 in the Fluency Notebook.

2. Have students read one or more of the following poems: "Bubble Gum" and "I Won't Eat Yams."

3. Circulate and listen to students read or gather a small group of students who need additional support.

Day 2

PHONEMIC AWARENESS: LISTEN	**1.** Give the directions. Say, "I am going to say a word. I want you to tell me the sounds in the word. So if I say 'map,' you say '/m/ /ă/ /p/.'"
	2. Say the following words:
	ram hem plum stem sum dim Tom swim jam gum

PUZZLE PIECE REVIEW	**1.** Say, "When I point to the piece, you tell me its name" (*hat, bed, zip, log, sun*).
	2. Say, "When I point to the piece, you tell me its sound" (/ă/, /ĕ/, /ĭ/, /ŏ/, /ŭ/).
	3. Say, "When I point to the piece, you tell me its spelling" (*a, e, i, o, u*).
	4. Say, "Write the spellings in the air with your finger" (students will form the patterns *a, e, i, o,* and *u*).

BLENDING: PUTTING SOUNDS TOGETHER TO MAKE NEW WORDS	**1.** Follow the Blending routine on page I-17 of the Introduction.
	2. Display the following words on the board one line at a time. Facilitate a discussion about the blending line focus after each line.
	3. Then display the weekly sight words and sentence.
	4. Discuss the question mark in the sentence and model reading with intonation and answering a *what* question.

ram	rim	trim	Discuss: *r* and *tr* blend as initial sound; *m* as final sound; contrast short vowel medial sounds
sum	Sam	stem	Discuss: *s* as initial sound; *m* as final sound; contrast short vowel medial sounds
hem	hum	him	Discuss: *h* as initial sound; *m* as final sound; contrast short vowel medial sounds

Sight Words: what   who

Sentence: What is the sun?

QUICK SWITCH: MANIPULATE YOUR WORDS	**1.** Have students turn to page 269 of the Learner's Notebook.
	2. Follow the Quick Switch routine on page I-23 of the Introduction to dictate the following words:
	rim → ram → ham → hem → stem
	3. Help students segment words and identify whether the vowel or consonant sound is changing. Help students segment and record the consonant blend in *stem*.

SORT: WHAT IS YOUR FOCUS PATTERN?	**1.** Have students take out their bag of words (created on Day 1) and follow the Sorting With Words routine on page I-27 of the Introduction.

PRACTICE: COMPLETE YOUR WORK ON YOUR OWN	**1.** Students will follow the Create a Puzzle Piece routine on page I-51 of the Introduction.
	2. Circulate as students work, which usually takes fifteen minutes, and coach as needed.

FLUENCY:
READING LIKE
YOU'RE SPEAKING

1. Have students turn to page 39 in the Fluency Notebook.

2. Have students read one or more of the following poems: "Bubble Gum" and "I Won't Eat Yams."

3. Circulate and listen to students read or gather a small group of students who need additional support.

Day 3

PHONEMIC AWARENESS: LISTEN

1. Give the directions. Say, "I am going to say a word. I want you to tell me the sounds in the word. So if I say '*map*,' you say '/m/ /ă/ /p/.'"

2. Say the following words:

hem   hop   tip   top   Tom   swim   hot   swim   step   sum

PUZZLE PIECE REVIEW

1. Say, "When I point to the piece, you tell me its name" (*hat, bed, zip, log, sun*).

2. Say, "When I point to the piece, you tell me its sound" (/ă/, /ĕ/, /ĭ/, /ŏ/, /ŭ/).

3. Say, "When I point to the piece, you tell me its spelling" (*a, e, i, o, u*).

4. Say, "Write the spellings in the air with your finger" (students will form the patterns *a, e, i, o,* and *u*).

BLENDING: PUTTING SOUNDS TOGETHER TO MAKE NEW WORDS

1. Follow the Blending routine on page I-17 of the Introduction.

2. Display the following words on the board one line at a time. Facilitate a discussion about the blending line focus after each line.

3. Then display the weekly sight words and sentence.

4. Discuss the question mark in the sentence and model reading with intonation and answering a *who* question.

sum	**jam**	**rim**	Discuss: mix of consonant and short vowel sounds
swim	**ham**	**gum**	Discuss: blend found in *swim*
plum	**hem**	**stem**	Discuss: blends found in *plum* and *stem*

Sight Words: what   who

Sentence: Who has the jam?

DICTATION: STRETCH OUT YOUR WORDS

1. Have students turn to page 270 of the Learner's Notebook.

2. Follow the Dictation routine on page I-21 of the Introduction to dictate the following words:

   I. ram   2. Tom   3. swim   4. plum

   Sight Word: who

   Sentence: Tom has gum.

3. Help students segment the words and reference puzzle pieces as necessary.

SORT: WHAT IS YOUR FOCUS PATTERN?

1. Have students take out their bag of words (created on Day 1) and follow the Sorting With Words routine on page I-27 of the Introduction.

PRACTICE: COMPLETE YOUR WORK ON YOUR OWN

1. Students will complete the Color-Code Writing routine on page I-52 of the Introduction.

2. Circulate as students work, which usually takes fifteen minutes, and coach as needed.

FLUENCY:
READING LIKE
YOU'RE SPEAKING

1. Have students turn to page 39 in the Fluency Notebook.

2. Have students read one or more of the following poems: "Bubble Gum" and "I Won't Eat Yams."

3. Circulate and listen to students read or gather a small group of students who need additional support.

Day 4

PHONEMIC AWARENESS: LISTEN	**1.** Give the directions. Say, "I am going to say a word. Your job is to tell me the vowel sound you hear in the word. Do the motion of the sound you hear. So if I say '*stem*,' you do the motion of the *bed* piece."
	2. Say the following words:
	jam plum sum hem gum swim Tom ram dim rim

PUZZLE PIECE REVIEW	**1.** Say, "When I point to the piece, you tell me its name" (*hat, bed, zip, log, sun*).
	2. Say, "When I point to the piece, you tell me its sound" (/ă/, /ĕ/, /ĭ/, /ŏ/, /ŭ/).
	3. Say, "When I point to the piece, you tell me its spelling" (*a, e, i, o, u*).
	4. Say, "Write the spellings in the air with your finger" (students will form the patterns *a, e, i, o, u*).

BLENDING: PUTTING SOUNDS TOGETHER TO MAKE NEW WORDS	**1.** Follow the Blending routine on page I-17 of the Introduction.
	2. Display the following words on the board one line at a time. Facilitate a discussion about the blending line focus after each line.
	3. Then display the weekly sight words and sentence.
	4. Discuss the quotation marks in the sentence. Model reading with students.

dim   rim   Rick   Discuss: contrast word families

Sam   sum   sock   Discuss: contrast word families

hum   ham   hill   Discuss: contrast word families

Sight Words: what   who

Sentence: Mom said, "Pick the plum."

QUICK SWITCH: MANIPULATE YOUR WORDS	**1.** Have students turn to page 270 of the Learner's Notebook.
	2. Follow the Quick Switch routine on page I-23 of the Introduction to dictate the following words:
	jam → ham → hand → sand → sum
	3. Help students segment the words and reference puzzle pieces as necessary.

SORT: WHAT IS YOUR FOCUS PATTERN?	**1.** Have students take out their bag of words (created on Day 1) and follow the Sorting With Words routine on page I-27 of the Introduction.

PRACTICE: COMPLETE YOUR WORK ON YOUR OWN	**1.** Have students complete the following Practice Pieces: Glue, Draw a Picture and Super Sentences (on pages I-50 and I-53 of the Introduction).
	2. Circulate as students work, which usually takes fifteen minutes, and coach as needed.

FLUENCY: READING LIKE YOU'RE SPEAKING	**1.** Have students turn to page 39 in the Fluency Notebook.
	2. Have students read one or more of the following poems: "Bubble Gum" and "I Won't Eat Yams."
	3. Circulate and listen to students read or gather a small group of students who need additional support.

PHONEMIC AWARENESS: LISTEN	**1.** Give the directions. Say, "I am going to say a word. Your job is to tell me the vowel sound you hear in the word. Do the motion of the sound you hear. So if I say '*stem*,' you do the motion of the *bed* piece."

2. Say the following words:

> stop   gum   sum   ram   drip   step   hem   Tom   plum   pup

REVIEW PATTERNS OF THE WEEK	**1.** Say, "Find a partner."

2. Say, "Tell your partner the names of this week's pieces" (*hat, bed, zip, log, sun*).

3. Say, "Tell your partner the sounds of this week's pieces" (/ă/, /ĕ/, /ĭ/, /ŏ/, /ŭ/).

4. Say, "Tell your partner the spellings of this week's pieces" (*a, e, i, o, u*).

5. Say, "Write the spellings on your partner's back with your finger" (students will form the letters *a, e, i, o,* and *u*).

SPELLING CHECK	**1.** Follow the Spelling Check routine on page I-34 of the Introduction.

2. Instruct students to sit in their word study groups and turn to page 271 of the Learner's Notebook.

3. Say, "I am going to say one word at a time to each group. Record the words as I say them to your group. Make sure you only record the words from your group."

4. Move back and forth between the groups and dictate the following words:

Words for Group I	Words for Group 2
I. dim	I. plum
2. gum	2. yam
3. stem	3. prom
4. jam	4. gem
5. Tom	5. him
Sentence: I see a ram.	**Sentence: Tom swam a bit.**

WORD HUNT	**1.** Students will follow the Word Hunt routine on page I-55 of the Introduction.

2. Instruct students to search texts and the classroom for words with short vowels.

COMPREHENSION CHECK	**1.** Have students turn to page 272 of the Learner's Notebook.

2. Students will follow the Comprehension Check routine on page I-36 of the Introduction.

3. Check students' work. Circled answers are as follows:

1. Dad will have ham.

2. Mom will have jam.

3. Bud will have a plum.

4. Possible written responses include the following:

1. Dad will have ham.

2. I have a _____. (Students may put any logical word or phrase into the blank. For example, "I have a sandwich.")

WEEKLY CELEBRATION	**1.** Display the celebratory message: "That's your jam! You are mastering the *hat, bed, zip, log,* and *sun* pieces!"

2. Encourage students to work together to read the message.

3. Have students copy the message onto their weekly certificate (see resources .corwin.com/puzzlepiecephonics-gradeK) and place it somewhere to take home.

Preparing for Your Week

Resources

PUZZLE PIECES

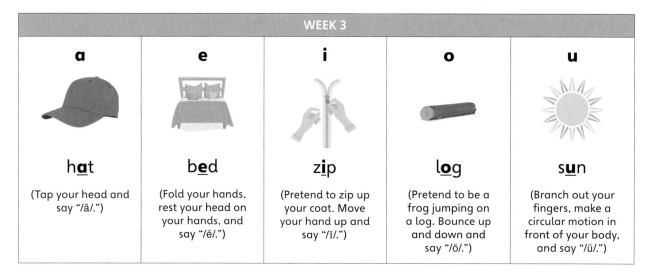

WEEK 3				
a	**e**	**i**	**o**	**u**
h**a**t	b**e**d	z**i**p	l**o**g	s**u**n
(Tap your head and say "/ă/.")	(Fold your hands, rest your head on your hands, and say "/ĕ/.")	(Pretend to zip up your coat. Move your hand up and say "/ĭ/.")	(Pretend to be a frog jumping on a log. Bounce up and down and say "/ŏ/.")	(Branch out your fingers, make a circular motion in front of your body, and say "/ŭ/.")

Hat: istock.com/stevezmina1; Bed: istock.com/vasilyevalara; Zip: istock.com/pe-art; Log: istock.com/bennyb; Sun: istock.com/StudioBarcelona

Preparing for Your Week

CORRESPONDING *LEARNER'S NOTEBOOK PAGES*

| Group 1 | Week 3 | Concept 9 |

Name _____ Date _____

Weekly Sort

–an	–en	–in
–on	–un	fin
van	men	skin
plan	hen	bin
con	bun	fun
pan	run	den

Concept 9 **273**

| Group 2 | Week 3 | Concept 9 |

Name _____ Date _____

Weekly Sort

–an	–en	–in
–on	–un	spin
clan	den	skin
scan	pen	tin
con	stun	fun
upon	run	twin

Concept 9 **275**

| Week 3 | Concept 9 |

Name _____ Date _____

A _____ has a _____ .

Circle the sentence that matches the picture.

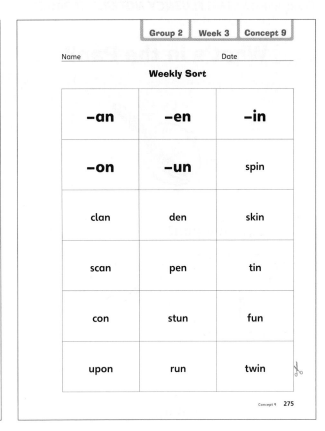

A fox has a den.
A fox has a hen.
A fox has a cub.

A fish has fun.
A fish has a van.
A fish has a fin.

A pen has an egg.
A hen has an egg.
A man has an egg.

Use the text to answer the questions.

1. What does a fox have? A fox has a _____.

2. What do you have? You have a _____.

280 PUZZLE PIECE PHONICS LEARNER'S NOTEBOOK, KINDERGARTEN

CORRESPONDING *FLUENCY NOTEBOOK PAGES*

What's in the Pan?

What's in the pan?
Eggs and ham.

What's in the pan?
Toast and jam.

What time is it?
It's time for breakfast!

What's in the pot?
Tater tots.

What's in the pot?
Soup—it's hot!

What time is it?
It's time for dinner!

There's a Hen in the Den

There's a hen in the den.
She belongs in a pen!
What should we do?
Call the boys!
Call the men!

There's a frog in my clogs.
Get him back to the bog!
What should we do?
Get the cat!
Get the dog!

There's a rabbit in the cabinet.
What a very bad habit!
What should we do?
We can nab it!
We can grab it!

Preparing for Your Week

Tips for Management and Differentiation

Refer to this section and to resources.corwin.com/puzzlepiecephonics-gradeK for resources and ideas to deepen your students' learning throughout the week. Feel free to put your own spin on the routines, too. For daily lesson plans, see pages 380–386 of this Teacher's Guide.

TIPS FOR PHONEMIC AWARENESS	• The focus for this week is segmenting words. • If you notice your students need additional practice, extend the activity with more words.
TIPS FOR THE PUZZLE PIECE REVIEW	• Students will review all of the short vowel pieces this week. • Spend more time on any vowels your students may be mixing up or struggling to identify.
TIPS FOR BLENDING	• If your students master words that end in *n* early in the week, then you can blend words similar to those for Day 4 earlier. On the other hand, if your students are still struggling to read words with mixed vowels by Day 4, then you can have them continue to blend words from their sorts. • Both of the sight words this week are question words. Your students may need additional practice with these words to understand how they are used and ways to start sentences that answer *when* and *where* questions. Give students time to answer the question with a partner, move around to music, and then answer the same question (or a different question) with a new partner.
TIPS FOR DICTATION AND QUICK SWITCH	• Support your students as much as necessary so they feel successful. You can complete the routine as a class or have students check their work after each letter, if necessary.

TIPS FOR SORTING	• Model and positively reinforce the sorting routine repeatedly throughout the week.
	• Discuss the vocabulary words that appear in the sort. Vocabulary words include the following:
	  • Sort 1: *van, con, bun, fin, bin, den*
	  • Sort 2: *clan, scan, con, upon, den, stun, tin*

TIPS FOR THE PRACTICE PIECES	• Review the routines for Create a Puzzle Piece, Color-Code Writing, and Super Sentences as necessary. You can complete the routines as a class if students still need additional support before working independently. • Give students time to play Read and Trade with words from this week and weeks in the previous concepts. Celebrate their success and the fact that they really can read all short vowels, even when they are mixed up.
TIPS FOR FLUENCY	• This week students will read poems with various short vowels. • Students can highlight words with a short vowel plus *n*. • You can assign students fluency partners. Students will work together to achieve fluency with the daily poems. • Students can participate in a "Fluency Celebration." Call on students who feel prepared to present a particular poem in front of the class. Other students can follow along in the Fluency Notebook.

Day 1

PHONEMIC AWARENESS: LISTEN

1. Give the directions. Say, "I am going to say a word. I want you to tell me the sounds in the word. So if I say 'map,' you say '/m/ /ă/ /p/.'"

2. Say the following words:

slip   jam   gem   step   rip   top   hum   plum   flip   map

THE BIG REVEAL

1. Say, "Remember that we now know our short vowels very well and are ready to mix them up! This week we will again read and write words with /ă/, /ĕ/, /ĭ/, /ŏ/, and /ŭ/. Let's review our short vowel pieces."

2. Say, "This is the *hat* puzzle piece. It represents the letter *a*. The *hat* piece says '/ă/' like in the middle of the word *hat*. Let's do the motion of the *hat* piece. Good!"

3. Say, "This is the *bed* puzzle piece. It represents the letter *e*. The *bed* piece says '/ĕ/' like in the middle of the word *bed*. Let's do the motion of the *bed* piece. Good!"

4. Say, "This is the *zip* puzzle piece. It represents the letter *i*. The *zip* piece says '/ĭ/' like in the middle of the word *zip*. Let's do the motion of the *zip* piece. Good!"

5. Say, "This is the *log* puzzle piece. It represents the letter *o*. The *log* piece says '/ŏ/' like in the middle of the word *log*. Let's do the motion of the *log* piece. Good!"

6. Say, "This is the *sun* puzzle piece. It represents the letter *u*. The *sun* piece says '/ŭ/' like in the middle of the word *sun*. Let's do the motion of the *sun* piece. Good!"

BLENDING: PUTTING SOUNDS TOGETHER TO MAKE NEW WORDS

1. Follow the Blending routine on page I-17 of the Introduction.

2. Display the following words on the board one line at a time. Facilitate a discussion about the blending line focus after each line.

3. Then display the weekly sight words and sentence.

4. Discuss the question mark in the sentence and model reading with intonation and answering a *where* question.

van	pan	pen	Discuss: compare and contrast the *–an* family words with *pen*
run	bun	bin	Discuss: compare and contrast the *–un* family words with *bin*
on	con	can	Discuss: compare and contrast the *–on* family words with *can*

Sight Words: when   where

Sentence: Where is the red hen?

DICTATION: STRETCH OUT YOUR WORDS

1. Have students turn to page 277 of the Learner's Notebook.

2. Follow the Dictation routine on page I-21 of the Introduction to dictate the following words:

l. fin   2. bin   3. pan   4. plan

Sight Word: when

Sentence: The plan is fun.

3. Use Dictation as an informal pretest of students' knowledge of this week's mixed vowels.

PRACTICE:
COMPLETE
YOUR WORK ON
YOUR OWN

1. Have students turn to page 273 (Group 1) or page 275 (Group 2) of the Learner's Notebook.

2. Instruct students to tear out the sort and complete the following Practice Pieces: Quick Color, Careful Cut, Highlighter Hunt, and Sorting With Words (see further directions on pages I-37, I-38, I-43, and I-27 of the Introduction).

3. Circulate as students work, which usually takes fifteen minutes, and coach as needed.

FLUENCY:
READING LIKE
YOU'RE SPEAKING

1. Have students turn to page 40 in the Fluency Notebook.

2. Have students read one or more of the following poems: "What's in the Pan?" and "There's a Hen in the Den."

3. Circulate and listen to students read or gather a small group of students who need additional support.

Day 2

PHONEMIC AWARENESS: LISTEN

1. Give the directions. Say, "I am going to say a word. I want you to tell me the sounds in the word. So if I say '*map*,' you say '/m/ /ă/ /p/.'"

2. Say the following words:

plan   den   skin   fin   run   con   bun   hen   van   spin

PUZZLE PIECE REVIEW

1. Say, "When I point to the piece, you tell me its name" (*hat, bed, zip, log, sun*).

2. Say, "When I point to the piece, you tell me its sound" (/ă/, /ĕ/, /ĭ/, /ŏ/, /ŭ/).

3. Say, "When I point to the piece, you tell me its spelling" (*a, e, i, o, u*).

4. Say, "Write the spellings in the air with your finger" (students will form the letters *a, e, i, o,* and *u*).

BLENDING: PUTTING SOUNDS TOGETHER TO MAKE NEW WORDS

1. Follow the Blending routine on page I-17 of the Introduction.

2. Display the following words on the board one line at a time. Facilitate a discussion about the blending line focus after each line.

3. Then display the weekly sight words and sentence.

4. Discuss short vowels that you read in the sentence.

pen	**pan**	**plan**	Discuss: *p* and *pl* blend as initial sound; *n* as final sound; contrast short vowel medial sounds
fun	**fan**	**fin**	Discuss: *f* as initial sound; *n* as final sound; contrast short vowel medial sounds
Dan	**den**	**dent**	Discuss: *d* as initial sound; *n* and *nt* blend as final sound; contrast short vowel medial sounds; capital *D* in name *Dan*

Sight Words: when   where

Sentence: I see six men in the van.

QUICK SWITCH: MANIPULATE YOUR WORDS

1. Have students turn to page 277 of the Learner's Notebook.

2. Follow the Quick Switch routine on page I-23 of the Introduction to dictate the following words:

con → can → pan → pin → skin

3. Help students segment words and identify whether the vowel or consonant sound is changing. Help students segment and record the consonant blend in *skin*.

SORT: WHAT IS YOUR FOCUS PATTERN?

1. Have students take out their bag of words (created on Day 1) and follow the Sorting With Words routine on page I-27 of the Introduction.

PRACTICE: COMPLETE YOUR WORK ON YOUR OWN

1. Students will follow the Create a Puzzle Piece routine on page I-51 of the Introduction.

2. Circulate as students work, which usually takes fifteen minutes, and coach as needed.

FLUENCY: READING LIKE YOU'RE SPEAKING

1. Have students turn to page 40 in the Fluency Notebook.

2. Have students read one or more of the following poems: "What's in the Pan?" and "There's a Hen in the Den."

3. Circulate and listen to students read or gather a small group of students who need additional support.

Day 3

PHONEMIC AWARENESS: LISTEN

1. Give the directions. Say, "I am going to say a word. I want you to tell me the sounds in the word. So if I say '*map*,' you say '/m/ /ǎ/ /p/.'"

2. Say the following words:

step   mop   men   stop   hem   bun   stem   flip   run   top

PUZZLE PIECE REVIEW

1. Say, "When I point to the piece, you tell me its name" (*hat, bed, zip, log, sun*).

2. Say, "When I point to the piece, you tell me its sound" (/ǎ/, /ě/, /ǐ/, /ǒ/, /ǔ/).

3. Say, "When I point to the piece, you tell me its spelling" (*a, e, i, o, u*).

4. Say, "Write the spellings in the air with your finger" (students will form the letters *a, e, i, o,* and *u*).

BLENDING: PUTTING SOUNDS TOGETHER TO MAKE NEW WORDS

1. Follow the Blending routine on page I-17 of the Introduction.

2. Display the following words on the board one line at a time. Facilitate a discussion about the blending line focus after each line.

3. Then display the weekly sight words and sentence.

4. Discuss the question mark in the sentence and model reading with intonation and answering a *where* question.

run	**rim**	**rip**	Discuss: initial sound of /r/; final sound of /n/, /m/, or /p/
hop	**ham**	**hen**	Discuss: initial sound of /h/; final sound of /p/, /m/, or /n/
skin	**skip**	**stem**	Discuss: initial sound of /s/; *sk–* and *st–* blends

Sight Words: when   where

Sentence: Where did the ram run?

DICTATION: STRETCH OUT YOUR WORDS

1. Have students turn to page 278 of the Learner's Notebook.

2. Follow the Dictation routine on page I-21 of the Introduction to dictate the following words:

I. den   2. plan   3. rim   4. pup

Sight Word: where

Sentence: The hen can run.

3. Help students segment the words and reference puzzle pieces as necessary.

SORT: WHAT IS YOUR FOCUS PATTERN?

1. Have students take out their bag of words (created on Day 1) and follow the Sorting With Words routine on page I-27 of the Introduction.

PRACTICE: COMPLETE YOUR WORK ON YOUR OWN

1. Students will complete the Color-Code Writing routine on page I-52 of the Introduction.

2. Circulate as students work, which usually takes fifteen minutes, and coach as needed.

(Continued)

Day 3 (Continued)

FLUENCY: READING LIKE YOU'RE SPEAKING

1. Have students turn to page 40 in the Fluency Notebook.

2. Have students read one or more of the following poems: "What's in the Pan?" and "There's a Hen in the Den."

3. Circulate and listen to students read or gather a small group of students who need additional support.

Day 4

PHONEMIC AWARENESS: LISTEN

1. Give the directions. Say, "I am going to say a word. Your job is to tell me the vowel sound you hear in the word. Do the motion of the sound you hear. So if I say 'hen,' you do the motion of the *bed* piece."

2. Say the following words:

den bin scan con plan van hen run men skin

PUZZLE PIECE REVIEW

1. Say, "When I point to the piece, you tell me its name" (*hat, bed, zip, log, sun*).

2. Say, "When I point to the piece, you tell me its sound" (/ă/, /ĕ/, /ĭ/, /ŏ/, /ŭ/).

3. Say, "When I point to the piece, you tell me its spelling" (*a, e, i, o, u*).

4. Say, "Write the spellings in the air with your finger" (students will form the letters *a, e, i, o,* and *u*).

BLENDING: PUTTING SOUNDS TOGETHER TO MAKE NEW WORDS

1. Follow the Blending routine on page I-17 of the Introduction.

2. Display the following words on the board one line at a time. Facilitate a discussion about the blending line focus after each line.

3. Then display the weekly sight words and sentence.

4. Discuss the question mark in the sentence and model reading with intonation and answering a *when* question.

bun	bin	bill	Discuss: contrast word families
run	ran	rag	Discuss: contrast word families
fun	fin	fill	Discuss: contrast word families

Sight Words: when   where

Sentence: When can I run?

QUICK SWITCH: MANIPULATE YOUR WORDS

1. Have students turn to page 278 of the Learner's Notebook.

2. Follow the Quick Switch routine on page I-23 of the Introduction to dictate the following words:

den → hen → hill → fill → fin

3. Help students segment the words and reference puzzle pieces as necessary. Review the *–ill* family with students.

SORT: WHAT IS YOUR FOCUS PATTERN?

1. Have students take out their bag of words (created on Day 1) and follow the Sorting With Words routine on page I-27 of the Introduction.

PRACTICE: COMPLETE YOUR WORK ON YOUR OWN

1. Have students complete the following Practice Pieces: Glue, Draw a Picture and Super Sentences (on pages I-50 and I-53 of the Introduction).

2. Circulate as students work, which usually takes fifteen minutes, and coach as needed.

FLUENCY: READING LIKE YOU'RE SPEAKING

1. Have students turn to page 40 in the Fluency Notebook.

2. Have students read one or more of the following poems: "What's in the Pan?" and "There's a Hen in the Den."

3. Circulate and listen to students read or gather a small group of students who need additional support.

Day 5

PHONEMIC AWARENESS: LISTEN	**1.** Give the directions. Say, "I am going to say a word. Your job is to tell me the vowel sound you hear in the word. Do the motion of the sound you hear. So if I say 'hen,' you do the motion of the *bed* piece."
	2. Say the following words:

men   hem   gum   stop   flip   gem   Tom   skin   pen   plop

REVIEW PATTERNS OF THE WEEK	**1.** Say, "Find a partner."
	2. Say, "Tell your partner the names of this week's pieces" (*hat, bed, zip, log, sun*).
	3. Say, "Tell your partner the sounds of this week's pieces" (/ă/, /ĕ/, /ĭ/, /ŏ/, /ŭ/).
	4. Say, "Tell your partner the spellings of this week's pieces" (*a, e, i, o, u*).
	5. Say, "Write the spellings on your partner's back with your finger" (students will form the letters *a, e, i, o,* and *u*).

SPELLING CHECK	**1.** Follow the Spelling Check routine on page I-34 of the Introduction.
	2. Instruct students to sit in their word study groups and turn to page 279 of the Learner's Notebook.
	3. Say, "I am going to say one word at a time to each group. Record the words as I say them to your group. Make sure you only record the words from your group."
	4. Move back and forth between the groups and dictate the following words:

Words for Group 1

1. run
2. pan
3. con
4. skin
5. men

Sentence: The hen is big.

Words for Group 2

1. stun
2. con
3. clan
4. tin
5. den

Sentence: I am a twin.

WORD HUNT	**1.** Students will follow the Word Hunt routine on page I-55 of the Introduction.
	2. Instruct students to search texts and the classroom for words with short vowels.

COMPREHENSION CHECK	**1.** Have students turn to page 280 of the Learner's Notebook.
	2. Students will follow the Comprehension Check routine on page I-36 of the Introduction.
	3. Check students' work. Circled responses are as follows:

1. A fox has a den.
2. A fish has a fin.
3. A hen has an egg.

4. Possible written responses include the following:

1. A fox has a den.
2. You have a _____. (Students may put any logical word or phrase into the blank. For example, "You have a bedroom.")

WEEKLY CELEBRATION	**1.** Display the celebratory message: "You're the man! You are mastering the *hat, bed, zip, log,* and *sun* pieces!"
	2. Encourage students to work together to read the message.
	3. Have students copy the message onto their weekly certificate (see resources .corwin.com/puzzlepiecephonics-gradeK) and place it somewhere to take home.

Preparing for Your Week

Resources

PUZZLE PIECES

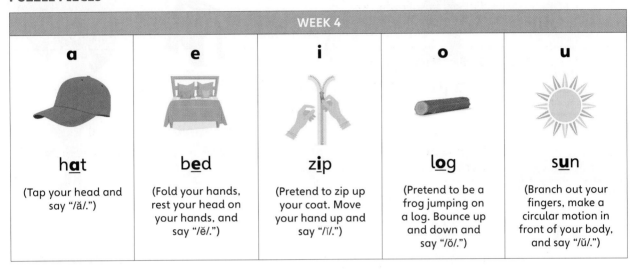

WEEK 4				
a	**e**	**i**	**o**	**u**
h**a**t	b**e**d	z**i**p	l**o**g	s**u**n
(Tap your head and say "/ă/.")	(Fold your hands, rest your head on your hands, and say "/ĕ/.")	(Pretend to zip up your coat. Move your hand up and say "/ĭ/.")	(Pretend to be a frog jumping on a log. Bounce up and down and say "/ŏ/.")	(Branch out your fingers, make a circular motion in front of your body, and say "/ŭ/.")

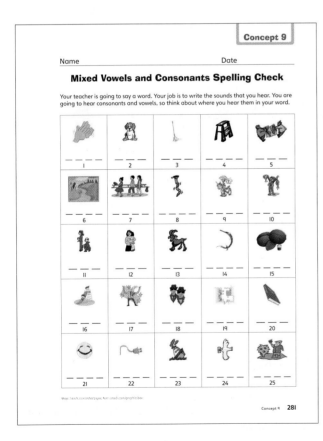

POSTASSESSMENT DIRECTIONS

This assessment is used to identify which consonant and short vowel sounds students can represent and which patterns students need to be retaught. Students may be able to master a Spelling Check when there is a sound taught in isolation. However, they may struggle when asked to produce multiple sounds. This check is to primarily look for mastery of short vowel sounds, but will check for students' mastery of consonant sounds.

You can give this postassessment any day during Concept 9, Week 4. You can split the rows and do parts on different days. Do what works for your class.

Instruct students to turn to **page 281 in the Learner's Notebook**.

Explain to students that they have studied all of the spellings in the words they will hear. The purpose of this check is to show what they know.

When giving this assessment, go row by row in saying the word represented by the picture. Students are not guessing what the picture is. You tell them the word.

Hat: istock.com/stevezmina1; Bed: istock.com/vasilyevalara; Zip: istock.com/pe-art; Log: istock.com/bennyb; Sun: istock.com/StudioBarcelona

Preparing for Your Week

POSTASSESSMENT: MIXED VOWELS AND CONSONANTS SPELLING CHECK

		ANSWER KEY		
1. clap	2. pup	3. mop	4. step	5. rip
6. mist	7. last	8. rust	9. lost	10. best
11. hem	12. mom	13. ram	14. slim	15. plum
16. fun	17. win	18. men	19. plan	20. non
21. glad	22. plug	23. sunk	24. send	25. pick

Mop: istock.com/mhatzapa; Fun: istock.com/graphic-bee

EVALUATING THE ASSESSMENT: WHAT TO LOOK FOR

- Knowledge of consonants
- Knowledge of short vowels
- Knowledge of basic blends

TIPS FOR SCORING

Row 1 contains words with short vowel plus –p ending. Row 2 contains words with short vowel plus –st ending. Row 3 contains words with short vowel plus –m ending. Row 4 contains words with short vowel plus –n ending. Row 5 contains mixed short vowels. Have students write all of the sounds they hear in the word.

Each word is worth one point. For each correctly spelled word, students earn one point. To show mastery of consonants and short vowels, students must show 80 percent mastery or correctly phonetically spell twenty out of twenty-five words.

Use teacher discretion when reviewing. If students need to solely focus on the short vowel sound, only grade them on the medial sound they hear.

Preparing for Your Week

CORRESPONDING *LEARNER'S NOTEBOOK PAGES*

| Group 1 | Week 4 | Concept 9 |

Name _____ Date _____

Weekly Sort

–ast	–est	–ist
–ost	–ust	rest
fast	dust	nest
last	must	list
cost	cast	fist
lost	best	rust

Concept 9 **283**

| Group 2 | Week 4 | Concept 9 |

Name _____ Date _____

Weekly Sort

–ast	–est	–ist
–ost	–ust	rest
cast	rust	pest
fast	gust	lost
cost	vast	fist
frost	vest	mist

Concept 9 **285**

| Week 4 | Concept 9 |

Name _____ Date _____

The Boy

Circle the sentence that matches the picture.

	The boy is fast! The boy is fist! The boy is cast!
	The boy is the rest. The boy is the test. The boy is the best.
	The boy must nest. The boy must rest. The boy must text.

Use the text to answer the questions.

1. Is the boy fast or slow? The boy is _____

2. Are you fast like the boy? I am _____

Preparing for Your Week

CORRESPONDING *FLUENCY NOTEBOOK PAGES*

Eggs in the Nest

Eggs in the nest,
1, 2.
Baby birds,
Here soon.

Eggs in the nest,
3, 4, 5.
Baby birds,
Here on time.

Eggs in the nest,
6, 7, 8.
Baby birds,
I cannot wait!

Be the Best

I want to be the best,
I say!
Better than the rest,
I say!
Put me to the test,
I say!
I want to impress,
I say!

I'm acting like a pest,
You say?
Just give it a rest,
You say?
Stop making such a mess,
You say?
I'll quiet down—oh yes,
For today …
I say!

Preparing for Your Week

Tips for Management and Differentiation

Refer to this section and to resources.corwin.com/puzzlepiecephonics-gradeK for resources and ideas to deepen your students' learning throughout the week. Feel free to put your own spin on the routines, too. For daily lesson plans, see pages 392–399 of this Teacher's Guide.

TIPS FOR PHONEMIC AWARENESS	• The focuses for this week are segmenting words and identifying the vowel sound in words. • If you notice your students need additional practice, extend the activity with more words.
TIPS FOR THE PUZZLE PIECE REVIEW	• Students will review all of the short vowel pieces this week. • Spend more time on any vowels your students may be mixing up or struggling to identify.
TIPS FOR BLENDING	• If your students master words that end in *st* early in the week, then you can blend words similar to those for Day 4 earlier. On the other hand, if your students are still struggling to read words with mixed vowels by Day 4, then you can have them continue to blend words from their sorts. • The sight words this week are opposites (*over, under*). Your students may need additional practice with these words to understand how they are related.
TIPS FOR DICTATION AND QUICK SWITCH	• Support your students as much as necessary so they feel successful. You can complete the routine as a class or have students check their work after each letter, if necessary.

TIPS FOR SORTING	• Model and positively reinforce the sorting routine repeatedly throughout the week.
	• Discuss the vocabulary words that appear in the sort. Vocabulary words include the following:
	  • Sort 1: *cost, dust, must, cast, fist, rust*
	  • Sort 2: *cast, cost, frost, rust, gust, vast, vest, pest, fist, mist*

TIPS FOR THE PRACTICE PIECES	• Review the routines for Create a Puzzle Piece, Color-Code Writing, and Super Sentences as necessary. You can complete the routines as a class if students still need additional support before working independently. • Give students time to play Read and Trade with words from this week and weeks in the previous concepts. Celebrate their success and the fact that they really can read all short vowels, even when they are mixed up!
TIPS FOR FLUENCY	• This week students will read poems with various short vowels. • Students can highlight words with a short vowel plus *st*. • You can assign students fluency partners. Students will work together to achieve fluency with the daily poems. • Students can participate in a "Fluency Celebration." Call on students who feel prepared to present a particular poem in front of the class. Other students can follow along in the Fluency Notebook.

Day 1

PHONEMIC AWARENESS: LISTEN	**1.** Give the directions. Say, "I am going to say a word. I want you to tell me the sounds in the word. So if I say '*map*,' you say '/m/ /ǎ/ /p/.'"
	2. Say the following words:
	bun stop clap men stem Tom van yam skin step

THE BIG REVEAL	**1.** Say, "Remember that we now know our short vowels very well and are ready to mix them up! This week we will again read and write words with /ǎ/, /ě/, /ǐ/, /ǒ/, and /ǔ/. Let's review our short vowel pieces."
	2. Say, "This is the *hat* puzzle piece. It represents the letter *a*. The *hat* piece says '/ǎ/' like in the middle of the word *hat*. Let's do the motion of the *hat* piece. Good!"
	3. Say, "This is the *bed* puzzle piece. It represents the letter *e*. The *bed* piece says '/ě/' like in the middle of the word *bed*. Let's do the motion of the *bed* piece. Good!"
	4. Say, "This is the *zip* puzzle piece. It represents the letter *i*. The *zip* piece says '/ǐ/' like in the middle of the word *zip*. Let's do the motion of the *zip* piece. Good!"
	5. Say, "This is the *log* puzzle piece. It represents the letter *o*. The *log* piece says '/ǒ/' like in the middle of the word *log*. Let's do the motion of the *log* piece. Good!"
	6. Say, "This is the *sun* puzzle piece. It represents the letter *u*. The *sun* piece says '/ǔ/' like in the middle of the word *sun*. Let's do the motion of the *sun* piece. Good!"

BLENDING: PUTTING SOUNDS TOGETHER TO MAKE NEW WORDS	**1.** Follow the Blending routine on page I-17 of the Introduction.
	2. Display the following words on the board one line at a time. Facilitate a discussion about the blending line focus after each line.
	3. Then display the weekly sight words and sentence.
	4. Model visualizing the sentence with your students. Have them explain what they are picturing in their minds as they read about the cat *under* the bed.

fast	**last**	**list**	Discuss: compare and contrast the *–ast* family words with *list*
best	**rest**	**rust**	Discuss: compare and contrast the *–est* family words with *rust*
last	**cast**	**cost**	Discuss: compare and contrast the *–ast* family words with *cost*

Sight Words: under   over

Sentence: The cat rests under the bed.

DICTATION: STRETCH OUT YOUR WORDS	**1.** Have students turn to page 287 of the Learner's Notebook.
	2. Follow the Dictation routine on page I-21 of the Introduction to dictate the following words:
	l. rust 2. dust 3. best 4. nest
	Sight Word: under
	Sentence: The dog is lost.
	3. Use Dictation as an informal pretest of students' knowledge of this week's mixed vowels.

PRACTICE:
COMPLETE
YOUR WORK ON
YOUR OWN

1. Have students turn to page 283 (Group 1) or page 285 (Group 2) of the Learner's Notebook.

2. Instruct students to tear out the sort and complete the following Practice Pieces: Quick Color, Careful Cut, Highlighter Hunt, and Sorting With Words (see further directions on pages I-37, I-38, I-43, and I-27 of the Introduction).

3. Circulate as students work, which usually takes fifteen minutes, and coach as needed.

FLUENCY:
READING LIKE
YOU'RE SPEAKING

1. Have students turn to page 41 in the Fluency Notebook.

2. Have students read one or more of the following poems: "Eggs in the Nest" and "Be the Best."

3. Circulate and listen to students read or gather a small group of students who need additional support.

Day 2

PHONEMIC AWARENESS: LISTEN	**1.** Give the directions. Say, "I am going to say a word. I want you to tell me the sounds in the word. So if I say '*map*,' you say '/m/ /ă/ /p/.'"
	2. Say the following words:
	must cast lost nest dust list rust rest must fist
PUZZLE PIECE REVIEW	**1.** Say, "When I point to the piece, you tell me its name" (*hat, bed, zip, log, sun*).
	2. Say, "When I point to the piece, you tell me its sound" (/ă/, /ĕ/, /ĭ/, /ŏ/, /ŭ/).
	3. Say, "When I point to the piece, you tell me its spelling" (*a, e, i, o, u*).
	4. Say, "Write the spellings in the air with your finger" (students will form the letters *a, e, i, o,* and *u*).
BLENDING: PUTTING SOUNDS TOGETHER TO MAKE NEW WORDS	**1.** Follow the Blending routine on page I-17 of the Introduction.
	2. Display the following words on the board one line at a time. Facilitate a discussion about the blending line focus after each line.
	3. Then display the weekly sight words and sentence.
	4. Model visualizing the sentence with your students. Have them explain what they are picturing in their minds as they read about running *over* the hill.

lost	list	blast	Discuss: *l* and *bl* blend as initial sound; *st* as final sound; contrast short vowel medial sounds
fast	fist	frost	Discuss: *f* and *fr* blend as initial sound; *st* as final sound; contrast short vowel medial sounds
rest	rust	dust	Discuss: *r* or *d* as initial sound; *st* as final sound; contrast short vowel medial sounds

Sight Words: under   over

Sentence: We ran over the hill.

QUICK SWITCH: MANIPULATE YOUR WORDS	**1.** Have students turn to page 287 of the Learner's Notebook.
	2. Follow the Quick Switch routine on page I-23 of the Introduction to dictate the following words:
	fast → fist → list → lost → cost
	3. Help students segment words and identify whether the vowel or consonant sound is changing.
SORT: WHAT IS YOUR FOCUS PATTERN?	**1.** Have students take out their bag of words (created on Day 1) and follow the Sorting With Words routine on page I-27 of the Introduction.
PRACTICE: COMPLETE YOUR WORK ON YOUR OWN	**1.** Students will follow the Create a Puzzle Piece routine on page I-51 of the Introduction.
	2. Circulate as students work, which usually takes fifteen minutes, and coach as needed.
FLUENCY: READING LIKE YOU'RE SPEAKING	**1.** Have students turn to page 41 in the Fluency Notebook.
	2. Have students read one or more of the following poems: "Eggs in the Nest" and "Be the Best."
	3. Circulate and listen to students read or gather a small group of students who need additional support.

PHONEMIC AWARENESS: LISTEN

1. Give the directions. Say, "I am going to say a word. I want you to tell me the sounds in the word. So if I say '*map*,' you say '/m/ /ă/ /p/.'"

2. Say the following words:

stop   skin   past   nest   run   men   hop   ham   last   van

PUZZLE PIECE REVIEW

1. Say, "When I point to the piece, you tell me its name" (*hat, bed, zip, log, sun*).

2. Say, "When I point to the piece, you tell me its sound" (/ă/, /ĕ/, /ĭ/, /ŏ/, /ŭ/).

3. Say, "When I point to the piece, you tell me its spelling" (*a, e, i, o, u*).

4. Say, "Write the spellings in the air with your finger" (students will form the letters *a, e, i, o,* and *u*).

BLENDING: PUTTING SOUNDS TOGETHER TO MAKE NEW WORDS

1. Follow the Blending routine on page I-17 of the Introduction.

2. Display the following words on the board one line at a time. Facilitate a discussion about the blending line focus after each line.

3. Then display the weekly sight words and sentence.

4. Model visualizing the sentence with your students. Have them explain what they are picturing in their minds as they read about the list being *under* the bin.

lost	list	flip	Discuss: initial sound of /l/ or /fl/
cost	cast	clam	Discuss: initial sound of /k/ or /kl/
fist	fast	fin	Discuss: initial sound of /f/

Sight Words: under   over

Sentence: The list is under the bin.

DICTATION: STRETCH OUT YOUR WORDS

1. Have students turn to page 288 of the Learner's Notebook.

2. Follow the Dictation routine on page I-21 of the Introduction to dictate the following words:

I. gust   2. den   3. rest   4. rim

Sight Word: over

Sentence: The big cup is best.

3. Help students segment the words and reference puzzle pieces as necessary.

SORT: WHAT IS YOUR FOCUS PATTERN?

1. Have students take out their bag of words (created on Day 1) and follow the Sorting With Words routine on page I-27 of the Introduction.

PRACTICE: COMPLETE YOUR WORK ON YOUR OWN

1. Students will complete the Color-Code Writing routine on page I-52 of the Introduction.

2. Circulate as students work, which usually takes fifteen minutes, and coach as needed.

(Continued)

Day 3 (Continued)

**FLUENCY:
READING LIKE
YOU'RE SPEAKING**

1. Have students turn to page 41 in the Fluency Notebook.

2. Have students read one or more of the following poems: "Eggs in the Nest" and "Be the Best."

3. Circulate and listen to students read or gather a small group of students who need additional support.

Day 4

PHONEMIC AWARENESS: LISTEN

1. Give the directions. Say, "I am going to say a word. Your job is to tell me the vowel sound you hear in the word. Do the motion of the sound you hear. So if I say '*hen*,' you do the motion of the *bed* piece."

2. Say the following words:

rest   van   rust   plum   flip   skin   top   Tom   list   cost

PUZZLE PIECE REVIEW

1. Say, "When I point to the piece, you tell me its name" (*hat, bed, zip, log, sun*).

2. Say, "When I point to the piece, you tell me its sound" (/ă/, /ĕ/, /ĭ/, /ŏ/, /ŭ/).

3. Say, "When I point to the piece, you tell me its spelling" (*a, e, i, o, u*).

4. Say, "Write the spellings in the air with your finger" (students will form the letters *a, e, i, o,* and *u*).

BLENDING: PUTTING SOUNDS TOGETHER TO MAKE NEW WORDS

1. Follow the Blending routine on page I-17 of the Introduction.

2. Display the following words on the board one line at a time. Facilitate a discussion about the blending line focus after each line.

3. Then display the weekly sight words and sentence.

4. Discuss the words with short vowels found in the sentence.

best	bun	band	Discuss: contrast word families
cast	clam	cuff	Discuss: contrast word families
lost	lip	luck	Discuss: contrast word families

Sight Words: under   over

Sentence: Ham is on the list.

QUICK SWITCH: MANIPULATE YOUR WORDS

1. Have students turn to page 288 of the Learner's Notebook.

2. Follow the Quick Switch routine on page I-23 of the Introduction to dictate the following words:

fast → fan → can → con → cost

3. Help students segment the words and reference puzzle pieces as necessary.

SORT: WHAT IS YOUR FOCUS PATTERN?

1. Have students take out their bag of words (created on Day 1) and follow the Sorting With Words routine on page I-27 of the Introduction.

PRACTICE: COMPLETE YOUR WORK ON YOUR OWN

1. Have students complete the following Practice Pieces: Glue, Draw a Picture and Super Sentences (on pages I-50 and I-53 of the Introduction).

2. Circulate as students work, which usually takes fifteen minutes, and coach as needed.

FLUENCY: READING LIKE YOU'RE SPEAKING

1. Have students turn to page 41 in the Fluency Notebook.

2. Have students read one or more of the following poems: "Eggs in the Nest" and "Be the Best."

3. Circulate and listen to students read or gather a small group of students who need additional support.

Day 5

PHONEMIC AWARENESS: LISTEN

1. Give the directions. Say, "I am going to say a word. Your job is to tell me the vowel sound you hear in the word. Do the motion of the sound you hear. So if I say 'hen,' you do the motion of the *bed* piece."

2. Say the following words:

> **dust   hen   gum   rim   pup   clap   test   him   stop   jot**

REVIEW PATTERNS OF THE WEEK

1. Say, "Find a partner."

2. Say, "Tell your partner the names of this week's pieces" (*hat, bed, zip, log, sun*).

3. Say, "Tell your partner the sounds of this week's pieces" (/ă/, /ĕ/, /ĭ/, /ŏ/, /ŭ/).

4. Say, "Tell your partner the spellings of this week's pieces" (*a, e, i, o, u*).

5. Say, "Write the spellings on your partner's back with your finger" (students will form the letters *a, e, i, o,* and *u*).

SPELLING CHECK

1. Follow the Spelling Check routine on page I-34 of the Introduction.

2. Instruct students to sit in their word study groups and turn to page 289 of the Learner's Notebook.

3. Say, "I am going to say one word at a time to each group. Record the words as I say them to your group. Make sure you only record the words from your group."

4. Move back and forth between the groups and dictate the following words:

Words for Group I	Words for Group 2
I. must	I. vest
2. list	2. frost
3. best	3. fist
4. lost	4. gust
5. cast	5. cast
Sentence: I am fast.	**Sentence: The bug is a pest.**

WORD HUNT

1. Students will follow the Word Hunt routine on page I-55 of the Introduction.

2. Instruct students to search texts and the classroom for words with short vowels.

COMPREHENSION CHECK

1. Have students turn to page 290 of the Learner's Notebook.

2. Students will follow the Comprehension Check routine on page I-36 of the Introduction.

3. Check students' work. Circled responses are as follows:

1. The boy is fast!

2. The boy is the best.

3. The boy must rest.

4. Possible written responses include the following:

1. The boy is fast.

2. I am _____. (Students may put any logical word or phrase into the blank. For example, "I am fast just like the boy.")

Day 5 (Continued)

**WEEKLY
CELEBRATION**

1. Display the celebratory message: "You're simply the best! You mastered the *hat, bed, zip, log,* and *sun* pieces!"

2. Encourage students to work together to read the message.

3. Have students copy the message onto their weekly certificate (see resources .corwin.com/puzzlepiecephonics-gradeK) and place it somewhere to take home.

Concept 10 Overview:

Short Vowels and Vowel_e

WHAT ARE LONG VOWELS?

Students have been studying short vowels all year long. When they see an *a* in a word, they will say /ă/. This concept introduces students to long vowels. Long vowels are vowels that "say their name." Students will contrast short vowels with long vowels and learn the spelling of vowel_*e* to represent a long vowel sound when writing.

GOALS FOR THE CONCEPT

Students will
- Identify and represent short vowels

- Identify and represent long vowels with the spelling of vowel_*e*
- Identify and represent consonant sounds
- Read and write sight words
- Recognize that words with a long vowel sound need to have a final *e*
- Manipulate words in order to create a new word
- Develop reading fluency and comprehension

WEEKS FOR THIS CONCEPT

Week 1: Short Vowels and Vowel_*e* (Short *a, a_e*)
Week 2: Short Vowels and Vowel_*e* (Short *e, e_e*)
Week 3: Short Vowels and Vowel_*e* (Short *i, i_e*)
Week 4: Short Vowels and Vowel_*e* (Short *o, o_e*)
Week 5: Short Vowels and Vowel_*e* (Short *u, u_e*)

Resources

PUZZLE PIECES

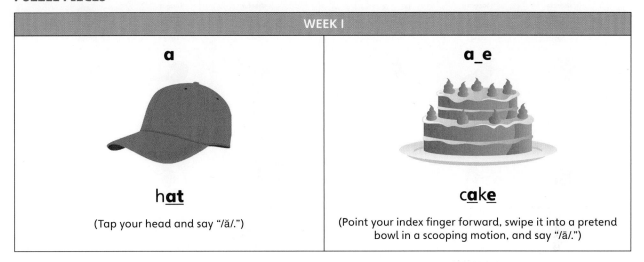

WEEK I	
a	**a_e**
h**at**	c**a**k**e**
(Tap your head and say "/ă/.")	(Point your index finger forward, swipe it into a pretend bowl in a scooping motion, and say "/ā/.")

Hat: istock.com/stevezmina1; Cake: istock.com/Tomacco

Preparing for Your Week

CORRESPONDING *LEARNER'S NOTEBOOK PAGES*

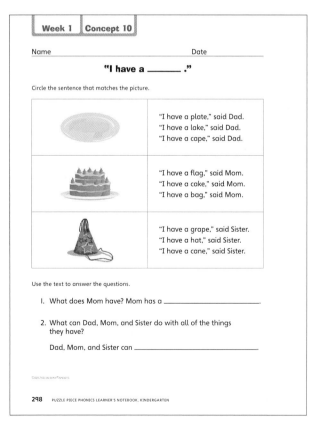

Preparing for Your Week

CORRESPONDING *FLUENCY NOTEBOOK PAGES*

Magic E

I have a friend.

His name is Magic E.

He can make new words, easily!

Magic E turns *tap* into *tape*.

Magic E turns *cap* into *cape*.

Magic E turns *rat* into *rate*.

Magic E turns *hat* into *hate*.

Magic E turns *can* into *cane*.

Magic E turns *pan* into *pane*.

Magic E turns *mad* into *made*.

Magic E turns *fad* into *fade*.

I have a friend.

His name is Magic E.

He can make new words, easily!

Poof! Magic E

Magic E puts on his cape—

Look at the words he can make.

Poof! Magic E creates the word *tape*.

Voilà! Magic E creates the word *cape*.

Abra! Magic E creates the word *made*.

Cadabra! Magic E creates the word *fade*.

Ala! Magic E creates the word *cane*.

Kazam! Magic E creates the word *pane*.

Magic E takes off his cape—

Look at the words that you can make.

Poof! You create the word *tap*.

Voilà! You create the word *cap*.

Abra! You create the word *mad*.

Cadabra! You create the word *fad*.

Ala! You create the word *can*.

Kazam! You create the word *pan*.

Preparing for Your Week

Tips for Management and Differentiation

Refer to this section and to resources.corwin.com/puzzlepiecephonics-gradeK for resources and ideas to deepen your students' learning throughout the week. Feel free to put your own spin on the routines, too. For daily lesson plans, see pages 406–411 of this Teacher's Guide.

TIPS FOR PHONEMIC AWARENESS	• The focus for this week is listening for long and short vowels. • If you notice your students need additional practice, extend the activity with more words. • Students can also put their thumbs up or down or go to the right or left side of the room to show their responses instead of standing up or sitting down.
TIPS FOR THE PUZZLE PIECE REVIEW	• Students will review short *a* (*hat* piece) this week. They will also be introduced to their first long vowel piece, *cake* (*a_e*). Point out the different color-coding on the puzzle pieces to reinforce to students that the *cake* puzzle piece represents a new type of vowel that sounds and is spelled differently. • Have students write spellings in the air, on the floor, on their arms, or on each other's backs with their fingers. • Come up with a class name for "silent *e*" ("Magic E," "Momma E," "Super E," etc.). • Take more time to introduce and review the *cake* piece throughout the week. Students are used to seeing an *a* and hearing the short *a* sound. It may take them a long time to connect the long *a* sound and the *a_e* spelling.
TIPS FOR BLENDING	• It may be necessary to reblend the lines with vowel_e words. Support students in making the long *a* sound. • Remind students that this is the first time they have been exposed to long *a*. It will take students a lot of practice to master this sound. • The sight words this week are *have* and *ate*. Discuss with students that both words have the *a_e* spelling pattern but only *ate* has a long *a* sound. Remind students that sight words are words that students need to memorize and will not always follow sound spelling patterns.
TIPS FOR DICTATION AND QUICK SWITCH	• Support your students as much as necessary so they feel successful. You can complete the routine as a class or have students check their work after each letter, if necessary. • Monitor students' work during Dictation and Quick Switch. If students are forgetting the *e* to make the vowel say its name, then read the way they are spelling the word and ask if that is the word they are intending to spell. For example, if you asked them to write *cake* and a student wrote *cak*, read the word and pronounce it /k/ /ă/ /k/. Ask them, "Does that spell *cake*? How can we fix it?"

TIPS FOR SORTING	• Model and positively reinforce the sorting routine repeatedly throughout the week. This week students go back to sorting with words and pictures.
	 • Discuss the vocabulary words that appear in the sort. Vocabulary words include the following:
	    • Sort 1: *mane, cape, cane, rate, mate*
	    • Sort 2: *rake, mane, fame, cape*

Preparing for Your Week

TIPS FOR THE PRACTICE PIECES

- Support students with the vocabulary words for this week. They may need assistance in writing sentences.
- Students can make a "magic *e*" on a Popsicle stick. Have students write consonant, vowel, consonant (CVC) words and then add their "magic *e*" stick to the end of their word to make a long vowel.
- Students can make a "magic *e*" flip-book by writing CVC words on one side of the page and the *e* on the edge of the backside. When they flip a portion of the paper to reveal the *e*, they turn the CVC word into a vowel_*e* word. Please reference resources.corwin.com/puzzlepiecephonics-gradeK for resources for a blackline master of this additional Practice Piece.

TIPS FOR FLUENCY

- Students can highlight words with short *a* or long *a*.
- You can assign students fluency partners. Students will work together to achieve fluency with the daily poems.
- Students can participate in a "Fluency Celebration." Call on students who feel prepared to present a particular poem in front of the class. Other students can follow along in the Fluency Notebook.

Day 1

THE PUZZLE PIECE FAMILY

Launch Concept 10: Short Vowels and Vowel_*e* by following the Puzzle Piece Family routine on page I-11 of the Introduction.

1. Show students the following words:

cap	cape
pet	Pete
pin	pine
not	note
cut	cute

2. Have students read the words with you. Assist students when reading words with long vowels. Underline the vowel(s) in each word.

3. Facilitate a discussion that leads them to discover the Puzzle Piece Family: Short Vowels and Vowel_*e*.

PHONEMIC AWARENESS: LISTEN

1. Give the directions. Say, "I am going to say a word. If you hear short *a* (/ă/), sit down. If you hear a word with a different sound, stand up."

2. Say the following words:

rat rate tap tape cat Kate mat mate mad made

THE BIG REVEAL

1. Say, "Class, we have learned all of our short vowel sounds. Let's say them all together: '/ă/ /ĕ/ /ĭ/ /ŏ/ /ŭ/.'"

2. Say, "For the next five weeks, we are going to study a new type of vowel called long vowels. We will learn the long vowel sound for each vowel. A long vowel is when the vowel says its own name. This week we will focus on short *a* and long *a*."

3. Say, "You know the *hat* puzzle piece. It represents the letter *a*. The hat piece says '/ă/ /ă/ /ă/' like in the middle of the word *hat*. Let's all do the motion for the *hat* piece together."

4. Say, "This is the *cake* piece. It represents the *a_e* spelling of long *a*. The *cake* piece says '/ā/ /ā/ /ā/' like in the word *cake*. Point your index finger forward, swipe it into a pretend bowl in a scooping motion, and say '/ā/.' We will study this sound all week. Let's make a list of words that have the *cake* sound in them" (record the words). If students suggest a word with the sound of /ā/ represented by a pattern other than *a_e*, say, "You're hearing the right sound, but that word has a different spelling pattern. Let's try another word."

BLENDING: PUTTING SOUNDS TOGETHER TO MAKE NEW WORDS

1. Follow the Blending routine on page I-17 of the Introduction.

2. Display the following words on the board one line at a time. Facilitate a discussion about the blending line focus after each line.

3. Then display the weekly sight words and sentence.

BLENDING: PUTTING SOUNDS TOGETHER TO MAKE NEW WORDS (Continued)	**4.** In the sentence, discuss the words *have* and *cape*. Point out to students that both words have the *a_e* spelling pattern but only *cape* has the sound of long *a*.

hat	hate	gate	Discuss: compare and contrast short *a* with long *a*
tap	tape	cape	Discuss: compare and contrast short *a* with long *a*
rat	rate	mate	Discuss: compare and contrast short *a* with long *a*

Sight Words: have   ate

Sentence: I have a cape.

DICTATION: STRETCH OUT YOUR WORDS	**1.** Have students turn to page 295 of the Learner's Notebook. **2.** Follow the Dictation routine on page I-21 of the Introduction to dictate the following words: 1. can 2. cane 3. rat 4. rate **Sight Word: have** **Sentence: I have a cap and a cape.** **3.** Use Dictation as an informal pretest of students' knowledge of vowel_e. Assist students with the spelling of long *a*.

PRACTICE: COMPLETE YOUR WORK ON YOUR OWN	**1.** Have students turn to page 291 (Group 1) or 293 (Group 2) of the Learner's Notebook. **2.** Instruct students to tear out the sort and complete the following Practice Pieces: Quick Color, Careful Cut, Highlighter Hunt, and Sorting With Separate Picture and Word Cards (see further directions on pages I-37, I-38, I-43, and I-26 of the Introduction). **3.** Circulate as students work, which usually takes fifteen minutes, and coach as needed.

FLUENCY: READING LIKE YOU'RE SPEAKING	**1.** Have students turn to page 42 in the Fluency Notebook. **2.** Have students read one or more of the following poems: "Magic E" and "Poof! Magic E." **3.** Circulate and listen to students read or gather a small group of students who need additional support.

Day 2

PHONEMIC AWARENESS: LISTEN

1. Give the directions. Say, "I am going to say a word. Your job is to tell me the vowel sound you hear in the word. Do you hear a short vowel or a long vowel? Do the motion of the sound you hear." Review the motions for *hat* and *cake*.

2. Say the following words:

make   pale   pat   nap   tale   tap   tape   fake   mat   rat

PUZZLE PIECE REVIEW

1. Say, "When I point to the piece, you tell me its name" (*hat, cake*).

2. Say, "When I point to the piece, you tell me its sound" (/ă/, /ā/).

3. Say, "When I point to the piece, you tell me its spelling" (*a, a_e*).

4. Say, "Write the spellings in the air with your finger" (students will form the patterns *a* and *a_e*).

BLENDING: PUTTING SOUNDS TOGETHER TO MAKE NEW WORDS

1. Follow the Blending routine on page I-17 of the Introduction.

2. Display the following words on the board one line at a time. Facilitate a discussion about the blending line focus after each line.

3. Then display the weekly sight words and sentence.

4. In the sentence, identify the rhyming words *ate* and *Kate*. Discuss with students that both words end in –*ate*.

mat	mate	Kate	Discuss: compare and contrast short and long *a*; capital *K* in the name *Kate*
mad	made	fade	Discuss: compare and contrast short and long *a*
can	cane	pane	Discuss: compare and contrast short and long *a*

Sight Words: have   ate

Sentence: I ate with Kate!

QUICK SWITCH: MANIPULATE YOUR WORDS

1. Have students turn to page 295 of the Learner's Notebook.

2. Follow the Quick Switch routine on page I-23 of the Introduction to dictate the following words:

mat → mate → Kate → cat → can

3. Assist students when going from *mat* to *mate* by identifying the change in the vowel sound and pointing to the *hat* and *cake* puzzle pieces. Help students when going from *Kate* to *cat* by identifying the change in the vowel sound and reminding students that both *k* and *c* can represent the sound of /k/.

SORT: WHAT IS YOUR FOCUS PATTERN?

1. Have students take out their bag of words (created on Day 1) and follow the Sorting With Separate Picture and Word Cards routine on page I-26 of the Introduction.

PRACTICE: COMPLETE YOUR WORK ON YOUR OWN

1. Students will follow the Color-Code Writing routine on page I-52 of the Introduction.

2. Circulate as students work, which usually takes fifteen minutes, and coach as needed.

FLUENCY: READING LIKE YOU'RE SPEAKING

1. Have students turn to page 42 in the Fluency Notebook.

2. Have students read one or more of the following poems: "Magic E" and "Poof! Magic E."

3. Circulate and listen to students read or gather a small group of students who need additional support.

PHONEMIC AWARENESS: LISTEN

1. Give the directions. Say, "I am going to say a word. Your job is to tell me the vowel sound you hear in the word. Do you hear a short vowel or a long vowel? Do the motion of the sound you hear." Review the motions for *hat* and *cake*.

2. Say the following words:

> take rat bait jam fat tape shake lap train tad

PUZZLE PIECE REVIEW

1. Say, "When I point to the piece, you tell me its name" (*hat, cake*).

2. Say, "When I point to the piece, you tell me its sound" (/ă/, /ā/).

3. Say, "When I point to the piece, you tell me its spelling" (*a, a_e*).

4. Say, "Write the spellings in the air with your finger" (students will form the patterns *a* and *a_e*).

BLENDING: PUTTING SOUNDS TOGETHER TO MAKE NEW WORDS

1. Follow the Blending routine on page I-17 of the Introduction.

2. Display the following words on the board one line at a time. Facilitate a discussion about the blending line focus after each line.

3. Then display the weekly sight words and sentence.

4. Discuss the examples of *a_e* in the sentence. Have students underline on the board what is making the *a* say its name in the words *ate* and *cake*.

can	ran	ban	Discuss: *–an* family
mate	rate	date	Discuss: *–ate* family
man	mane	sane	Discuss: compare and contrast short *a* and long *a*

Sight Words: have   ate

Sentence: The man ate a cake.

DICTATION: STRETCH OUT YOUR WORDS

1. Have students turn to page 296 of the Learner's Notebook.

2. Follow the Dictation routine on page I-21 of the Introduction to dictate the following words:

> l. tap   2. tape   3. mad   4. made

Sight Word: ate

Sentence: I made a trap out of tape.

3. Help students segment the words and reference puzzle pieces as necessary. Assist students with spelling of *a_e*.

SORT: WHAT IS YOUR FOCUS PATTERN?

1. Have students take out their bag of words (created on Day 1) and follow the Sorting With Separate Picture and Word Cards routine on page I-26 of the Introduction.

PRACTICE: COMPLETE YOUR WORK ON YOUR OWN

1. Students will complete the Read and Trade routine on page I-47 of the Introduction.

2. Circulate as students work, which usually takes fifteen minutes, and coach as needed.

FLUENCY: READING LIKE YOU'RE SPEAKING

1. Have students turn to page 42 in the Fluency Notebook.

2. Have students read one or more of the following poems: "Magic E" and "Poof! Magic E."

3. Circulate and listen to students read or gather a small group of students who need additional support.

Day 4

PHONEMIC AWARENESS: LISTEN	**1.** Give the directions. Say, "I am going to say a word. Your job is to tell me the vowel sound you hear in the word. Do you hear a short vowel or a long vowel? Do the motion of the sound you hear." Review the motions for *hat* and *cake*.
	2. Say the following words:
	<div align="center">bad tail gap hat bake Sam pad yam hate trade</div>

PUZZLE PIECE REVIEW	**1.** Say, "When I point to the piece, you tell me its name" (*hat, cake*).
	2. Say, "When I point to the piece, you tell me its sound" (/ă/, /ā/).
	3. Say, "When I point to the piece, you tell me its spelling" (*a, a_e*).
	4. Say, "Write the spellings in the air with your finger" (students will form the patterns *a* and *a_e*).

BLENDING: PUTTING SOUNDS TOGETHER TO MAKE NEW WORDS	**1.** Follow the Blending routine on page I-17 of the Introduction.
	2. Display the following words on the board one line at a time. Facilitate a discussion about the blending line focus after each line.
	3. Then display the weekly sight words and sentence.
	4. Discuss the question mark in the sentence and model reading with intonation and answering a *what* question.

fame	dame	blame	Discuss: –*ame* family
flag	stand	sad	Discuss: short *a*; blends
bake	grape	plate	Discuss: long *a* spelled *a_e*

Sight Words: have   ate

Sentence: What will we name the pet snake?

QUICK SWITCH: MANIPULATE YOUR WORDS	**1.** Have students turn to page 296 of the Learner's Notebook.
	2. Follow the Quick Switch routine on page I-23 of the Introduction to dictate the following words:
	<div align="center">at → ate → gate → rate → rat</div>
	3. Assist students when going from *at* to *ate* and from *rate* to *rat* by identifying the change in the vowel sound and pointing to the *hat* and *cake* puzzle pieces.

SORT: WHAT IS YOUR FOCUS PATTERN?	**1.** Have students take out their bag of words (created on Day 1) and follow Sorting With Separate Picture and Word Cards routine on page I-26 of the Introduction.

PRACTICE: COMPLETE YOUR WORK ON YOUR OWN	**1.** Have students complete the following Practice Pieces: Glue, Draw a Picture and Super Sentences (on pages I-50 and I-53 of the Introduction).
	2. Circulate as students work, which usually takes fifteen minutes, and coach as needed.

FLUENCY: READING LIKE YOU'RE SPEAKING	**1.** Have students turn to page 42 in the Fluency Notebook.
	2. Have students read one or more of the following poems: "Magic E" and "Poof! Magic E."
	3. Circulate and listen to students read or gather a small group of students who need additional support.

PHONEMIC AWARENESS: LISTEN

1. Give the directions. Say, "I am going to say a word. Your job is to tell me the vowel sound you hear in the word. Do you hear a short vowel or a long vowel? Do the motion of the sound you hear." Review the motions for *hat* and *cake*.

2. Say the following words:

> bail   bath   pale   tack   dad   rap   whale   Dale   frame   Dan

REVIEW PATTERNS OF THE WEEK

1. Say, "Find a partner."

2. Say, "Tell your partner the names of this week's pieces" (*hat, cake*).

3. Say, "Tell your partner the sounds of this week's pieces" (/ă/, /ā/).

4. Say, "Tell your partner the spellings of this week's pieces" (*a, a_e*).

5. Say, "Write the spellings on your partner's back with your finger" (students will form the patterns *a* and *a_e*).

SPELLING CHECK

1. Follow the Spelling Check routine on page I-34 of the Introduction.

2. Instruct students to sit in their word study groups and turn to page 297 of the Learner's Notebook.

3. Say, "I am going to say one word at a time to each group. Record the words as I say them to your group. Make sure you only record the words from your group."

4. Move back and forth between the groups and dictate the following words:

Words for Group I	Words for Group 2
1. at	1. flag
2. ate	2. grape
3. mate	3. lake
4. mad	4. fame
5. made	5. stand
Sentence: I have a cape.	**Sentence: Dan ate all of the cake.**

WORD HUNT

1. Students will follow the Word Hunt routine on page I-55 of the Introduction.

2. Instruct students to search texts and the classroom for words with long *a* spelled *a_e*.

COMPREHENSION CHECK

1. Have students turn to page 298 of the Learner's Notebook.

2. Students will follow the Comprehension Check routine on page I-36 of the Introduction.

3. Check students' work. Circled answers are as follows:

   1. "I have a plate," said Dad.

   2. "I have a cake," said Mom.

   3. "I have a hat," said Sister.

4. Possible written responses include the following:

   1. Mom has a cake.

   2. Dad, Mom, and Sister can _____. (Students may put any phrase that is supported by the text and pictures into the blank. For example, "Dad, Mom, and Sister can have a party.")

WEEKLY CELEBRATION

1. Display the celebratory message: "Piece of cake! You learned the *hat* and *cake* pieces!"

2. Encourage students to work together to read the message.

3. Have students copy the message onto their weekly certificate (see resources .corwin.com/puzzlepiecephonics-gradeK) and place it somewhere to take home.

Preparing for Your Week

Resources

PUZZLE PIECES

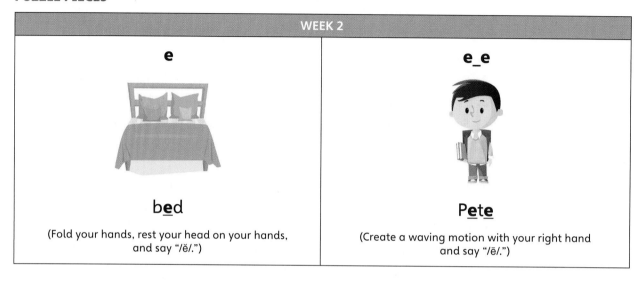

WEEK 2

e

b<u>e</u>d

(Fold your hands, rest your head on your hands, and say "/ĕ/.")

e_e

P<u>e</u>t<u>e</u>

(Create a waving motion with your right hand and say "/ē/.")

Bed: istock.com/vasilyevalara; Pete: istock.com/pijama61

Preparing for Your Week

CORRESPONDING *LEARNER'S NOTEBOOK PAGES*

GROUP 1 ANSWER KEY
Weekly Sort

short e	long e	
bed	Pete	pet
Pete	Jen	hen
pen	net	wet
eve	Steve	here
step	jet	men
fed	led	10 ten

GROUP 2 ANSWER KEY
Weekly Sort

short e	long e	
bed	Pete	pet
Pete	delete	hen
theme	rest	west
eve	Steve	here
step	blend	men
fled	tent	10 ten

	Week 2	Concept 10

Name _____ Date _____

Pete and the dog _____.

Circle the sentence that matches the picture.

	The dog is lost. The dog is here. The dog is late.
	Pete and the dog run. Pete and the dog stand. Pete and the dog pet.
	Pete and the dog fled. Pete and the dog step. Pete and the dog rest.

Use the text to answer the questions.

1. Where is the dog? The dog is _____

2. Why do Pete and the dog rest? Pete and the dog rest because

_____

306 PUZZLE PIECE PHONICS LEARNER'S NOTEBOOK, KINDERGARTEN

Preparing for Your Week

CORRESPONDING *FLUENCY NOTEBOOK PAGES*

Pet Fish

Fish, fish! In the net.

Fish, fish! I want a pet.

Catch them, catch them

Just like that.

Count them, count them.

Ready? Set!

1, 2,

3, 4, 5!

6, 7,

8, 9, 10!

Fish, fish! In a bowl.

Fish, fish! My house is full.

Delete

I hit delete,

And there it went!

Who knows where

It all was sent?

I hit delete.

Poof—it's gone!

Now I think

That I was wrong.

I hit delete.

What can I do?

Fix it, fix it!

Please, will you?

Preparing for Your Week

Tips for Management and Differentiation

Refer to this section and to resources.corwin.com/puzzlepiecephonics-gradeK for resources and ideas to deepen your students' learning throughout the week. Feel free to put your own spin on the routines, too. For daily lesson plans, see pages 417–424 of this Teacher's Guide.

TIPS FOR PHONEMIC AWARENESS	• The focus for this week is listening for long and short vowels. • If you notice your students need additional practice, extend the activity with more words. • Students can also put their thumbs up or down or go to the right or left side of the room to show their responses instead of standing up or sitting down. • If your students master short *e* versus long *e* early in the week, then you can add words with short and long *a* as a cumulative review and challenge.
TIPS FOR THE PUZZLE PIECE REVIEW	• Students will review short *e* (*bed* piece) this week. They will also be introduced to another long vowel piece, *Pete* (e_e). Review the different color-coding on the puzzle pieces and remind students that the *Pete* puzzle piece represents a new type of vowel that sounds and is spelled differently. • Have students write spellings in the air, on the floor, on their arms, or on each other's backs with their fingers. • Come up with a class name for "silent *e*" ("Magic E," "Momma E," "Super E," etc.). • Take more time to introduce and review the *Pete* piece throughout the week. Students are used to seeing an *e* and hearing the short *e* sound. It may take them a long time to connect the long *e* sound and the e_e spelling. • You can display the Long Vowels: Vowel_e horizontal header piece to connect the *cake* and *Pete* puzzle pieces. Explain to students that they are similar sound spelling patterns.
TIPS FOR BLENDING	• Help students connect the e_e spelling to the a_e spelling. Review the name your class decided on for silent *e* and remind students that silent *e* always works in the same way. It makes a vowel say the name of the letter. • It may be necessary to reblend the lines with vowel_e words. Support students in making the long *e* sound. If students still need focused practice to master vowel_e by Day 3, then you can continue to blend words from this week's sort during Blending, instead of adding words with long *a*. • Remind students that this is the first time they have been exposed to long *e*. It will take students a lot of practice to master this sound. • Help students connect the sight word *eat* to the sight word *ate* (from last week). Encourage students to use the words in sentences and write them in the air to help them remember the spellings.

(Continued)

Preparing for Your Week

TIPS FOR DICTATION AND QUICK SWITCH

- Support your students as much as necessary so they feel successful. You can complete the routine as a class or have students check their work after each letter, if necessary.
- Monitor students' work during Dictation and Quick Switch. If students are forgetting the *e* to make the vowel say its name, then read the way they are spelling the word and ask if that is the word they are intending to spell. For example, if you asked them to write *Pete* and a student wrote *pet*, read the word and pronounce it /p/ /ĕ/ /t/. Ask them, "Does that spell *Pete*? How can we fix it?"
- If students still need focused practice to master vowel_e by Day 3, then you can continue to dictate words from this week's sort, instead of adding words with long *a*.
- As students are ready, release more responsibility to them for recording the sentences in Dictation.

TIPS FOR SORTING

- Model and positively reinforce the sorting routine repeatedly throughout the week. During this concept, students go back to sorting with words and pictures.
- Discuss the vocabulary words that appear in the sort. Vocabulary words include the following:
  - Sort 1: *hen, eve, jet, led*
  - Sort 2: *delete, theme, west, eve, blend, fled*

TIPS FOR THE PRACTICE PIECES

- Support students with the vocabulary words for this week. They may need assistance in writing sentences.
- Students can make a "magic *e*" on a Popsicle stick. Have students write CVC words and then add their "magic *e*" stick to the end of their word to make a long vowel.
- Students can make a "magic *e*" flip-book by writing CVC words on one side of the page and the *e* on the edge of the backside. When they flip a portion of the paper to reveal the *e*, they turn the CVC word into a vowel_e word. Please reference resources.corwin.com/puzzlepiecephonics-gradeK for resources for a blackline master of this additional Practice Piece.

TIPS FOR FLUENCY

- Students can highlight words with short *e* or long *e*.
- You can assign students fluency partners. Students will work together to achieve fluency with the daily poems.
- Students can participate in a "Fluency Celebration." Call on students who feel prepared to present a particular poem in front of the class. Other students can follow along in the Fluency Notebook.

PHONEMIC AWARENESS: LISTEN

1. Give the directions. Say, "I am going to say a word. Your job is to tell me the vowel sound you hear in the word. Do you hear a short vowel or a long vowel? Do the motion of the sound you hear." Review the motions for *hat* and *cake*.

2. Say the following words:

pack plate save mat sad lake rap fake race ape

THE BIG REVEAL

1. Say, "Class, we have learned all of our short vowel sounds. Let's say them all together: '/ă/ /ĕ/ /ĭ, /ŏ/ /ŭ/.'"

2. Say, "Remember that now we are studying a new type of vowel called long vowels. A long vowel is when the vowel says the name of the letter. What is the long vowel sound of *a*? Good job! The long vowel sound of *a* is /ā/. This week we will learn a new long vowel. We will focus on short *e* and long *e*."

3. Say, "You know the *bed* puzzle piece. It represents the letter *e*. The *bed* piece says '/ĕ/ /ĕ/ /ĕ/' like in the middle of the word *bed*. Let's all do the motion for the *bed* piece together."

4. Say, "This is the *Pete* puzzle piece. It represents the spelling *e_e*. The *Pete* piece says '/ē/ /ē/ /ē/' like in the word *Pete*. Create a waving motion with your right hand and say '/ē/.' We will study this sound all week. Let's make a list of words that have the *Pete* sound in them" (record the words). If students suggest a word with the sound of /ē/ represented by a pattern other than *e_e*, say, "You're hearing the right sound, but that word has a different spelling pattern. Let's try another word."

BLENDING: PUTTING SOUNDS TOGETHER TO MAKE NEW WORDS

1. Follow the Blending routine on page I-17 of the Introduction.

2. Display the following words on the board one line at a time. Facilitate a discussion about the blending line focus after each line.

3. Then display the weekly sight words and sentence.

4. Compare and contrast the spellings and sounds of short *e* and long *e* in the sentence.

net	pet	Pete	Discuss: compare and contrast short *e* with long *e*
men	hen	here	Discuss: compare and contrast short *e* with long *e*
Bev	eve	Steve	Discuss: compare and contrast short *e* with long *e*; capital letters at the beginning of names

Sight Words: eat done

Sentence: Steve fed the hen.

DICTATION: STRETCH OUT YOUR WORDS

1. Have students turn to page 303 of the Learner's Notebook.

2. Follow the Dictation routine on page I-21 of the Introduction to dictate the following words:

  l. pet 2. wet 3. get 4. Pete

  Sight Word: eat

  Sentence: I have a pet hen named Pete.

3. Use Dictation as an informal pretest of students' knowledge of vowel_e. Assist students with the spelling of long *e*.

(Continued)

Day 1 (Continued)

PRACTICE: COMPLETE YOUR WORK ON YOUR OWN	**1.** Have students turn to page 299 (Group 1) or 301 (Group 2) of the Learner's Notebook. **2.** Instruct students to tear out the sort and complete the following Practice Pieces: Quick Color, Careful Cut, Highlighter Hunt, and Sorting With Separate Picture and Word Cards (see further directions on pages I-37, I-38, I-43, and I-26 of the Introduction). **3.** Circulate as students work, which usually takes fifteen minutes, and coach as needed.
FLUENCY: READING LIKE YOU'RE SPEAKING	**1.** Have students turn to page 43 in the Fluency Notebook. **2.** Have students read one or more of the following poems: "Pet Fish" and "Delete." **3.** Circulate and listen to students read or gather a small group of students who need additional support.

PHONEMIC AWARENESS: LISTEN	**1.** Give the directions. Say, "I am going to say a word. Your job is to tell me the vowel sound you hear in the word. Do you hear a short vowel or a long vowel? Do the motion of the sound you hear." Review the motions for *bed* and *Pete*. **2.** Say the following words: **wet feet red pen sheep lead green men fed beep**

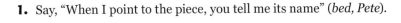

PUZZLE PIECE REVIEW 	**1.** Say, "When I point to the piece, you tell me its name" (*bed, Pete*). **2.** Say, "When I point to the piece, you tell me its sound" (/ĕ/, /ē/). **3.** Say, "When I point to the piece, you tell me its spelling" (*e, e_e*). **4.** Say, "Write the spellings in the air with your finger" (students will form the patterns *e* and *e_e*).

BLENDING: PUTTING SOUNDS TOGETHER TO MAKE NEW WORDS	**1.** Follow the Blending routine on page I-17 of the Introduction. **2.** Display the following words on the board one line at a time. Facilitate a discussion about the blending line focus after each line. **3.** Then display the weekly sight words and sentence. **4.** Discuss examples of vowel_e words in the sentence. Compare and contrast long *e* with long *a*.

bet	**set**	**Pete**	Discuss: compare and contrast short and long e
stem	**hem**	**here**	Discuss: compare and contrast short and long e
Jen	**Eve**	**Steve**	Discuss: compare and contrast short and long e; capital letters for names

Sight Words: eat   done

Sentence: Steve can eat the cake.

QUICK SWITCH: MANIPULATE YOUR WORDS	**1.** Have students turn to page 303 of the Learner's Notebook. **2.** Follow the Quick Switch routine on page I-23 of the Introduction to dictate the following words: **hen → pen → pet → Pete → set** **3.** Assist students when going from *pet* to *Pete* by reminding them of silent *e* and reviewing that names begin with a capital letter. Assist students when going from *pet* to *Pete* by listening for the vowel sound.

SORT: WHAT IS YOUR FOCUS PATTERN?	**1.** Have students take out their bag of words (created on Day 1) and follow the Sorting With Separate Picture and Word Cards routine on page I-26 of the Introduction.

PRACTICE: COMPLETE YOUR WORK ON YOUR OWN	**1.** Students will follow the Color-Code Writing routine on page I-52 of the Introduction. **2.** Circulate as students work, which usually takes fifteen minutes, and coach as needed.

FLUENCY: READING LIKE YOU'RE SPEAKING	**1.** Have students turn to page 43 in the Fluency Notebook. **2.** Have students read one or more of the following poems: "Pet Fish" and "Delete." **3.** Circulate and listen to students read or gather a small group of students who need additional support.

Day 3

PHONEMIC AWARENESS: LISTEN

1. Give the directions. Say, "I am going to say a word. Your job is to tell me the vowel sound you hear in the word. Do you hear a short vowel or a long vowel? Do the motion of the sound you hear." Review the motions for *bed* and *Pete*.

2. Say the following words:

seat   west   pen   heap   read   keep   fed   meal   bet   tent

PUZZLE PIECE REVIEW

1. Say, "When I point to the piece, you tell me its name" (*bed, Pete*).

2. Say, "When I point to the piece, you tell me its sound" (/ĕ/, /ē/).

3. Say, "When I point to the piece, you tell me its spelling" (*e, e_e*).

4. Say, "Write the spellings in the air with your finger" (students will form the patterns *e* and *e_e*).

BLENDING: PUTTING SOUNDS TOGETHER TO MAKE NEW WORDS

1. Follow the Blending routine on page I-17 of the Introduction.

2. Display the following words on the board one line at a time. Facilitate a discussion about the blending line focus after each line.

3. Then display the weekly sight words and sentence.

4. Discuss examples of vowel_e words in the sentence. Compare and contrast long *e* with long *a*.

neck	nest	best	Discuss: short *e*; short vowel –*ck* and blend *st*
eve	here	Pete	Discuss: long *e*; capital letter in the name *Pete*
crave	hare	late	Discuss: long *a*; compare with line above

Sight Words: eat   done

Sentence: We will rake over here.

DICTATION: STRETCH OUT YOUR WORDS

1. Have students turn to page 304 of the Learner's Notebook.

2. Follow the Dictation routine on page I-21 of the Introduction to dictate the following words:

l. cap   2. cape   3. pet   4. Pete

Sight Word: done

Sentence: Pete is late.

3. Assist students with identifying the vowel sound and referencing the puzzle pieces from this week and last week to correctly spell each word. In the sentence, help students segment the words *Pete* and *late*, identify the different vowel sounds, and reference the puzzle pieces.

SORT: WHAT IS YOUR FOCUS PATTERN?

1. Have students take out their bag of words (created on Day 1) and follow the Sorting With Separate Picture and Word Cards routine on page I-26 of the Introduction.

PRACTICE: COMPLETE YOUR WORK ON YOUR OWN

1. Students will complete the Read and Trade routine on page I-47 of the Introduction.

2. Circulate as students work, which usually takes fifteen minutes, and coach as needed.

**FLUENCY:
READING LIKE
YOU'RE SPEAKING**

1. Have students turn to page 43 in the Fluency Notebook.

2. Have students read one or more of the following poems: "Pet Fish" and "Delete."

3. Circulate and listen to students read or gather a small group of students who need additional support.

Day 4

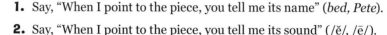

PHONEMIC AWARENESS: LISTEN

1. Give the directions. Say, "I am going to say a word. Your job is to tell me the vowel sound you hear in the word. Do you hear a short vowel or a long vowel? Do the motion of the sound you hear." Review the motions for *bed* and *Pete*.

2. Say the following words:

feel   week   left   men   set   feet   bead   let   peel   send

PUZZLE PIECE REVIEW

1. Say, "When I point to the piece, you tell me its name" (*bed, Pete*).

2. Say, "When I point to the piece, you tell me its sound" (/ĕ/, /ē/).

3. Say, "When I point to the piece, you tell me its spelling" (*e, e_e*).

4. Say, "Write the spellings in the air with your finger" (students will form the patterns *e* and *e_e*).

BLENDING: PUTTING SOUNDS TOGETHER TO MAKE NEW WORDS

1. Follow the Blending routine on page I-17 of the Introduction.

2. Display the following words on the board one line at a time. Facilitate a discussion about the blending line focus after each line.

3. Then display the weekly sight words and sentence.

4. In the sentence, help students read "New Year's Eve." You can preread those words for students or scaffold them by displaying a picture and helping students use the initial consonant sounds plus the picture to read the words.

band	bend	blade	Discuss: contrast short and long vowels
stamp	step	Steve	Discuss: contrast short and long vowels
hand	help	here	Discuss: contrast short and long vowels

Sight Words: eat   done

Sentence: We eat ham on New Year's Eve.

QUICK SWITCH: MANIPULATE YOUR WORDS

1. Have students turn to page 304 of the Learner's Notebook.

2. Follow the Quick Switch routine on page I-23 of the Introduction to dictate the following words:

Pete → pet → pat → mat → mate

3. Assist students with identifying the vowel sound and referencing the puzzle pieces from this week and last week to correctly spell each word. Remind students that *Pete* is a name, so it begins with a capital letter.

SORT: WHAT IS YOUR FOCUS PATTERN?

1. Have students take out their bag of words (created on Day 1) and follow the Sorting With Separate Picture and Word Cards routine on page I-26 of the Introduction.

PRACTICE: COMPLETE YOUR WORK ON YOUR OWN

1. Have students complete the following Practice Pieces: Glue, Draw a Picture and Super Sentences (on pages I-50 and I-53 of the Introduction).

2. Circulate as students work, which usually takes fifteen minutes, and coach as needed.

FLUENCY: READING LIKE YOU'RE SPEAKING

1. Have students turn to page 43 in the Fluency Notebook.

2. Have students read one or more of the following poems: "Pet Fish" and "Delete."

3. Circulate and listen to students read or gather a small group of students who need additional support.

PHONEMIC AWARENESS: LISTEN

1. Give the directions. Say, "I am going to say a word. Your job is to tell me the vowel sound you hear in the word. Do you hear a short vowel or a long vowel? Do the motion of the sound you hear." Review the motions for *bed* and *Pete*.

2. Say the following words:

> **bail   bath   pale   tack   dad   rap   whale   Dale   frame   Dan**

REVIEW PATTERNS OF THE WEEK

1. Say, "Find a partner."

2. Say, "Tell your partner the names of this week's pieces" (*bed, Pete*).

3. Say, "Tell your partner the sounds of this week's pieces" (/ĕ/, /ē/).

4. Say, "Tell your partner the spellings of this week's pieces" (e, e_e).

5. Say, "Write the spellings on your partner's back with your finger" (students will form the patterns *e* and *e_e*).

SPELLING CHECK

1. Follow the Spelling Check routine on page I-34 of the Introduction.

2. Instruct students to sit in their word study groups and turn to page 305 of the Learner's Notebook.

3. Say, "I am going to say one word at a time to each group. Record the words as I say them to your group. Make sure you only record the words from your group."

4. Move back and forth between the groups and dictate the following words:

Words for Group I	Words for Group 2
I. hen	I. west
2. here	2. eve
3. pet	3. Steve
4. Pete	4. tent
5. eve	5. Pete
Sentence: The men eat.	**Sentence: I will rest when I am done.**

WORD HUNT

1. Students will follow the Word Hunt routine on page I-55 of the Introduction.

2. Instruct students to search texts and the classroom for words with long *e* spelled *e_e*.

COMPREHENSION CHECK

1. Have students turn to page 306 of the Learner's Notebook.

2. Students will follow the Comprehension Check routine on page I-36 of the Introduction.

3. Check students' work. Circled answers are as follows:

1. The dog is here.

2. Pete and the dog stand.

3. Pete and the dog rest.

4. Possible written responses include the following:

1. The dog is here.

2. Pete and the dog rest because _____. (Students may put any phrase that is supported by the text and pictures into the blank. For example, "Pete and the dog rest because they had to stand.")

(Continued)

Day 5 (Continued)

WEEKLY CELEBRATION

1. Display the celebratory message: "Completed! You learned the *bed* and *Pete* pieces!"

2. Encourage students to work together to read the message.

3. Have students copy the message onto their weekly certificate (see resources .corwin.com/puzzlepiecephonics-gradeK) and place it somewhere to take home.

Preparing for Your Week

Resources

PUZZLE PIECES

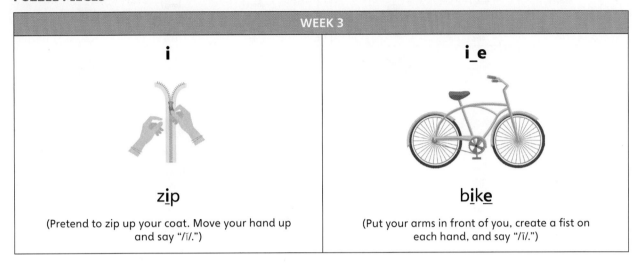

WEEK 3

i	i_e
z**i**p	b**i**k**e**
(Pretend to zip up your coat. Move your hand up and say "/ĭ/.")	(Put your arms in front of you, create a fist on each hand, and say "/ī/.")

Zip: istock.com/pe-art; Bike: istock.com/heather_mcgrath

Preparing for Your Week

CORRESPONDING *LEARNER'S NOTEBOOK PAGES*

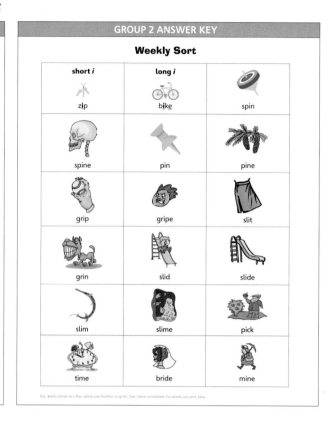

GROUP 1 ANSWER KEY

Weekly Sort

short *i*	long *i*	
zip	bike	spin
spine	pin	pine
hid	hide	bit
bite	slid	slide
fin	fine	fine
kite	Tim	time

GROUP 2 ANSWER KEY

Weekly Sort

short *i*	long *i*	
zip	bike	spin
spine	pin	pine
grip	gripe	slit
grin	slid	slide
slim	slime	pick
time	bride	mine

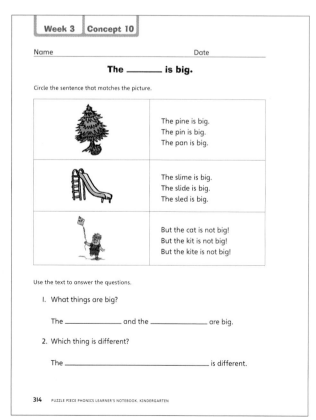

Week 3	Concept 10

Name _____ Date _____

The _____ is big.

Circle the sentence that matches the picture.

	The pine is big. The pin is big. The pan is big.
	The slime is big. The slide is big. The sled is big.
	But the cat is not big! But the kit is not big! But the kite is not big!

Use the text to answer the questions.

1. What things are big?

   The _____ and the _____ are big.

2. Which thing is different?

   The _____ is different.

CORRESPONDING *FLUENCY NOTEBOOK PAGES*

Hiking

Hike, hike, hike
Three more miles to go.
"Are we there yet?"
asks Mom.

Hike, hike, hike.
Two more miles to go.
"Are we there yet?"
asks Dad.

Hike, hike, hike.
One more mile to go.
"Are we there yet?"
asks Tim.

Hike, hike, hike.
No more miles to go.
"Are we there yet?"
asks Matt.

YES!

Mike's Bike

Look, see?
Look at Mike
Take a ride
On his bike!

He can ride
From side to side.
He can pump,
And he can glide.

His bike is tall
And has red stripes,
But, uh oh, Mike!
W—, w—, wipeout.

Preparing for Your Week

Tips for Management and Differentiation

Refer to this section and to resources.corwin.com/puzzlepiecephonics-gradeK for resources and ideas to deepen your students' learning throughout the week. Feel free to put your own spin on the routines, too. For daily lesson plans, see pages 430–435 of this Teacher's Guide.

TIPS FOR PHONEMIC AWARENESS	• The focus for this week is listening for long and short vowels. • If you notice your students need additional practice, extend the activity with more words. • Students can also put their thumbs up or down or go to the right or left side of the room to show their responses instead of standing up or sitting down. • If your students master short *i* versus long *i* early in the week, then you can add words with short and long *a* and *e* as a cumulative review and challenge.
TIPS FOR THE PUZZLE PIECE REVIEW	• Students will review short *i* (*zip* piece) this week. They will also be introduced to another long vowel piece, *bike* (*i_e*). Review the different color-coding on the puzzle pieces and remind students that the *bike* puzzle piece represents a new type of vowel that sounds and is spelled differently. • Have students write spellings in the air, on the floor, on their arms, or on each other's backs with their fingers. • Come up with a class name for "silent *e*" ("Magic E," "Momma E," "Super E," etc.). • Take more time to introduce and review the *bike* piece throughout the week than the *zip* piece. Students are used to seeing an *i* and hearing the short *i* sound. It may take them a long time to connect the long *i* sound and the *i_e* spelling. • You can display the Long Vowels: Vowel_e horizontal header piece to connect the *cake*, *Pete*, and *bike* puzzle pieces. Explain to students that they are similar sound spelling patterns.
TIPS FOR BLENDING	• Help students connect the *i_e* spelling to the *a_e* and *e_e* spellings. Review the name your class decided on for silent *e* and remind students that silent *e* always works in the same way. It makes a vowel say the name of the letter. • Review the short *i* families learned in Concept 6 (including *–ick* and *–ill*) as needed before Blending. • It may be necessary to reblend the lines with vowel_e words. Support students in making the long *i* sound. If students still need focused practice to master vowel_e by Day 4, then you can continue to blend words from this week's sort during Blending, instead of adding words with long *a* and long *e*. • Remind students that this is the first time they have been exposed to long *i*. It will take students a lot of practice to master this sound. • This week starts the sight word review. Select words that your students need the most practice with.

Preparing for Your Week

TIPS FOR DICTATION AND QUICK SWITCH

- Monitor students' work during Dictation and Quick Switch. If students are forgetting the *e* to make the vowel say its name, then read the way they are spelling the word and ask if that is the word they are intending to spell. For example, if you asked them to write *fine* and a student wrote *fin*, read the word and pronounce it /f/ /ĭ/ /n/. Ask them, "Does that spell *fine*? How can we fix it?"
- If students still need focused practice to master vowel_e by Day 4, then you can continue to dictate words from this week's sort, instead of adding words with long and short *a* and *e*.
- As students are ready, release more responsibility to them for recording the sentences in Dictation.

TIPS FOR SORTING

- Model and positively reinforce the sorting routine repeatedly throughout the week. During this concept, students go back to sorting with words and pictures.
- Discuss the vocabulary words that appear in the sort. Vocabulary words include the following:
  - Sort 1: *spine, pine, fin, slid, kite*
  - Sort 2: *spine, pine, grip, gripe, slit, grin, slim, bride*

TIPS FOR THE PRACTICE PIECES

- Support students with the vocabulary words for this week. They may need assistance in writing sentences.
- Students can make a "magic *e*" on a Popsicle stick. Have students write CVC words and then add their "magic *e*" stick to the end of their word to make a long vowel.
- Students can make a "magic *e*" flip-book by writing CVC words on one side of the page and the *e* on the edge of the backside. When they flip a portion of the paper to reveal the *e*, they turn the CVC word into a vowel_e word. Please reference resources.corwin.com/puzzlepiecephonics-gradeK for resources for a blackline master of this additional Practice Piece.
- Students can identify words that are the same except for the vowel sound (e.g., *time* and *tame* or *line* and *lane*). They can practice reading the words quickly on flashcards and illustrate their meaning.

TIPS FOR FLUENCY

- Students can highlight words with short *i* or long *i*.
- You can assign students fluency partners. Students will work together to achieve fluency with the daily poems.
- Students can participate in a "Fluency Celebration." Call on students who feel prepared to present a particular poem in front of the class. Other students can follow along in the Fluency Notebook.

Day 1

PHONEMIC AWARENESS: LISTEN

1. Give the directions. Say, "I am going to say a word. Your job is to tell me the vowel sound you hear in the word. Do you hear a short vowel or a long vowel? Do the motion of the sound you hear." Review the motions for *hat, cake, bed*, and *Pete*.

2. Say the following words:

snack   stand   lake   green   peace   red   clap   name   waste   pet

THE BIG REVEAL

1. Say, "Class, we have learned all of our short vowel sounds. Let's say them all together: '/ă/ /ĕ/ /ĭ/ /ŏ/ /ŭ/.'"

2. Say, "Remember that now we are studying a new type of vowel called long vowels. A long vowel is when the vowel says the name of the letter. Do you remember the long vowel sound for *a*? Good job! The long vowel sound of *a* is /ā/. What is the long vowel sound of *e*? Good job! The long vowel sound of *e* is /ē/. This week we will learn a new long vowel. We will focus on short *i* and long *i*."

3. Say, "You know the *zip* puzzle piece. It represents the letter *i*. The *zip* piece says '/ĭ/ /ĭ/ /ĭ/' like in the middle of the word *zip*. Let's all do the motion for the *zip* piece together."

4. Say, "This is the *bike* puzzle piece. It represents the spelling *i_e*. The *bike* piece says '/ī/ /ī/ /ī/' like in the middle of the word *bike*. Put your arms in front of you, create a fist on each hand, and say '/ī/.' We will study this sound all week. Let's make a list of words that have the *bike* sound in them" (record the words). If students suggest a word with the sound of /ī/ represented by a pattern other than *i_e*, say, "You're hearing the right sound, but that word has a different spelling pattern. Let's try another word."

BLENDING: PUTTING SOUNDS TOGETHER TO MAKE NEW WORDS

1. Follow the Blending routine on page I-17 of the Introduction.

2. Display the following words on the board one line at a time. Facilitate a discussion about the blending line focus after each line.

3. Then display the weekly sight words and sentence.

4. In the sentence, compare and contrast the short *i* and long *i* sounds and spellings.

spin	spine	line	Discuss: compare and contrast short *i* with long *i*
slid	slide	ride	Discuss: compare and contrast short *i* with long *i*
kit	kite	bite	Discuss: compare and contrast short *i* with long *i*

Sight Words: when   where

Sentence: Where did Sid hide?

DICTATION: STRETCH OUT YOUR WORDS

1. Have students turn to page 311 of the Learner's Notebook.

2. Follow the Dictation routine on page I-21 of the Introduction to dictate the following words:

I. spin   2. spine   3. slid   4. slide

Sight Word: when

Sentence: I like the kite.

3. Use Dictation as an informal pretest of students' knowledge of vowel_e. Assist students with the spelling of long *i*.

**PRACTICE:
COMPLETE
YOUR WORK ON
YOUR OWN**

1. Have students turn to page 307 (Group 1) or 309 (Group 2) of the Learner's Notebook.

2. Instruct students to tear out the sort and complete the following Practice Pieces: Quick Color, Careful Cut, Highlighter Hunt, and Sorting With Separate Picture and Word Cards (see further directions on pages I-37, I-38, I-43, and I-26 of the Introduction).

3. Circulate as students work, which usually takes fifteen minutes, and coach as needed.

**FLUENCY:
READING LIKE
YOU'RE SPEAKING**

1. Have students turn to page 44 in the Fluency Notebook.

2. Have students read one or more of the following poems: "Hiking" and "Mike's Bike."

3. Circulate and listen to students read or gather a small group of students who need additional support.

PHONEMIC AWARENESS: LISTEN	**1.** Give the directions. Say, "I am going to say a word. Your job is to tell me the vowel sound you hear in the word. Do you hear a short vowel or a long vowel? Do the motion of the sound you hear." Review the motions for *zip* and *bike*.
	2. Say the following words:

lid lime fine fin flip lip like hike tick try

PUZZLE PIECE REVIEW	**1.** Say, "When I point to the piece, you tell me its name" (*zip, bike*).
	2. Say, "When I point to the piece, you tell me its sound" (/ĭ/, /ī/).
	3. Say, "When I point to the piece, you tell me its spelling" (*i, i_e*).
	4. Say, "Write the spellings in the air with your finger" (students will form the patterns *i* and *i_e*).

BLENDING: PUTTING SOUNDS TOGETHER TO MAKE NEW WORDS	**1.** Follow the Blending routine on page I-17 of the Introduction.
	2. Display the following words on the board one line at a time. Facilitate a discussion about the blending line focus after each line.
	3. Then display the weekly sight words and sentence.
	4. Discuss examples of vowel_e words in the sentence. Compare and contrast long *e* with long *i*.

fin	fine	mine	Discuss: compare and contrast short and long *i*
Tim	time	slime	Discuss: compare and contrast short and long *i*; capital letter in the name *Tim*
slick	like	Mike	Discuss: compare and contrast short and long *i*; capital letter in the name *Mike*

Sight Words: over under

Sentence: Pete did a trick on the slide.

QUICK SWITCH: MANIPULATE YOUR WORDS	**1.** Have students turn to page 311 of the Learner's Notebook.
	2. Follow the Quick Switch routine on page I-23 of the Introduction to dictate the following words:

fin → fine → line → pine → pin

	3. Assist students in identifying whether the vowel or consonant sounds are changing. Help students reference the *bike* piece to represent *i_e*.
SORT: WHAT IS YOUR FOCUS PATTERN?	**1.** Have students take out their bag of words (created on Day 1) and follow the Sorting With Separate Picture and Word Cards routine on page I-26 of the Introduction.
PRACTICE: COMPLETE YOUR WORK ON YOUR OWN	**1.** Students will follow the Color-Code Writing routine on page I-52 of the Introduction.
	2. Circulate as students work, which usually takes fifteen minutes, and coach as needed.
FLUENCY: READING LIKE YOU'RE SPEAKING	**1.** Have students turn to page 44 in the Fluency Notebook.
	2. Have students read one or more of the following poems: "Hiking" and "Mike's Bike."
	3. Circulate and listen to students read or gather a small group of students who need additional support.

PHONEMIC AWARENESS: LISTEN

1. Give the directions. Say, "I am going to say a word. Your job is to tell me the vowel sound you hear in the word. Do you hear a short vowel or a long vowel? Do the motion of the sound you hear." Review the motions for *zip* and *bike*.

2. Say the following words:

bid   Mike   bike   hide   spin   lick   pin   slid

PUZZLE PIECE REVIEW

1. Say, "When I point to the piece, you tell me its name" (*zip, bike*).

2. Say, "When I point to the piece, you tell me its sound" (/ĭ/, /ī/).

3. Say, "When I point to the piece, you tell me its spelling" (*i, i_e*).

4. Say, "Write the spellings in the air with your finger" (students will form the patterns *i* and *i_e*).

BLENDING: PUTTING SOUNDS TOGETHER TO MAKE NEW WORDS

1. Follow the Blending routine on page I-17 of the Introduction.

2. Display the following words on the board one line at a time. Facilitate a discussion about the blending line focus after each line.

3. Then display the weekly sight words and sentence.

4. Discuss the meaning of –*s* in the sentence ("more than one").

stick	still	spill	Discuss: short *i*; short vowel –*ck* and doubling the consonant *l*
dime	time	slime	Discuss: -*ime* family
bit	bite	site	Discuss: compare and contrast long and short *i*

Sight Words: what   who

Sentence: I like grapes and limes.

DICTATION: STRETCH OUT YOUR WORDS

1. Have students turn to page 312 of the Learner's Notebook.

2. Follow the Dictation routine on page I-21 of the Introduction to dictate the following words:

l. sit   2. site   3. dim   4. dime

Sight Word: what

Sentence: I took a big bite out of the lime.

3. Assist students to identify whether the vowels are long or short and reference the puzzle pieces before recording each word.

SORT: WHAT IS YOUR FOCUS PATTERN?

1. Have students take out their bag of words (created on Day 1) and follow the Sorting With Separate Picture and Word Cards routine on page I-26 of the Introduction.

PRACTICE: COMPLETE YOUR WORK ON YOUR OWN

1. Students will complete the Read and Trade routine on page I-47 of the Introduction.

2. Circulate as students work, which usually takes fifteen minutes, and coach as needed.

FLUENCY: READING LIKE YOU'RE SPEAKING

1. Have students turn to page 44 in the Fluency Notebook.

2. Have students read one or more of the following poems: "Hiking" and "Mike's Bike."

3. Circulate and listen to students read or gather a small group of students who need additional support.

Day 4

PHONEMIC AWARENESS: LISTEN

1. Give the directions. Say, "I am going to say a word. Your job is to tell me the vowel sound you hear in the word. Do you hear a short vowel or a long vowel? Do the motion of the sound you hear." Review the motions for _zip_ and _bike_.

2. Say the following words:

        pie   big   win   dry   dime   dim   hip   fine   mine   tin

PUZZLE PIECE REVIEW

1. Say, "When I point to the piece, you tell me its name" (_zip_, _bike_).

2. Say, "When I point to the piece, you tell me its sound" (/ĭ/, /ī/).

3. Say, "When I point to the piece, you tell me its spelling" (_i_, _i_e_).

4. Say, "Write the spellings in the air with your finger" (students will form the patterns _i_ and _i_e_).

BLENDING: PUTTING SOUNDS TOGETHER TO MAKE NEW WORDS

1. Follow the Blending routine on page I-17 of the Introduction.

2. Display the following words on the board one line at a time. Facilitate a discussion about the blending line focus after each line.

3. Then display the weekly sight words and sentence.

4. In the sentence, have students come up and underline the _i_e_ spelling pattern. Discuss with students that there is no _e_ on the end of _zip_, so the vowel is short.

pine	prize	pride	Discuss: _i_e_
bite	mite	kite	Discuss: _-ite_ family
hare	here	hire	Discuss: vowel_e

Sight Words: its   ask

Sentence: I like to ride the zip line.

QUICK SWITCH: MANIPULATE YOUR WORDS

1. Have students turn to page 312 of the Learner's Notebook.

2. Follow the Quick Switch routine on page I-23 of the Introduction to dictate the following words:

        pin → pine → pane → pan → pen

3. Help students identify the vowel sound and reference the puzzle pieces before recording.

SORT: WHAT IS YOUR FOCUS PATTERN?

1. Have students take out their bag of words (created on Day 1) and follow the Sorting With Separate Picture and Word Cards routine on page I-26 of the Introduction.

PRACTICE: COMPLETE YOUR WORK ON YOUR OWN

1. Have students complete the following Practice Pieces: Glue, Draw a Picture and Super Sentences (on pages I-50 and I-53 of the Introduction).

2. Circulate as students work, which usually takes fifteen minutes, and coach as needed.

FLUENCY: READING LIKE YOU'RE SPEAKING

1. Have students turn to page 44 in the Fluency Notebook.

2. Have students read one or more of the following poems: "Hiking" and "Mike's Bike."

3. Circulate and listen to students read or gather a small group of students who need additional support.

PHONEMIC AWARENESS: LISTEN

1. Give the directions. Say, "I am going to say a word. Your job is to tell me the vowel sound you hear in the word. Do you hear a short vowel or a long vowel? Do the motion of the sound you hear." Review the motions for *zip* and *bike*.

2. Say the following words:

    pine   spine   Mike   dim   pick   ride   win   fin   hiss   lime

REVIEW PATTERNS OF THE WEEK

1. Say, "Find a partner."

2. Say, "Tell your partner the names of this week's pieces" (*zip, bike*).

3. Say, "Tell your partner the sounds of this week's pieces" (/ĭ/, /ī/).

4. Say, "Tell your partner the spellings of this week's pieces" (*i, i_e*).

5. Say, "Write the spellings on your partner's back with your finger" (students will form the patterns *i* and *i_e*).

SPELLING CHECK

1. Follow the Spelling Check routine on page I-34 of the Introduction.

2. Instruct students to sit in their word study groups and turn to page 313 of the Learner's Notebook.

3. Say, "I am going to say one word at a time to each group. Record the words as I say them to your group. Make sure you only record the words from your group."

4. Move back and forth between the groups and dictate the following words:

Words for Group I	Words for Group 2
I. pin	I. grip
2. pine	2. gripe
3. hid	3. slit
4. hide	4. slid
5. bite	5. slide
Sentence: Tim is fine.	**Sentence: The slime is fake.**

WORD HUNT

1. Students will follow the Word Hunt routine on page I-55 of the Introduction.

2. Instruct students to search texts and the classroom for words with long *i* spelled *i_e*.

COMPREHENSION CHECK

1. Have students turn to page 314 of the Learner's Notebook.

2. Students will follow the Comprehension Check routine on page I-36 of the Introduction.

3. Check students' work. Circled answers are as follows:

   1. The pine is big.

   2. The slide is big.

   3. But the kite is not big!

4. Possible written responses include the following:

   1. The pine and the slide are big.

   2. The kite is different.

WEEKLY CELEBRATION

1. Display the celebratory message: "Nice work! You learned the *zip* and *bike* pieces!"

2. Encourage students to work together to read the message.

3. Have students copy the message onto their weekly certificate (see resources .corwin.com/puzzlepiecephonics-gradeK) and place it somewhere to take home.

Preparing for Your Week

Resources

PUZZLE PIECES

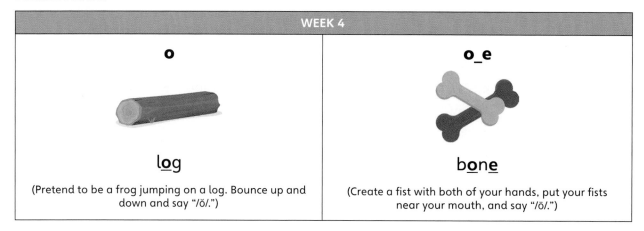

WEEK 4	
o	**o_e**
<u>log</u>	b<u>one</u>
(Pretend to be a frog jumping on a log. Bounce up and down and say "/ŏ/.")	(Create a fist with both of your hands, put your fists near your mouth, and say "/ō/.")

Log: istock.com/bennyb; Bone: istock.com/adekvat

CORRESPONDING *LEARNER'S NOTEBOOK PAGES*

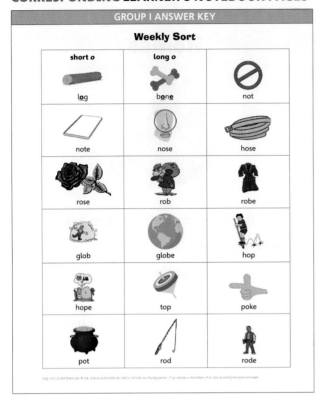

Week 4   Concept 10

Name _____   Date _____

This _____ is for you, Mom.

Circle the sentence that matches the picture.

	This not is for you, Mom. This note is for you, Mom. This net is for you, Mom.
	This rag is for you, Mom. This ride is for you, Mom. This rose is for you, Mom.
	This joke is for you, Mom. This jack is for you, Mom. This jet is for you, Mom.

Use the text to answer the questions.

1. What does Mom get?

   Mom gets a _____, a _____, and a
   _____.

2. Why do you think Mom gets things?

   Mom gets things because _____

Preparing for Your Week

CORRESPONDING *FLUENCY NOTEBOOK PAGES*

Find a Friend

"I am all alone," said Mole.
"I hope I find a friend."

"I am all alone," said Snake.
"I hope I find a friend."

"I am all alone," said Ape.
"I hope I find a friend."

"I am all alone," said Crane.
"I hope I find a friend."

"Turn around and see," says Duck.
"Look, we all are friends!"

Homes

What is home for a mole, you ask?
Moles dig down,
        down,
              down.
What is home for a mole, you ask?
Big holes underground!

What is home for an ape, you ask?
Apes swing from here
        to
      there.
What is home for an ape, you ask?
Where trees are everywhere!

What is home for a pig, you ask?
It's **mud**, and *mess*, and SLOP!

What is home for a pig, you ask?
Where mud goes drip, drip, drop!

Preparing for Your Week

Tips for Management and Differentiation

Refer to this section and to resources.corwin.com/puzzlepiecephonics-gradeK for resources and ideas to deepen your students' learning throughout the week. Feel free to put your own spin on the routines, too. For daily lesson plans, see pages 441–447 of this Teacher's Guide.

TIPS FOR PHONEMIC AWARENESS	• The focus for this week is listening for long and short vowels. • If you notice your students need additional practice, extend the activity with more words. • Students can also put their thumbs up or down or go to the right or left side of the room to show their responses instead of standing up or sitting down. • If your students master short *o* versus long *o* early in the week, then you can add words with short and long *a, e,* and *i* as a cumulative review and challenge.
TIPS FOR THE PUZZLE PIECE REVIEW	• Students will review short *o* (*log* piece) this week. They will also be introduced to another long vowel piece, *bone* (*o_e*). Review the different color-coding on the puzzle pieces and remind students that the *bone* puzzle piece represents a new type of vowel that sounds and is spelled differently. • Have students write spellings in the air, on the floor, on their arms, or on each other's backs with their fingers. • Come up with a class name for "silent *e*" ("Magic E," "Momma E," "Super E," etc.). • Take more time to introduce and review the *bone* piece throughout the week than the *log* piece. Students are used to seeing an *o* and hearing the short *o* sound. It may take them a long time to connect the long *o* sound and the *o_e* spelling. • You can display the Long Vowels: Vowel_e horizontal header piece to connect the *cake, Pete, bike,* and *bone* puzzle pieces. Explain to students that they are similar sound spelling patterns.
TIPS FOR BLENDING	• Help students connect *o_e* to the other vowel_e spellings. Review the name your class decided on for silent *e* and remind students that silent *e* always works in the same way. It makes a vowel say the name of the letter. • Review the short *o* families learned in Concept 7 (including *–ock* and *–ong*) as needed before Blending. • It may be necessary to reblend the lines with vowel_e words. Support students in making the long *e* sound. If students still need focused practice to master vowel_e by Day 4, then you can continue to blend words from this week's sort during Blending, instead of adding review words. • Remind students that this is the first time they have been exposed to long *o*. It will take students a lot of practice to master this sound.

(Continued)

Preparing for Your Week

TIPS FOR DICTATION AND QUICK SWITCH

- Monitor students' work during Dictation and Quick Switch. If students are forgetting the *e* to make the vowel say its name, then read the way they are spelling the word and ask if that is the word they are intending to spell. For example, if you asked them to write *robe* and a student wrote *rob*, read the word and pronounce it /r/ /ŏ/ /b/. Ask them, "Does that spell *robe*? How can we fix it?"
- If students still need focused practice to master vowel_e by Day 4, then you can continue to dictate words from this week's sort, instead of adding words with long and short *a*, *e*, and *i*.
- As students are ready, release more responsibility to them for recording the sentences in Dictation.

TIPS FOR SORTING

- Model and positively reinforce the sorting routine repeatedly throughout the week. During this concept, students go back to sorting with words and pictures.
- Discuss the vocabulary words that appear in the sort. Vocabulary words include the following:
  - Sort 1: *rob, robe, glob, globe, hope, rode*
  - Sort 2: *plot, robe, glob, globe, lob, lobe, wrote, rot*

TIPS FOR THE PRACTICE PIECES

- Support students with the vocabulary words for this week. They may need assistance in writing sentences.
- Students can make a "magic *e*" on a Popsicle stick. Have students write CVC words and then add their "magic *e*" stick to the end of their word to make a long vowel.
- Students can make a "magic *e*" flip-book by writing CVC words on one side of the page and the *e* on the edge of the backside. When they flip a portion of the paper to reveal the *e*, they turn the CVC word into a vowel_e word. Please reference resources.corwin.com/puzzlepiecephonics-gradeK for resources for a blackline master of this additional Practice Piece.
- Students can identify words that are the same except for the vowel sound (e.g., *lone, line,* and *lane*). They can practice reading the words quickly on flashcards and illustrate their meaning.

TIPS FOR FLUENCY

- Students can highlight words with short vowels and vowel_e.
- Students can participate in a "Fluency Celebration." Call on students who feel prepared to present a particular poem in front of the class. Other students can follow along in the Fluency Notebook.
- Students can illustrate their poems to support fluency and comprehension.

PHONEMIC AWARENESS: LISTEN

1. Give the directions. Say, "I am going to say a word. Your job is to tell me the vowel sound you hear in the word. Do you hear a short vowel or a long vowel? Do the motion of the sound you hear." Review the motions for the short and long *a*, *e*, and *i* pieces.

2. Say the following words:

mix game tale steam step pin hike fly bat heap

THE BIG REVEAL

1. Say, "Class, we have learned all of our short vowel sounds. Let's say them all together: '/ǎ/ /ě/ /ǐ/ /ǒ/ /ǔ/.'"

2. Say, "Now we are studying long vowels. A long vowel is when the vowel says the name of the letter. What is the long vowel sound of *a*? Good job! The long vowel sound of *a* is /ā/. What is the long vowel sound of *e*? Good job! The long vowel sound of *e* is /ē/. What is the long vowel sound of *i*? Good job! The long vowel sound of *i* is /ī/. This week we will learn a new long vowel. We will focus on short *o* and long *o*."

3. Say, "You know the *log* puzzle piece. It represents the letter *o*. The *log* piece says '/ǒ/ /ǒ/ /ǒ/' like in the middle of the word *log*. Let's all do the motion for the *log* piece together."

4. Say, "This is the *bone* puzzle piece. It represents the spelling *o_e*. The *bone* piece says '/ō/ /ō/ /ō/' like in the middle of the word *bone*. Create a fist with both of your hands, put your fists near your mouth, and say '/ō/.' We will study this sound all week. Let's make a list of words that have the *bone* sound in them" (record the words). If students suggest a word with the sound of /ō/ represented by a pattern other than *o_e*, say, "You're hearing the right sound, but that word has a different spelling pattern. Let's try another word."

BLENDING: PUTTING SOUNDS TOGETHER TO MAKE NEW WORDS

1. Follow the Blending routine on page I-17 of the Introduction.

2. Display the following words on the board one line at a time. Facilitate a discussion about the blending line focus after each line.

3. Then display the weekly sight words and sentence.

4. In the sentence, compare and contrast the short *o* and long *o* sounds and spellings.

not	note	nose	Discuss: compare and contrast short *o* with long *o*
rob	robe	globe	Discuss: compare and contrast short *o* with long *o*
hop	hope	rope	Discuss: compare and contrast short *o* with long *o*

Sight Words: got hot

Sentence: I am hot in my robe.

DICTATION: STRETCH OUT YOUR WORDS

1. Have students turn to page 319 of the Learner's Notebook.

2. Follow the Dictation routine on page I-21 of the Introduction to dictate the following words:

I. rod   2. rode   3. not   4. note

Sight Word: got

Sentence: I got a note.

3. Use Dictation as an informal pretest of students' knowledge of vowel_e. Help students identify the vowel and reference the puzzle pieces before recording each word. In the sentence, help students hear the difference between the short vowel in *got* and the long vowel in *note*.

(Continued)

Day 1 (Continued)

PRACTICE: **COMPLETE** **YOUR WORK ON** **YOUR OWN**	**1.** Have students turn to page 315 (Group 1) or 317 (Group 2) of the Learner's Notebook. **2.** Instruct students to tear out the sort and complete the following Practice Pieces: Quick Color, Careful Cut, Highlighter Hunt, and Sorting With Separate Picture and Word Cards (see further directions on pages I-37, I-38, I-43, and I-26 of the Introduction). **3.** Circulate as students work, which usually takes fifteen minutes, and coach as needed.
FLUENCY: **READING LIKE** **YOU'RE SPEAKING**	**1.** Have students turn to page 45 in the Fluency Notebook. **2.** Have students read one or more of the following poems: "Find a Friend" and "Homes." **3.** Circulate and listen to students read or gather a small group of students who need additional support.

PHONEMIC AWARENESS: LISTEN	**1.** Give the directions. Say, "I am going to say a word. Your job is to tell me the vowel sound you hear in the word. Do you hear a short vowel or a long vowel? Do the motion of the sound you hear." Review the motions for *log* and *bone*.
	2. Say the following words:
	hot rob robe stone slow pot mop groan lost phone
PUZZLE PIECE REVIEW	**1.** Say, "When I point to the piece, you tell me its name" (*log, bone*).
	2. Say, "When I point to the piece, you tell me its sound" (/ŏ/, /ō/).
	3. Say, "When I point to the piece, you tell me its spelling" (o, o_e).
	4. Say, "Write the spellings in the air with your finger" (students will form the patterns o and o_e).
BLENDING: PUTTING SOUNDS TOGETHER TO MAKE NEW WORDS	**1.** Follow the Blending routine on page I-17 of the Introduction.
	2. Display the following words on the board one line at a time. Facilitate a discussion about the blending line focus after each line.
	3. Then display the weekly sight words and sentence.
	4. Discuss the quotation marks in the sentence. Identify who is speaking.

glob	**globe**	**robe**	Discuss: compare and contrast short and long o
rod	**rode**	**code**	Discuss: compare and contrast short and long o
moss	**mope**	**hope**	Discuss: compare and contrast short and long o; doubled consonant in *moss*

Sight Words: its ask

Sentence: "It's a globe," said Mom.

QUICK SWITCH: MANIPULATE YOUR WORDS	**1.** Have students turn to page 319 of the Learner's Notebook.
	2. Follow the Quick Switch routine on page I-23 of the Introduction to dictate the following words:
	rob → robe → rose → hose → hot
	3. Assist students in identifying whether the vowel or consonant sound is changing. Help students reference the *bone* puzzle piece to represent o_e.
SORT: WHAT IS YOUR FOCUS PATTERN?	**1.** Have students take out their bag of words (created on Day 1) and follow the Sorting With Separate Picture and Word Cards routine on page I-26 of the Introduction.
PRACTICE: COMPLETE YOUR WORK ON YOUR OWN	**1.** Students will follow the Color-Code Writing routine on page I-52 of the Introduction.
	2. Circulate as students work, which usually takes fifteen minutes, and coach as needed.
FLUENCY: READING LIKE YOU'RE SPEAKING	**1.** Have students turn to page 45 in the Fluency Notebook.
	2. Have students read one or more of the following poems: "Find a Friend" and "Homes."
	3. Circulate and listen to students read or gather a small group of students who need additional support.

Day 3

PHONEMIC AWARENESS: LISTEN	**1.** Give the directions. Say, "I am going to say a word. Your job is to tell me the vowel sound you hear in the word. Do you hear a short vowel or a long vowel? Do the motion of the sound you hear." Review the motions for *log* and *bone*.
	2. Say the following words:
	shop home woke dot hop joke rose note toast fox
PUZZLE PIECE REVIEW	**1.** Say, "When I point to the piece, you tell me its name" (*log, bone*).
	2. Say, "When I point to the piece, you tell me its sound" (/ŏ/, /ō/).
	3. Say, "When I point to the piece, you tell me its spelling" (*o, o_e*).
	4. Say, "Write the spellings in the air with your finger" (students will form the patterns *o* and *o_e*).
BLENDING: PUTTING SOUNDS TOGETHER TO MAKE NEW WORDS	**1.** Follow the Blending routine on page I-17 of the Introduction.
	2. Display the following words on the board one line at a time. Facilitate a discussion about the blending line focus after each line.
	3. Then display the weekly sight words and sentence.
	4. In the sentence, review the vocabulary words *broke* and *cone* with students.
	long lock lot Discuss: medial sound of short *o*
	hope rope nope Discuss: -*ope* family
	spoke smoke broke Discuss: blends; -*oke* family
	Sight Words: sit very
	Sentence: He broke the cone.
DICTATION: STRETCH OUT YOUR WORDS	**1.** Have students turn to page 320 of the Learner's Notebook.
	2. Follow the Dictation routine on page I-21 of the Introduction to dictate the following words:
	I. hose 2. rose 3. note 4. vote
	Sight Word: sit
	Sentence: The hose is long.
	3. Help students identify pairs of words as words within a family. Remind students they can use word families to help them spell new words. In the sentence, review the −*ong* family from Blending.
SORT: WHAT IS YOUR FOCUS PATTERN?	**1.** Have students take out their bag of words (created on Day 1) and follow the Sorting With Separate Picture and Word Cards routine on page I-26 of the Introduction.
PRACTICE: COMPLETE YOUR WORK ON YOUR OWN	**1.** Students will complete the Read and Trade routine on page I-47 of the Introduction.
	2. Circulate as students work, which usually takes fifteen minutes, and coach as needed.
FLUENCY: READING LIKE YOU'RE SPEAKING	**1.** Have students turn to page 45 in the Fluency Notebook.
	2. Have students read one or more of the following poems: "Find a Friend" and "Homes."
	3. Circulate and listen to students read or gather a small group of students who need additional support.

Day 4

PHONEMIC AWARENESS: LISTEN

1. Give the directions. Say, "I am going to say a word. Your job is to tell me the vowel sound you hear in the word. Do you hear a short vowel or a long vowel? Do the motion of the sound you hear." Review the motions for *log* and *bone*.

2. Say the following words:

moth   soap   row   hot   got   poke   honk   home   pose   jot

PUZZLE PIECE REVIEW

1. Say, "When I point to the piece, you tell me its name" (*log, bone*).

2. Say, "When I point to the piece, you tell me its sound" (/ŏ/, /ō/).

3. Say, "When I point to the piece, you tell me its spelling" (*o, o_e*).

4. Say, "Write the spellings in the air with your finger" (students will form the patterns *o* and *o_e*).

BLENDING: PUTTING SOUNDS TOGETHER TO MAKE NEW WORDS

1. Follow the Blending routine on page I-17 of the Introduction.

2. Display the following words on the board one line at a time. Facilitate a discussion about the blending line focus after each line.

3. Then display the weekly sight words and sentence.

4. In the sentence, contrast all of the words that contain a short *o* with the word *poke*.

line	**lane**	**lone**	Discuss: initial sound of /l/; vowel *–ne* pattern
dome	**dime**	**dame**	Discuss: initial sound of /d/; vowel *–me* pattern
wove	**wave**	**eve**	Discuss: vowel *–ve* pattern

Sight Words: we   and

Sentence: Do not poke the hot pot.

QUICK SWITCH: MANIPULATE YOUR WORDS

1. Have students turn to page 320 of the Learner's Notebook.

2. Follow the Quick Switch routine on page I-23 of the Introduction to dictate the following words:

rode → ride → ripe → rope → hope

3. Help students identify the vowel sound and reference the puzzle pieces before recording.

SORT: WHAT IS YOUR FOCUS PATTERN?

1. Have students take out their bag of words (created on Day 1) and follow the Sorting With Separate Picture and Word Cards routine on page I-26 of the Introduction.

PRACTICE: COMPLETE YOUR WORK ON YOUR OWN

1. Have students complete the following Practice Pieces: Glue, Draw a Picture and Super Sentences (on pages I-50 and I-53 of the Introduction).

2. Circulate as students work, which usually takes fifteen minutes, and coach as needed.

FLUENCY: READING LIKE YOU'RE SPEAKING

1. Have students turn to page 45 in the Fluency Notebook.

2. Have students read one or more of the following poems: "Find a Friend" and "Homes."

3. Circulate and listen to students read or gather a small group of students who need additional support.

PHONEMIC AWARENESS: LISTEN	**1.** Give the directions. Say, "I am going to say a word. Your job is to tell me the vowel sound you hear in the word. Do you hear a short vowel or a long vowel? Do the motion of the sound you hear." Review the motions for *log* and *bone*.
	2. Say the following words:
	wrote shone mom lone frog hop stone shop snow float

REVIEW PATTERNS OF THE WEEK	**1.** Say, "Find a partner."
	2. Say, "Tell your partner the names of this week's pieces" (*log, bone*).
	3. Say, "Tell your partner the sounds of this week's pieces" (/ŏ/, /ō/).
	4. Say, "Tell your partner the spellings of this week's pieces" (*o, o_e*).
	5. Say, "Write the spellings on your partner's back with your finger" (students will form the patterns *o* and *o_e*).

SPELLING CHECK	**1.** Follow the Spelling Check routine on page I-34 of the Introduction.
	2. Instruct students to sit in their word study groups and turn to page 321 of the Learner's Notebook.
	3. Say, "I am going to say one word at a time to each group. Record the words as I say them to your group. Make sure you only record the words from your group."
	4. Move back and forth between the groups and dictate the following words:

Words for Group I	**Words for Group 2**
I. hop	I. glob
2. hope	2. globe
3. rod	3. lob
4. rode	4. lobe
5. note	5. woke
Sentence: I see a rose.	**Sentence: The red rake broke.**

WORD HUNT	**1.** Students will follow the Word Hunt routine on page I-55 of the Introduction.
	2. Instruct students to search texts and the classroom for words with long *o* spelled *o_e*.

COMPREHENSION CHECK	**1.** Have students turn to page 322 of the Learner's Notebook.
	2. Students will follow the Comprehension Check routine on page I-36 of the Introduction.
	3. Check students' work. Circled answers are as follows:
	1. This note is for you, Mom.
	2. This rose is for you, Mom.
	3. This joke is for you, Mom.
	4. Possible written responses include the following:
	1. Mom gets a note, a rose, and a joke.
	2. Mom gets things because _____. (Students may put any phrase that makes sense into the blank. For example, "Mom gets things because it is her birthday.")

WEEKLY CELEBRATION

1. Display the celebratory message: "I hope you had fun! You learned the *log* and *bone* pieces!"

2. Encourage students to work together to read the message.

3. Have students copy the message onto their weekly certificate (see resources .corwin.com/puzzlepiecephonics-gradeK) and place it somewhere to take home.

Preparing for Your Week

Resources

PUZZLE PIECES

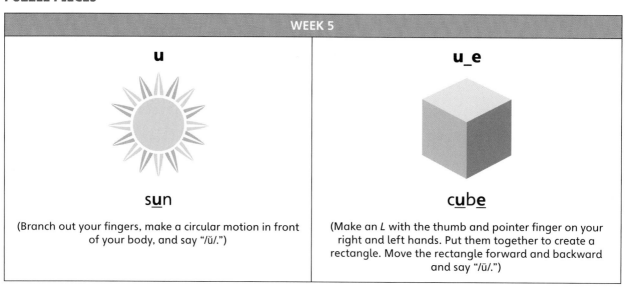

WEEK 5
u ... **sun** (Branch out your fingers, make a circular motion in front of your body, and say "/ŭ/.")	**u_e** ... **cube** (Make an *L* with the thumb and pointer finger on your right and left hands. Put them together to create a rectangle. Move the rectangle forward and backward and say "/ū/.")

POSTASSESSMENT DIRECTIONS

This End Check is used to identify which consonants, short vowels, blends, and vowel_e sounds students mastered and retained during kindergarten.

You can give this End Check any day during the last week of Concept 10. You can split the rows and do parts on different days. Do what works for your class.

Instruct students to turn to **page 323 in the Learner's Notebook**.

Explain to students that they have studied all of the spellings in the words they will hear during this End Check. The purpose of this check is to show what they know and mastered in kindergarten.

When giving this assessment, go row by row in saying the word represented by the picture. Students are not guessing what the picture is. You tell them the word.

Sun: istock.com/StudioBarcelona; Cube: istock.com/Physicx

Preparing for Your Week

POSTASSESSMENT: CONSONANTS, SHORT VOWELS, AND VOWEL_e SPELLING CHECK

ANSWER KEY				
1. ten	2. tux	3. step	4. cap	5. cape
6. pop	7. yam	8. must	9. pin	10. pine
11. fit	12. vet	13. frog	14. cub	15. cube
16. dab	17. jog	18. fast	19. pet	20. Pete
21. gum	22. quiz	23. slit	24. hop	25. hope

Pin: istock.com/jane_Kelly; Cube: istock.com/Physicx; Jog: istock.com/graphic-bee; Fast: istock.com/funnybank; Pete: istock.com/pijama61; Gum: istock.com/elinedesignservices

EVALUATING THE ASSESSMENT: WHAT TO LOOK FOR

- Knowledge of consonants
- Knowledge of short vowels
- Knowledge of basic blends
- Knowledge of vowel_e
- Knowledge that each word contains a vowel

TIPS FOR SCORING

Columns 1 and 2 contain words with short vowels and consonants. Column 3 contains words with short vowels and consonant blends. Column 4 contains words with short vowels and consonants. Column 5 contains words with the vowel_e spelling pattern.

Each word is worth one point. For each correctly spelled word, students earn one point. To show mastery of kindergarten spelling patterns, students must show 80 percent mastery or correctly phonetically spell twenty out of twenty-five words.

Use teacher discretion when reviewing.

Preparing for Your Week

CORRESPONDING *LEARNER'S NOTEBOOK PAGES*

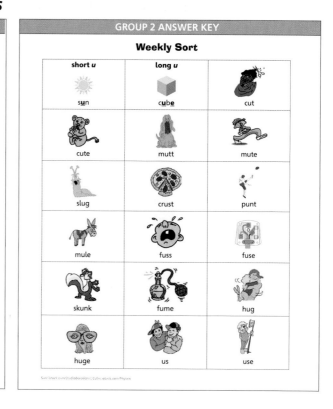

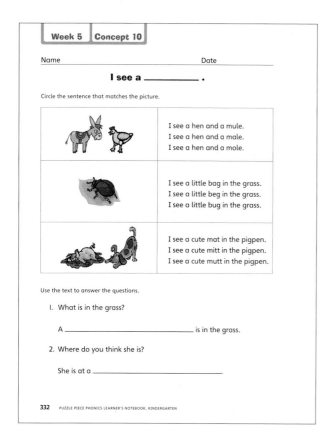

CORRESPONDING *FLUENCY NOTEBOOK PAGES*

Wait, Bus, Wait!

The bus goes up the hill.
Up, up, up!
The bus goes very slow.
Putt, putt, putt!

The bus goes down the hill.
Down, down, down.
The bus goes very fast.
See it now!

The bus is out of gas.
Clug, clug, clug.
The bus runs on fumes.
Glug, glug, glug.

No-Good Pets

For a pet,
I had a skunk.
He was so cute
But really stunk.

For a pet,
I had a mule.
He kicked and stomped.
He was not cool.

For a pet,
I had a slug.
He left behind
Slime on the rug.

This summer,
I will find a pet
Who does not stink,
Who does not kick,
Who does not slime.
What should I get?

Preparing for Your Week

Tips for Management and Differentiation

Refer to this section and to resources.corwin.com/puzzlepiecephonics-gradeK for resources and ideas to deepen your students' learning throughout the week. Feel free to put your own spin on the routines, too. For daily lesson plans, see pages 454–461 of this Teacher's Guide.

TIPS FOR PHONEMIC AWARENESS	• The focus for this week is listening for long and short vowels. • If you notice your students need additional practice, extend the activity with more words. • Students can also put their thumbs up or down or go to the right or left side of the room to show their responses instead of standing up or sitting down. • If your students master short *u* versus long *u* early in the week, then you can add words with short and long *a, e, i,* and *o* as a cumulative review and challenge.
TIPS FOR THE PUZZLE PIECE REVIEW	• Students will review short *u* (*sun* piece) this week. They will also be introduced to another long vowel piece, *cube* (*u_e*). Review the different color-coding on the puzzle pieces and remind students that the *cube* puzzle piece represents a new type of vowel that sounds and is spelled differently. • Have students write spellings in the air, on the floor, on their arms, or on each other's backs with their fingers. • Come up with a class name for "silent *e*" ("Magic E," "Momma E," "Super E," etc.). • Take more time to introduce and review the *cube* piece throughout the week than the *sun* piece. Students are used to seeing a *u* and hearing the short *u* sound. It may take them a long time to connect the long *u* sound and the *u_e* spelling. • You can display the Long Vowels: Vowel_e horizontal header piece to connect the *cake, Pete, bike, bone,* and *cube* puzzle pieces. Explain to students that they are similar sound spelling patterns.
TIPS FOR BLENDING	• Help students connect *u_e* to the other vowel_e spellings. Review the name your class decided on for silent *e* and remind students that silent *e* always works in the same way. It makes a vowel say the name of the letter. • Review the short *u* families learned in Concept 8 (including *–uck, –uff,* and *–unk*) as needed before Blending. • It may be necessary to reblend the lines with vowel_e words. Support students in making the long *u* sound. If students still need focused practice to master vowel_e by Day 4, then you can continue to blend words from this week's sort during Blending, instead of adding review words. • Remind students that this is the first time they have been exposed to long *u*. It will take students a lot of practice to master this sound.

Preparing for Your Week

TIPS FOR DICTATION AND QUICK SWITCH

- Help students segment the words for Dictation and Quick Switch quickly and accurately. Students are more likely to associate the long *u* sound with *y* if they draw it out when segmenting words.
- Monitor students' work during Dictation and Quick Switch. If students are forgetting the *e* to make the vowel say its name, then read the way they are spelling the word and ask if that is the word they are intending to spell. For example, if you asked them to write *cute* and a student wrote *cut*, read the word and pronounce it /c/ /ŭ/ /t/. Ask them, "Does that spell *cute*? How can we fix it?"

TIPS FOR DICTATION AND QUICK SWITCH

- If students still need focused practice to master vowel_e by Day 4, then you can continue to dictate words from this week's sort, instead of adding words with long and short *a*, *e*, *i*, and *o*.
- Encourage students to independently record the sentences during Dictation. Tell them that in first grade, they will record sentences all year long! This is their chance to act like a first grader.

TIPS FOR SORTING

- Model and positively reinforce the sorting routine repeatedly throughout the week. During this concept, students go back to sorting with words and pictures.
- Discuss the vocabulary words that appear in the sort. Vocabulary words include the following:
  - Sort 1: *mutt, mute, cub, cube, mule, fuss, fuse, fume*
  - Sort 2: *mutt, mute, slug, punt, mule, fuss, fuse, fume, huge*

TIPS FOR THE PRACTICE PIECES

- Support students with the vocabulary words for this week. They may need assistance in writing sentences.
- Students can make a "magic *e*" on a Popsicle stick. Have students write CVC words and then add their "magic *e*" stick to the end of their word to make a long vowel.
- Students can make a "magic *e*" flip-book by writing CVC words on one side of the page and the *e* on the edge of the backside. When they flip a portion of the paper to reveal the *e*, they turn the CVC word into a vowel_e word. Please reference resources.corwin.com/puzzlepiecephonics-gradeK for resources for a blackline master of this additional Practice Piece.
- Students can identify words that are the same except for the vowel sound (e.g., *mule, mole, mile,* and *male*). They can practice reading the words quickly on flashcards and illustrate their meaning.

TIPS FOR FLUENCY

- Students can highlight words with short vowels and vowel_e.
- Students can participate in a "Fluency Celebration." Call on students who feel prepared to present a particular poem in front of the class. Other students can follow along in the Fluency Notebook.
- Students can illustrate their poems to support fluency and comprehension.

Day 1

PHONEMIC AWARENESS: LISTEN

1. Give the directions. Say, "I am going to say a word. Your job is to tell me the vowel sound you hear in the word. Do you hear a short vowel or a long vowel? Do the motion of the sound you hear." Review the motions for the short and long *a, e, i,* and *o* pieces.

2. Say the following words:

spin spine hot frog nose bat bake flame red teeth

THE BIG REVEAL

1. Say, "Class, we have learned all of our short vowel sounds. Let's say them all together: '/ă/ /ĕ/ /ĭ/ /ŏ/ /ŭ/.'"

2. Say, "Now we are studying long vowels. A long vowel is when the vowel says the name of the letter. What is the long vowel sound of *a*? Good job! The long vowel sound of *a* is /ā/. What is the long vowel sound of *e*? Good job! The long vowel sound of *e* is /ē/. What is the long vowel sound of *i*? Good job! The long vowel sound of *i* is /ī/. What is the long vowel sound of *o*? Good job! The long vowel sound of *o* is /ō/. This week we will learn the last long vowel. We will focus on short *u* and long *u*."

3. Say, "You know the *sun* puzzle piece. It represents the letter *u*. The *sun* piece says '/ŭ/ /ŭ/ /ŭ/' like in the middle of the word *sun*. Let's all do the motion for the *sun* piece together."

4. Say, "This is the *cube* puzzle piece. It represents the spelling *u_e*. The *cube* piece says '/ū/ /ū/ /ū/' like in the word *cube*. Make an L with your thumb and your pointer finger on your right and left hands. Put them together to make a rectangle. Move the rectangle forward and backward and say '/ū/.' We will study this sound all week. Let's make a list of words that have the *cube* sound in them" (record the words). If students suggest a word with the sound of /ū/ represented by a pattern other than *u_e*, say, "You're hearing the right sound, but that word has a different spelling pattern. Let's try another word."

BLENDING: PUTTING SOUNDS TOGETHER TO MAKE NEW WORDS

1. Follow the Blending routine on page I-17 of the Introduction.

2. Display the following words on the board one line at a time. Facilitate a discussion about the blending line focus after each line.

3. Then display the weekly sight words and sentence.

4. In the sentence, underline the word that contains the short *u* sound.

cub	cube	cute	Discuss: compare and contrast short *u* with long *u*
fuss	fuse	fume	Discuss: compare and contrast short *u* with long *u*
us	use	muse	Discuss: compare and contrast short *u* with long *u*

Sight Words: run ran

Sentence: I ran to get on the bus.

DICTATION: STRETCH OUT YOUR WORDS

1. Have students turn to page 329 of the Learner's Notebook.

2. Follow the Dictation routine on page I-21 of the Introduction to dictate the following words:

l. cub 2. cube 3. cut 4. cute

Sight Word: run

Sentence: I have a cube.

3. Use Dictation as an informal pretest of students' knowledge of vowel_e. Help students identify the vowel and reference the puzzle pieces before recording each word.

PRACTICE:
COMPLETE
YOUR WORK ON
YOUR OWN

1. Have students turn to page 325 (Group 1) or 327 (Group 2) of the Learner's Notebook.

2. Instruct students to tear out the sort and complete the following Practice Pieces: Quick Color, Careful Cut, Highlighter Hunt, and Sorting With Separate Picture and Word Cards (see further directions on pages I-37, I-38, I-43, and I-26 of the Introduction).

3. Circulate as students work, which usually takes fifteen minutes, and coach as needed.

FLUENCY:
READING LIKE
YOU'RE SPEAKING

1. Have students turn to page 46 in the Fluency Notebook.

2. Have students read one or more of the following poems: "Wait, Bus, Wait!" and "No-Good Pets."

3. Circulate and listen to students read or gather a small group of students who need additional support.

PHONEMIC AWARENESS: LISTEN

1. Give the directions. Say, "I am going to say a word. Your job is to tell me the vowel sound you hear in the word. Do you hear a short vowel or a long vowel? Do the motion of the sound you hear." Review the motions for *sun* and *cube*.

2. Say the following words:

> hug   run   cute   huge   fuse   fun   rug   mute   tub   fume

PUZZLE PIECE REVIEW

1. Say, "When I point to the piece, you tell me its name" (*sun, cube*).

2. Say, "When I point to the piece, you tell me its sound" (/ŭ/, /ū/).

3. Say, "When I point to the piece, you tell me its spelling" (*u, u_e*).

4. Say, "Write the spellings in the air with your finger" (students will form the patterns *u* and *u_e*).

BLENDING: PUTTING SOUNDS TOGETHER TO MAKE NEW WORDS

1. Follow the Blending routine on page I-17 of the Introduction.

2. Display the following words on the board one line at a time. Facilitate a discussion about the blending line focus after each line.

3. Then display the weekly sight words and sentence.

4. Discuss the adjective *cute* in the sentence. Ask students to describe the type of dog they are visualizing in their heads while reading.

mutt	mute	mule	Discuss: compare and contrast short and long *u*; doubled consonant in *mutt*
fuss	fuse	use	Discuss: compare and contrast short and long *u*; doubled consonant in *fuss*
cub	cube	cute	Discuss: compare and contrast short and long *u*

Sight Words: to   you

Sentence: **The dog is a cute mutt.**

QUICK SWITCH: MANIPULATE YOUR WORDS

1. Have students turn to page 329 of the Learner's Notebook.

2. Follow the Quick Switch routine on page I-23 of the Introduction to dictate the following words:

> bus → us → use → fuse → fuss

3. Help students get from *us* to *use* and *fuse* to *fuss* by identifying the vowel sound and referencing the correct puzzle piece before recording. Also remind students to double the *s* in *fuss*.

SORT: WHAT IS YOUR FOCUS PATTERN?

1. Have students take out their bag of words (created on Day 1) and follow the Sorting With Separate Picture and Word Cards routine on page I-26 of the Introduction.

PRACTICE: COMPLETE YOUR WORK ON YOUR OWN

1. Students will follow the Color-Code Writing routine on page I-52 of the Introduction.

2. Circulate as students work, which usually takes fifteen minutes, and coach as needed.

FLUENCY: READING LIKE YOU'RE SPEAKING

1. Have students turn to page 46 in the Fluency Notebook.

2. Have students read one or more of the following poems: "Wait, Bus, Wait!" and "No-Good Pets."

3. Circulate and listen to students read or gather a small group of students who need additional support.

PHONEMIC AWARENESS: LISTEN	**1.** Give the directions. Say, "I am going to say a word. Your job is to tell me the vowel sound you hear in the word. Do you hear a short vowel or a long vowel? Do the motion of the sound you hear." Review the motions for *sun* and *cube*.
	2. Say the following words:
	use mute mug fume stuck plug huge cube cute stuff

PUZZLE PIECE REVIEW

1. Say, "When I point to the piece, you tell me its name" (*sun, cube*).

2. Say, "When I point to the piece, you tell me its sound" (/ŭ/, /ū/).

3. Say, "When I point to the piece, you tell me its spelling" (*u, u_e*).

4. Say, "Write the spellings in the air with your finger" (students will form the patterns *u* and *u_e*).

BLENDING: PUTTING SOUNDS TOGETHER TO MAKE NEW WORDS

1. Follow the Blending routine on page I-17 of the Introduction.

2. Display the following words on the board one line at a time. Facilitate a discussion about the blending line focus after each line.

3. Then display the weekly sight words and sentence.

4. In the sentence, review the vocabulary word *mute* with students.

stuck	stuff	stunk	Discuss: medial sound of short *u*
cute	mute	mate	Discuss: vowel_e
fuse	use	vase	Discuss: vowel_e

Sight Words: for   go

Sentence: The TV is stuck on mute.

DICTATION: STRETCH OUT YOUR WORDS

1. Have students turn to page 330 of the Learner's Notebook.

2. Follow the Dictation routine on page I-21 of the Introduction to dictate the following words:

I. fume   2. fuse   3. mule   4. mute

Sight Word: go

Sentence: The mule is stuck.

3. Help students identify similar words (words that start with the same initial consonant and have the same vowel sound but have a different final consonant). Remind students that they can use words that they know to spell other words that sound similarly. Review the –uck family from Blending before students record *stuck* in the sentence.

SORT: WHAT IS YOUR FOCUS PATTERN?

1. Have students take out their bag of words (created on Day 1) and follow the Sorting With Separate Picture and Word Cards routine on page I-26 of the Introduction.

PRACTICE: COMPLETE YOUR WORK ON YOUR OWN

1. Students will complete the Read and Trade routine on page I-47 of the Introduction.

2. Circulate as students work, which usually takes fifteen minutes, and coach as needed.

(Continued)

Day 3 (Continued)

FLUENCY: READING LIKE YOU'RE SPEAKING

1. Have students turn to page 46 in the Fluency Notebook.

2. Have students read one or more of the following poems: "Wait, Bus, Wait!" and "No-Good Pets."

3. Circulate and listen to students read or gather a small group of students who need additional support.

Day 4

PHONEMIC AWARENESS: LISTEN	**1.** Give the directions. Say, "I am going to say a word. Your job is to tell me the vowel sound you hear in the word. Do you hear a short vowel or a long vowel? Do the motion of the sound you hear." Review the motions for *sun* and *cube*. **2.** Say the following words: cube lump tug dug use cube mule fun hut nut
PUZZLE PIECE REVIEW 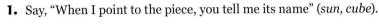	**1.** Say, "When I point to the piece, you tell me its name" (*sun, cube*). **2.** Say, "When I point to the piece, you tell me its sound" (/ŭ/, /ū/). **3.** Say, "When I point to the piece, you tell me its spelling" (*u, u_e*). **4.** Say, "Write the spellings in the air with your finger" (students will form the patterns *u* and *u_e*).
BLENDING: PUTTING SOUNDS TOGETHER TO MAKE NEW WORDS	**1.** Follow the Blending routine on page I-17 of the Introduction. **2.** Display the following words on the board one line at a time. Facilitate a discussion about the blending line focus after each line. **3.** Then display the weekly sight words and sentence. **4.** In the sentence, compare and contrast the words *mule* and *mile*. cube cave cove Discuss: initial sound of /k/; vowel_e pattern mule mile mole Discuss: initial sound of /m/; vowel_e pattern fume fame flame Discuss: initial sound of /f/; vowel –*me* pattern **Sight Words: be he** **Sentence: The mule can go a mile.**
QUICK SWITCH: MANIPULATE YOUR WORDS	**1.** Have students turn to page 330 of the Learner's Notebook. **2.** Follow the Quick Switch routine on page I-23 of the Introduction to dictate the following words: cute → cut → cat → cap → cape **3.** Help students identify the vowel sound and reference the puzzle pieces before recording.
SORT: WHAT IS YOUR FOCUS PATTERN?	**1.** Have students take out their bag of words (created on Day 1) and follow the Sorting With Separate Picture and Word Cards routine on page I-26 of the Introduction.
PRACTICE: COMPLETE YOUR WORK ON YOUR OWN	**1.** Have students complete the following Practice Pieces: Glue, Draw a Picture and Super Sentences (on pages I-50 and I-53 of the Introduction). **2.** Circulate as students work, which usually takes fifteen minutes, and coach as needed.
FLUENCY: READING LIKE YOU'RE SPEAKING	**1.** Have students turn to page 46 in the Fluency Notebook. **2.** Have students read one or more of the following poems: "Wait, Bus, Wait!" and "No Good Pets." **3.** Circulate and listen to students read or gather a small group of students who need additional support.

PHONEMIC AWARENESS: LISTEN

1. Give the directions. Say, "I am going to say a word. Your job is to tell me the vowel sound you hear in the word. Do you hear a short vowel or a long vowel? Do the motion of the sound you hear." Review the motions for *sun* and *cube*.

2. Say the following words:

slug   mutt   huge   mule   dug   bun   rust   cute   fume   run

REVIEW PATTERNS OF THE WEEK

1. Say, "Find a partner."

2. Say, "Tell your partner the names of this week's pieces" (*sun, cube*).

3. Say, "Tell your partner the sounds of this week's pieces" (/ŭ/, /ū/).

4. Say, "Tell your partner the spellings of this week's pieces" (*u, u_e*).

5. Say, "Write the spellings on your partner's back with your finger" (students will form the patterns *u* and *u_e*).

SPELLING CHECK

1. Follow the Spelling Check routine on page I-34 of the Introduction.

2. Instruct students to sit in their word study groups and turn to page 331 of the Learner's Notebook.

3. Say, "I am going to say one word at a time to each group. Record the words as I say them to your group. Make sure you only record the words from your group."

4. Move back and forth between the groups and dictate the following words:

Words for Group I	Words for Group 2
I. cub	I. fuss
2. cube	2. fuse
3. us	3. cut
4. use	4. cute
5. fume	5. fume
Sentence: The bug is cute.	Sentence: The slug is huge.

WORD HUNT

1. Students will follow the Word Hunt routine on page I-55 of the Introduction.

2. Instruct students to search texts and the classroom for words with long *u* spelled *u_e*.

COMPREHENSION CHECK

1. Have students turn to page 332 of the Learner's Notebook.

2. Students will follow the Comprehension Check routine on page I-36 of the Introduction.

3. Check students' work. Circled answers are as follows:

1. I see a hen and a mule.
2. I see a little bug in the grass.
3. I see a cute mutt in the pigpen.

4. Possible written responses include the following:

1. A little bug is in the grass.
2. She is at a _____. (Students may put any phrase that is supported by the text and pictures into the blank. For example, "She is at a farm.")

WEEKLY CELEBRATION

1. Display the celebratory message: "You used your brain! You learned the *sun* and *cube* pieces!"

2. Encourage students to work together to read the message.

3. Have students copy the message onto their weekly certificate (see resources .corwin.com/puzzlepiecephonics-gradeK) and place it somewhere to take home.

Notes

Notes

Notes